CHINESE
Wit &
Humor

CHINESE Wit & Humor

Edited by GEORGE KAO
Introduction by LIN YUTANG
Including a translation by Pearl Buck

A DISCOVERY HOUSE BOOK

STERLING PUBLISHING CO., INC. NEW YORK
Oak Tree Press Co., Ltd. London & Sydney

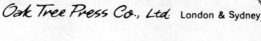

Published by Sterling Publishing Co., Inc.
419 Park Avenue South, New York, N.Y. 10016
British edition published by Oak Tree Press Co., Ltd., Nassau, Bahamas
Distributed in Australia and New Zealand by Oak Tree Press Co., Ltd.,
P.O. Box J34, Brickfield Hill, Sydney 2000, N.S.W.
Distributed in the United Kingdom and elsewhere in the British Commonwealth
by Ward Lock Ltd., 116 Baker Street, London W 1
Manufactured in the United States of America
Library of Congress Catalog Card No.: 74–82322
Sterling ISBN 0–8069–8002–8 Trade   Oak Tree 7061–2021–1
8003–6 Library

To Maeching

Contents

II. THE HUMOR OF THE PICARESQUE *(Old)*

III. HUMOR—PRACTICAL AND OTHERWISE *(All Time)*

IV. THE HUMOR OF PROTEST *(Modern)*

ACKNOWLEDGMENTS

THE editor is grateful to the many authors and translators who have allowed their work to be reprinted in this book. Every care has been taken to obtain permission from the owners to reprint material which is in copyright; any errors are unintentional and will be gladly corrected in future printings if notification is sent to the publishers, Coward-McCann, Inc., who wish to acknowledge with thanks the courtesy of the following for permission to reprint as indicated:

Kelly and Walsh, Ltd., Shanghai, for selections from *Chuang Tzŭ: Mystic, Moralist and Social Reformer* and from *Quips from a Chinese Jest Book,* both by Herbert A. Giles.

The John Day Company for Liehtze's "The Old Man Who Lost a Horse" from *My Country and My People* by Lin Yutang; "In Memoriam of the Dog-Meat General" from *With Love and Irony* by Lin Yutang. Thanks are also due to the John Day Company and Pearl S. Buck for "The Adventures of the Tattooed Monk" from *All Men Are Brothers,* copyright, 1933 by Pearl S. Buck.

Arthur Probsthain, London, for selections from *The Complete Works of Han Fei Tzŭ,* translated by W. K. Liao.

G. P. Putnam's Sons for "Hsi Men and the Gold Lotus" from *Chin P'ing Mei,* copyright, 1940, by G. P. Putnam's Sons.

Doubleday, Doran and Company, Inc. for "Liu *Lao-Lao* in the Garden of Spectacular Sights" from *Dream of the Red Chamber,* translated by Chi-Chen Wang.

T. Werner Laurie, Ltd., London, for "The Inconstancy of Madame Chuang" from the book of the same title, translated by E. B. Howell.

Columbia University Press for "Ah Q's Victories" and "The Cake of Soap" both from *Ah Q and Others: Selected Stories of Lusin,* translated by Chi-Chen Wang.

John Murray, London, for selections from *Taoist Teachings: From the Book of Lieh Tzu,* in the Wisdom of the East Series, translated by Lionel Giles.

The editor also wishes to acknowledge his debt to the following for material included from books published in China:

The Commercial Press, Ltd., Shanghai, and Lin Yutang for "If I Were a Bandit" and "An Open Letter to an American Friend" from *The Little Critic,* First Series (1930-1932); also for "Talking Pictures," "Ah Chuan Goes to School" and "Salt, Sweat and Tears" from *A Nun of Taishan and Other Translations* (1936).

Pei Hsin Book Company, Shanghai, for selections from *Ku Cha An Hsiao Hua Hsuan* (*Laugh Talks from the Bitter-Tea Studio*) by Chou Tso-jen.

Jen Chien Book House, Shanghai, for "Dr. Mao" from the story "Sacrifice" from *Ying Hai Chi* (*The Cherry Blossom Collection*) by Lao Sheh (1935).

Lunyu (*The Analects*) fortnightly, Shanghai, for "National Salvation Through Haircut" by Lao Hsiang and "Don't Say Your Own Writing Is No Good" by Yao Ying (1933).

EDITOR'S NOTE

FOR the compilation of this anthology I owe much to Lin Yutang and Chi-Chen Wang. Dr. Lin really should take on the job himself, but instead he passed it to me along with many valuable suggestions. He did contribute an introduction, which adds to what he has so wisely said about Chinese humor in his own books. Also, if he had not made the Chinese reading public humor-conscious in the prewar days, there would hardly have been any sample of modern Chinese humorous writing to include in this book. Professor Wang of Columbia University generously let me use many of his unpublished translations from the Chinese classics. He gave me a number of the short items in the first section; the second section, consisting of excerpts from Chinese novels, is mainly his.

I am not one of those who insist on using their own and "new" translations where there are perfectly good translations available. And I found, to the delight of my editorial eye and scissors, good translations, already printed or out of print, of many of the things I wanted to put in this book. I relied on Legge and Giles not only for their sound scholarship but also because their English carries a quaint flavor that in each case suits the original and, so it seems to me, imparts an additional drollness. Pearl Buck's fine rendition of that robust passage from *Shui Hu Chuan* is so representative of the whole that I wish I could include more.

G. K.

EDITOR'S PREFACE

DURING the late unlamented war more than once I was confronted with the American editor who wanted something on Chinese humor, for a syndicated newspaper article, for a magazine piece, for radio dramatization, and even to fill a book. That the Chinese people possess a sense of humor somewhat akin to your own has been one of the minor American myths about China that never ceases to amaze. The difficult thing about this myth is that it is at once so true and so hard to prove. And yet, your editor demands to know, doesn't every news photo of a Chungking crowd display a sea of grinning faces? And doesn't this ability to laugh have a lot to do with sustaining the Chinese people in their long resistance against a grim, unsmiling enemy?

I suppose this American assumption is correct on both scores. Still it is a difficult job when it comes to telling a typical Chinese joke or retailing a particularly pointed anecdote that would serve to illustrate the part humor played in China's war effort and to amuse American readers, to boot. There is no wartime cartoon from a Chinese *Punch* that could be readily reproduced to inspire a sense of admiration in an ally's bosom and a smile on his lips, however faint and delayed.

There is, furthermore, a much more serious obstacle to the assignment. A Chinese could not understand why, of all the heroic and tragic things there are to write about in this war—things that can "make you want to sing and make you want to cry"—one should want to write about *humor*. Wartime, to the Chinese mind, is no time for comedy, and no Chinese in his right mind would care to buck against public opinion in this matter. In vain would you seek to show that it is being done in America: that American wartime reading taste runs to the lighter fare; that radio and movie comedians are given priorities to travel far and wide to do their part by trying to uplift troop "morale"; that the English, the Belgians, the Dutch, and even the Russians have all had their sense of humor written up to prove that they are jolly good allies. It would still be considered callous to laugh, or rather to show that the Chinese laughed when they were really suffering, to "fiddle" while the good earth burned.

I mention this not in order to disprove the thesis that the Chinese are a humorous people, for I still want to produce this book, but to explain a basic difference in the American and the Chinese attitudes toward humor. This difference has been best summarized in the dictum of Judge John C. H. Wu, that "whereas Westerners are seriously humorous, the Chinese are humorously serious." The Chinese believe there is a time and place for everything and, by common consent, the War of Resistance and Reconstruction is not to be exploited for its humorous potentialities, even though there may have been such aplenty.

By common consent, as a matter of fact, the Chinese have for centuries assigned a definite time and place for humor in literature. It is, to put it negatively, not to be admitted in the Hall of Great and Good Taste. Since the Chinese conception of good government and the good society is based on rule by scholars, literature itself has been straitjacketed to include nothing but formalized and dehydrated essays and verses. Even drama and the novel, more likely productive of humor, have for so long been relegated to the literary ash can in China that their contemporary development has been seriously crippled, not to mention humorous writing *per se,* which was something unpracticed and unheard of until recent years.

Again I must be careful lest I should build up too good a case against Chinese humor. The Chinese have humor, as I believe all peoples do to a greater or lesser degree depending on the kind of weather they are used to and how good a breakfast they have packed in their belly. The Chinese, for reasons of their own, are a more irrepressible lot than a good many. That is what makes them seem like the Americans. Self-imposed conditions, however, have served rather effectively to cramp their literary and artistic expressions of this humor which they live and laugh by and possess in abundance.

In almost all essays on humor somewhere or other a definition is ventured. Perhaps at this point it devolves on me to offer a definition of the word "humor" as the Chinese understand it, or, maybe, a definition of the Chinese equivalent to the word "humor."

The Chinese term that readily comes to mind for "humor" is *huachi.* Literally, the character *hua* means "smoothe," or "slippery"; the character *chi,* meaning "to check" (to see if it tallies), or "a trick," is a perfect pun for the character *chi,* which means "chicken." An unscholarly translation of the word *huachi,* for which I shall be condemned, would therefore be "slick chick." After coming up with a little research, however, I find that the term *huachi* was first used by the ancient poet-patriot Chü Yuan (343–290 B.C.), a rather sad person, in the *Ch'u Tze* to characterize, according to his annotators, a "smoothe and ingratiating manner" with the prince which he obviously did not possess. Before Chü Yuan's time, during the Spring and Autumn Age (722–481 B.C.) celebrated by Confucius, the ruling princes were apparently highly unreasonable people and the only way to reason with them was to paint your face, put on a funny costume, and crack a few jokes, hoping they would see your point. If they didn't of course you might lose your head. In other words, court jesters were born, or "fools," as they are sometimes called, who in reality are not such fools as you might think. The term *huachi*, as it first came into use, was probably applied to these gentlemen, of whom the two most famous were Shunyu Kun and Tungfang Shuo.

In the classic *Shih Chi (Historical Records)* by Ssuma Chien, (140–80? B.C.), in which he wrote biographical sketches of ancient kings and the nobility, there appears a profile of Shunyu Kun in a series entitled *"Huachi Lieh Chuan,"* or "Biographies of Humor." These two anecdotes are told as illustrative of Shunyu Kun's life and deeds:

King Wei of the state of Ch'i led an indolent and dissipated life. He was so fond of the cup that he often indulged in all-night drinking, leaving state affairs in the hands of his ministers. As a result, his rule suffered neglect and chaos and the several princes concertedly invaded his land, threatening momentarily the existence of his state. Still, among those at his side, there was none who dared to speak up. It happened that King Wei loved to solve riddles, so Shunyu Kun came up and offered this riddle for his amusement. "There is a big bird in the land," said Shunyu Kun, "who stopped in the King's court. For three years this bird neither flew nor crowed. What manner of bird does Your Highness think this is?"

King Wei replied: "You know, this bird, once he takes flight, will pierce the sky; once he starts to crow he will awe all men!" So saying, the King summoned together the seventy-two magistrates in his realm and, then and there, singled out one for reward and another for punishment. Then he ordered out his troops to the astonishment of the several princes, who promptly returned to Ch'i all the invaded areas.

Another time, during the eighth year of King Wei's reign, the state of Ch'u dispatched a huge expedition against Ch'i. The King of Ch'i ordered that Shunyu Kun be sent on a mission to the state of Chao for aid, to take with him as a gift one hundred catties of gold and ten teams of coach and four. Shunyu Kun looked up to the sky and laughed and laughed until he snapped the tassels on his cap. The King asked, "Sir, you think it's too little?"

"How dare I think that?" Kun said.

"Then how do you explain your outburst of laughter?" the King asked.

"Well, now," Shunyu Kun began, "your humble servant happened to come from the east and saw by the wayside a man praying for a good harvest from his fields. He had a leg of roast pork in one hand and a cup of wine in the other and mumbled the following wish: 'May the God bless me with big hampers heaped full of ripe grains and wagons loaded with hay!' Your humble servant had to laugh, seeing that he offered so little and desired so much."

Whereupon, King Wei of Ch'i increased his gift to a thousand pieces of yellow gold, ten pairs of white jade, and a hundred teams of coach and four. The state of Ch'u, upon wind of this, evacuated its troops overnight.

In the Age of the Warring Kingdoms (403–221 B. C.), which followed the Spring and Autumn Age, this trick of the court jesters was taken up by the scholars in order to make their rulers behave. Confucius, Mencius, and many of their disciples, who started the tradition of the scholar in government, all sought with varying degrees of success to make their moral teachings more palatable by clothing them in the guise of a parable or a fable. It was really more wit than humor, but it was the first time anything that came close to being funny was set down in Chinese writings, and it gives substance to the claim that the Chinese are "humorously serious."

The history of *huachi* since those days was somewhat lost under the weight of succeeding generations of orthodox literature. There was evidence that it had lost its original meaning or didactic purpose and become more and more a matter of conduct or fad on the part of scholars who lost out in the pursuit of government office; at the same time *huachi* came to be less and less expressed in writing and more and more in deeds. The great exception is, of course, in the drama and fiction of the Sung and Yuan dynasties (A. D. 960–1367), which represented living literature sprung from among the folk. These were never considered legitimate by the scholars and were allowed no room for development, though the robust laughter that coursed through their pages rings true to this day.

The word *huachi* as I personally came to know it was always associated with jokes or with vaudeville comedy which has since expired but, unlike its American counterpart, has shown no' signs of coming back. Pretty soon Hollywood was upon us in China, and the first thing you know the cinemas were using the elegant lines of Chü Yuan— "*T'u t'i huachi*"—to advertise the antics of Charlie Chaplin and the Keystone cops. Thus in my own mind (such is the power of progressive education!) the word *huachi* has always stood for slapstick, and not humor in its ancient Chinese or Greek sense. I did not get to read Chü Yuan until at a more advanced age and, since *hua* does mean "slippery," the slipping-on-the-banana-peel act for a long time epitomized humor to me. Not until much later was I able to share the sentiment of the dowager in a Gardner Rea cartoon who, watching the involuntary downfall of a hapless old gent, remarked: "That's the sort of comedy that leaves me cold."

Parenthetically, I should note that the Chinese, old and young, have always been much taken with the art of Charlie Chaplin in his silent days. Without belatedly embroidering on the theme that Chaplin is really a great tragedian, I can see why his brand of humor should have found ready response in Chinese audiences. Again citing the authority of Judge Wu, we can say that while the Westerners are better acquainted with the misery of being funny (Bob Hope), the Chinese are better acquainted with the fun of being miserable (Charlie Chaplin). Chinese humor, to a greater degree than that of any other people, sees the ludicrous in the pathos of life. It is the result of a philosophical reaction to adversity coupled with innate optimism about the future. If wartime China yielded any humor it was certainly nothing but symptomatic of the misery pervading the land.

To go back to our philological research on Chinese humor, I must now reluctantly part with our "slick chick," with which I did have some fun, and come to a more contemporary Chinese word, *yumeh*. The literal meaning of these two characters (*yu* means "charming in seclusion"; *meh* means "silent") cannot by any stretch of the imagination be associated with "humor" even in its most subtle sense. But if you repeat the Chinese word *yumeh* often enough you will see that it is just a slow-motion approximation of the sound of the English word "humor"; in other words, a new coinage in the Chinese language whose component characters are not supposed to mean anything at all.

In Chinese this trick of transliteration is often resorted to for the representation of a foreign name, or an idea foreign to the Chinese vocabulary. Thus, in the old days when Western literature was first introduced to China, translators were hard put to it to find an accurate Chinese equivalent for the word "inspiration," so they simply transliterated its syllables and coined a cumbersome new Chinese term, *yen-ssu-pi-li-shun,* which would have something to do with smoke if the Chinese characters were to be taken literally. Similarly, President Truman's Chinese name, Tu-lu-men, would be some kind of a door if you take it seriously rather than phonetically.

Anyway, the point is, there came a day when Chinese writers realized that, save for the obsolete and corrupted *huachi,* they had no word that could adequately convey the shades of meaning implicit in the English word "humor," as currently understood. Hence *yumeh* was coined, and it has since gained such currency that, unlike *yen-ssu-pi-li-shun,* it is widely accepted today and destined to remain as much a part of the Chinese language as "chop suey" is a part of Mr. Mencken's American language.

Yumeh first made its appearance in 1923 in the literary supplement of the Peking *Chen Pao,* proposed by a comparatively unknown young professor named Lin Yutang, who wrote several essays about humor and the lack of it in Chinese writing. Ten years later Lin Yutang started *The Analects* fortnightly in Shanghai for the expressed purpose of promoting this product called *yumeh.* For his trouble, Dr. Lin became all but *persona non grata* to the government hierarchy and earned the hearty contempt of the communist and left-wing writers. But he also succeeded in rallying around him a group of writers who had a good time writing *yumeh* articles, samples of which are reproduced in this anthology, and in gaining a huge public following who honored him with the title *Yumeh Ta Shih,* or The Humor Master.

What Lin and his followers sought to do, with varying degrees of success, in the pages of *The Analects* and of many other magazines that followed and imitated it right up to the outbreak of war in 1937, was to give humor for the first time its rightful place in Chinese literature. They were the first to admit that the Chinese are an extremely funny people. But humor in China, they claimed, is more in deeds than in words; it is more practiced than preached. As a result, too many ludicrous things in Chinese life and politics were simply laughed off and forgotten for want of a chronicler, too many of the high and mighty who cut a ridiculous figure in the eyes of the people nevertheless got where they were because nobody dared laugh in their faces. The nation was in danger of losing its sense of humor, and *The Analects* was founded admittedly as a magazine "devoted to unconscious Chinese humor," to calling attention to the fact that the emperor was without clothes.

True to Chinese tradition, this conscious promotion and celebration of the role of humor had at its bottom a serious purpose. But the almost revolutionary concept which *The Analects* brought to Chinese popular literature, or journalism, was no less significant. For the first time the make-up of "humor" was looked into and analyzed, its presentation refined in both style and substance, and a more adult approach adopted toward the problem of what makes people laugh. No longer was it considered enough to assemble a shoddy collection of "laugh talks" and make your readers "hold their belly" in the American side-splitting sense or "spew the rice," as they would in appreciation of the efforts of a Chinese after-dinner speaker. Real humor in writing, now it was recognized, should be that which is capable of evoking what is known as the more meaningful *huei-hsin-ti-wei-hsiao,* or the "smile of the meeting of hearts." As to importation of Western examples, the *huachi* of Charlie Chaplin made way for the *yumeh* of *Punch* and *The New Yorker.*

If it is difficult to set up a national standard of humor it is much more so to establish an international standard whereby one nation's jokes would appear just as funny to citizens of another. The further one comes from the elementary appeal in humor the more restricted and provincial one is sure to become. After all, slipping-on-the-banana-peel speaks a universal language, whereas the weekly output of *The New Yorker,* so far from being intended for the old lady in Dubuque, produces its optimum enjoyment probably only in the area bounded by Madison Avenue and the East River, in the East Sixties.

The editor who sets out to export his native humor overseas, therefore, faces additional hazards. I can well sympathize with the English, for instance, who have been much maligned by unthinking Americans as a people with a peculiarly low humor content. Is this not because the English-speaking peoples are so nearly alike in manner and appearance that they have deprived one another of a most obvious source of humor, the outlandishness of the other fellow, and are constrained to appreciate humor at a more subtle level? If this is true, small wonder you can't make the average American appreciate a typically British reference to having "mulligatawny" in the jungles of Africa. It will be as difficult to make an Englishman share all the hilarious associations evoked in this land by the mere mention of Brooklyn.

With Americans vis-à-vis Chinese humor, we have a different kind of problem. The Chinese, as I am aware, are generally regarded in this country as having a sense of humor. The problem is to prove it, and live up to it. But what makes the Americans think the Chinese humorous? Is it not because of the unconsciously accepted premise that we two peoples are widely different from each other? When the Chinese are so different and strange, coming from the opposite end of the earth, as it were, anything they do or say, the very way they look, may strike you Americans as funny. They may not be funny—Chinamen eating with chopsticks and talking in a "singsong" tone are a commonplace in China—but it is enough, and perfectly natural, that they are funny in American eyes.

Thus, on closer inspection, what passes as Chinese humor in this country is often not Chinese humor, but American humor about the Chinese. Living in a melting pot, you have a humorous stereotype for almost every race and nationality, the Chinese, the Scotch, the Italians, the Jews, the Negroes. Your jokes about them are entirely your own; any similarity with the respective native brands is purely coincidental. Willie Howard's mimicry of the Gallic *professeur* is American humor; the same can be said of Fred Allen's celestial sleuth, One Long Pan.

Ever since the beginning of the war in China I have heard this allegedly Chinese story going the rounds in this country. It was first attributed, I think, to Will Rogers, and in his *Pocket Book of Wartime Humor* Bennet Cerf retells it as the only entry in his Chinese department. A Chinese laundryman, Foo Ling shall we call him, has an American customer who comes in every day and gives him the gist of the day's war news. The first time he reports the casualty list as one hundred Chinese killed and five Japs dead. Foo Ling looks up from his ironing board with a bland expression and says, "Good!" Things go bad for the Chinese Army and one day the friend drops in with the distressing news that one thousand Chinese troops were reported killed against only a hundred Jap casualties. The Chinaman, inscrutable as ever, responds with "Good! Velly good!" Finally the American rushes in with the day's headlines announcing the worst news yet: ten thousand Chinese killed, fifteen hundred Japs dead; whereupon Foo Ling exclaims, "Wonderful!" "What's so wonderful about that?" the American demands to know. "Pretty soon no Japanese!" Foo Ling says with a broad grin.

A very good American story that is, and so is this one which I heard over a radio program at one stage of the war when the American public was constantly enjoined against waste. A distinguished Chinese visitor, it seems, was being shown around New York City. Of course, they had the dignitaries and the motorcycle escort and everything. Suddenly this caravan got caught in a traffic jam, and just as the car came to a stop near an apartment house a man and his wife on the third floor got to the end of a terrific argument. The wife hauled off and knocked her husband out the window and he landed headfirst in the garbage can on the sidewalk. The Chinese visitor solemnly took in this scene, turned to a member of his party, and said: "American housewives velly wasteful. That man good for ten years yet."

The American humorous conception of the Chinese is generally good-natured, although Chinese do get sensitive about the fact that they are invariably portrayed in newspaper cartoons and on the vaudeville stage as pigtailed characters mouthing Confucian-like epigrams and concealing hatchets in their sleeves. American stereotypes of other peoples are not always so kind and sometimes can be cruel. Once I had the pleasure of visiting the studio of the well-known photographer, Alexander Alland, who is a fond portrayer of the polyglot American scene, and there were present Americans representing a great many nationalities and racial strains. It turned out to be a joke-swapping evening, in which everybody contributed with zest until somebody told one about a "Polack" which, by the way, I thought rather funny. Quite unexpectedly, it precipitated a heated debate among those present on the kind of stereotypes that might hurt racial relations, and the party broke up in a mirthless mood. Without investigating into this dire consequence of innocent humor, I do believe that it is entirely possible for many recipients of American humor about the Chinese to confuse it with Chinese humor itself.

Again, because the Chinese are expected to act differently and to go by a different, if not contrary, set of values, Americans are likely to be unduly impressed when they discover some points of similarity between the two peoples. This, I think, is another reason that accounts for the American myth according to which the Chinese have a great sense of humor "just like our own." When some professional promoters of international good will happen to be told some Chinese jokes that they readily recognize they exclaim: "Look, the Chinese laugh at the same things that we do! Their standard of values must be the same as ours." To me this is a sanguine but somewhat superficial view of the basis of international understanding. Yes, the Chinese do have miser jokes, moron jokes, doctor jokes, and mother-in-law jokes. But what is so wonderful about that? In all likelihood the Germans and the Japanese also have their versions of the same jokes to enjoy, when they are not too busy heeding their warmongering leaders.

The point seems to be not what you laugh at but how often you laugh. The former is governed by artificial rules of place and time, customs and usage. Anything that goes against the norm will seem funny, and, outside of a few elementary sure-fire formulas such as slipping-on-the-banana-peel, what seems funny will vary from land to land. The latter, however, is a matter of nature and temperament. An individual may be more lighthearted than another, and you say he has a greater sense of humor. Similarly, a nation, according to its natural endowments, may be considered as a whole as possessing a greater sense of humor than another. The Americans and the Chinese, fortunately, are each in its own way such a nation. As to whether Chinese humor would appear humorous to Americans, and vice versa, I can only say that the more you know of a people's manners and mores, its social background and literary heritage, the greater part of its humor you will appreciate and the more of its jokes you will understand. Only then will you be able to graduate from the belly laugh of the country rustic at the sight of a foreigner in his strange costume into the more sophisticated "smile of the meeting of hearts."

To this noble end the present humble collection is dedicated. I have no illusion about the laugh-provoking powers of an anthology of Chinese humor edited for American consumption, when humor is so much a part of the Chinese people but so little a part of Chinese literature. In the face of the very popular American humor about the Chinese I have to announce that what is assembled here is not so much to make you laugh as to show you what makes the Chinese laugh, or chuckle, or smile.* Come to think of it, I cannot exactly claim all of that either, for what appears funniest to the Chinese is oftentimes (1)

---

* An index of the Chinese sense of humor is the number and variety of Chinese terms used in describing the different kinds of laughter. In the onomatopoeic department there is the *ha-ha* laugh, the *ho-ho* laugh, the laugh *he-he,* the *chi-chi* laugh, the *pu-chi* laugh, and the *ke-ke* laugh. For the visually descriptive we have such expressions as "hold the belly," "spew the rice," the "open face" or grin, the "tumbling over" laugh, which corresponds to the English "rolling in the aisles," and the "looking-at-heaven" laugh.

outside the realm of writing, (2) untranslatable even if in writing, and (3) unfunny to the Westerner even if translated.

Thus circumscribed, the editing here is necessarily along somewhat different lines from those followed in anthologies of other national humors already published in this series. For one thing, in the whole book there are not more than twenty identifiable individual authors. For another, as my title indicates, the barbed point of wit seems more in evidence than the soothing tonic of humor. However, I do share with my fellow anthologists a subjective point of view and include only things that I have liked. It is, in a way, an impressionistic rather than comprehensive collection. My fond hope is that it should at least prove entertaining.

The scheme of the book is chronological as well as organic, though both only roughly and arbitrarily so. In simple terms, the four main sections are: ancient anecdotes, excerpts from novels, traditional jokes, and contemporary essays. The pungent aphorisms of Confucius are purposely left out, many of them being almost as familiar to us as the pseudo-Confucianisms. Laotze's humor is too much of the spiritual and, between other covers, he has lately been often and admirably introduced. At one point I toyed with the idea of establishing a section called "The Humor of Personalities," to pin down specimens like Su Tung-po, one or another of the Ming dynasty bohemians, or Mr. Wu Chih-hui, venerated as the "Living Laughing Buddha." But I am afraid they would make the book even more diffused than it is. I don't know whether I should feel regretful or relieved that the salacious appeal and the play on words which account for much of China's laughing matter are both inadmissible in an anthology for the Western reader.

GEORGE KAO

New York City

INTRODUCTION

INVARIABLY those writers who have visited China and come out with a book on that vast country and who are, in my opinion, successful at the job, have been people with a keen sense of humor. Two of the earliest good books on China, still among the best, are *Chinese Characteristics* and *Village Life in China,* both by the witty Reverend Arthur Smith, published some forty years ago. More recent instances are the works of Pearl Buck and Carl Crow. The serious students of China's affairs are not only a sad lot, but they usually manage to miss the subtle, indefinable, human quality of the Chinese people and Chinese politics, which carries with it a sense of convincing reality. The difference between those who have a sense of humor and those who do not is that the latter make the Chinese appear bizarre and paradoxical, living either in utopian bliss or in depths of degradation, while the former make them human and understandable by the magic touch of humor. Those very earnest students and critics of Chinese affairs give me the impression of plodding, conscientious Ph. D. candidates who try to analyze a Shakespearean comedy in a very serious frame of mind. That is why I am glad that, for a change, there is a Chinese writer like George Kao, who is not a Ph. D., to try to present China from the standpoint of humor—and to do so, not by his own interpretation and theorizing, but through a collection of Chinese writing itself.

The fact is, the Chinese are both a funny and humorous people. The Chinese people do many fantastic and contrary things. Intrinsically, these are funny to Westerners, as Western things are funny to the Chinese. And if you can make the Chinese see that many of their own things are funny, they are quick to laugh at them, for have they not been laughing at them all their lives? I think they laugh longer than the Western critics; the line must be drawn somewhere when things cease to be funny to foreigners in China, while they are still funny to the Chinese themselves. Professor Toynbee once told me something very sad. Outside Nanking, he saw a skinny pony with a heavy load stuck on an uphill path, while the old driver vainly tried to prod him with his whip. The pony tried frantically, but it seemed the cart and its load were threatening to submerge both the pony and his driver. Professor Toynbee, quite understandably, got down and helped the cart forward. The driver laughed, and the Chinese passengers laughed, instead of coming to help. But Professor Toynbee could not understand that the sight of a gray-haired white man pushing a cart in his shirt sleeves was so screamingly funny and contradictory to the general assumptions of the oriental world that the Chinese pony was laughing, too. On the other hand, the Christian point of view is that the sight of a poor animal struggling uphill under a staggering load is not a proper subject for laughter.

In a recent issue of *Life* there is an extraordinary photograph of a Chinese refugee family fleeing the Japs from Kweilin, curiously perched and lashed on the underside of a railroad boxcar; extraordinary because every face of that family, from the grandmother to the young girl, looks enviably comfortable and shows a wholehearted smile. These smiles are authentic and have nothing of the synthetic grin of United States Senators and bathing beauties. They are the smiles of the American common men and women. It is with this type of humor and good cheer that the Chinese people have been carrying on for the last three or four thousand years.

All good, pervading, solid, lasting humor, I believe, is based on a philosophy, a way of looking at things. We say the Chinese are humorous because they are philosophic. Such a dangerous, sweeping generalization may nevertheless be true. Chinese philosophy, or Confucianism, is a philosophy of common sense, and this common sense, I have no doubt, is the basis of Chinese humor.

There is a story about a Chinese farmer which illustrates this point of view. Once a farmer was going home after his day's work. On his way he had bought a pot of soybean sauce, and this he carried at the back end of a bamboo pole swung across his shoulder. The pot of soybean sauce slipped off the pole and crashed on the stone pavement, but the farmer walked on as if nothing had happened. A passenger thought he hadn't noticed it and called it to his attention. "I know," replied the farmer. "But if it's broken, it's broken, isn't it?" In the circumstances, there was just nothing to do about it. He didn't stop for it, and he didn't cry.

Given this general point of view, it is inevitable that we should find the Chinese laughing at the theater and in the novel and in the idle, literary, and political gossip that pervades both Chinese life and Chinese literature. The Chinese, I believe, are the world's greatest gossipers. The goal of gossiping is to prick the bubbles of the great of the world and re-establish a comfortable sense of equality of all mankind. In American terms, it proves that you are as good as anybody else.

There is, however, a peculiar twist which prevented the output of Chinese humorous literature from being as prolific as it should have been. That is Confucian puritanism. Confucian decorum put a damper on light, humorous writing, as well as on all imaginative literature, except poetry. Drama and the novel were despised as unworthy of a respectable scholar's occupation, and we had the greatest difficulty establishing the authorship of some of the greatest Chinese novels. This puritanical, austere public attitude has persisted to this day. While President Roosevelt took care to salt his speeches and broadcasts with some attempts at humor, it is inconceivable that President Chiang Kai-shek should. The thing isn't being done. While a respectable paper like the *New York Times* would publish an editorial on some perfectly inconsequential topic like "The Decline of Beef Stew," when a war was going on, no respectable Chinese editor would think of enlivening his political and economic discourses with a flash of humor. The recognition of the role of humor in general Chinese writing, and as an element of style, is what I fought for by founding and editing the first Chinese humor magazine, *The Analects,* some twelve years ago. I ran right into the Kuomintang rulers who are still very serious, and also right in to the communist and leftist writers, who, encumbered with youth's crabbed sense of responsibility to reshape the universe along Marxist lines, rather looked askance at a joke. The communists, especially, were howling that Lin Yutang, by preaching humor, was "ruining the country." I could not convince them that humor had a proper role in literature and life by referring them to ancient Chinese sources, including Confucius himself, for the leftists held all Chinese literature in utter Marxist contempt. In desperation, I had to show them that humor was something considered quite proper by foreigners, and therefore "modern." I pointed out that Charles Lamb did not ruin England and that *The Golden Calf* did not ruin their beloved postrevolutionary Soviet Russia. And they quietly shut up, although they are still unconvinced.

But humorous literature and jokes flourished in a joke-loving people in spite of Confucian puritanism and outside the sanctimonious territory of "orthodox literature," just as the drama and the novel did.

So long as gifted writers were willing to ignore "the cold pork at the Confucian Temple" and degrade themselves by writing anonymous novels and memoirs bristling with anecdotes and gossip, the literary priestcraft could do nothing about it; and so, along happy and unrestricted literary bypaths, this literature grew. There was quite a distinguished and, in parts, humorous long novel, *Yeh Sao Pao Yen.* Its hero was conceived as a Confucian model gentleman. The author employed the well-known formula for creating salacious sex appeal by placing the hero constantly in compromising positions with women and making him stop just short of a moral catastrophe. The whole novel was an ardent defense of the Confucian way of life. Yet both the author and his grandson omitted this novel, his literary masterpiece, from the list of his works in his official biography. It mentions only his puerile poetry and his earnest discourses on philosophy and the art of government. The point is, this situation did not prevent Hsia Erh-ming from writing the novel for his own amusement. Probably the most typical Chinese humorous novel, *Julin Waishih,* was a book devoted solely to poking fun at the Confucian scholars, and it was written by one who was himself a scholar.

One would have therefore to go to "unorthodox" literature to find the best examples of humor, to drama and the novel. Humorous sketches were almost completely absent. I do not think the *huachi,* or "funny," pieces that the Confucian writers wrote when they set out to be funny are funny at all; e.g., the *Farewell to Poverty,* by Han Yu, and *Drive out the Cats,* by Li Yu, which are disappointing to me. When these writers wrote *huachi* pieces, they told themselves they were going to be facetious, and were consciously so, which spoils the humorous effect for the reader. On the other hand, there is that vast realm of anecdotage—humor in the daily lives of the gentry and kings and their wives—which is a comic kingdom in itself. I may give two examples here, one ancient and the other modern.

Su Tung-po, the Sung poet, was a man of great charm and genial humor, and there are any number of anecdotes told about him. He had an incorrigible propensity for cracking jokes at the expense of his enemies, his friends, and himself.

Once Su Tung-po went to call on a Mr. Lu, and was kept waiting an unusually long time because the latter, a very fat person, was taking an unusually long afternoon nap. At last, when Lu came down to see him, Su pointed to an earthen jar containing a tortoise with a green water plant growing on its back, and said, "A tortoise with water plant on its shell is not so rare. What is really difficult to obtain is a tortoise with six eyes." Lu asked what he meant, and Su replied, "Emperor Chung of Tang dynasty once received a six-eyed tortoise, given him by a minister as a rarity. On being asked what was the virtue of a six-eyed tortoise, the minister replied, 'A six-eyed tortoise has three pair of eyes, while others have only one. Therefore, when a six-eyed tortoise takes a nap, it is equal to the nap of three tortoises together.'"

During the National Revolution of 1927, there was a riot of slogans and placards pasted on the walls of offices and public places. There was one Mr. Wang who had started a campaign against foot binding, and among the propaganda posters he put up there was one reading, "We ought to place the small feet of the million and a half sisters in Honan upon our own shoulders." A modern wit remarked that if you multiplied that by two, there would be three million small feet of the Honan women upon Wang's shoulders.

"One excellent test of the civilization of a country I take to be the flourishing of the comic idea and comedy," says George Meredith; "and the test of true comedy is that it shall awaken thoughtful laughter." All popular folk humor, I believe, is more or less alike, depending on a common assent as to what is to be laughed at—the miser, the cheat, the quack doctor, the mother-in-law, and, above all, the henpecked husband—and on a sudden ease of tension which provides the comic relief. Thoughtful humor, however, is based on the perception of human errors, incongruities, cant, and hypocrisy, which admittedly are shared by all of us. The comic spirit is that human understanding which, being higher than academic intelligence, rises above the confusion and self-deception of our common notions, and points its finger at life's sham, futility, and follies. The true comic genius is really a higher, because subtler, form of intelligence because it sees what the others do not see, and under the cloak of fun exercises the criticism of man's ideas. Man is a laughing animal, an honor doubtfully shared by anthropoid apes, and that is why to err is bestial, but to laugh at our errors is human. Only that culture which, by its own intellectual richness, rises above itself through its more penetrating minds to exercise criticism of its ideas, vogues, and fetishes could qualify for the name of a human culture. In this sense Meredith is right, and the best humor is that which is infused with the light of intellectual understanding.

In this sense, Laotze, the antagonist of Confucius, must he regarded as the true comic spirit of China, and Chuangtze, his follower and inventor of a great many libelous stories about Confucius, may be regarded as the most intelligent humorist of China. Laotze's laughter was dry and small, sounding low through his thin beard, while Chuangtze, being a younger man, often broke out into boisterous laughter. At times it sounded like a bitter laugh, because he was a campaigner for ideas. The laughter of these two men has reverberated down the ages. The interaction of two forces, the constructive, positive, humanizing outlook of Confucianism and the destructive, negative outlook and distrust of human agencies of Taoism, has conditioned and fashioned the fabric of Chinese thought through the centuries.

It was about seven hundred years later, after these two forces had met and mixed, that there emerged what seems to my mind the most mature humorous spirit of China. I refer to Tao Chien the poet, in whose spirit the last slightly sour note which existed in Chuangtze was lost, and humor, joined to an understanding acceptance of life, evoked only a kindly, leisurely smile. Confucianism and Taoism had sufficiently combined to make his appearance possible. Tao Chien was both responsible and irresponsible, and we see at last neither a crusader nor a cynic, but a family man, one of us, and therefore truly a great human spirit, conscious of the limitations of human existence, but nevertheless achieving his own freedom without abandon and peace of mind without rebellion. It would be difficult, though possible, to point to some particular piece of Tao's as showing his humorous spirit, but that is so with the greatest and best kind of humor when it becomes a pervading view of life. In him, humor becomes perfectly natural. Tao had come to terms with himself and with his relations with the human world.

When, after *The Analects* fortnightly, I started in Shanghai the *Yuchoufeng* magazine, whose object it was to enlarge the scope of humorous writing in China and merge it with the familiar essay, I received from New York a series of articles on the American scene by George Kao which read refreshingly different from the general run of Chinese "foreign correspondence." Though each was an example of careful reporting, his pieces were free from stuffy politico-economic pontificating and showed that blending of ease and familiar grace that delighted its readers. Since he himself practices the art of the familiar essay, which is the art of delving into the depths of erudition and coming up to the surface with the agility and grace of an accomplished swimmer, we are assured that he knows his job in making this anthology of Chinese humor.

The present anthology is the first of its kind, regarding humor in the sense the Americans understand it. To this end, Mr. Kao has amassed a good and comprehensive collection of Chinese humor, from popular jokes to Rabelaisian and picaresque humor of the Chinese novelists. The humor of ideas is well represented in the first section. I am glad also to see modern humor included in the last section. It is in this section that I believe humor as an element of style is most developed and comes closest to the Western humorous sketches.

LIN YUTANG

I

THE HUMOR OF PHILOSOPHY
(Ancient)

I. The Humor of Philosophy
(Ancient)

CHINA is known as a philosophical nation, so even Chinese humor must have its philosophy. Actually this is not unusual. When you hear something funny told you are not satisfied, you want to know what is the point to the story. That "point" is where the philosophy comes in. To put it another way, Chinese philosophy sometimes has its humor. Moral teachings have ever a tendency to be dull and tiresome to the receiver, and the teacher, if he knows his psychology, would seek to sugar-coat his pills of wisdom with a fable, an allegory, or just a touch or two of levity.

I would not go so far as to claim that all Chinese philosophers of ancient times made a practice of enlivening their preachments with a colorful and anecdotal style. As a matter of fact, taking the body of Chinese philosophy as a whole, the evidence points the other way. But there are enough examples of wisdom served up with wisecracks to justify starting our anthology of Chinese humor with this section.

For purposes of humor, Chinese philosophers may be divided into the usual two great schools: on the one hand, the Confucianists with the Great Sage himself, the Second Sage Mencius, and the Confucian disciples of all ages; on the other hand, the Taoist school, rooted in Laotze the "Old Boy," flowering in Chuangtze, and bearing fruit in Liehtze and Hanfeitze. Confucianism, with its precept of the moral man, has molded the serious thoughts and habits of the Chinese gentleman for all time; the Taoists have taken care of him in his off moments. Being resigned to nature, the Taoist can see man in his limitations; being the perennial outsider, he can afford to relax and laugh.

The samples collected in the following pages range from the gossamer essence of naturalistic philosophy to quick-witted court repartee. Authorship is indicated only as far as can be established—which is not very far. Not enough is known definitely about each man to set him up as a true humorist on the strength of either his personality or his work. The nearest approach to one, Liehtze, for instance, may not even have existed. The one thing common to all the pieces gathered here is their age, dating back two thousand years, or nearly as old.

Confucius and Disciples

IT MUST be said that a good deal of the forbidding seriousness about the Confucian classics is a result of the "orthodox" interpretation placed upon them by succeeding generations of scholar-officials for the benefit of the public and for posterity. Read with unjaundiced eye, the quoted sayings of Confucius are not lacking in pungency and jolly good fellowship (even if they do not exactly correspond to the latter-day Broadway conception of Confucian humor). As a humorist, however, Master Kung is more sinned against than sinning. The spectacle of a great sage bent on a career of doing positive good for society but roaming "like a lost dog" (his own words) from kingdom to kingdom in search of official sponsorship somehow piques the risibility of more detached onlookers. Hence the vast number of stories, apocryphal or otherwise, that have been built around his personality from shortly after his own time down to the present day.

THE TYRANT AND THE TIGER

Confucius once passed by the foot of the Tai Mountain. There he saw a woman crying her heart out beside a newly finished grave.

The Master stopped and listened. Then he sent Tselu over to inquire of the mourner, saying, "You cry as if you are in great sorrow."

"True!" the woman answered. "First my father-in-law was killed by the tiger; then my husband was killed by the tiger; and now my son—he also died at the mouth of the tiger."

"Why, then," the Master asked, "didn't you leave the place and go somewhere else?"

"But there is no tyrant here!" was the woman's reply.

Confucius turned to Tselu and said: "Mark it, my lad! A tyrant is worse than a tiger."

All items in this section translated by George Kao.

4

THE "HEY-YOU" FOOD

A great famine occurred in Ch'i. A rich man named Chien Ao set up a relief stand by the wayside to feed the hungry.

Presently a hungry man, in shreds and tatters, tottered along. With food in his left hand and drink in his right, Chien Ao called out to him, saying, "Hey, you, come and get it!"

The man flung him a glance and said, "It is just because I do not eat any 'hey-you' food that I have come to this."

Chien Ao apologized, but the man refused the proffered food to the end and died starving.

The philosopher Tsengtze heard of it and said, "My word! It is all right to balk at the 'hey'; but after the apologies it seems that the man could have eaten."

CONFUCIUS AND TZELU

Once Confucius went hiking in the hills, and he sent his disciple Tzelu to fetch some water. Tzelu was set upon by a tiger at the mountain stream. After a fierce struggle he succeeded in killing the beast by first grabbing its tail.

When he returned with the water he brought back the tail tucked away as a trophy. He was anxious to boast of his feat, but first he asked Confucius: "How does the higher man kill a tiger?" The Master said, "The higher man kills a tiger by aiming at its head." Then he asked, "How does the middling man kill a tiger?" The Master said, "The middling man kills a tiger by taking hold of its ears." Again he asked, "How does the lower man kill a tiger?" The Master said, "The lower man kills a tiger by grabbing at its tail." Tzelu, abashed, turned and discarded the tiger tail.

He was chagrined at Confucius, and he reasoned thus: "The Master sent me for water in the mountain, knowing there was a tiger lurking by the stream. It was because he wanted to see me killed." So he tucked away a stone with which he intended to hit Confucius, but first he asked, "How does the higher man kill a man?" The Master said, "The higher man kills a man with his pen." Then he asked, "How does the middling man kill a man?" The Master said, "The middling man kills a man with his tongue." Finally he asked, "How does the lower man kill a man?" The Master said, "The lower man kills a man with a stone." Tzelu turned around and sheepishly tossed away the stone, and his heart was convinced.

DEAD MEN TELL NO TALES

Tzekung once asked Confucius: "Do dead men know what is going on, or do they not?"

Confucius answered: "If I were to say that dead men know what's going on I am afraid all of the filial sons and grandsons would inconvenience the living in order to accommodate the dead. But if I were to say that dead men don't know what's going on, I am afraid that unfilial offspring would just leave their dead unburied. Now, Ssu, if you wish to know whether or not dead men know, wait until you die and you will know soon enough!"

THE LOST BOW

King Kung of Ch'u went ahunting and lost his bow. His men begged leave to go and look for it. The King said: "Never mind. Some man of Ch'u lost his bow and some man of Ch'u will find it. So why bother to look?"

When Confucius heard of this he commented: "What a pity that he was not big enough. He could have said simply, 'Some man lost his bow and some man will find it.' Why limit it to Ch'u?"

ABANDONED FISH

When Confucius went to Ch'u he met a fishmonger who insisted on making him a present of a fish. Confucius at first declined. But the fishmonger said, "The day is warm and I missed the market and could not sell this fish. I thought to myself, rather than throw the fish away I would do well to present it to the gentleman." When Confucius heard this he thanked the man and accepted the fish; then he ordered his disciples to sweep up the room preparatory to offering it as sacrifice. His disciples protested, saying: "Now, this is a fish that the man was about to abandon; yet our master thinks so much of it as to wish to offer it for sacrifice. Why?" Confucius said: "As I heard it, he is a sage who gives away his wealth instead of letting it rot on his hands. Today I had a gift from a sage, how can I help but offer if for sacrifice?"

A GIFT DECLINED

When Tzesse lived in the kingdom of Wei he was so poor that he wore a cotton robe without lining and had only nine meals in a fortnight. Tien Tze-fang heard of this and he sent Tzesse a fine fur coat. Because he was afraid that Tzesse would decline he added, "When I lend people anything I simply forget about it; when I give people anything I just consider it lost." Still Tzesse thanked him and refused to accept the gift. Tze-fang said, "Since I have and you have not what reason is there to decline my gift?" Tzesse replied, "According to what I hear, to give away something without call is like throwing it in the sewer. Although I am poor I could not bear to think of myself as a sewer. That is the reason I dare not accept."

FILIAL THOUGHTS

Po-yu did wrong and he cried when his mother chastised him with a stick. "You never used to cry when I thrashed you," said his mother. "Why do you cry today?" He answered, "When I did wrong and you thrashed me it always used to hurt. But this time Mother's strength is such that it does not hurt. That is why I cry."

CONFUCIUS BLAMED TSENGTZE

Tsengtze was hoeing melons and, by mistake, he cut off a root. His aged father, Tseng Hsi, greatly enraged, swung a big stick and hit him. The blow felled Tsengtze to the ground and knocked him unconscious. After a while he came to and got up with a jerk. Then he spoke to his father thus: "Just now when I incurred your displeasure, sir, you hit me hard. Did you not strain yourself?" After this he withdrew to the next room and started to play the lute and sing, so that Tseng Hsi might hear his song and know that his feelings were unruffled.

When Confucius heard about this he told his gateman: "When

Tseng Ts'an comes don't let him in." Tsengtze, believing he had done no wrong, sent someone over to Confucius to know the reason for his rebuff. Confucius said: "You have heard of the Blind Old Man whose son was the great Emperor Shun. The way Shun served his father, he would always be present when he was wanted for an errand, but he would never let himself be found when he was wanted to be killed; if his father wished to give him a mild thrashing he would wait, but if it threatened to be a big thrashing he would run. That was in order to escape blind fury. Now you expose yourself to blind fury, plant yourself in its way, and risk having yourself killed and your father plunged into wrongdoing. What greater unfilial conduct is there than this? For are you not the subject of the Son of Heaven? And what greater crime is there than to kill a subject of the Son of Heaven?"

To think that, with all of Tsengtze's talent, besides being a disciple of Confucius, still he did not know wherein he had erred. Is it not difficult to be right?

THREE TIMES A MURDERER

When Tseng Ts'an, one of the chief disciples of Confucius, was living in Fei, a namesake of his in the district killed a man in a brawl. Someone rushed to Tseng Ts'an's mother and said, "Tseng Ts'an has killed a man!" "My son can't do such a thing," said Tseng Ts'an's mother, and went on weaving as if nothing had happened. Presently someone else came to her and said, "Tseng Ts'an has killed a man!" but she paid no attention to him and went on weaving as before. But when a third man came to her and said, "Tseng Ts'an has killed a man!" her confidence was shaken and she fled the house.

Mencius

MENCIUS, who made the remark that "the great man is he who has not lost his childish heart," demonstrates a more conscious type of humor than Confucius has been enabled to show. His man of Ch'i who had two wives is a masterpiece of comic characterization. His position in relation to the kings of Ch'i, moreover, was ever that of mentor and adviser. While not above enlightening some particularly dim-witted ruler by means of a metaphor or parable, there is not the least in Mencius that suggests the court jester. This cannot be said of some of the others given in these pages who could only "get away" with a piece of daring advice to their liege by masquerading it under some ludicrously farfetched paradox.

THE MAN OF CH'I

A man of Ch'i had a wife and a concubine, and lived together with them in his house. When their husband went out, he would get himself well filled with wine and flesh, and then return, and, on his wife's asking him with whom he ate and drank, they were sure to be all wealthy and honorable people.

The wife informed the concubine, saying, "When our good man goes out, he is sure to come back having partaken plentifully of wine and flesh. I asked him with whom he ate and drank, and they are all, it seems, wealthy and honorable people. And yet no people of distinction ever come here. I will spy out where our good man goes."

Accordingly, she got up early in the morning and privately followed wherever her husband went. Throughout the whole city there was no one who stood or talked with him. At last he came to those who were sacrificing among the tombs in the eastern suburbs, and begged what they had over. Not being satisfied, he looked about, and went to another party; and this was the way in which he got himself satiated.

The wife returned and informed the concubine, saying, "It was to our husband that we looked up in hopeful contemplation with whom our lot is cast for life—and now these are his ways!" On this, along

All selections from Mencius are from the translation by James Legge.

with the concubine she reviled their husband, and they wept together
in the middle hall.

In the meantime the husband, knowing nothing of all this, came in
with a jaunty air, carrying himself proudly to his wife and concubine.

In the view of a superior man, as to the ways by which men seek
for riches, honors, gain, and advancement, there are few of their wives
and concubines who would not be ashamed and weep together on
account of them.

A SHEEP FOR AN OX

King Hsuan of Ch'i asked, "Is such a one as I competent to love and
protect the people?"

Mencius said, "Yes."

"From what do you know that I am competent to do that?"

"I heard the following incident from Hoo Heih: 'The King,' said
he, 'was sitting aloft in the hall, when a man appeared, leading an ox
past the lower part of it. The King saw him and asked, 'Where is the
ox going?' The man replied, 'We are going to consecrate a bell with
its blood.' The King said, 'Let it go. I cannot bear its frightened appearance, as if it were an innocent person going to the place of death.'
The man answered, 'Shall we then omit the consecration of the bell?'
The King said, 'How can that be omitted? Change it for a sheep.' I
do not know whether this incident really occurred."

The King replied, "It did," and then Mencius said, "The heart seen
in this is sufficient to carry you to the imperial sway. The people all
supposed that Your Majesty grudged the animal, but your servant
knows surely that it was Your Majesty's not being able to bear the
sight which made you do as you did."

The King said, "You are right. And yet there really was an appearance of what the people condemned. But though Ch'i be a small and
narrow state, how should I grudge one ox? Indeed, it was because I
could not bear its frightened appearance, as if it were an innocent person going to the place of death, that therefore I changed it for a sheep."

Mencius pursued, "Let not Your Majesty deem it strange that the
people should think you were grudging the animal. When you changed
a large one for a small, how should they know the true reason? If you
felt pained by its being led without guilt to the place of death, what
was there to choose between an ox and a sheep?"

The King laughed and said, "What really was my mind in the matter? I did not grudge the expense of it, and changed it for a sheep! There was reason in the people's saying that I grudged it."

"There is no harm in their saying so," said Mencius. "Your conduct was an artifice of benevolence. You saw the ox, and had not seen the sheep. So is the superior man affected toward animals, that, having seen them alive, he cannot bear to see them die; having heard their dying cries, he cannot bear to eat their flesh. Therefore he keeps away from his cook room."

The King was pleased, and said, "It is said in the book of Poetry, 'The minds of others, I am able by reflection to measure'; This is verified, my master, in your discovery of my motive. I indeed did the thing, but when I turned my thoughts inward, and examined into it, I could not discover my own mind. When you, Master, spoke those words, the movements of compassion began to work in my mind. How is it that this heart has in it what is equal to the imperial sway?"

Mencius replied, "Suppose a man were to make this statement to Your Majesty: 'My strength is sufficient to lift three thousand catties, but it is not sufficient to lift one feather; my eyesight is sharp enough to examine the point of an autumn hair, but I do not see a wagonload of fagots'; would Your Majesty allow what he said?"

"No," was the answer, on which Mencius proceeded, "Now here is kindness sufficient to reach to animals, and no benefits are extended from it to the people. How is this? Is an exception to be made here? The truth is, the feather's not being lifted is because the strength is not used; the wagonload of firewood's not being seen is because the vision is not used; and the people's not being loved and protected is because the kindness is not employed. Therefore, Your Majesty's not exercising the imperial sway is because you do not do it, not because you are not able to do it.

THE KING TALKED OF OTHER THINGS

"Suppose," Mencius said to King Hsuan of Ch'i, "one of Your Majesty's subjects should entrust his wife and children to the care of a friend before he went on a journey to the state of Ch'u and should find, on his return, that his wife and children had suffered from hunger and cold. What then would Your Majesty do?"

"I would no longer consider that man a friend," the King replied.

"What if a teacher is unable to manage his pupils?"

"I would discharge him."

"What if the entire state is neglected?"

The King thereupon turned to his attendants right and left and talked of other things.

THE FARMER OF SUNG

There was a man of Sung who was grieved that his growing corn was not longer, and so he pulled it up. Having done this, he returned home, looking very stupid, and said to his people, "I am tired today. I have been helping the corn to grow long." His son ran to look at it, and found the corn all withered. There are few in the world who do not deal with their passion nature as if they were assisting the corn to grow long. Some indeed consider it of no benefit to them, and let it alone—they do not weed their corn. They who assist it to grow long pull out their corn. What they do is not only of no benefit to the nature, but it also injures it.

THE TOUCH OF HANDS

Shunyu Kun said, "Is it the rule that males and females shall not allow their hands to touch in giving or receiving anything?" Mencius replied, "It is the rule." Kun asked, "If a man's sister-in-law be drowning, shall he rescue her with his hand?" Mencius said, "He who would not so rescue a drowning woman is a wolf.* For males and females not to allow their hands to touch in giving and receiving is the general rule; when a sister-in-law is drowning, to rescue her with the hand is a peculiar expediency."

Kun said, "The whole empire is drowning. How strange it is that you will not rescue it!"

Mencius answered, "A drowning empire must be rescued with right principles, as a drowning sister-in-law has to be rescued with the hand. Do you wish me to rescue the empire with my hand?"

THE ARCHERY STUDENT

Pang Meng learned archery of Yi. When he had acquired completely all the science of Yi, he thought that in all the empire only Yi was

* Not to be taken as having the same meaning as in the current American slang.

superior to himself, and so he slew him. Mencius said, "In this case Yi also was to blame. Kungming Yi indeed said, 'It would appear as if he were not to be blamed,' but he thereby only meant that his blame was slight. How can he be held without any blame?

"The people of Cheng sent Tzecho Ju to make a stealthy attack on Wei, which sent Yukung Sze to pursue him. Tzecho Ju said, 'Today I feel unwell, so that I cannot hold my bow. I am a dead man!' At the same time he asked his driver, 'Who is it that is pursuing me?' The driver said, 'It is Yukung Sze,' on which he exclaimed, 'I shall live.' The driver said, 'Yukung Sze is the best archer of Wei. What do you mean by saying, "I shall live?"' Ju replied, 'Yukung Sze learned archery from Yinkung To, who again learned it from me. Now, Yinkung To is an upright man, and the friends of his selection must be upright also.' When Yukung Sze came up he said, 'Master, why are you not holding your bow?' Ju answered him, 'Today I am feeling unwell, and cannot hold my bow.' On this Sze said, 'I learned archery from Yinkung To, who again learned it from you. I cannot bear to injure you with your own science. The business of today, however, is the prince's business, which I dare not neglect.' He then took his arrows, knocked off their steel points against the carriage wheel, discharged four of them, and returned."

THE NEIGHBOR'S DAUGHTER

A man of Jen asked the disciple Wulu, saying, "Is an observance of the rules of propriety in regard to eating, or the eating, the more important?" The answer was, "The observance of the rules of propriety is the more important."

"Is the gratifying the appetite of sex, or the doing so only according to the rules of propriety, the more important?" The answer again was, "The observance of the rules of propriety in the matter is the more important."

The man pursued, "If the result of eating only according to the rules of propriety will be death by starvation, while by disregarding those rules we may get food, must they still be observed in such a case? If according to the rule that he shall go in person to meet his wife a man cannot get married, while by disregarding that rule he may get married, must he still observe the rule in such a case?"

Wulu was unable to reply to these questions, and the next day he went to Tsou, and told them to Mencius. Mencius said, "What difficulty is there in answering these inquiries?

"If you do not adjust them at their lower extremities, but only put their tops on a level, pieces of wood an inch square may be made to be higher than the pointed peak of a high building.

"Gold is heavier than feathers; but does that saying have reference, on the one hand, to a single clasp of gold, and, on the other, to a wagonload of feathers?

"If you take a case where the eating is of the utmost importance and the observing the rules of propriety is of little importance, and compare the things together, why stop with saying merely that the eating is more important? So, taking the case where gratifying the appetite of sex is of the utmost importance and observing the rules of propriety is of little importance, why stop with merely saying that gratifying the appetite is the more important?

"Go and answer him thus: 'If by twisting your elder brother's arm and snatching from him what he is eating you can get food for yourself, while if you do not do so you will not get anything to eat, will you so twist his arm? If by getting over your neighbor's wall and dragging away his virgin daughter you can get a wife, while if you do not do so you will not be able to get a wife, will you so drag her away?'"

THE RETIRED TIGER FIGHTER

When Ch'i was suffering from famine, Chen Tsin said to Mencius, "The people are all thinking that you, Master, will again ask that the granary of T'ang be opened for them. I apprehend that you will not do so a second time."

Mencius said, "To do it would be to act like Feng Fu. There was a man of that name in Chin, famous for his skill in seizing tigers. Afterward he became a scholar of reputation, and going once out to the wild country, he found the people all in pursuit of a tiger. The tiger took refuge in a corner of a hill, where no one dared to attack him, but when they saw Feng Fu, they ran and met him. Feng Fu immediately bared his arms, and descended from the carriage. The multitude were pleased with him, but those who were scholars laughed at him."

Chuangtze

THE "do-nothing" philosophy of Laotze lately has been much talked about by Western authors. Chuang Chou was the harmonious personality who expounded the Way by living it and by brilliant and ironical sallies against Confucian activity. The humor of Chuangtze pertains to an attitude, a way of life, rather than to any trick of expression. The following samples are some of the best-known jewels of Chuangtzean philosophy. They convey a serious message; yet, depending on the way you look at it, items like "Butterfly Dream" and "The Pleasure of Fishes" could almost serve as basic script for one of those mad exchanges between Abbott and Costello.

DIALOGUE WITH A SKULL

Chuangtze one day saw an empty skull, bleached, but still preserving its shape. Striking it with his riding whip, he said, "Wert thou once some ambitious citizen whose inordinate yearnings brought him to this pass?—some statesman who plunged his country in ruin and perished in the fray?—some wretch who left behind him a legacy of shame?—some beggar who died in the pangs of hunger and cold? Or didst thou reach this state by the natural course of old age?"

When he had finished speaking, he took the skull, and placing it under his head as a pillow, went to sleep. In the night he dreamed that the skull appeared to him and said, "You speak well, sir; but all you say has reference to the life of mortals, and to mortal troubles. In death there are none of these. Would you like to hear about death?"

Chuangtze having replied in the affirmative, the skull began: "In death, there is no sovereign above, and no subject below. The workings of the four seasons are unknown. Our existences are bounded only by eternity. The happiness of a king among men cannot exceed that which we enjoy."

Chuangtze, however, was not convinced, and said, "Were I to prevail upon God to allow your body to be born again, and your bones and

All selections from Chuangtze are from the translation by Herbert A. Giles.

flesh to be renewed, so that you could return to your parents, to your wife, and to the friends of your youth, would you be willing?"

At this, the skull opened its eyes wide and knitted its brows and said, "How should I cast aside happiness greater than that of a king and mingle once again in the toils and troubles of mortality?"

THE DEATH OF CHUANGTZE'S WIFE

When Chuangtze's wife died, Huitze went to condole. He found the widower sitting on the ground, singing, with his legs spread out at a right angle, and beating time on a bowl.

"To live with your wife," exclaimed Huitze, "and see your eldest son grow to be a man, and then not to shed a tear over her corpse—this would be bad enough. But to drum on a bowl, and sing; surely this is going too far."

"Not at all," replied Chuangtze. "When she died, I could not help being affected by her death. Soon, however, I remembered that she had already existed in a previous state before birth, without form, or even substance; that while in that unconditioned condition, substance was added to spirit; that this substance then assumed form; and that the next stage was birth. And now, by virtue of a further change, she is dead, passing from one phase to another like the sequence of spring, summer, autumn, and winter. And while she is thus lying asleep in Eternity, for me to go about weeping and wailing would be to proclaim myself ignorant of these natural laws. Therefore I refrain."

A TORTOISE IN THE MUD

Chuangtze was one day fishing, when the Prince of Ch'u sent two high officials to interview him, saying that His Highness would be glad of Chuangtze's assistance in the administration of his government. The latter quietly fished on, and without looking around replied, "I have heard in the state of Ch'u there is a sacred tortoise, which has been dead three thousand years, and which the Prince keeps packed up in a box on the altar in his ancestral shrine. Now do you think that tortoise would rather be dead and have its remains thus honored, or be alive and wagging its tail in the mud?" The two officials answered that no doubt it would rather be alive and wagging its tail in the mud;

whereupon Chuangtze cried out, "Begone! I, too, elect to remain wagging my tail in the mud."

BUTTERFLY DREAM

Once upon a time I dreamed I was a butterfly, fluttering hither and thither, to all intents and purposes a butterfly. I was conscious only of following my fancies (as a butterfly), and was unconscious of my individuality as a man. Suddenly, I awaked; and there I lay, myself again. I do not know whether I was then dreaming I was a butterfly, or whether I am now a butterfly dreaming that it is a man.

THE PLEASURE OF FISHES

Chuangtze and Huitze had strolled onto the bridge over the Hao, when the former observed, "See how the minnows are darting about! That is the pleasure of fishes."

"You not being yourself a fish," said Huitze, "how can you possibly know in what the pleasure of fishes consists?"

"And you not being I," retorted Chuangtze, "how can you know that I do not know?"

"That I, not being you, do not know what you know," replied Huitze, "is identical with my argument that you, not being a fish, cannot know in what the pleasure of fishes consists."

"Let us go back to your original question," said Chuangtze. "You ask me how I know in what consists the pleasure of fishes. Your very question shows that you knew I knew. I knew it from my own feelings on this bridge."

THE BUTCHER'S WAY

Prince Hui's cook was cutting up a bullock. Every blow of his hand, every heave of his shoulders, every tread of his foot, every thrust of his knee, every *whshh* of rent flesh, every *chhk* of the chopper, was in perfect harmony—rhythmical like the dance of the Mulberry Grove, simultaneous like the chords of the "Ching Shou."

"Well done!" cried the Prince. "Yours is skill indeed."

"Sire," replied the cook, "I have always devoted myself to Tao. It is better than skill. When I first began to cut up bullocks, I saw before me simply *whole* bullocks. After three years' practice, I saw no more whole animals. And now I work with my mind and not with my eye. When my senses bid me stop, but my mind urges me on, I fall back upon eternal principles. I follow such openings or cavities as there may be, according to the natural constitution of the animal. I do not attempt to cut through joints; still less through large bones.

"A good cook changes his chopper once a year—because he cuts. An ordinary cook, once a month—because he hacks. But I have had this chopper nineteen years, and although I have cut up many thousand bullocks, its edge is as if fresh from the whetstone. For at the joints there are always interstices, and the edge of a chopper being without thickness, it remains only to insert that which is without thickness into such an interstice. By these means the interstice will be enlarged, and the blade will find plenty of room. It is thus that I have kept my chopper for nineteen years as though fresh from the whetstone.

"Nevertheless, when I come upon a hard part where the blade meets with difficulty, I am all caution. I fix my eye on it. I stay my hand, and gently apply my blade, until with a *hwah* the part yields like earth crumbling to the ground. Then I take out my chopper and stand up, and look around, and pause, until with an air of triumph I wipe my chopper and put it carefully away."

"Bravo!" cried the Prince. "From the words of this cook I have learned how to take care of my life."

CHUANGTZE AND THE STRANGE BIRD

When Chuangtze was wandering in the park at Tiao-ling, he saw a strange bird which came from the south. Its wings were seven feet across. Its eyes were an inch in circumference. And it flew close past Chuangtze's head to alight in a chestnut grove.

"What manner of bird is this?" cried Chuangtze. "With strong wings it does not fly away. With large eyes it does not see."

So he picked up his skirts and strode toward it with his crossbow, anxious to get a shot. Just then he saw a cicada enjoying itself in the shade, forgetful of all else. And he saw a mantis spring and seize it, forgetting in the act its own body, which the strange bird immediately pounced upon and made its prey. And this it was which had caused the bird to forget its own nature.

"Alas!" cried Chuangtze with a sigh. "How creatures injure one another! Loss follows the pursuit of gain."

So he laid aside his bow and went home, driven away by the park keeper, who wanted to know what business he had there.

For three months after this, Chuangtze did not leave the house; and at length Lin Chü asked him, saying, "Master, how is it that you have not been out for so long?"

"While keeping my physical frame," replied Chuangtze, "I lost sight of my real self. Gazing at muddy water, I lost sight of the clear abyss. Besides, I have learned from the Master as follows: 'When you go into the world, follow its customs.' Now when I strolled into the park at Tiao-ling, I forgot my real self. That strange bird which flew close past me to the chestnut grove forgot its nature. The keeper of the chestnut grove took me for a thief. Consequently I have not been out."

CONFUCIUS HEMMED IN

When Confucius was hemmed in between Chen and Tsai, he passed seven days without food.

The minister Jen went to condole with him, and said, "You were near, sir, to death."

"I was indeed," replied Confucius.

"Do you fear death, sir?" inquired Jen.

"I do," said Confucius.

"Then I will try to teach you," said Jen, "the way not to die.

"In the eastern sea there are certain birds, called the *i-erh*. They behave themselves in a modest and unassuming manner, as though unpossessed of ability. They fly simultaneously; they roost in a body. In advancing, none strives to be first; in retreating, none ventures to be last. In eating, none will be the first to begin; it is considered proper to take the leavings of others. Therefore, in their own ranks they are at peace, and the outside world is unable to harm them. And thus they escape trouble.

"Straight trees are the first felled. Sweet wells are soonest exhausted. And you, you make a show of your knowledge in order to startle fools. You cultivate yourself in contrast to the degradation of others. And you blaze along as though the sun and moon were under your arms; consequently, you cannot avoid trouble. . . ."

"Good indeed!" replied Confucius; and forthwith he took leave of his friends and dismissed his disciples and retired to the wilds, where he dressed himself in skins and serge and fed on acorns and chestnuts. He passed among the beasts and birds and they took no heed of him."

THE HUNCHBACK

There was a hunchback named Su. His jaws touched his navel. His shoulders were higher than his head. His hair knot looked up to the sky. His viscera were upside down. His buttocks were where his ribs should have been. By tailoring, or washing, he was easily able to earn his living. By sifting rice he could make enough to support a family of ten.* When orders came down for a conscription, the hunchback stood unconcerned among the crowd. And, similarly, in matters of public works, his deformity shielded him from being employed.

On the other hand, when it came to donations of grain, the hunchback received as much as three *chung,* and of firewood ten faggots. And if physical deformity was thus enough to preserve his body until its alloted end, how much more would not moral and mental deformity avail!

CONFUCIUS AND NO-TOES

There was a man of the Lu state who had been mutilated—Shue Shan No-Toes. He came walking on his heels to see Confucius; but Confucius said, "You did not take care, and so brought this misfortune upon yourself. What is the use of coming to me now?"

"In my ignorance," replied No-Toes, "I made free with my body and lost my toes. But I come with something more precious than toes which I now seek to keep. There is no man, but Heaven covers him; there is no man, but Earth supports him; and I thought that you, sir, would be as Heaven and Earth. I little expect to hear these words from you."

"I must apologize," said Confucius. "Pray walk in and let us discuss." But No-Toes walked out.

"There!" said Confucius to his disciples. "There is a criminal with-

* In all of these occupations a man would necessarily stoop.

out toes who seeks to learn in order to make atonement for his previous misdeeds. And if he, how much more those who have no misdeeds for which to atone?"

No-Toes went off to Laotze and said, "Is Confucius a sage, or is he not? How is it he has so many disciples? He aims at being a subtle dialectician, not knowing that such a reputation is regarded by real sages as the fetters of a criminal."

"Why do you not meet him with the continuity of life and death, the identity of can and can not," answered Laotze, "and so release him from these fetters?"

"He has been thus punished by God," replied No-Toes. "It would be impossible to release him."

Liehtze

LIEHTZE, who possessed the somewhat odd name of Yu-kou ("Resist-the-enemy"), was the best storyteller of the Taoist thinkers. Many of his fables—such as the man who worried about heaven, the old man who lost a horse, and the old man who would move a mountain—are retold today in readers and enjoyed by school children. Some of them, like other tales in this section, have been distilled into four-word proverbs which have become household patter. It is generally accepted that Liehtze never lived and that what passed as his work consisted of the contributions of later Taoist disciples.

THE THIEF

A man lost an ax and suspected his neighbor's son. Everything that his neighbor's son did looked suspicious to him: the way he walked, the tone of his voice, his countenance, and his gestures. But when he recovered his ax in digging a ditch, he could not see anything suspicious in his neighbor's son at all.

This and the following items translated by Chi-Chen Wang.

THREE AND FOUR VS. FOUR AND THREE

In Sung there lived a man known as Tsu Kung who was fond of monkeys and kept large flocks of them. He understood the monkeys' ways and the monkeys, too, seemed to appreciate his kindness to them. He denied himself and his family in order to feed his pets. But at last his growing poverty made it necessary to cut down on the monkeys' rations. Being afraid that the monkeys would object, he thus prepared them: "I am sorry that I shall have to cut down your rations. Do you think that you can get along on three measures in the morning and four at night?" The monkeys rose and jabbered their protest. When they had quieted down, Tsu Kung said, "I see that you don't like my proposal. Then how about four measures in the morning and three at night?" At this the monkeys quieted down and were satisfied.

Just as Tsu Kung fools the monkeys so do the sages fool the people.

THE MAN OF YEN

A native of Yen was born in Yen but brought up in Lu. In his old age he set out for his native land. Passing through Chin his fellow travelers decided to play a trick on him. They pointed to a city and said to him, "There is a Yen city," whereupon the man of Yen was deeply moved. Then pointing to a temple they said, "This is your village temple." The man heaved a deep sigh. Then pointing to a house they said, "This is your ancestral home." The man's tears started to flow. Finally they pointed to a cemetery and said to him, "These are your ancestors' tombs." The man burst into lamentations. Thereupon his companions laughed and said, "We have been only fooling. This is the state of Chin!" The man felt sheepish and when he did reach Yen and beheld real Yen cities and temples and the actual house and tombs of his ancestors his heart barely fluttered.

THE SECRET TO GOOD RULE

"It is as easy to govern the world as to turn the palm of your hand," Yang Chu said to the King of Liang. To this retorted the King: "You, sir, have a wife and concubine and are unable to manage them; you have a garden of only three acres and you cannot keep them free from weeds. And yet you say that it is as easy to govern the world as to turn the palm of your hand. Does that not seem odd?"

"Has not Your Majesty ever seen a flock of sheep?" Yang Chu replied. "They surge around in hundreds and yet with a switch of bamboo a boy of five feet can make them go east or west as he wishes. On the other hand, if you were to have Emperor Yao drag a sheep in front and Emperor Shun follow behind with a switch, they would not be able to make the sheep budge. Moreover I have heard it said that a fish big enough to swallow a boat cannot swim in a tiny brook and that sky-dominating swans would not alight in stagnant pools. Similarly the slow and solemn cadence of the Yellow Bell cannot be used for the quick and confused steps of the popular dance. He that is destined for great things cannot be expected to manage trivial matters."

THE MAN WHO FORGOT

Yangli Huatze, of the Sung state, was afflicted in middle age by the disease of amnesia. Anything he received in the morning he had forgotten by evening; anything he gave away in the evening he had forgotten the next morning. Out-of-doors, he forgot to walk; indoors, he forgot to sit down. At any given moment, he had no recollection of what had just taken place; and a little later on, he could not even recollect what had happened then. All his family were perfectly disgusted with him. Fortunetellers were summoned, but their divinations proved unsuccessful; wizards were sought out, but their exorcisms were ineffectual; physicians were called in, but their remedies were of no avail. At last, a learned professor from the Lu state volunteered his services, declaring that he could effect a cure. Huatze's wife and family immediately offered him half their landed property if only he would tell them how to set to work. The professor replied: "This is a case which cannot be dealt with by means of auspices and diagrams; the evil cannot be removed by prayers and incantations, nor successfully combated by drugs and potions. What I shall try to do is to influence his mind and turn the current of his thoughts; in that way a cure is likely to be brought about."

Accordingly, the experiment was begun. The professor exposed his patient to cold, so that he was forced to beg for clothes; subjected him to hunger, so that he was fain to ask for food; left him in darkness, so that he was obliged to search for light. Soon, he was able to report progress to the sons of the house, saying gleefully: "The disease can be checked. But the methods I shall employ have been handed down as a secret in my family, and cannot be made known to the public. All attendants must, therefore, be dismissed, and I must be shut up alone with my patient." The professor was allowed to have his way, and for the space of seven days no one knew what was going on in the sick man's chamber. Then, one fine morning, the treatment came to an end, and, wonderful to relate, the disease of so many years' standing had entirely disappeared!

No sooner had Huatze regained his sense, however, than he flew into a great rage, drove his wife out-of-doors, beat his sons, and, snatching up a spear, hotly pursued the professor through the town. On being arrested and asked to explain his conduct, this is what he said: "Lately, when I was steeped in forgetfulness, my senses were so benumbed that

I was quite unconscious of the existence of the outer world. But now I have been brought suddenly to a perception of the events of half a lifetime. Preservation and destruction, gain and loss, sorrow and joy, love and hate have begun to throw out their myriad tentacles to invade my peace; and these emotions will, I fear, continue to keep my mind in the state of turmoil that I now experience. Oh! if I could but re-capture a short moment of that blessed oblivion!"

This and the following items translated by Lionel Giles

MASTER AND SERVANT

Mr. Yin of Chou was the owner of a large estate who harried his servants unmercifully, and gave them no rest from morning to night. There was one old servant in particular whose physical strength had quite left him; yet his master worked him all the harder. All day long he was groaning as he went about his work, and when night came he was reeling with fatigue and would sleep like a log. His spirit was then free to wander at will, and every night he dreamed that he was a king, enthroned in authority over the multitude, and controlling the affairs of the whole state. He took his pleasure in palaces and belvederes, fol-lowing his own fancy in everything, and his happiness was beyond compare. But when he awoke, he was a servant once more. To some-one who condoled with him on his hard lot the old man replied: "Hu-man life may last a hundred years, and the whole of it is equally divided into nights and days. In the daytime I am only a slave, it is true, and my misery cannot be gainsaid. But by night I am a king, and my happiness is beyond compare. So what have I to grumble at?"

Now Mr. Yin's mind was full of worldly cares, and he was always thinking with anxious solicitude about the affairs of his estate. Thus he was groaning as he went about his work, and when night came he, too, fell asleep utterly exhausted. Every night he dreamed that he was another man's servant, running about on menial business of every de-scription, and subjected to every possible kind of abuse and ill treat-ment. He would mutter and groan in his sleep, and obtained no relief until morning came. This state of things at last resulted in a serious illness, and Mr. Yin besought the advice of a friend. "Your station in life," his friend said, "is a distinguished one, and you have wealth and property in abundance. In these respects you are far above the average. If at night you dream that you are a servant and exchange ease for affliction, that is only the proper balance in human destiny. What you want is that your dreams should be as pleasant as your waking moments. But that is beyond your power to compass." On hearing what his friend said, Mr. Yin lightened his servant's toil, and allowed his own mental worry to abate; whereupon his malady began to decrease in proportion.

HOW TO BE A THIEF

Mr. Kuo of the Ch'i state was very rich, while Mr. Hsiang of the Sung state was very poor. The latter traveled from Sung to Ch'i and asked the other for the secret of his prosperity. Mr. Kuo told him. "It is because I am a good thief," he said. "The first year I began to be a thief, I had just enough. The second year, I had ample. The third year, I reaped a great harvest. And, in the course of time, I found myself the owner of whole villages and districts."

Mr. Hsiang was overjoyed; he understood the word "thief" in its literal sense, but he did not understand the true way of becoming a thief. Accordingly, he climbed over walls and broke into houses, grabbing everything he could see or lay hands upon. But before very long his thefts brought him into trouble, and he was stripped of even what he had previously possessed. Thinking that Mr. Kuo had basely deceived him, Hsiang went to him with a bitter complaint.

"Tell me," said Mr. Kuo, "how did you set about being a thief?" On learning from Mr. Hsiang what had happened, he cried out: "Alas and alack! You have been brought to this pass because you went the wrong way to work. Now let me put you on the right track. We all know that Heaven has its seasons, and that earth has its riches. Well, the things that I steal are the riches of Heaven and earth, each in their season—the fertilizing rain water from the clouds, and the natural products of mountain and meadow land. Thus I grow my grain and ripen my crops, build my walls and construct my tenements. From the dry land I steal winged and four-footed game, from the rivers I steal fish and turtles. There is nothing that I do not steal. For corn and grain, clay and wood, birds and beasts, fishes and turtles are all products of nature. How can I claim them as mine?

"Yet, stealing in this way from Providence, I bring on myself no retribution. Gold, jade, and precious stones, corn, silk stuffs, and all manner of riches are simply appropriated by men. How can Providence be said to give them away? Yet if we commit a crime in stealing them, who is there to resent it?"

Mr. Hsiang, in a state of great perplexity, and fearing to be led astray a second time by Mr. Kuo, went off to consult Tung Kuo, a man of learning. Tung Kuo said to him: "Are you not already a thief in respect of your own body? You are stealing the harmony of the Yin and the Yang in order to keep alive and maintain your bodily form. How much more, then, are you a thief with regard to external possessions! Assuredly, Heaven and earth cannot be dissociated from the myriad objects of nature. To claim any one of these as your own betokens confusion of thought. Mr. Kuo's thefts are carried out in a spirit of justice, and therefore bring no retribution. But your thefts were carried out in a spirit of self-seeking, and therefore landed you in trouble. Those who take possession of property, whether public or private, are thieves. Those who abstain from taking property, public or private, are also thieves. The great principle of Heaven and earth is to treat public property as such and private property as such. Knowing this principle, which of us is a thief, and at the same time which of us is not a thief?"

BLACK AND WHITE

Yang Pu, the younger brother of Yang Chu, one day went out wearing a light-colored coat. It started to rain so he shed his light-colored coat and changed into a dark-colored one. When he came back his own dog did not recognize him and met him with loud barks. This made Yang Pu angry and he was about to cane the dog. Yang Chu intervened, saying: "Better not hit him, for you wouldn't have acted any differently. Imagine that your dog should go out white and come home black. Would you not be surprised?"

This and the following items translated by George Kao.

THE INVADER INVADED

Duke Wen of Chin had mobilized his troops and set out to invade the Kingdom of Wei. Prince Tsu lifted his head and laughed out loud. The Duke asked him what he was laughing at, and he answered: "I laugh as I recall the man in the neighborhood who was taking his wife back to her mother's for a visit. On the way he was charmed by the sight of a pretty mulberry maid, and he stopped to chat with her. Even as he did so he looked back over his shoulder and saw that somebody else was flirting with his wife! That was what I was laughing to myself about."

The Duke got his point and right away called off the expedition and withdrew his troops. He barely returned when he found that invaders had already penetrated the northern outskirts of his kingdom.

THE MAN WHO SAW GOLD

Once there was a man of Ch'i who desired gold. One morning he rose and dressed and went to market. He went straight to a shop that sold gold, grabbed some of the gold, and ran. The police arrested him and questioned him, saying, "How could you rob somebody else's gold in broad daylight and in front of all these people, too?" The man of Ch'i answered, "When I reached for the gold I only saw gold, I didn't see any people."

A GOOD DEED

On the occasion of the first day of the year the people of Hantan offered a wild duck to Prince Chien of Chao. The Prince was well pleased and rewarded the men amply. One of his guests asked to know the reason why. Prince Chien said, "To set free a live bird on New Year's Day is to do an extraordinarily good deed." The guest said, "If the people know that their prince loves to set birds free they will vie with one another in catching them for him, and many birds will therefore be killed. If you really wish to see the birds live you would do better forbidding the people to catch them. When you catch a bird in order to set it free again, your good deed and bad cancel each other." "Right you are," said Prince Chien.

CONFUCIUS AND THE TWO BOYS

Confucius journeyed east and encountered two boys in heated argument. He inquired the cause of the argument, whereupon one boy said, "I believe when the sun first rises it is nearer to men and when it is in the middle of the sky it is farther away." The other boy, however, thought the rising sun farther away and the noonday sun nearer.

The first boy said in support of his theory, "When the sun rises it is as big as a carriage hood, but by the time it reaches the middle of the sky it is the size of a dish. Is it not so that distant objects look small and near-by objects look big?" The other boy countered by saying, "When the sun rises it is cool, but by the time it reaches high noon it is hot as boiling water. Does this not prove that it is nearer when it is hot and farther away when it is cool?" Confucius was at a loss to judge which of the two was in the right. The two boys laughed and said, "Who said you were full of wisdom?"

THE WOODEN COCK

Chi Hsiaotze was retained by King Hsuan of Chou to raise a cock for the cockfight. After ten days the King asked: "Is the bird ready for the fight?" "No," he answered, "it is still full of pride and wrath." Another ten days and the King asked again. "Not yet," was the answer. "The bird still crows back at any sound and struts at its own shadow." Another ten days and the King asked once more. "Not yet," he advised, "it is still staring and putting on airs." Finally, after ten more days, the King asked once more whether the cock was ready to fight. This time Chi answered: "It is about time. The bird no longer changes its attitude when challenged. Looking at it you would think it is a wooden cock; it has just about reached perfect form." By this time, no other cocks dared answer its crow, but instead turned and fled it.

THE DREAM AND THE DEER

A man was gathering fuel in the Cheng state when he fell in with a deer that had been startled from its usual haunts. He gave chase, and succeeded in killing it. He was overjoyed at his good luck; but, for fear of discovery, he hastily concealed the carcass in a dry ditch, and covered it up with brushwood. Afterward he forgot the spot where he had hidden the deer, and finally became convinced that the whole affair was only a dream. He told the story to people he met as he went along; and one of those who heard it, following the indications given, went and found the deer. On reaching home with his booty, this man made the following statement to his wife: "Once upon a time," he said, "a woodcutter dreamed that he had got a deer, but couldn't remember the place where he had put it. Now I have found the deer, so it appears that his dream was a true dream."

"On the contrary," said his wife, "it is you who must have dreamed that you met a woodcutter who had caught a deer. Here you have a deer, true enough. But where is the woodcutter? It is evidently your dream that has come true."

"I have certainly got a deer," replied her husband; "so what does it matter to us whether it was his dream or mine?"

Meanwhile, the woodcutter had gone home, not at all disgusted at having lost the deer. But the same night, he saw in a dream the place where he had really hidden it, and he also dreamed of the man who had taken it. So, the next morning, in accordance with his dream, he went to seek him out in order to recover the deer. A quarrel ensued, and the matter was finally brought before the magistrate, who gave judgment in these terms: "You," he said to the woodcutter, "began by really killing a deer, but wrongly thought it was a dream. Then you really dreamed that you had got the deer, but wrongly took the dream to be a reality. The other man really took your deer, which he is now disputing with you. His wife, on the other hand, declares that he saw both man and deer in a dream, so that nobody can be said to have killed the deer at all. Meanwhile, here is the deer itself in court, and you had better divide it between you."

The case was reported to the prince of the Cheng state, who said: "Why, the magistrate must have dreamed the whole thing himself!" The question was referred to the prime minister, but the latter confessed himself unable to disentangle the part that was a dream from the part that was not a dream. "If you want to distinguish between waking and dreaming," he said, "you would have to go back to the Yellow Emperor or Confucius. Both these sages are dead, and there is nobody now alive who can draw any such distinction. So the best thing you can do is to uphold the magistrate's decision."

This and the following item translated by Lionel Giles

THE OLD MAN WHO MOVED MOUNTAINS

The two mountains T'ai-hsing and Wang-wu, which cover an area of seven hundred square *li,* and rise to an enormous altitude, originally stood in the south of the Chi district and north of Ho-yang. The Simpleton of the North Mountain, an old man of ninety, dwelt opposite these mountains, and was vexed in spirit because their northern flanks blocked the way to travelers, who had to go all the way round. So he called his family together, and broached a plan.

"Let us," he said, "put forth our utmost strength to clear away this obstacle, and cut right through the mountains until we come to Hanyin. What say you?"

They all assented except his wife, who made objections and said: "My good man has not the strength to sweep away a dunghill, let alone two such mountains as T'ai-hsing and Wang-wu. Besides, where will you put all the earth and stones that you dig up?" The others replied that they would throw them on the promontory of P'o-hai.

So the old man, followed by his son and grandson, sallied forth with their pickaxes, and the three of them began hewing away at the rocks, and cutting up the soil, and carting it away in baskets to the promontory of P'o-hai. A widowed woman who lived near had a little boy who, though he was only just shedding his milk teeth, came skipping along to give them what help he could. Engrossed in their toil, they never went home except once at the turn of the season.

The Wise Old Man of the River Bend burst out laughing and urged them to stop. "Great indeed is your witlessness!" he said. "With the poor remaining strength of your declining years you will not succeed in removing a hair's breadth of the mountain, much less the whole vast mass of rock and soil."

With a sigh the Simpleton of the North Mountain replied: "Surely it is you who are narrow-minded and unreasonable. You are not to be compared with the widow's son, despite his puny strength. Though I myself must die, I shall leave a son behind me, and through him a grandson. That grandson will beget sons in his turn, and those sons will also have sons and grandsons. With all this posterity, my line will not die out, while on the other hand the mountains will receive no increment or addition. Why then should I despair of leveling it to the ground at last?" The Wise Old Man of the River Bend had nothing to say in reply.

One of the serpent-brandishing deities heard of the undertaking and, fearing that it might never be finished, went and told God Almighty, who was touched by the old man's simple faith, and commanded the two sons of K'ua O to transport the mountains, one to the extreme northeast, the other to the southern corner of Yung. Ever since then, the region lying between Chi in the north and Han in the south has been an unbroken plain.

THE OLD MAN WHO LOST A HORSE

An old man was living with his son at an abandoned fort on the top of a hill, and one day he lost a horse. The neighbors came to express their sympathy for this misfortune, and the old man asked, "How do you know this is bad luck?" A few days afterward, his horse returned with a number of wild horses, and his neighbors came again to congratulate him on this stroke of fortune, and the old man replied, "How do you know this is good luck?" With so many horses around, his son began to take to riding, and one day he broke his leg. Again the neighbors came around to express their sympathy, and the old man replied, "How do you know this is bad luck?" The next year, there was a war, and because the old man's son was crippled, he did not have to go to the front.

Translated by Lin Yutang.

Hanfeitze

HANFEITZE is known as the founder of the legalist school of Chinese philosophy. He was the cold, logical realist; unfortunately for him, the Chinese as a people are warm and human. He would make such a fetish of "system" that, in buying a pair of shoes, he would rather trust the ruler than his own feet. Sometimes one almost wishes that the Chinese could learn to go by a ruler for a change, instead of always going by their own feet.

THE SELF-CONSCIOUS BEAUTY

Once Yangtze passed through Sung and stayed in an inn. The inn had two waitresses. The ugly one of them was esteemed but the beautiful one was despised. Therefore Yangtze asked the reason. In reply the old innkeeper said: "The beautiful one thinks so much of her own beauty, but I never notice her being so beautiful. The ugly one is so conscious of her own ugliness, but I never notice her being so ugly." Thereupon Yangtze said to his disciples: "Who practices worthiness and abandons the aptitude for self-esteem, would be praised wherever he goes."

This and the following items translated by Chi-Chen Wang.

SHIELD AND SPEAR

There was a man of Ch'u who sold shields and spears. First he praised his shields, saying, "My shields are so strong that nothing can pierce them"; then he praised his spears, saying, "My spears are so sharp that nothing can stop them." Then someone said to him, "What if one should use your own spears to attack your own shields?" To this the man of Ch'u was unable to answer.

Just as a shield that stops everything cannot exist at the same time with a spear that pierces everything, so Yao and Shun cannot both surpass all in virtue and wisdom.

MEASUREMENT FOR SHOES

A man of Cheng was about to buy a pair of shoes. He measured the length of his feet but forgot to take the measurement with him when he went to the market place. "I must go back and get my measurement," he said to the shoe man when he discovered his oversight, and forthwith went back home. When he returned to the market, the market had already closed. "Why didn't you try the shoes with your feet?" someone asked him. "I'd rather trust my measurement than my feet," was his reply.

AN HONEST MAN'S WORD

The Kingdom of Chi invaded the Kingdom of Lu and, as a trophy of war, demanded Lu's treasured incense burner. The Kingdom of Lu surrendered a faked object. The men of Chi said, "This is faked." The men of Lu said, "No, this is the real thing." Chi said, "If you send Yocheng Tzechuen with this, then we will believe you." Thereupon the King of Lu sent for Yocheng Tzechuen. Yocheng Tzechuen asked his Emperor, "Why don't you give them the real one?" The Emperor replied, "Because I prize it highly." Yocheng Tzechuen answered, "Your servant also prizes highly his good faith."

Translated by George Kao.

THE ELIXIR OF DEATH

A certain person having forwarded some elixir of immortality to the Prince of Ching, it was received as usual by the doorkeeper. "Is this to be swallowed?" inquired the chief warden of the palace. "It is," replied the doorkeeper. Thereupon the chief warden purloined and swallowed it. At this the Prince was exceedingly wroth, and ordered his immediate execution; but the chief warden sent a friend to plead for him, saying, "Your Highness' servant asked the doorkeeper if the drug was to be swallowed; and as he replied in the affirmative, your servant accordingly swallowed it. The blame rests entirely with the doorkeeper. Besides, if the elixir of life is presented to Your Highness, and because your servant swallows it, your Highness slays him, that

elixir is clearly the elixir of death; and for Your Highness thus to put
to death an innocent official is simply for Your Highness to be made
the sport of men."

The Prince spared his life.

Translated by Herbert A. Giles.

THE IVORY MULBERRY LEAVES

Once a man of Sung made for the ruler mulberry leaves of ivory.
It took him three years to complete them. Having stems and branches,
wide and narrow, and tiny buds and colorful gloss, they were scattered
amidst real mulberry leaves and showed no difference from them.
After all, this man was on account of his skillfulness endowed with a
bounty in the Sung state.

When Liehtze heard this, he said: "Supposing heaven and earth
made a leaf in three years, then things that have leaves would be few."

This and the following items translated by W. K. Liao.

IVORY CHOPSTICKS

Of old, Chow made chopsticks of ivory. Thereby was the Viscount
of Ch'i frightened. He thought: "Ivory chopsticks would not be used
with earthenwares but with cups made of jade or rhinoceros horns.
Further, ivory chopsticks and jade cups would not go with the soup
made of beans and coarse greens but with the meat of long-haired
buffaloes and unborn leopards. Again, eaters of the meat of long-haired
buffaloes and unborn leopards would not wear short hemp clothes and
eat in a thatched house but would put on nine layers of embroidered
dresses and move to live in magnificent mansions and on lofty ter-
races. Afraid of the ending, I cannot help trembling with fear at the
beginning."

In the course of five years, Chow made piles of meat in the form of
flower beds, raised roasting pillars, walked upon mounds of distiller's
grains, and looked over pools of wine. In consequence ended the life
of Chow. Thus by beholding the ivory chopsticks, the Viscount of Ch'i
foreknew the impending catastrophe of All-under-Heaven. Hence the
saying: "Who beholds smallness is called enlightened."

SELF-CONQUEST

Once, when Tzehsia saw Tsengtze, Tsengtze asked, "Why have you become so stout?" "Because I have been victorious in warfare," replied Tzehsia. "What do you mean by that?" asked Tsengtze. In reply Tzehsia said: "Whenever I went in and saw the virtue of the early kings I rejoiced in it. Whenever I went out and saw the pleasure of the rich and noble I rejoiced in it, too. These two conflicting attractions waged a war within my breast. When victory and defeat still hung in the balance, I was thin. Since the virtue of the early kings won the war, I have become stout." Therefore the difficulty of volition lies not in conquering others but in conquering oneself. Hence the saying: "One who conquers himself is mighty."

Yentze

DIPLOMATS are among the people the Chinese hero-worship. Whether it is the Lord Li Hung-chang ignoring Western table manners at a state banquet tendered him by Bismarck or Dr. V. K. Wellington Koo speaking in three tongues with equal ease at the council of the late lamented League, a Chinese envoy is always very extraordinary and capable of outwitting the other fellow. Perhaps this legend dated from the days of Yen Yin, when representatives of one of the warring kingdoms to another had to talk fast or lose their heads. From the numerous anecdotes about Yentze we can see that, when he was not on some mission or other abroad, he was a pretty hard taskmaster to his own king, too.

THE ROBBER FROM CH'I

Yentze of the state of Ch'i was about to leave on a mission to the kingdom of Chin.

The King of Chin got wind of it and he asked of his court: "Yentze is known as a sage. Now he is coming here, how could we find some way to humiliate him?"

One of the ministers suggested: "Wait until he comes—your servant begs leave to have a man bound and paraded before the King . . ."

So, when the time came when the King of Chin was receiving Yentze in audience, there came a man bound and paraded before the court.

The King asked: "Wherefore is this?"

He was told: "It is a man from Ch'i."

The King asked: "And what are the charges?"

The answer was: "Robbery."

The King said: "So the men of Ch'i are robbers!"

Yentze turned to face him and said: "South of the river there grows an orange which the King of Ch'i ordered transplanted to the north. When it bears fruit it is no longer oranges but tangerines; they look alike but taste different. And why is it so? A matter of environment. Now this man of Ch'i was never a robber in Ch'i; come to Chin and he is a robber. Could it not also be a matter of environment?"

37

The King of Chin said: "It is my wish to hurt you, but it seems that I have brought it down upon myself!"

This and the following items translated by George Kao.

THE SMALL DOOR

Once Yentze was sent to Ch'u as ambassador. As Yentze was very short of stature, the people of Ch'u made a small gate beside the regular gate, much in the manner of the opening in the wall through which dogs and flood water pass, and invited Yentze to enter through it. Yentze refused, saying, "In a dog country one enters by the dog gate. I am now in Ch'u and should not enter by this gate." The master of ceremonies admitted the mistake and ushered Yentze through the regular gate.

When the King of Ch'u saw Yentze he asked him, "Is there no one in Ch'i?"

"Lintzu, the capital of Ch'i, is so large that it is divided into three hundred wards, and so populous that when people brush off their sweat it forms a rainstorm and when they open their sleeves they form huge tents. There are such crowds of them that they press upon one another, shoulder to shoulder and toe to heel. How could Your Majesty ask if there is anyone in Ch'i?"

"Then why is it that they have sent you?"

"Because Ch'i selects ambassadors according to the worth of the countries to which they are sent, worthy men being sent to worthy countries, while unworthy men are sent to unworthy countries. I am the least worthy of all and I have accordingly been sent to Ch'u."

THE THREE UNLUCKY OMENS

Prince Ching went ahunting and encountered a tiger in the mountains and a snake in the swamps. Upon his return he summoned Yentze and asked him, saying, "Today in the hunt we went up the mountain and saw a tiger, then we descended to the swamps and what did we find there but a snake! Are those not what you would call unlucky omens?"

"There are three unlucky omens in the land," Yentze answered, "but these are not among them. The first unlucky omen is when you have good men and you do not know them. The second unlucky omen is when you know that there are good men and you do not use them. The third unlucky omen is when you use them and do not trust them. These are the so-called unlucky omens for a country. As to finding a tiger in the mountain, you ought to know that it is the tiger's natural abode. When you go down to the swamps and find a snake, that's the snake's own home. What's so unlucky about the tiger's being in his natural abode and the snake's being in his own home?"

A FASHION DECREE

Prince Ling was fond of seeing his women in mannish garb. Before long all the women in the kingdom had taken to wearing men's clothes. The Prince then issued an ordinance against the fad in the following words:

"Any woman who is found wearing men's clothes shall have her robe torn and her belt ripped." Soon the streets were filled with women with torn robes and broken belts, but the mannish fashion persisted.

When Yentze was in audience, the Prince asked, "I have issued an order prohibiting women from wearing men's clothes. All those who offended have had their clothes torn, and yet the fashion persists. How do you account for that?" Yentze answered, "Your Highness has caused your women to wear it within the palace at the same time that you banned it without; it is as if you had hung a cow's head at your door and sold horse meat inside. Why don't you ask that this habit be ended in your own house? Then there would be no one who would dare practice it abroad."

"Fine!" said the Prince, and ordered that the fashion be abolished within his household. After a month there was not a woman in the kingdom who affected mannish fashion.

YENTZE AS MAGISTRATE

Prince Ching commissioned Yentze to be the magistrate of Tungo. After three years Yentze's bad name as an administrator was known throughout the kingdom. Prince Ching was not pleased, and he summoned Yentze in order to dismiss him. Yentze apologized, saying, "Yin is well aware of his own fault, but if you could but permit him to administer Tungo for another three years he guarantees that he

could produce results that would be known all over the country."
Prince Ching did not have the heart to refuse, so he sent Yentze back
to be magistrate of Tungo.

Three years later, to be sure, Yentze's name as a good administrator
had spread throughout the kingdom. Prince Ching, greatly pleased,
summoned him again in order to reward him. Yentze declined the
reward with thanks. The Prince asked him why, and he stated in reply:

"Formerly when Yin managed Tungo he built roads and hastened
public works, thereby incurring the displeasure of the wicked citizens;
he cited the thrifty and the filial, thereby incurring the displeasure of
the indolent citizens; in trying cases he did not make any allowance
for the strong and the powerful, thereby incurring the displeasure of
the strong and the powerful; when people at his right and at his left
had any request he would grant it if it was proper and refuse it if it
was unlawful, thereby incurring the displeasure of those at his right
and at his left; in serving the person of his superiors he did not exceed
the demands of propriety, thereby incurring the displeasure of his superiors. That was how it came that wicked tongues started wagging
without and damaging words were planted within, and in three years
criticism had reached the ears of the Prince.

"Now this time your servant took care to amend his ways: He would
neglect road-building and delay other public works, thereby pleasing
the wicked citizens; he would overlook the thrifty and the filial and
condone the thieves and the robbers, thereby pleasing the indolent citizens; in trying cases he would make allowances for the strong and the
powerful, thereby pleasing the strong and the powerful; he would
grant every request from those at his right and at his left, thereby
pleasing those at his right and at his left; in serving the persons of his
superiors he would go beyond the requirements of propriety, thereby
pleasing his superiors. That was why tongues started to wag in my
favor and words were planted in my behalf, and in three years my
praise has reached your ears. To my mind, Yin deserved reward formerly when he was ordered done away with; whereas today he merits
dismissal and yet reward is coming to him. That is why he dares not
accept."

From this Prince Ching realized that Yentze was an honest man. So
he gave him the whole kingdom to administer, and in three years' time
great prosperity came to the kingdom of Ch'i.

THE KING WONDERED ABOUT THE WEATHER

Once during the reign of Prince Ching it rained and snowed for three days without stop. The Prince, ensconced in his white fox furs, was sitting near the steps of the hall enjoying the snow. Yentze came in and stood by for a while. Presently the Prince exclaimed, "How strange! Rain and snow for three days and it is not cold!"

Yentze replied, "Is it not cold?" The Prince laughed. Yentze said, "Yin has heard about the good rulers of old: When they were fed they knew that the people were hungry; when they were warm they knew that the people were cold; when they were at ease they knew that the people were hard at work. Now you, my Prince, do not seem to know."

"Well said!" the Prince responded. "Your prince has learned his lesson." Forthwith he ordered furs and grain distributed for the relief of the hungry and the cold.

THE LOST FALCON

Prince Ching was fond of falconry. He put Shu Ts'o in charge of his favorite falcon, but soon afterward the man lost it. The Prince was angry and ordered that the man be executed. Yentze said: "Shu Ts'o is guilty of three crimes. May I not enumerate his crimes before we execute him?" The Prince gave him permission to do so, whereupon he summoned the culprit and read off the charges before the Prince in these words:

"Shu Ts'o, you were put in charge of His Highness's falcon and you lost it; that's your first crime. On account of a bird you would cause our prince to kill a man; that's your second crime. As a consequence to this incident you would proclaim to the several princes that our prince is one who valued his falcon above his official; that's your third crime."

When Yentze had finished counting Shu Ts'o crimes thus he asked that the execution be carried out. "Don't kill him," the Prince said. "Your prince has got the point."

YENTZE'S DRIVER

When Yentze was prime minister of Ch'i he had a driver in his employ whose wife one day peeped through a crack in the door as Yentze was going out. She saw her husband, the Prime Minister's driver, sitting ensconced under a great hood, holding a team of four by the reins, and displaying a high-flying, self-satisfied air. When the driver returned home his wife told him that she intended to leave him. The husband demanded to know the reason why. The wife answered, "You look at Yentze, a man not quite six feet in height and already the prime minister of Ch'i whose name is renowned among the princes of the several kingdoms. And yet as I watched him while he was going out, I could see that he looked deeply thoughtful and modest of mien. Now you who are more than eight feet tall and nothing but a servant and driver to others, judging by your airs you seem to be perfectly satisfied. That is why your wife asks to leave you."

As a result of this, the driver husband began to conduct himself in a modest and self-deprecating manner. Yentze was surprised to note the change in the man and asked him for an explanation. The driver told him the truth, whereupon Yentze recommended his driver to be a minister to the king.

YENTZE DECLINED THE PRINCE'S GIFT

Once Prince Ching's messenger arrived while Yentze was having his meal. Yentze invited the messenger to partake of his meal; as a result, the messenger went away hungry and Yentze was also hungry. The messenger reported this to the Prince upon his return, and the Prince said, "Ah, so Yentze's family is so poor! And your prince did not know it—that was the fault of your prince."

So he dispatched an official to Yentze with a gift of a thousand taels of gold as entertainment expenses. Yentze declined the gift. It was insisted on him thrice, but finally Yentze bowed and declined in these words:

"Who said Yin is poor? With such a gift from the Prince, he is blessed unto kinsmen and friends and honored as an example for the Hundred Names. What a rich gift it is from the Prince already! Really Yentze is not poor. The way Yin has heard it, to receive richly from the Prince and pass it on to the people would be usurping the role of the Prince unto his people—a thing that a loyal servant would not do; to receive richly from the Prince and withhold it from the people would be lining one's own trunks and boxes—a thing that a virtuous man would not do; to receive from the Prince and incur the displeasure of your fellows, and then to die and have your wealth transferred to others, would be hoarding—a thing that a wise man would not do. Your servant is content with a suit of rough cloth and a meal of beans, so please excuse him from taking the Prince's gift."

Prince Ching later asked Yentze, saying, "There was a time when my late father Prince Huan offered his minister Kuan Chung a gift of five estates, and Kuan Chung accepted the gift without demur. Why is it that you should decline my gift?" The answer was: "Yin has heard that if the sage has a thousand ideas there is bound to be one wrong, and if the fool has a thousand ideas there is bound to be one right. Perhaps it is that Kuan Chung just missed it that time and Yin just happened to get it. That is why I bowed twice and dared not accept."

TWO PEACHES AMONG THREE MEN

There were three braves who served Prince Ching, named Kungsun Chieh, Tien Kai-chiang, and Ku Yeh-tze, who were so strong that they were known to be tiger fighters. One day Yentze went to pay them his respects, and the three gentlemen did not even bother to get up. Later, when Yentze went to see the Prince, he remarked, "Your servant has heard that the way an enlightened ruler keeps his strong men is to be careful that they observe the proprieties with their prince and their elders and set a moral example to their juniors. Thus, they would prove useful internally to suppress violence and externally to discourage aggression. They would be elevated to high ranks and rewarded with heavy stipends, because their superiors profit from their usefulness and their inferiors bow to their strength. Now the way you, my prince, keep your strong men, they do neither observe the proprieties with their prince and their elders nor set a moral example for their juniors; internally they could not be counted upon to suppress violence, nor externally to discourage aggression. Thus they have become instruments to the kingdom's potential danger. It is better to do away with them."

Prince Ching replied, "But how can you get these three fellows?

Fight them? I fear you will lose. Shoot them? I fear you will miss."

Yentze said, "They are all of them the type of men who overcome their foe by brute strength; however, they are ignorant of the proprieties that rule among the elders and the young." He therefore asked that the Prince dispatch a messenger to them bearing a gift of two peaches together with a message, saying, "Would the three gentlemen not divide the peaches among them according to their own estimation of their respective merits?"

Kungsun Chieh looked up to the sky and sighed, saying, "This Yentze is a clever man! He knew that if he asked the Prince to test our merits in this manner we would have to accept the peaches; to decline would be an admission that we are all cowards who have earned no merit. And yet there are three of us—one more than there are peaches—so what can we do but to reckon our merits and eat the peaches accordingly? As for myself, I have first fought and conquered a wild boar and then fought and conquered a cub tiger. Judging from these accomplishments, I believe I can eat a peach over and above any one of you." So saying, Kungsun Chieh snatched a peach and rose to his feet.

Tien Kai-chiang then jumped up and said: "I have with my sword twice repulsed the enemy's massed troops. Such a merit as I have earned should give me the right to eat a peach over and above any one of you." So saying, he also snatched a peach and rose to his feet.

Then Ku Yeh-tze spoke up and said: "Once I attended the Prince's carriage while crossing a river. All of a sudden a monster tortoise reared its head and bit into the horse on the left flank, dragging him off to midstream. At that moment, though I knew not how to swim, I dived into the water, waded a hundred paces against the current, and drifted nine *li* with the current before I seized the monster and killed it. Then, grabbing the horse by the tail with my left hand and with the tortoise head in my right, I leaped up like a stork from under the water while people on the bank exclaimed: 'Here comes the God of the River!' They looked again and saw that it was only the huge tortoise head. With such a feat as mine, I can surely eat a peach over and above any of you. Why don't you two hand the peaches over?" So saying, he rose, drawing his sword.

Kungsun Chieh and Tien Kai-chiang both said, "We are not as brave as you are, nor can our merits match yours. It is covetous not to give up the peach; and it is cowardly not to die." They both gave the peaches to Ku Yeh-tze and hanged themselves. Ku Yeh-tze said, "To live alone while the two of them perished is unvirtuous; to have humiliated others with words and crowed of your own success is ungentlemanly. To hate myself for what I have done and not die for it is lacking in courage." So saying, he returned the peaches to the Prince's messenger and hanged himself. The messenger came back and reported, "They are all dead!" Whereupon the Prince ordered the three braves buried with ministerial rites.

THE INTERPRETER OF DREAMS

After the Duke Ching of Ch'i had been sick with an excess of water for more than ten days, he dreamed one night that he fought against two suns and was defeated by them. At his audience with Yentze the following morning the Duke told him of the dream and asked him if it did not portend that he was going to die. "Let the Interpreter of Dreams be called and consulted," Yentze said. Then Yentze went out to the gate of the palace and intercepted the Dream Interpreter and said to him, "Last night the Duke dreamed that he fought against two suns and was defeated and the Duke is afraid that he is going to die. That is why you have been summoned."

"Then I must go back and consult my books," the Interpreter said.

"That is not necessary," said Yentze. "The Duke's illness is due to Darkness and it has been defeated by two suns, the symbol of Light. It means that the Duke will soon get well. Thus you must interpret the Duke's dream."

The Dream Interpreter went into the palace and interpreted the Duke's dream in the manner suggested by Yentze. Three days later the Duke became well and was about to reward the Interpreter. "It is Yentze who should be rewarded, for it was he who told me how to interpret the dream," the Interpreter said. Yentze was then summoned but he also declined the reward, saying, "My interpretation was efficacious only because the Dream Interpreter had told it. If I had told it myself, you would not have taken comfort in it. Therefore it was not to my credit."

The Duke rewarded them both.

This and the following item translated by Chi-Chen Wang.

THE SON OF HEAVEN

When the King of Wu was about to receive Yentze, ambassador from Ch'i, he decided to test the latter's presence and familiarity with the rites. Therefore he instructed his master of ceremonies thus: "When the visitor arrives, say that the Son of Heaven wishes to see him." The master of ceremonies acted as he was instructed and said to Yentze, "The Son of Heaven wishes to see you." Yentze assumed a puzzled look but said nothing. Again the master of ceremonies said, "The Son of Heaven wishes to see you," and again Yentze assumed a puzzled look but said nothing. For a third time the master of ceremonies said, "The Son of Heaven wishes to see you," and for the third time Yentze assumed a puzzled look and then said, "I have been ordered by my prince to visit the court of the King of Wu, but I have been stupid and have lost my way, and come to the court of the Son of Heaven. Would you be good enough to tell me, sir, where I might find the King of Wu?" It was not until the master of ceremonies amended, after a hurried consultation with the King, the form of his request to "Fuchai, the King of Wu, wishes to see you," that Yentze entered the palace and saluted the King of Wu as a vassal of the Son of Heaven.

Tales of the Warring Kingdoms

THE LARGEST group of anecdotes in this section is taken from Chan-kuo Tseh (Stratagems of the Warring Kingdoms). *With a few exceptions, the other stories, from such works as* Shuoyuan (A Garden of Talks) *and* Hsiaolin (A Forest of Laughs), *also concern witty and epigrammatic gentlemen who lived by their clever "three-inch tongues" in this period of Chinese history (403–221 B.C.) when Machiavellian politics was the order of the day and feudal kingdoms engaged in perpetual back-stabbing warfare. As a matter of fact, Chuangtze, Liehtze, and Hanfeitze, given separate sections above, also lived in the Age of the Warring Kingdoms; and Yentze, just a little before that time. Perhaps a world of strife and intrigue is particularly fruitful of bizarre deeds and words,*

A FUND-RAISING SCHEME

Chang Yi found himself in straitened circumstances in the kingdom of Ch'u; his followers grumbled and hinted their wish to go back to their native land. He went, therefore, to see the King and asked for permission to go to Chin. The King was in a bad humor and readily gave his consent.

"Has Your Majesty no commission for me in Chin?" he asked of the King.

"Nothing," the King answered, "for Ch'u is the land where gold and pearls, rhinoceros's horns and elephant tusks are produced."

"That is only because Your Majesty cares not for beautiful women," Chang Yi said. "The women in the Middle Land are so beautiful that those who do not know mistake them, because of the whiteness of their skin and the ebony black of their eyebrows, for goddesses that have strayed to the earth."

"I have never seen women from the Middle Land," said the King of Ch'u. "If they are indeed as beautiful as you say, rest assured that I shall not be unappreciative of them." Thereupon he gave Chang Yi jade and pearls and commissioned him to bring back the most beautiful women that he could find.

Now in the palace of Ch'u, Nan Hou and Cheng Pao were the King's favorites. When they heard of Chang Yi's commission, they became alarmed, and each sent him a thousand measures of gold. A farewell banquet was held in the palace, and, emboldened by wine, Chang Yi begged to drink a toast to the King's favorites. Nan Hou and Cheng Pao were summoned. After gazing upon them for a moment Chang Yi fell on his knees and said to the King, "I deserve death for having deceived Your Majesty!" Pressed for an explanation, he continued, "I have traveled everywhere under heaven but I have never seen ladies as beautiful as these two. Because of my ignorance I had undertaken even to secure beautiful women for Your Majesty from elsewhere."

"Be not disturbed," the King said. "I have always thought that there could be no woman more beautiful than these two."

This and the following items translated by Chi-Chen Wang.

CHENG PAO AND THE NEW LADY

The King of Wei presented the King of Ch'u with a beautiful lady and the King of Ch'u took great delight in her. Instead of showing the slightest signs of jealousy, Cheng Pao, who had been the King's chief favorite, went out of her way to be kind to the new lady; she provided her with the most gorgeous dresses, put at her disposal the finest suite in the palace, and tried to please her more than she tried to please the King. "It is with their beauty that women serve their lord," the King declared, "and it is in their nature to be jealous. And yet Cheng Pao serves the new lady more faithfully than she does me and shows not the slightest signs of jealousy. She is indeed like a filial son and a faithful minister to me."

Convinced that she had impressed the King with her lack of jealousy, Cheng Pao went and said to the new beauty, "The King indeed loves you and admires your beauty; however, he does not like your nose. You should take care, therefore, to cover your nose in the King's presence." The new lady took her advice and covered up her nose whenever she saw the King. The King was puzzled and asked Cheng Pao about the new lady's behavior. "I know the reason," Cheng Pao said, "but I dare not say it."

"You must tell me, even though it may be distasteful," the King insisted.

"It appears that she does not like Your Majesty's breath," Cheng Pao said. Thereupon the King was so outraged that he ordered the new lady's nose cut off.

THE KING'S FAVORITE

After the death of the consort of the King of Ch'i there were seven rivals for the position. Wishing to know which of the seven the King favored most, the Duke of Hsueh presented the King with seven pieces of jade, one of them surpassing all the others in beauty and quality. On the following day he spotted the lady that wore the finest piece of jade and recommended her to the King as his new consort.

THE TIGER AND THE FOX

King Hsuan of Ch'u asked his ministers, saying, "I have been told that the people in the north are in mighty fear of Chao Hsi-hsu. Is it true?"

For a moment no one answered, but finally Chiang I answered thus: "The tiger hunts all beasts and devours them. One day it caught a fox and was about to devour it when the fox said, 'You must not eat me, for I have been appointed by God as the king of beasts and you will be disobeying the mandate of God if you eat me. If you do not believe me, follow me and see for yourself if the animals do not flee from me.' The tiger agreed and indeed all the beasts of the forest fled when they saw the fox and tiger. The tiger did not realize that the animals fled because of fear of himself but thought that they were indeed afraid of the fox. Now Your Majesty rules over a land of five thousand *li* and has a million men bearing arms. You have delegated your powers to Chao Hsi-hsu. Therefore, in fearing Chao Hsi-hsu, the people of the north are actually fearing your army, just as the animals in reality fear the tiger and not the fox."

SU CHIN IN THE KINGDOM OF CH'U

When Su Chin was finally received by the King of Ch'u after three days of waiting, he intimated, at the end of the audience, that he was leaving Ch'u right away. "But you have just come from a thousand *li* away," the King said in surprise. "Pray, why are you in such haste to go away?"

Thereupon Su Chin answered, "I have found that in Ch'u food is dearer than jade and fuel dearer than cassia wood and that the gate-keeper is as difficult to see as a ghost and the King as difficult as God himself. I confess that I can neither afford to eat jade and burn cassia wood nor wish to try to see God through ghosts."

"Kindly return to the guest house," the King said, "and we shall see what can be done to remedy the situation."

THE SWALLOWED PEARL

Chang Ch'ou, while hostage in Yen, had reason to believe that the King of Yen would have him executed unless he yielded a rare pearl that he was reputed to have. He fled Yen but was stopped by the border guard. Thereupon Chang Ch'ou said to his captor: "The King wants to kill me because he would not believe that I no longer have the pearl that he covets. If you should return me to the King, I shall tell him that you have robbed me of the pearl and swallowed it. The King is covetous and values pearls far above human lives; he will certainly have you disemboweled in order to recover the pearl. I shall die if you return me to the King; but your intestines, too, will be cut to pieces."

The guard let Chang Ch'ou pass.

THE STOLEN HORSE

Duke Mu of Ch'in lost his favorite horse and went to look for it himself. Finally he came upon the horse thieves and caught them feasting upon its flesh. "This is my favorite horse that you are eating," the Duke said to them. Then as the men rose in terror, he continued, "I've heard it said that horse meat without wine will cause death, so you must let me offer you some wine." The horse thieves drank of the Duke's wine and went away in shame and gratitude.

Three years later Chin attacked Ch'in and beseiged the Duke Mu. "Now is our chance to repay the Duke," the horse thieves said to one another. They broke through the seige and rescued Duke Mu, who was then able to rally his forces and defeat the invading army, capturing Duke Hui of Chin as his prize.

THE HEIR APPARENT

King Kung of Ch'u had many favorite sons and was not able to decide whom to make his heir. "Dissension and war will beset Ch'u," commented Chü Chien. "For when a hare runs wild through the street, it will be pursued by ten thousand men; but as soon as one man catches it, all others will cease pursuing. When proprietorship has not been fixed, a hare will cause riot and confusion among ten thousand men, but when proprietorship had been determined, even a greedy man knows where to stop. Now the King has many favorite sons and yet the position of heir apparent is still vacant. The uncertainty will cause dissension and war in Ch'u just as an ownerless hare will attract ten thousand pursuers."

When the King heard this, he set up one of his sons as heir apparent, known to posterity as King Kang.

THE DRAGON AND THE FISHERMAN

The King of Wu expressed the wish to go among his people incognito and to carouse with them. Wu Tzu-hsü advised against this, saying, "This is a dangerous thing to do. Once upon a time the White Dragon descended into a mountain pool and changed itself into a fish. The fisherman Yü Tsu shot at him and injured him in the eye. The White Dragon went back to Heaven and complained to God. 'What shape did you assume when this happened?' God asked the dragon. 'I was in the shape of a fish and was swimming in a mountain pool,' the dragon answered. 'Then Yü Tsu is without fault, for there is no taboo against men shooting fish,' God said. Now the White Dragon is a favored beast of God while Yü Tsu was only a common fisherman of Sung, yet because the dragon changed its shape Yü Tsu could shoot it with impunity. If Your Majesty should leave your exalted throne of ten thousand chariots and carouse with the cotton-clothed, your subject fears that you will be exposed to the danger of some Yü Tsu."

The King heeded the advice and abandoned his idea of carousing with his people.

THE CUCKOO AND THE OWL

"Where are you going, my friend?" asked a cuckoo of an owl.

"I am moving out east," the owl replied.

"Why?" asked the cuckoo.

"Because people hereabouts don't like my song."

"Why not change your tune?" said the cuckoo. "For unless you do people out there won't like your song any better."

THE PRAYING MANTIS LEAF

A poor man of Ch'u read in the works of Huainantze that a leaf from behind which a praying mantis pounces on the cicada would enable one to conceal oneself from mortal eyes. He went into the woods and looked from tree to tree until he found what he wanted, but the leaf fell to the ground among myriads of other fallen leaves and it was impossible to distinguish the magic leaf from the rest. He swept up all the leaves, several basketsful of them, and carried them home. Then taking one leaf at a time, he held it in front of him and asked his wife if she could see him. "Of course I can see you," his wife said, laughing at the absurd question. But as the day wore on she got tired of being asked everlastingly the same question and answered, "No, I can't see you now."

The man was overjoyed and went to the market place with his magic leaf and helped himself to the first thing that struck his fancy, right under the merchant's eyes. He was arrested and taken to the magistrate, who laughed and set him free when he heard the man's explanation of his extraordinary behavior.

THE FARMER OF SUNG

A farmer of Sung had a tree on his farm. One day a startled rabbit ran and broke his neck on the tree trunk. The farmer forthwith abandoned his hoe and kept watch all the day long by the tree, expecting to obtain another rabbit in the same manner. He failed to obtain any more rabbits but only succeeded in making a laughingstock of himself in Sung.

This and the following items translated by George Kao.

THE TWO BRAVES

There were two braves in the Kingdom of Ch'i: one of them lived in the East City and the other lived in the West City. One day they met in the street and said to each other: "Let's have a drink!" After a few rounds they said: "Let's have some flesh to eat!" Then one of them said: "You are flesh, and I am flesh. Why should we look further?"

So they drew their swords and ate of each other until they died.

Rather no bravery than bravery like this.

THE DARING MAGISTRATE

Emperor Chuang Tsung was fond of the hunt. Once, hunting in the district of Chung Mou, his horses trampled all over the people's rice fields. The magistrate of the district stopped his horse and sought to dissuade the Emperor from despoiling the crops. The Emperor was outraged and shouted to have the official taken away and beheaded. The actor Chin Hsin-mo knew that this was not right, so, at the head of a group of actors, he dashed in front of the magistrate and scolded him in these words:

"You call yourself a magistrate. How is it that you condone your people and allow them to grow their crops so that taxes can be paid? Why don't you let your people starve so that the ground could be cleared for the hunting pleasure of the Son of Heaven? Surely you are guilty and deserve to die!"

So saying, he asked the Emperor that the execution be promptly carried out. Chuang Tsung understood, laughed, and set the magistrate free.

MR. NANKUO

King Hsuan of Ch'i was fond of listening to flute music, and frequently he would have three hundred men play for him in a concert. Mr. Nankuo was not adept at the flute, but he passed himself among the ranks of the three hundred and enjoyed official patronage.

King Hsuan passed away. King Ming succeeded to the throne, and he commanded the flutists to play before him one by one. Mr. Nankuo got away in a hurry.

AN ARMY OF DEER

Once the Premier Emperor of Ch'in talked of laying out a hunting ground of gigantic dimensions, one that would extend from Hanku-kwan in the east to Yungchentsan in the west.

Yu Tan said: "Splendid! Let us turn loose a great number of birds and beasts into it, so that when invaders come from the east all we need to do is to set the army of deer on them."

Hearing this, the Emperor abandoned his scheme.

CHIEN KU-YANG KILLED HIS MASTER

During a battle between King Kung of Ch'u and Prince Li of Chin at a place called Yenning, General Tze-fang of Ch'u felt thirsty and wanted a drink. Chien Ku-yang offered his master wine. Tze-fang said, "Take it away, that's wine!"

Ku-yang said, "It's not wine."

Tze-fang repeated, "Take it away, that's wine!"

Ku-yang insisted, "No, it's not wine."

Tze-fang took it and drank it up. Afterward he was drunk and went to sleep. When King Kung wanted to resume battle he sent for Tze-fang, and Tze-fang excused himself saying he suffered heart trouble. So King Kung went to see him and, upon entering his tent, smelled wine. "I was counting on the General in today's battle," the King said, "and now the General got himself as drunk as this. This shows that he did not care if our country should perish and if our people should be enslaved. How could I carry on this war!" Thereupon he ordered Tze-fang executed. Now when Ku-yang offered the wine he had no intention of hurting Tze-fang; it was out of his loyalty and devotion to him, but it was enough to kill him. That is why it is said, small loyalty hurts big loyalty and small profit ruins big profit.

SEVEN SCHOLARS A DAY

Shunyu Kun recommended seven scholars to King Hsuan in one day. The King said, "You come here. As we heard it, if scholars could be found every thousand miles they are already lining up shoulder to shoulder; if sages could be born a hundred generations apart they are already falling over one another's heels. Now you have recommended to me seven scholars in one day. Isn't that too many scholars?"

"No," replied Shunyu Kun. "As the saying goes, birds of a feather flock together and beasts of the same paws walk together. Also, if you go to seek dry firewood in rivers and streams you would be looking all your life in vain; but if you go to seek it in the fields of Yi Shu and Liang Fu then you could get it by the carload. In other words, there is a place to go for everything. As for Kun, he is the place to go for scholars. When the King asked Kun for scholars it is like going to the stream for water and going to the wood for fire. Not to mention seven scholars, Kun is going to recommend more!"

THE NEW PRIME MINISTER

The Prime Minister of Liang died. When Huitze heard this he was in such a hurry to get to Liang that he missed his step in the ferry boat and fell into the river. He was rescued by the boatman, who asked him, "Why are you in such a hurry?"

"There is no prime minister in Liang now," he answered. "I am anxious to go and be its prime minister."

The boatman said, "You cannot even manage yourself in the boat— if it were not for me you would have drowned—how could you expect to be prime minister of Liang?"

Huitze replied, "Here in the boat, I am not as good as you. But in governing the land and upholding society, compared to me, you are like a blind dog."

THE JADE AND THE SWORD

Yu Shu had in his possession a jade which the Prince of Yu demanded to have. At first he refused to give it up, but then he regretted his decision, reasoning thus: "There is a proverb in the Chou dynasty which says, 'A fellow has not committed any crime, but the fact that he posseses a jade is his crime.' This jade of mine will do me no good and will perhaps bring me much harm." So he offered it to his prince. Soon the Prince came around again and demanded to have his treasured sword. Then Shu said, "That's what you call insatiable. If he is insatiable he will get me sooner or later." So he revolted against the Prince of Yu and, as a result, the Prince fled for refuge to a place called Kung Chih.

DISTANT WATER: NEAR-BY FIRE

Prince Mu of Lu sent several of his sons to serve in the court of Chin and others in the court of Ch'in. Li Tsu said, "Suppose your son is drowning and you send for a rescuer from the Kingdom of Yueh, although the Yueh people are known as fine swimmers, your son will surely drown. Suppose there is a fire in your house and you wait until water is fetched from the sea, then although there is much water in the sea, your house will surely burn down. Why? Because distant water will not put out a near-by fire. Now it is true that Chin and Ch'in are strong countries, but Ch'i is the nearest one to us. If Lu should be in trouble do you not think that we should count on Ch'i?"

RECOMMENDING AN ENEMY

Prince Wen of Chin inquired of Chiu Fan, saying, "Who in your opinion is fit to be the superintendent of West River?"

Chiu Fan answered, "Yu Tze-kao is the man."

"Isn't he an enemy of yours?" asked the Prince.

"Yes, but Your Highness asked who is fit to be the superintendent, not whom I hate as my enemy," was the answer.

When this incident was known Yu Tze-kao came to Chiu Fan and thanked him, saying, "It's my good fortune that you not only have forgiven me but even recommended me to the Prince so that I can be superintendent of the West River."

Chiu Fan answered, "My recommending you is public; my hating you is private. I would not want to let my private feelings hurt the public good. But you'd better be off, or I'll shoot you!"

THE STATE OF A NATION

King Chuang of Ch'u wished to invade the kingdom of Chen, but first he sent a scout to look over the country. The scout came back and reported, "We must not invade Chen."

"Why?" King Chuang demanded to know.

The scout answered, "The country is surrounded with a high wall and a deep moat. Its granary is well stocked. All things indicate that it is a well-governed country."

The King said, "I believe that it is all right to invade Chen. Now Chen is a small kingdom. When a small country has a well-stocked granary it means that it levies heavy taxes; when a country levies heavy taxes it means that the people are aggrieved against their ruler. When a small country surrounds itself with a high wall and a deep moat it means that the strength of the people has been sapped." Thereupon King Chuang sent an expedition against the kingdom of Chen, and annexed it.

SELF-ACCUSATION

Once Emperor Yu went for a ride and saw a criminal by the wayside. The Emperor descended from his carriage, questioned the man, and wept for him. The Emperor's attendants asked, "The man has become a criminal because he violated the law; why should Your Majesty be so sorrowful for him?"

Yu said, "The people under Emperor Yao and Shun all made the heart of Yao and Shun as their own heart. Now, with me as the emperor, the Hundred Names * each follows his own heart. That is why I am pained."

The *Classics* have it, "When there is crime among the Hundred Names, the crime is in myself."

*Hundred Names, *pai-hsing,* is the Chinese term for the common people.

II

THE HUMOR OF THE PICARESQUE
(Old)

II. The Humor of the Picaresque
(Old)

AN EARLY and imperfect recollection of such Western novels as *Tom Jones* and *Roderick Random* caused me to light on the word "picaresque" as an appropriate label for this part of the book, which is filled with slices from Chinese novels. The meaning of "picaresque" I had only a vague notion of until I consulted Webster, which says, "Of, pertaining to, or characteristic of, rogues or rascals." Also, "designating, or pertaining to, a type of prose fiction . . . in which the principal character is a rogue or vagabond (*picaro*), and the narrative a series of incidents or episodes connected chronologically but with little or no motivation or complication of plot."

By this definition the characters in the selections I have made are mostly picaresque. The Tattooed Monk, Lu Chi-Shen, and Monkey, who calls himself "The Great Sage Equal of Heaven," are certainly rogues or rascals or both. The band of travelers in *The Romance of the Mirrored Flowers* whose voyages bring them to all sorts of strange lands are vagabonds of the first water. Even Liu *lao-lao,* the old country dame who looks ridiculous in fashionable society, is more roguish than some of those smart young ladies in Red Chamber seem to realize.

Old Chinese novels are almost all episodic, which makes them the more convenient to excerpt. The last two items are included here for their sardonic satire, but there is enough of the picaresque to make them not out of place.

Shih Nai-an

MY FIRST *acquaintance with the classic* Shih Hu Chuan *was not in its seventy-one-chapter original but through an adaptation for the juvenile reader called* The Tattooed Monk Raising Hell on the Wutai Mountain. *Since then I have read the whole book backward, forward, and opened-at-any-page, for at least a hundred times, but the passage devoted to the adventures of the rough and ready officer who takes to the ecclesiastic robes through no fault of his own still brings me the most unadulterated pleasure. For elegance of metaphor I recommend the description of how Lu Ta finishes the town bully with three blows of the fist to the best picturesque language connoisseur in America. And nothing so convulses me as the two magnificent drunken sprees on which Lu Chi-Shen (the latter, "Profound Wisdom," being his Buddhist name) embarks before giving up the monastery for the greenwoods of the bandit lair.*

The novel itself tells of a band of 108 bandits and how they came to be that way. The great Ch'ing dynasty critic Chin Sheng-t'an, who listed it as one of his ten "Books of Genius," has classified its main characters each according to his worth—"top-top," "middling-top," "middling-low," or "low-low." The Tattooed Monk is rated a "top-top" character for his goodness of heart.

THE ADVENTURES OF THE TATTOOED MONK

Let it be told of Shih Chin as he left the mountain with his spear. He went on the Kuangsi road toward Yien An Fu. When he was hungry he ate and when athirst he drank and at night he slept in wayside inns. Alone he went for more than half a month and he came to a city called Wei Chou, where there was a great general's palace. There he thought to himself, "I wonder if my teacher Wang is here?" And he went into the city to see, and there of course were great streets and markets. But then he saw a little teashop just at the mouth of the road. Shih Chin went into this place and he chose a seat and sat down. The serving man in the shop came to him and asked him, saying, "Sir Guest, what tea would you like to drink?"

From *All Men Are Brothers*, translated by Pearl S. Buck.

Shih Chin answered, "I will drink a bowl with the tea leaves in it."

Then the serving man brought the tea and put it before Shih Chin and Shih Chin asked him, saying, "Where is the court of the general here?"

The serving man replied, "It is just in front of us."

Shih Chin said, "I wish to ask you if there is a man surnamed Wang and named Ching there, who is a teacher of military tactics and he came from the eastern capital."

The serving man replied, "There are many such persons in the general's halls and there are three or four surnamed Wang, and I do not know which is Wang Ching."

Before they had finished speaking they saw a tall man enter the tea-shop with great strides. Shih Chin gave him a look. He was in appearance a leader in wars. On his head he wore a hat of spotted silk, on the back of which were two twisted golden circles from T'ai Yuan Fu. On his upper body he wore a coat of the blue of a parrot's feathers. About his waist was a double girdle the color of the greenish black of a crow's plumage. On his feet were leather boots, and they were like the claws of an old eagle, dry yellow in color, and with four seams. His face was round, his ears were very large, his nose was straight and his mouth square. He wore a fan-shaped beard clean around his jaws. His body was eight feet in height, and his girth was enormous.

As this man came in and sat down, the serving man said to Shih Chin, "Sir Guest, if you look for an Instructor Wang, ask this honorable one. He knows them all."

So Shih Chin rose quickly and made an obeisance and he said, "Sir, pray sit down and drink tea."

Now the other man saw Shih Chin was tall and large and strong and that he looked a good fellow, and he also made an obeisance, therefore, and the two sat down and Shih Chin said, "I, who am but a humble person, yet dare greatly enough to ask your honorable surname."

The other replied, "I am a captain of Chin Lo Fu. My surname is Lu, my name is Ta. I also dare to ask, Elder Brother, what is your surname?"

Shih Chin said, "This small one is a man from Hua Chou in the county of Hua Ying, and my surname is Shih and my name is Chin. I wish to ask my lord this; I, humble one that I am, have had a teacher from the eastern capital surnamed Wang and named Ching. I do not know whether he is in this military camp or not."

Captain Lu said, "Elder Brother, perhaps you are from the Village of the Shih Family, and are even perhaps that big fellow, The Nine Dragoned Shih Chin?"

Shih Chin bowed and said, "That humble person am I."

Captain Lu quickly returned the bow and replied, "To see you is to know that you are even better than that which I have heard of you. As to that Instructor Wang whom you seek, is not he the one who offended the Commander Kao Ch'iu at the eastern capital?"

Shih Chin said, "It is even he."

Lu Tao said, "I have heard of his name. That elder brother is not here. I have heard people say he is in Yien An Fu working in the border camp under the old general there. This Wei Chou of ours is guarded by the younger general, and that man is not here. If you are that big fellow, Shih Chin, I have heard of your great fame. Now come on to the street with me and have a cup of wine."

And Lu Ta took Shih Chin's hand and they went out of the teashop and Lu Ta turned his head and said, "This money for the tea I will give you later!"

The serving man made reply, "Sir Captain, drink and it does not matter. Pray go without troubling yourself about it."

Lu Ta and Shih Chin, still holding each other's arms, came out from the teashop and went on the street and when they had gone some thirty to fifty paces they saw a crowd of people encircling a piece of empty ground. Shih Chin said, "Elder Brother, let us go and see."

Then they parted the crowd and looked. In the midst of the crowd was a man who had at his back some ten-odd wooden staves and placed on the ground before him one by one were ten-odd plasters for medicine. He had a plate and he put the plasters on the plate and on top he put a piece of paper. Now from the beginning such medicine has been sold by wandering fencers who use their fighting tricks to collect a crowd to whom they can sell medicine. This man was such a one, and when Shih Chin saw him he recognized him. The man had once taught him military gymnastics, and his name was Li The Warrior Who Wars Against Tigers.

Shih Chin called out of the crowd to him, saying, "Teacher, we have not met this long time!"

Li, whose name was Chung, answered, "Good Brother, how have you come here?"

Lu Ta said, "If you are my good comrade Shih Chin's teacher, then come and let us drink three cups of wine."

Li Chung said, "Wait until I have sold three plasters and have some money back and then I will come with you."

Lu Ta said, "Who can take the trouble to wait for you? If you want to come with us come at once."

Li Chung said, "This is my means for food and clothing and no other have I. Captain, pray then do you go on. This humble person, who am I, will come and find you." Turning to Shih Chin then he said, "Sir, go on."

Then Lu Ta grew angry and he pushed the crowd this way and that and he began to curse, saying, "Get out of here! If anyone does not get out of here, I will beat him!"

When the crowd saw it was Captain Lu, they cried out and all ran away. Li Chung, seeing how fierce Lu Ta was, grew angry in his heart but he did not dare to speak. He had no recourse and he could only smile at Lu and say, "Good, impetuous fellow!" and quickly collected his weapons and his medicine bags and put them in someone's house. The three men then turned a corner here and there, and so came to the Bridge of the Chou, where there was a famous wine shop kept by a man surnamed P'an. In front of the door was a flag pole on which hung the sign of this shop, and the flag blew back and forth in the wind.

The three then went upstairs in the wine shop and they saw a little clean veranda and there they sat down. The captain sat in the host's place, Li Chung sat opposite, and Shih Chin sat below him. The wine shop owner came in and called out a greeting and he recognized Captain Lu and he said, "Sir Captain, how much wine do you wish brought in?"

Lu answered, "First bring four measures of wine and then place fruits and meats and things suitable for drinking down with the wine."

Then the man asked again, "Sir and what will you have to drink down with your wine?"

Lu answered, "And why do you ask? Just bring along what you have. I will pay for it with the wine. You good-for-nothing, to be asking this and that and making a pother!"

The keeper of the wine shop went down then, and quickly he brought the heated wine upstairs and he brought all the meats he had ready and he covered the table with food.

These three then drank several cups of wine and they talked together idly, comparing methods of using various weapons. Just as they found themselves in good accord, they heard in the little veranda next to them someone crying and sobbing softly. Lu Ta grew angry and took his cup and bowl and plate and flung them upon the floor. The servant heard the noise and came running up and he saw Lu Ta there mad with fury and the servant cried, "Sir, what is it you want? Tell me and I will bring it."

Lu Ta said, "What do I want? You ought to know who I am! Why have you put someone next to us who sobs and cries and troubles us as we drink? I have always paid for my wine!"

The servant said, "Sir, do not be angry. How would so humble a person as I dare to let anyone come here and weep and trouble a lord as he drinks? This weeping comes from a father and daughter, singers, who sing at the wine tables and beg a little money thus. They do not know that such honorable ones are here drinking wine. Just now they are weeping because of their own bitter fate."

Lu Ta said, "This is very strange! Go and call them for me."

The servant man went and called them and in a moment the three saw the pair coming in. In front was a girl eighteen or nineteen years of age, and behind her a man fifty or sixty years old, in whose hand were a pair of castanets. When the two had come into their presence, the three saw that the girl, although she was not very pretty, was still comely enough to move a man somewhat. She wiped her eyes with the back of her hand as she came before them. Then she put her hands into her sleeves and bowed deeply three times. The man came also and made obeisances.

Lu Ta then said, asking them, "Who are you and from whence do you come and why are you weeping?"

The girl answered, saying, "Sir, you do not know. Let this humble one, who am I, tell you. I am from the eastern capital and I came here with my parents to a relative's home in Wei Chou, and we never dreamed they had moved to Nanking. My mother became ill in an inn and died there. We two, father and daughter, cannot return, but we must stay here to eat out our lives in bitterness. There is a rich man here, a lord whom all fear, east and west, and he is surnamed Cheng. He saw me, and he sent someone to force me to become his concubine. Who could have thought when he wrote it down that he would give three thousand strings for me that really he gave nothing, although he took my person too, and that before three months had passed his first wife, who was very jealous and cruel, would drive me out and would not let me stay with our husband? She also told the landlord in this inn to compel me to return the money which we never received. My father is too weak and ignorant to reason with her and she is rich and powerful. We have never had one penny from them. Now from whence can we find this money to pay them? There is no way, indeed.

"Nevertheless, my father from my childhood has taught me to sing little songs from plays and now we go into wine shops and sing, and every day as soon as we get a little money we give the larger half of it to this lord Cheng and there is only a very little left for our own use. These last two days the guests have been very few and yet he compels us to give as much as any other day, a certain amount, and we have not been able. Perhaps today when he comes to ask us for the money he will make us suffer for it. We two, father and daughter, when we think of this bitterness, have no one to whom we can talk of it and nowhere to seek redress, and for this reason we sit and weep. I did not think that we were not careful and so made you angry. Noble Sir, I pray you to forgive us our sin. Pray, Sir, lift your hand high that I may pass under it as under your mercy!"

Then Lu Ta asked again, "What is your surname? At what inn do you live? Where does this Cheng live?"

The old man answered, saying, "I am an old fellow and I am surnamed Chin. I am the second son in my father's family. My daughter is named Jade Lotus. The lord Cheng lives across the Bridge of the First Degree, and he is a pig butcher by trade and his nickname is Cheng The Bully Of Kuangsi. We two live just inside the east gate of the city in an inn kept by a fellow surnamed Lo."

As he spoke Lu Ta interrupted, saying, "P'u—that fellow? I thought you meant the real lord Cheng who is an official. It is only that pig butcher! That filthy, vile thing! He is a butcher near our place and he opens a meat shop there. This is how he cheats the people, is it?" Then he turned around and looked at Shih Chin and at Li Chung and he said, "You two sit here and wait until I go and beat that fellow to death and then I will be back straightway!"

At this Shih Chin and Li Chung threw their arms about Lu Ta and they besought him, saying, "Elder Brother, do not be so angry! Tomorrow we will go and talk with him."

Both of them thus begged him, three and five times they begged, until Lu Ta gave up going. Then he said, "Old fellow, come here! I will give you some money for travel. Tomorrow go back to the eastern capital—how is that?"

Father and daughter replied to him, saying, "If we can go home it is like giving us life again, like nurturing us to strength again! But how will the landlord of the inn let us go? The lord Cheng will surely demand the money from him."

Lu Ta said, "That does not matter. Of course I will have a way."

Then he felt on his person and brought out five ounces and more of silver and put it on the table, and he looked at Shih Chin and said, "I have not brought much silver with me today. Do you have any to lend me? I will repay you tomorrow."

Shih Chin said, "What small matter is this that I should seek repayment!"

From his bundle he took out a ten-ounce piece of silver and put it on the table and Lu Ta looked at it and then at Li Chung and he said, "You lend a little to me, too!"

Then Li Chung took out from his girdle something over two ounces of silver. When Lu Ta saw it he thought it too little and he said to himself, "What a stingy fellow, too!" He gave the fifteen ounces of the silver to the old man and he commanded himself, saying, "You two, father and daughter, take this for your travel expenses. Prepare your goods and tomorrow at dawn I will come and tell you when to start. I will see what landlord of an inn will dare to stop you!"

The old fellow Chin and his daughter knocked their heads on the ground before him and thanked him. Lu Ta then took the two ounces of silver and threw it back to Li Chung. The three men drank two measures more of wine and then went downstairs, and Lu Ta called, "Innkeeper, as for this money for the wine, I will pay it to you tomorrow!"

The innkeeper replied hastily, "Yes—yes—yes—do not trouble! Just come and drink wine—never mind! We are only afraid you will not come and so will not owe us anything!"

The three then went out of the wine shop and on the street they parted and Shih Chin and Li Chung went each to his inn.

Let it be further told that Lu Ta returned to his own dwelling place, and went into his sleeping room, but he did not eat any night meal. He went angry to his sleep and the landlord did not dare ask him for anything.

Let us now speak of the old man Chin. After he had received the fifteen ounces of silver, he went back to his inn and after his daughter had gone to bed he went outside the city to a distant place and found a wheelbarrow. When he came back to the inn he arranged all his possessions and paid his bill at the inn and paid for all the fuel and rice he had used, and then he could do no more than wait for the dawn of the next day. Nothing befell them during the night.

On the next morning before dawn he arose and the two of them, father and daughter, lit the fire first and cooked their early meal and after they had eaten they put things to rights. The sky was faintly light with the dawn and as they waited, Lu Ta came with great strides to the inn and in a loud voice he called aloud, "Ho, you serving man, where is the sleeping place of that old fellow Chin?"

The serving man called, "Old Chin, Captain Lu is here looking for you!"

Old Chin opened the door of his room and said, "Sir Captain, pray come in and sit down."

Lu Ta answered, "Why should I sit? If you are going, go at once! For what are you waiting?"

Old Chin then called his daughter and took up his load and thanked Lu Ta.

But even as he was going out the door the waiter stopped him and said, "Old Chin, where are you going?"

Lu Ta then asked, "And does he owe you any room money?"

The man replied, "The room money he settled last night, but he still owes the lord Cheng some money for his concubine. That one bade me to watch them and demand the money of them."

"That pig butcher, Cheng?" asked Lu Ta. "I will return his money. You let this old man go home."

How could the man be willing to let them go? Then Lu Ta grew mightily angry. He opened his five fingers and flung wide his arm and slapped the serving man full in the face so that blood burst out of his mouth. Then Lu Ta lifted up his fist and slapped the man again and knocked out his two front teeth. The serving man crawled up and, swift as a streak of smoke, he ran to hide in the inn. Then the landlord himself did not dare to come out to stop the trouble, and Old Chin and his daughter quickly left the inn and went outside the city and there found the wheelbarrow hired the day before.

But Lu Ta had a thought. It was that perhaps this serving man would pursue the pair and bring them back and so he took a bench out from the inn and sat there on it for two watches. Then in his heart he thought, "By now they will have gone a long way," and he stood up and went straight to the Bridge of the First Degree.

Let it be told now of the Pig Butcher Cheng. He had double doors to his shop and it opened to the street and on either side were the counters with meat for sale. There were three or five whole hogs hanging there. As for Cheng Tu, which was the butcher's name, on that day he sat in front of his counter at the door, and he was watching his ten-odd clerks as they sliced off meat.

Lu Ta came to the door and he called out, "Butcher Cheng!"

Cheng looked and saw that it was Lu Ta and he quickly came out to the front of the counter and he bowed and called a greeting and said, "Captain, pray excuse my rudeness that I did not come to meet you." And he commanded a clerk to bring out a bench, and he said again, "Captain, pray sit down."

Then Lu Ta sat down and he said, "I have just received a command from the General. He wants ten catties of lean meat cut into strips. He will not see the smallest piece of fat in it at all."

Then Cheng The Butcher said to his clerks, "Quickly find some good lean meat and cut up ten catties of it!"

Lu Ta said, "I will not have those dirty things cut the meat for us! I want you to cut it up yourself."

Cheng The Pig Butcher said, "You are right. This humble person will do it."

Then he himself went to the counter and he chose out ten pounds of lean meat and he cut it finely into strips. By this time the servant from the inn had arrived with his head tied up in a large handkerchief to tell Cheng of the affair with Old Chin, but when he saw Lu Ta sitting beside the meat table he stood afar off, not daring to come near, and he watched from under the distant eaves.

Cheng The Butcher, when he had sliced for half a watch, tied the meat into a lotus leaf and he said, "Captain, shall I bid someone to take it for you?"

Lu Ta said, "Take what? Wait a minute—we still want ten pounds of fat and it must be cut into shreds too."

Cheng said, "Just now you wanted lean and I thought the magistrate wanted it to make dumplings. But what can be the use of shredded fat?"

Lu Ta opened his eyes wide and he said, "This is what I was commanded! Who dares to ask what it is for?"

Cheng Tu said, "If it is to be used, this humble one will slice it and there is an end to it."

So again he chose ten pounds of the best firm fat and he sliced it finely and he tied it into a lotus leaf. He spent exactly the whole morning in this. By this time it was time to have eaten the noon meal, and the servant from the inn still did not dare to come near. Even some of the old customers did not dare to come near. Cheng said, "Shall I bid someone to take it to the court for you, Captain?"

Lu Ta said, "I still want ten pounds of gristle and it also must be shredded. There must not be a particle of meat in it."

At this Cheng The Butcher laughed and he said, "Are you not making a joke of me?"

Lu Ta hearing this leaped up and he took the two bundles of shredded meat and he opened his eyes enormously and he stared at the butcher and he said, "I did indeed come to make a joke of you!"

Then he threw the two bundles of shredded meat into Cheng's face, and it rained meat everywhere. Cheng The Butcher was very angry. Two flames of anger seemed to run from the soles of his feet to the crown of his head. His heart was like a lump of dark fire in his breast and it flamed up in him, and was not to be pressed down. From the counter he seized a sharp pointed knife used to split bones and he leaped up from the ground.

But Lu Ta was long since in the middle of the street and of all the neighbors and ten-odd clerks, not one dared to come forward and persuade the two to peace. The passers-by all stopped and the servant from the inn was frightened stupid. Cheng The Butcher raised his knife in his hand and stretched out his left hand to grasp Lu Ta's throat, but Lu grasped Cheng's left hand as he rushed forward and Lu ran forward first and he kicked Cheng in the lower belly and knocked him down on the street. Then Lu Ta went forward another step and as Cheng sprawled there, Lu put one foot on his breast. Lu Ta's fists, each as big as a coarse earthen bowl, were outstretched and his eyes glared down at Cheng as he said, "I was at first a guard before the general's gate, and then I was raised to be an official over five different districts, and I do not think I held the title of lord in vain, and are you fit to be called by that name, who are but a meat-selling, knife-holding butcher—a man like a dog. Shall you be called an official? How did you dare to use force to cheat the maid surnamed Chin and named Jade Lotus?"

And as he spoke he lifted his fist and with a dull thud he hit Cheng on the bridge of the nose and the fresh blood flowed out. Cheng's nose was broken and bent to the side and of a sudden he smelled as many smells as though he had opened a condiment shop—soy bean sauce, salt, sour, sweet, hot—all in a second he smelled them all. He tried to get up but he could not. He had cast the pointed knife to one side and he kept yelling, "That's right—you hit me—go on and hit me!"

Lu Ta cursed him, saying, "You incestuous beast, do you still dare to answer me?"

And he lifted his great fist and hit Cheng on the eye socket and split open the corner of his eye so that his eyeball burst out. It was now to Cheng as though he had opened a silk shop wherein were silks of many colors, for he saw black and purple and red from the bursting of his eyeball. The onlookers on all sides were afraid of Lu Ta and which one dared to go before him to placate him? But Cheng could endure no more and he begged Lu Ta to forgive him.

Then Lu Ta yelled at him, "Ho, you rascal, if you had been stubborn to the end I could have forgiven you! But now you are begging forgiveness and I will purposely not forgive you!" And he gave him another hit on the temple with his clenched fist.

By now it seemed to Cheng that he was in an assembly of priests in great mass and he heard in his head the reverberations of the great musical instruments, and the clanging of cymbals great and small, all going on together. Lu Ta, taking a look, only saw Cheng lying very straight on the ground and stiff, and from his mouth the breath came out but did not go in and he did not move. Lu Ta pretended to curse him again, saying, "You thing, you are pretending to be dead! I will hit you again."

But Lu Ta looked and he saw that Cheng's face was changing color. Then Lu Ta thought a little to himself thus: "I only hoped to hit him hard the once. I did not dream that in three blows I would really kill him. I shall be arrested for this, and I have not a soul who could fetch me anything to eat in jail! I had better run away as soon as I can."

So he lifted up his legs and he went off, and as he went away he turned back his head to the corpse and called to it, "You are pretending to be dead! I shall come back and finish this affair at another time!"

Thus cursing and taking great strides, he went away. And of the neighbors in the street and of the clerks in the shop, which one dared to come forward and stop him?

Lu Ta went back to his rented room and quickly he bundled up his clothes and some money for travel; his good clothes and silver he took thus, but his old things and all heavy things he left behind. In his hand he took a staff as high as his eyebrows and he ran out of the south gate and was away like a puff of smoke.

Let it be told now of the people in Cheng The Pig Butcher's house and the servant from the inn. They tried for half a day to revive him, and they could not bring him to life. Alas, he was dead! Old and young among the neighbors then went to the local governor's office to report the case, and they waited until the governor went into The Hall Of Justice for audience. Then they presented their written account of the matter.

When the governor had read this to the end he said, "Lu Ta is a captain in the military court. I cannot go straight off and arrest the murderer."

Nevertheless he went at once into his sedan and was carried to the military court and he got out of his sedan and the soldiers at the gates went in and told the general, and this one, when he heard it was the governor, told them to invite him to come in. When the governor therefore had entered the hall and had seen the general and made obeisance to him, that general asked the governor, saying, "What is your business here?"

The governor answered, saying, "There is a matter I wish your Lordship to know. There is a captain in your guard called Lu Ta, who without any cause lifted up his fists and killed Cheng The Pig Butcher. I would not have reported this matter but I did not dare go alone and arrest the murderer."

When the general heard this, he gave a start of fright and in his heart he thought, "This Lu Ta, in spite of his great ability in war, is too coarse and rough a fellow! Now he has committed a murder, and how can I protect him? Certainly it seems better to let him suffer for this deed." Then he said aloud to the governor, "This man Lu Ta is a captain who served under my father. Because I had no one here to act as chief guard I told him to come here and be captain. If he has committed the crime of murder, take him according to the law and punish him. If he records his act clearly and you have fixed his punishment, then pray let my father know of it when you carry out the sentence, lest my father may want to use him on the border, and then it will not look well if we have killed him."

The governor said to him, "Assuredly so small a governor as I, when I have enquired clearly into the matter should tell the aged official and my lord and let them know before I dare to sentence him."

The governor then bade the general farewell and the governor went out and got into his sedan and returned to his own court and went into The Hall Of Justice and sat down. He called the men out for duty on this day, and he gave the chief of them written authority to go and catch the offender, Lu Ta.

At that time this chief, who was surnamed Wang, took the written proclamation and with him twenty-odd men and they went straight to the inn where Lu Ta lived. There they saw the landlord who said, "He has just taken up his bundle and his staff and gone out. I, humble man that I am, guessed that he was going out on some duty and I did not dare to question him."

Wang, hearing this, called his men to break open Lu Ta's door and look in. There were only some old clothes in the room and some bedding. Then Wang, taking the landlord along with him, went east and west and everywhere in all four directions and he went from the north to the south of the city, but he could not find Lu Ta to seize him. Wang then went and summoned two of the neighbors, and they all went to the governor's court and Wang said, "Lu Ta was frightened and he has escaped. Now we do not know where he is gone. I have brought only his landlord here and his neighbors."

When the governor heard this he at once told Wang to cast these persons into jail and he also commanded that some of the neighbors of Cheng The Pig Butcher be put there also. Then he sent for the coroner and the two local small officials and the police of that street and the body of Cheng The Pig Butcher was examined many times.

Then Cheng's wife prepared a coffin and put Cheng's body into it and she had the coffin placed temporarily in a temple. She had an account of the whole affair written down, and she sent people to the court to ask for a definite date for the arrest of the murderers. The accusers of Lu Ta left guarantors in their places and went home. As for the magistrate, he ordered the neighbors beaten because they had not come out to help Cheng and he accused the landlord and neighbors of Lu Ta also because they should not have let Lu Ta escape. The governor then sent out a proclamation everywhere that Lu Ta was to be arrested and to the man who caught him would be given a thousand strings of cash. In the proclamation was given also the age of Lu Ta, his home, the description of his countenance, and everywhere this proclamation was hung up. Then all who had been imprisoned he sent home and told them to be prepared for further call.

As for the people in Cheng The Pig Butcher's house, they went home themselves and prepared for the funeral and of this there is no more to be told.

Let it be told now of Lu Ta. From the time he left Wei Chou he ran east and west and here and there in the greatest haste. He passed through several cities and he ate anything he could get and he covered himself with what he had and in his exigency he was like any poor fellow who fares any way he can and who cannot get what he wants but must take what he can get, even though it be an ugly wife. And Lu Ta's temper was exceedingly impatient and he went in the greatest haste, not knowing in his heart which was the best way of escape.

Thus speeding for more than half a month he came to a city in Shansi called T'ai Chou. After he had entered this city he saw that trade here was very brisk, people crowded, and carts and horses without number. Of the one hundred and twenty trades there were all of them here, and the place was most assuredly prosperous in appearance. Although it was only a county seat, it was larger than the capital of a province. Lu Ta, as he was walking along the road, saw a crowd of people gathered at a crossroad looking at a sign that hung there, and seeing how many there were of them, he ran into their midst to listen. Now Lu Ta could not read, and he only heard people reading aloud thus:

"The magistrate of T'ai Chou has received a notice from the high official who has received a proclamation from Wei Chou saying that a certain criminal named Lu Ta is to be arrested. He is a captain in the military camp. Whoever takes him in to live and to eat food, he shall be considered equal with the criminal in guilt. If anyone arrests him and brings him here, or secretly comes and tells the magistrate where he is, to that man will be given one thousand strings of cash."

Lu Ta had just listened thus far when someone called loudly behind him, "Elder Brother Chang, why are you come here?" and he felt himself embraced and dragged away from the crossroad.

Lu Ta then turned himself about to see who this was and the one who dragged him away was none other than the Old Chin whom he had rescued in the wine shop in Wei Chou. The old man now took him straight to a place where no one was and he said to him, "Gracious One, how daring you are! The accusation hangs there openly against you now, offering a reward of a thousand strings for you. Why do you run and look at it? If it had not been I that chanced upon you, would you not have been taken to the magistrate's court? On that sign is written your age, your appearance, and the place of your home!"

Lu Ta said, "I will not deceive you. All this came out of the day when you escaped and when I met this Pig Butcher Cheng, and I killed him with three blows of the fist. Because of this I had to run away. I have run hither and thither everywhere for the last forty or fifty days, and I did not dream when I reached here that you had not gone to the eastern capital. Why did you come here, too?"

Old Chin replied, "Gracious One, you are high above me. When you saved me I found a wheelbarrow and I planned then to go back to the eastern capital. But I was afraid that fellow would catch me there again and then the Gracious One would not be there to save us. For this reason I did not go to the eastern capital. We went as the road winds to the north and we found an old man on the way who was from the capital and he came here to do business, and he brought us, father and daughter, to this place. Luckily he helped us and was go-between for me, an old man, and for my daughter, with a great rich man of this place who is surnamed Chao. My daughter is now mistress to the lord Chao and she has plenty to eat and wear. This all comes from your kindness to us. My daughter constantly says to her lord, 'It is by the captain's great mercy.' As for that noble lord, he also likes to use a staff and weapons and he always asks, 'How can we meet with this savior of yours? How well it would be if we could meet!' In his heart he is always planning how he may meet with you. Pray, Gracious One, come to my house for a few days and we will plan further."

Lu Ta then went with Old Chin and in less than a quarter of a mile they came to his door, and Lu Ta saw the old man draw aside the curtain and he heard him call out, "My daughter, the Great Merciful One is here!"

Then the girl, beautifully dressed and coifed, came out from within the house, and she invited Lu to come and sit inside in the middle place. And it was as though she had lit a candle before a god, and she bowed herself to the ground before him six times. Then she said, "If the Great Merciful One had not saved our lives how could we have come to our present good fortune?" Then when she had finished bowing she besought Lu Ta saying, "Merciful One, pray go upstairs and sit down."

Lu Ta said, "Do not let me trouble you. I go on very soon."

Old Chin then said, "Merciful One, since you have come here, how can we let you go at once?"

And the old man took Lu Ta's staff and his bundle and he asked him to go upstairs and sit down. The old man then commanded his daughter, saying, "Daughter, go upstairs and entertain him as he sits. I will go and arrange for foods and meats."

Lu Ta said, "Do not go and be busy. Give me anything that you have—that is best."

The old man said, "Merciful One and Captain, even though I killed my body I could not repay you for your mercy to us. I am going to prepare a little coarse food of no fine flavor. Do not mention it, therefore."

The girl then took Lu Ta upstairs and the old man came down and called the small maidservant in his house and bade her light the fire in the kitchen, and then together they went on the street and bought some fresh fish and tender chicken, some salted goose that had been soaked in the lees of wine, some fat fish, and some newly ripened fruit and other such things, and they returned. They opened the wine for the table and prepared the meats and soon all was ready. Then they placed the wine cups, the three pairs of chopsticks, and at last the meat and fruits and other things. Then the servant brought out a silver wine jug, and heated the wine, and the father and daughter each in turn invited Lu Ta to drink. Old Chin bowed to the ground and knocked his head and the Captain said, "Old man, why do you knock your head like this before me? You put me in the wrong and shame me."

Old Chin said, "Merciful One, hear me speak! When I had just come to this place I wrote your name on a piece of red paper and morning and evening I burned a stick of incense to it. We two, father and daughter, knocked our heads before it. Today the Merciful One has come here of his own accord and shall I not knock my head before him?"

Lu Ta replied, "It is not easy to find a heart like yours."

The three then drank wine slowly and feasted until almost night. Suddenly they heard a great noise downstairs. Lu Ta opened the window to look out and he saw some twenty or thirty people below. Each one carried a white wooden staff and they all shouted out, "Bring him down!" In the midst was one who looked like a lord and he rode a horse and he shouted loudly, "Do not let the thief escape!" Lu Ta, seeing that things looked badly for him, took up his stool and flung it out of the window. Old Chin wrung his hands and cried out, saying, "Let no one move!"

Then the old man went quickly down and he ran to the lord mounted on his horse and said a few sentences. The lord laughed and shouted to the twenty or thirty people to be scattered and each went away. Then he came down from his horse and went inside and the old man invited Lu Ta to come and the lord dropped himself down and knocked his head on the ground and he said, "What I have heard is not as great as the reality. Pray let the noble captain accept my obeisances."

Lu Ta then asked Old Chin, saying, "Who is this lord? I have never known him. Why is he knocking his head to do me reverence?"

The old man said, "This is even that lord to whom my daughter is mistress. He thought that I had brought a bad man here to come upstairs to feast and drink and so he brought his tenants for a fight. But I have made the matter clear and he has sent them away."

Lu Ta then went upstairs and sat down again. Old Chin again arranged the wine cups and again prepared wine and meats. Chao let Lu Ta sit in the highest seat, but Lu Ta said, "How dare I?"

The lord replied, "This expresses but a little of my respect for you. I have heard much of your great feats and today Heaven has given me the chance of meeting you face to face. This is great happiness."

Lu Ta said, "I am but a coarse and common man. Now I have done a crime for which I am sentenced to death. If by your mercy you will overlook my low estate I can be a friend. If afterwards you can use me in any place, I will go anywhere for you."

At this the lord was very pleased and he asked Lu Ta how he had come to kill a man and they talked idly together and compared certain methods of fighting, and they drank a half night of wine and then each went to his rest.

The second day at dawn the lord said, "This place is neither safe nor convenient for you. Pray come to my humble village."

Lu Ta asked, saying, "And where is your honorable village?"

The lord replied, "It is about three miles from here and the village is named The Village Of The Seven Precious Things. That is it."

Lu Ta then said, "It is well."

The lord therefore told someone to go to the village and bring back another horse and before noon the horse was come and the lord then invited Lu Ta to mount the horse and he bade his tenants carry the baggage. Lu Ta bade farewell to the two, Old Chin and his daughter, and with the lord Chao, he mounted his horse and the two rode side by side the whole way and on the road they talked idle talk and thus they came to The Village Of The Seven Precious Things.

In a little while they reached the front of the village and they went into the great hall and each sat in his proper seat. Chao commanded people to kill sheep and to prepare wine for Lu Ta and to prepare the guest room for him to sleep in that night. On the second day a feast was prepared for him.

Lu Ta then said to Chao, "Your affection for me is a mistaken one. How can I repay you?"

The lord Chao replied, "'Around the four seas all men are brothers.' Why do you speak of repaying?"

But the story must not be told in tiresome detail. From this time on Lu Ta lived in that village and so he lived for seven or eight days. Suddenly one day when he sat with Chao in the library talking they saw the old man Chin running in a mighty haste to the village and he came straight into the library and he saw Lu Ta and Chao there and that there was no one else, and he said to Lu Ta, "Merciful One, it is not that I am suspicious, but the other day when you were feasting and drinking wine with this old man upstairs, this honorable lord was wrongly told by the people and he brought in tenants and came to the street to make a quarrel, and afterwards he sent them away again. This has set people to wondering and this one talks to that one. Yesterday three or four runners from the magistrate's court came to our neighbor's house on the same street with us and questioned them very closely. I fear lest they will come to this village and arrest us all unless we are very careful. If trouble comes of it what shall we do, then?"

Lu Ta said, "If this is so, I must go straight away and that is an end to it."

But Chao said, "If I let the captain stay here it will be as dangerous as mountains too high and waters too deep. Then if trouble comes, you will hate me. If I do not let you stay, it will look badly too. Now I have a way, and I can keep you from any danger, and surely I can make your person safe and at peace. I only fear you, My Captain, will not be willing."

Lu Ta said, "I am a man who ought to die, and if I can find a refuge it is enough. How then should I not be willing?"

Then Chao said, "If it be thus it is well. There is a mountain some ten miles from here, and it is called The Five Crested Mountain. On that mountain is a temple to the god Wen Ch'u, for it is the place where Wen Ch'u, the great Buddhist, preached. In this large temple there are some five to seven hundred priests, and the abbot is named Chi Chen. He is my sworn brother. My ancestors formerly gave a great deal of money to this temple, and were its loyal adherents, and once I made a vow before the god that I would persuade someone to become a priest before him. I have already bought a certificate of priesthood in the five colors, but I have not found a trustworthy man to help me fulfill my vow. If you, Sir Captain, will do it, I will prepare all the necessary money. But when you come to the truth of it, are you willing to shave your head and become a priest?"

Lu Ta meditated awhile in his heart and said to himself, "If I go away now, where shall I go and to whom? This road is the best after all." So he said aloud, "If the Merciful One so helps me, I am willing to be a priest. I can only trust you to help me." Thus was it decided.

In the night of that same day they prepared Lu Ta's clothing, and they prepared money and some bolts of satin and all that was needed. On the next day they rose early in the morning and told the villagers to carry these things, and Chao and Lu Ta both went up the road until they reached the foothills. They sat in two chairs, then, and were carried up the mountain, while they bade the tenants to go ahead and tell the temple priests. When they came to the front of the temple the chief priests of the temple were there to meet them. The two came down out of their chairs then and sat down in the little pavilion outside the temple gate.

When the abbot heard of it he came also with his attendants outside the temple gate to meet him. Chao and Lu, when they saw the abbot coming, rose and came forward and made obeisance and the abbot returned the obeisance with his blessing and he said to Chao, "Our disciple, you have come a long way to see us and for what reason?"

Chao answered this, saying, "I have some small matters to tend, and I came especially to your honored temple to beg something of you, Sir Abbot."

The abbot said, "But first I must ask you, the lord, to come into the hall of the temple to drink tea."

Chao went in front and Lu followed him at his back, but they went together into the great hall. The abbot then invited the lord Chao to sit in the most honored guest's seat. Lu Ta sat in a lower place on the great couch where priests usually sat cross-legged, but the lord Chao put his mouth to Lu's ear and reproved him, saying, "You are come to this place as a priest to renounce the world. How is it you can sit in the abbot's presence?"

Lu said, "I do not understand." Nevertheless, he rose and stood beside Chao's shoulder.

In front of them were the abbot, the elder who had charge of the discipline of the priests, the attendants upon the elder, the master of the temple, the chief priest, the priest in charge of guests, the scribes; according to rank they stood east and west on either side. The tenants put the chairs right and brought all the boxes in and put them down. The abbot said, "Have you brought gifts again also? We have many places in the temple that need your help."

Chao answered, "These are but a few poor things, and why need you thank me for them?"

The temple servants received the gifts and took them away. Then Chao stood up and said, "There is something I wish to say. Once I had a certain hope fulfilled and I promised before the god that I would send one to serve as a priest in his temple. The priestly proofs and the accounts I have already prepared, but until now I have not found a person who could come and be priest. Today my brother friend, sur-named Lu, who has been a captain of imperial soldiers, now sees that life upon this earth is too difficult and he wishes to leave it and become a priest. I hope the elders will receive him and shave his head and let him become a priest. It will be a great mercy and a compassion if you thus receive him for my sake and repay my slender gifts in the past to the temple. All that he needs for use in his novitiate I will prepare. I hope a thousand times that the abbot will complete all with his ap-proval, for this will make me very happy."

When the abbot heard this he answered, "This is an honor to our temple. It is easy—easy—but first, pray drink tea!"

The servants then brought tea and when it had been drunk, took the tea things out again. The abbot then called to the elders to come aside for consultation as to shaving this man and making him into a priest, and he told them to prepare the vegetarian meal that was usual to the temple, and meanwhile the other priests went away to discuss the matter. They said among themselves, "This man does not look like one who renounces the world. How fierce are his two eyes!" And they said to the priest in charge of the guests, "Sir, do you go and sit with the guests and we will consult with the elders on this matter."

Just then the priest who was master of the temple came out and asked Chao and Lu to come into the guest room to sit down and the other priests went humbly to the abbot and they said, "The face and likeness of this man who has just come in to renounce the world are dreadful and hideous and he looks very fierce. We do not think he should be allowed to remain. Perhaps afterwards we may be impli-cated in his crimes."

But the abbot replied, "He is our disciple Chao's friend. Why should we not receive him for Chao's sake? You must not suspect such things. Wait a little until I see." He then lit a stick of incense of a certain length and went to the seat for meditation and there he sat down and crossed his legs. He began to chant and in his meditation his soul went out of his body. When the incense had burned to its set end the abbot's soul returned to its body and he said to the priests, "We must let this man stay and be a priest. He is born of a Star in Heaven. His heart is exceedingly single and sincere, although he is a man of fierceness. Yes, even though his destiny is full of evil and difficult things, yet afterwards he will assuredly go to the pure regions of the gods and he will become more than man and in the end none of you will equal him. Remember what I have said, and do not refuse him or send him away."

The head priest then said, "The abbot is prejudiced in his favor! But we can only do as he commanded. If we do not reason with him, that will be our fault; if he will not listen he must just have his way."

The abbot then called out, "Prepare the vegetable meal and invite Chao and the others to come into the guest hall and we will eat!" After they had eaten, the scribe wrote an account of what one would need for his novitiate and Chao brought out silver and told a servant to buy the things according to the account, while in the temple they made a priest's hat and garments and shoes and cloak and a cushion for his worship. In a day or two all were prepared.

Then the abbot chose a lucky day and hour, and he commanded the priests to strike the bell and beat the drum and he called everyone together in the assembly hall. There were some five or six hundred priests in all and they wrapped themselves in their square cloaks and went before the dais and made obeisance, each priest with his palms pressed together, and so they worshipped. Then they divided in two rows and sat down. The lord Chao took out silver and gifts and incense and knocked his head on the ground before the abbot. A priest then read aloud from a written paper an account of the lord Chao's vow and a small servant led Lu Ta to the foot of the dais and the abbot called to Lu to take off his hat and divide his hair into nine parts and knot it. The barber first shaved his head all round and then prepared to shave his beard, but Lu Ta cried, "Leave me this little thing anyway!"

When the priests heard this they all laughed. But the abbot said, "Hear me read the sacred words!"

Then he began to read, " 'One spear of hair cannot be left on the head. The six senses must be utterly removed.' Now I must take these from you in order that all unrest may be taken away." When he had said this he cried in one shout, "Away with it."

And the barber with one sweep of his razor shaved Lu Ta clean.

Then the scribe put the certificate in front of the abbot and asked the abbot to give the new priest a name. The abbot took a blank page on the certificate and he wrote and as he wrote he chanted, "Of Budha's light a fragment, but the price of it is beyond gold! By the power of the gods will I give him a name and it shall be Chi Shen!"

The abbot when he had given the name bade someone take the paper, and the scribe wrote the name in its place and gave the paper to Lu Chi Shen to keep. Then the abbot gave him clothes and a square red cloak and told him to put these on. At the same time the master of temple discipline led him to the dais and the abbot put his hand on the crown of Lu's head and commanded him, saying, "First, you must believe in the doctrines of Buddha. Second, you must believe in the true denomination of Buddhism. Third, you must revere your teachers and friends. These are the three commandments. Beyond these are the five forbidden acts. First, you must not take life; second, you must not steal; third, you must not commit adultery; fourth, you must not drink wine; fifth, you must not lie."

Lu Chi Shen did not know the customs of the temple that to these commands must be given the answer "I can," so at this time he merely said, "I will remember." When the priests heard this they all laughed again.

After the rites were over, the lord Chao asked all the priests to come into the great hall and there they seated themselves and they burned incense and ate a vegetable meal that had been prepared and they sacrificed to the gods. To all the priests high and low Chao gave a congratulatory present. Then the abbot took Lu Chi Shen and introduced him to each one, and he took him also into the priest's inner room, and showed him the seat there for his meditation. There is no more to be told concerning that night.

On the second day the lord Chao wished to return, so he went to the abbot to say farewell. The abbot could not persuade him to linger, and after they had eaten the morning vegetable meal all the monks escorted Chao outside the temple gate. The lord Chao put his hands together and said to them, "Sir Abbot, abide here, and, sir monks, do you stay. Whatever happens, I beg you to forgive my younger brother in Lu Chi Shen. He is a simple-minded and stupid man. If he is sometimes deficient in manners or if what he says offends you, or if he is not careful and he breaks the laws of Buddha, I greatly hope you will consider my poor honor and forgive him."

The abbot then replied, "Sir, let your heart be at rest. This old priest will teach him slowly how to read the books and how to repeat the magic rituals and how to examine the sacred ways, and how to go into meditation."

The lord Chao then said, "Surely I will reward you." And out of the many persons he called to Lu Chi Shen to come under the pine tree and in a low voice he said, "Good Brother, from now on you cannot be as you once were. Whatever comes, you must be careful and you cannot be proud. If you do not behave well, we cannot easily meet again. Take good care of your body. What you need for clothing I will bid someone to bring you."

Lu Chi Shen said, "I do not need my elder brother to tell me. I will obey in everything."

Then the lord Chao left the abbot and said farewell to all and went into his sedan chair and his villagers went with him carrying the empty sedan. Then they took the boxes and went down the mountain and to their homes and the abbot led all the priests back into the temple.

Let it be told further of Lu Chi Shen. He went into the temple again and into the great hall and then he went to the long seat and threw himself down and fell asleep. The two monks next him pulled him up and said, "You may not do thus. If you renounce the world then why do you not learn to sit the night through?"

But Lu Chi Shen said, "I will sleep my sleep, and what has it to do with you?"

The two priests, unwilling to speak an evil word, only stammered, "We-ll—We-ll——"

Lu Chi Shen gave a great grunt and he muttered, "Turtle meat I can eat too, and why do you speak of eels?"

The two priests then said, "This is too bad—it is too bitter to bear!"

Lu Chi Shen said, "Turtle's meat is sweet and good to eat and fat and why do you talk of bitterness?"

But the two priests on either side of him would not talk with him longer, and so they let him go to sleep.

On the second day they wished to go and tell the abbot how mannerless Lu Chi Shen had been, but the head monk besought them, saying, "The abbot has already told us that this man would become a Buddha and that he would be greater than any of us. We must protect him in every way. There is no recourse; we cannot quarrel with him at all."

The monks then went away. Lu Chi Shen, seeing that no one reproved him, lay out straight every night, his arms outspread crosswise, and he fell upon the long seat like this and slept. His snoring was like thunder and when he rose in the night to piss he would shout out this and that in a great voice, and he went and pissed behind the very Buddha so that the water and filth ran over the whole floor. Then the monks went to the abbot and they said, "This Chi Shen is indeed too mannerless! He is altogether unlike a priest. How can we in our temple allow such a one as this to live here?"

But the abbot replied in a loud voice, "You foolish talkers! We can now consider nothing except Chao's pride. This man will change after a while."

From this time on no one dared to say a word against Lu Chi Shen.

Thus Lu Chi Shen created a turmoil for four or five months in the mountain temple without even knowing that he did. Winter drew near and he grew weary of being quiet for so long and he wished to go out. One day the air was very clear, and Lu Chi Shen put on a priest's robe, long and black, and he tied a silken girdle about him and he changed his priest's shoes and in great strides he went out of the temple gate.

Letting his feet go as they would, he went to a little pavilion half way up the mountain and he sat there on a long bench. He thought thus in his heart: "What is all this about? I used before to eat good meat and good wine and every day such food was upon my lips. Now they have made me into a priest and I am half starved and I am grown all dry and withered. And Chao these last days does not send anyone to bring me something to seat. My mouth is so cursed tasteless I cannot bear it! How can I get hold of some wine somehow to make me right again?"

Even as his heart thought of wine he saw in the distance a man who climbed the hill and who was singing as he climbed. He carried two buckets slung on a pole, and they were covered with lids. In his hand was a wine jug. Singing and climbing he came, and thus he sang:

"Three miles long is the mountain—it looks on old battlefields.
At its foot a small cowherd an old battle axe wields.
The kind wind ruffles the waters of the River Wu,
It seems the voice of I Chi, weeping her lord the day through."

Lu Chi Shen, seeing the man with his pair of buckets coming near, sat in the pavilion and watched him. The man approached and put his buckets down and Chi Shen said, "Ha, you fellow, those buckets of yours—what have they inside?"

"Good wine!" the man answered.

"How much is it a bucket?" asked Chi Shen.

"Priest," replied the man, "surely you are joking with me."

"I am joking what with you?" Chi Shen asked.

The man replied, "This wine of mine that I carry up here is only to sell to the servants in the temple and to chair carriers and for such men to drink. There is a rule in the temple that if I sell to any priest the abbot will punish me and he will take back the money he lent us for capital, and he will drive us out of our house. We use temple money now to carry on our business and we live in a house rented from the temple. How can I dare to sell wine to you to drink?"

Chi Shen asked, "You truly will not sell it to me?"

The man replied, "Even if you kill me for it I will not sell to you."

"I will not kill you," said Chi Shen. "I will only ask you to sell the wine to me to drink."

The man saw the outlook was bad for him and he lifted up his buckets to run away. But Lu Chi Shen rushed out of the pavilion and with both hands he seized the man's carrying pole and with one foot he kicked him in the buttocks. The man grasped himself where he had been kicked and bowed himself over and for a long time he could not stand up. Chi Shen then took a bucket and went into the pavilion and he picked up the jug from the road, took off the cover of the bucket, and dipping the jug into the cold wine, he drank. In a short time one of the two big buckets of wine was gone, for he had drunk it all. Chi Shen said then, "Man, come here tomorrow for the money!"

But the man, whose pain was only just now eased, was afraid the monks in the temple would know of it and deprive him of his living, and so he swallowed his anger and dared say nothing. How then could he dare to ask for money? He divided the remaining wine into the two buckets and lifted them up and he took the wine jug and he went down that mountain as though he flew.

Let it be told further of Lu Chi Shen. He sat in the pavilion for a long time, and the wine came up into his head. He went down out of the pavilion and sat under a pine tree for another long while. The wine came up into his head more than ever. Then he took off his black robe and tied it by the sleeves into his girdle. The upper part of his body was left bare and showed his tattooing, and thus he went up the mountain, swinging his arms as he went. As he approached the temple gate, the two gate priests saw him from afar. They took up their split bamboo staves and they went to the gate and stopped him and cried loudly, "You are a disciple of Buddha, and how can you come up the mountain as drunk as this? Your eyes are not blind—you can see the sign hanging there! 'If any monk disobeys and is drunken he must be beaten forty times with the split bamboo and he shall be driven from the temple. If the gate priests allow a drunken monk to come into the temple they shall be beaten ten times.' Quickly go back down the mountain and we will forgive you these blows of the bamboo!"

Now Lu Chi Shen in the first place had only just become a priest; in the second place, his former temper was not changed; therefore he opened his two eyes wide and he cursed, saying, "You two thieves, do you two seek to fight me? I will fight you!"

One of the two temple priests, seeing the outlook was bad for them, went flying to tell the chief priest who was master of the temple; the other held up the split bamboo and made as if to strike Lu Chi Shen and stop him. Then Chi Shen flung his hand up and spread his five fingers out and struck that priest in the face so that he staggered forward, and as he staggered Lu Chi Shen gave him another blow of the fist and knocked him down. There in front of the temple gate, he fell, crying, "Bitterness—bitterness!"

Lu Chi Shen then cried, "I will forgive you, you good-for-naught!" and staggering back and forth he went into the temple.

When the chief priest heard what the gate priest said he called together some workmen and some kitchen serving men and chair bearers, twenty or thirty men in all. Each had a wooden staff and they ran forth out of the western veranda and thus they met Lu Chi Shen. He saw them and with a roar like a great clap of thunder he plunged into the middle of the crowd with great strides. At first they did not know that he had been a man who led soldiers; then, seeing him beat about so savagely, they ran back into the hall where the books were kept and shut the windows. Lu Chi Shen rushed to the foot of the steps and with one blow of his fist he burst open the window, and he so besieged the twenty or thirty persons that they had no way to turn. Then he seized a stick and rushed out again.

The master of the temple then ran to tell the abbot. When the abbot heard it he quickly brought several of his attendants and came to the veranda and he cried out in a great voice, saying, "Chi Shen, you cannot so act without manners!"

Now Chi Shen, although he was still drunken, yet recognized the abbot, and he threw down his stick and went into the abbot's presence and he said, "Your pardon, my father!" Then he pointed with his finger below the veranda and he said, "I did but drink a couple of bowls of wine—I did not do anything to anger them. But those people brought many others to beat me."

The abbot said, "Consider my favor! Go quickly and sleep. Tomorrow we will talk again."

Lu Chi Shen said, "If I did not care for the abbot's favor I would kill those scab-headed donkeys!"

The abbot called to an attendant to support Lu Chi Shen to the long couch, and there Chi Shen fell over and began to snore in his sleep. The higher priests surrounded the abbot and said to him, "Formerly our novices had but to come and ask of the abbot, and how is it today? How can our temple suffer such a wild cat as this who so sullies the clear rectitude of our Buddhist habits?"

The abbot replied, "Although there is now such confusion and lack of peace, yet afterwards he is assuredly to become a god. There is no way, except that we are to consider our disciple Chao, and forgive him this time. Tomorrow I will call him here and reprove him."

The priests smiled cold smiles and they said, "Undiscerning abbot!" Then each went his way to his rest.

The next day after the morning vegetable meal, the abbot told his attendant to go to the priest's general hall and call Lu Chi Shen. But Lu had not yet arisen. The attendant waited and Lu Chi Shen rose and put on his outer robe and then without any stockings he dashed out of the hall. The attendant, seeing him come out thus to approach the abbot, was frightened and ran after him to see what he did. There was Lu Chi Shen behind the big Buddha, passing his waste! The attendant could not keep from laughing and he waited until Lu Chi Shen had washed his hands and he said, "The abbot invites you to come and talk with him."

Lu Chi Shen then went with the attendant into the abbot's room, and the abbot said, "Chi Shen, although you are a captain of soldiers, yet the lord Chao has spent a great deal of money to make you into a priest. At that time I also put my hand upon your head in consecration. I told you that in the first place you must not take life; in the second, you must not steal; third, you must not commit adultery;

fourth, you must not drink wine; fifth, you must not lie. These five things forbidden you are common rules among the priestly orders. Those who have renounced the world must first of all not drink wine. How is it that last night you became so greatly drunken and beat the gate priests and broke open the red windows of the temple and beat the servants too, until they ran away, shouting to know why you behave like this?"

Then Chi Shen knelt down and replied, "I will not dare to do it again."

The abbot said, "If you have renounced the world, how then did you first of all break the vow against drinking? And now you have broken the habit of peace among the priests. If it were not out of consideration for your guarantor the lord Chao I would certainly drive you out of the temple. After this, do not break rules again!"

Lu Chi Shen stood up and put his palms together and he said, "I will not dare—I will not dare!"

The abbot allowed him to remain therefore and prepared to breakfast. With good words he exhorted him and he brought a priest's robe and a pair of priest's shoes and he gave them to Chi Shen and told him to go back to the general hall.

. . . No one should drink to his capacity. It is a common saying, "Wine can accomplish a deed but it can also bring about a downfall." But if a man of small courage drinks, and seems then to change into a man of great courage, how much more is this true with a brave, haughty fellow?

Let it be told further of Lu Chi Shen. After he was drunken and had made such a turmoil for three or four months he did not dare to go out of the temple. But there came a day in the second month of the year when it grew suddenly very hot, and he left the place where he lived and he let his feet wander as they would from the temple gate.

Then he stood and looked at The Five Crested Mountain and was murmuring, "Beautiful—beautiful!" when all at once he heard below the mountain a ringing sound wafted up by the favoring wind. He went back to his hall and fetched some silver and thrust it into his bosom and step by step he went down the mountain.

And he passed through an archway at the foot of the mountain upon which was written, "The Happy Place Of The Five Crested Mountain." Lu Chi Shen looked about and he saw that here was a street of trade and shops, and there were some five to seven hundred families living there. Looking down the busy street, Lu Chi Shen saw there were some shops that sold meats and some that sold vegetables and some wine shops and some noodle shops. Then Lu Chi Shen said in his own heart, "Am I dazed? If I had known before there was such a place I would not have robbed that man of his bucket of wine. I would have come here and bought myself some to drink. All these days my mouth has been longing and watering. Now let me go and see what there is to buy and eat."

He listened to the ringing sounds and he found they came from an ironsmith's shop. On the house opposite to it hung a sign saying, "The Inn Of Father And Son."

Lu Chi Shen went to the door of the ironsmith to look and there he saw three men beating out iron on the forge and he asked them, saying, "Fellows, have you good steel?"

One of the ironsmith's apprentices, seeing Lu Chi Shen and how his cheeks were covered with a short beard newly shaven just now growing out, and stiff and rough looking, was half afraid of him and he stopped his hand and said, "Sir Priest, pray sit down. What do you want us to make for you?"

Chi Shen replied, "I want a priest's iron staff and a priest's girdle knife. But I do not know whether or not you have the best grade of iron."

The apprentice said, "This lowly one assuredly has some very good iron. But we do not know how heavy a staff is wanted. Only command, and it is enough."

Lu Chi Shen then said, "I want a staff weighing a hundred catties."

The apprentice laughed and said, "That is heavy, Sir Priest! I fear I cannot beat out so heavy a thing, and how can you wield it. Even the sword of King Kuan was only eighty-one catties!"

Lu Chi Shen grew angry then and he cried, "And may I not measure to King Kuan? He was no more than a man!"

The apprentice said, "This lowly one but speaks usually. I can make a staff no heavier than forty or fifty catties, and that is called very heavy."

Chi Shen said, "Do as you said first and make it as heavy as King Kuan's was, then. Make it eighty-one catties!"

But the apprentice replied, "Sir Priest, the staff will be too thick for its length and it will be both ugly and hard to wield. Do as this lowly one thinks best, and we will make you a fine staff of sixty-two catties, and we will polish it well with stone and water. If it is too heavy for you, you must not blame me. As to a knife, you have already spoken of it and you need not mention it more. I will use the very best iron and make it."

Lu Chi Shen asked, "How many ounces of silver will these two things cost?"

The apprentice replied, "The fixed price is five ounces of silver."

Lu Chi Shen said, "I will allow you five ounces of silver. If you make it well wrought, I will add something."

The apprentice took the silver and said, "I will make it well for you."

Lu Chi Shen said, "I have some odd silver here. Let us go and buy a bowl of wine and drink it together."

The apprentice replied, "Sir Priest, you do as you will. But I have my work and I cannot go with you."

Lu Chi Shen then left the ironsmith's shop and he had not gone more than twenty or thirty paces when he saw a wine flag hanging on a bamboo on a shop roof. He pushed aside the door curtain and he went in and sat down and knocked on the table and he shouted out, "Bring wine here!"

The wine seller came out, saying, "Sir Priest, I crave your pardon, but this humble person's house belongs to the temple, and the capital with which we opened the shop was also the temple's and the abbot has given us a command that if we sell wine to a priest from the temple our capital will be taken back and we will be driven from the house. Pray do not blame me, then, that I cannot sell you wine."

Lu Chi Shen said, "But sell me a little wine anyhow to drink! I will not tell that it was at your shop I bought it."

The wine shop keeper said, "I cannot do as I would, Sir Priest. Pray go elsewhere to drink. Pray do not blame me."

Lu Chi Shen stood up then, but he said, "Though I drink wine elsewhere yet I will come back and have something to say to you."

He passed out of the shop and went a few steps and there he saw another flag hanging down straight in front of a door. Lu Chi Shen went in at once and sat down and he called out, "Wine seller! Bring me wine quickly and sell me some that I may drink!"

The wine seller said, "Sir Priest, you do not understand. The abbot has given a command and surely you must know it. Why do you come here to spoil my business?"

But Lu Chi Shen would not go. Three times and five times he demanded the wine and the man would not sell to him. Then Lu Chi Shen, seeing that the man really would not sell, stood up and went forth again and thus he went to some three or five shops and none would sell to him. Chi Shen then thought of a way, for he had said to himself, "If I do not think of a way, how can I ever get any wine to drink?"

In the distance he saw some blossoming apricot trees and at the end of the street there was a shop and before it was a rough straw rope twisted to make a sign for a wine shop. Chi Shen went to see it and it was a small wine shop on the edge of the village. He went into the shop and sat down close to the window and he called out, "Wine seller, I am a passing priest and I wish to buy a bowl of wine."

The wine seller looked at him and said, "Priest, from whence have you come?"

Lu Chi Shen answered, "I am a wandering priest and I am passing through here and I would buy a bowl of wine to drink."

The wine seller said, "Priest, if you were from The Five Crested Mountain Temple I would not dare to sell for you to drink."

"I am not," said Lu Chi Shen. "Quickly sell me the wine!"

The innkeeper, seeing his looks and his voice were not like those of other priests, said then, "How much wine would you have me draw?"

Lu Chi Shen replied, "Do not ask how much—only pour out this great bowl full!"

After he had drunk some ten-odd bowls of wine Chi Shen asked, "What meats have you? Bring a plateful for me to eat."

The innkeeper replied, "This morning we had some cow's flesh, but I have sold it all."

But Lu Chi Shen at that moment smelled the fragrance of meat and he went out to see and he saw beside the wall an earthenware pot in which was boiling a dog. Chi Shen cried, "You have some dog's flesh in your house—why do you not sell it to me to eat?"

The innkeeper answered, "I feared you were one who had renounced the world and so would not eat dog's flesh. For this reason I did not ask you."

Chi Shen said, "My silver is here and it is plenty." He fumbled for the silver then and gave it to the innkeeper, saying, "First give me half the dog."

The innkeeper hastily fetched half the cooked dog and he put some chopped leeks on it and brought it and placed it before Lu Chi Shen. Lu Chi Shen was very glad to see it. He tore the meat apart with his hands and dipped it into the leeks and ate of it, and he drank some ten-odd bowls of wine, and wine and food poured down his slippery throat. He only wanted wine and more wine and he would not stop. The innkeeper stared in a daze and he cried, "Priest, let this be enough!"

But Chi Shen opened his eyes wide and cried out, "I am not eating your food without paying for it! Why do you try to rule me?"

The innkeeper said, "But how much more do you want?"

"Bring yet another bucket of wine!" said Chi Shen.

The innkeeper dipped up another bucketfull and brought it in and soon Lu Chi Shen had drunk this also. He had left at last only a dog's leg and this he thrust into his bosom. When he went out the door he said, "I will come back tomorrow and eat to the amount of silver I have left with you."

At this the innkeeper was so frightened that his eyes stared woodenly and his jaw hung, for he perceived that after all Chi Shen was a priest of the mountain temple, and he did not know what to do. He watched him turn to the mountain.

Lu Chi Shen went halfway up the mountain and sat down for a little while in the pavilion. The wine rose into his head then and he leaped up and spoke, saying, "For a long time I have not done my postures of hand and fist. I feel my body is all soft and languid. I will try a few movements of my hands and feet and see how it goes."

He came out of the pavilion then and he wrapped his long sleeves into balls and held them in his hands and thus up and down and right and left he postured and as he did this his strength rose, so that when he flung out one arm it struck a pillar of the pavilion and he heard a rattling sound. He had broken the pillar and the pavilion was half fallen.

The gate priests heard the noise and they looked down from above and saw Lu Chi Shen coming up the mountain, his head nodding with every stride. They cried out, saying, "Ah, here is bitterness, for this wild animal has again drunk no little!"

They closed the gate and drew the bar across it and peeped through a crack. They saw Lu Chi Shen rush up to the gate and when he found it was locked he lifted his great fist that was like a hammer and began to knock with a loud noise. But the two gate priests did not dare to open the gate. When Lu Chi Shen had knocked for a while he turned around and he saw at the left the great guardian idol that stands at the front of the temple gate and he shouted at it, saying, "You great accursed fellow, why do you not beat for me? You only raise your fist to scare me! I am not afraid of you——"

He then leaped upon the pedestal where the god stood and he tore away the palings about it as easily as pulling up an onion and he took one of the broken staves and he beat the legs of the god. The earth and the paint broke, clattering off. The gate priests, seeing this, could but cry bitterness, and all they could do was to go and tell the abbot. Chi Shen waited awhile and then he turned and saw the other guardian god standing on the right side of the gate and he shouted, "You great thing stretching wide your mouth, you have come to laugh at me too!"

And he leaped on that pedestal and he beat the god's legs twice. Suddenly he heard a sound of falling great enough to shake the heavens. The guardian god had fallen from his pedestal. Chi Shen stood with the broken stave in his hand and guffawed loudly. But when the two gate priests went to tell the abbot, he only said, "Do not annoy him. Leave me."

By this time all the working priests and all the others came into the hall to address the abbot, and they said, "This wild cat has again drunk too deeply and he has broken the halfway pavilion and the guardian gods. What shall be done now?"

The abbot replied, "From ancient times even until now the Emperor has overlooked drunken persons. Why should not I, therefore, who am but an old priest? If he has broken the gods we will ask his guarantor Chao to make new ones. As for the fallen pavilion, we will ask for that to be repaired also. Let him go."

All the priests said, "But these guardian gods are the lords of the gate. How can we change them to others?"

The abbot replied, "Do not say the guardian gods are broken—though he broke the great Buddha himself we could not help it. We can only overlook him. Did you not see how fierce he was before?"

The priests came out of the hall then and they said among themselves, "What a stupid old abbot! Gate priests, you are not to open the gate and do you but listen from the inside."

Then Lu Chi Shen from outside the gate yelled in a great voice, "You incestuous scab-headed donkeys! If you do not let me come into the temple I will stay out here and take a torch and burn the accursed temple."

Hearing this, the priests could only command the gate priests to draw back the bar then, and let that wild beast come in. They said, "If we do not open the gate he will really do such a thing."

The gate priests tiptoed silently to the gate and drew back the bar and then as though they flew they ran into the house and hid. As for the other priests each ran also and hid.

Now let it be told of Lu Chi Shen. He pushed against the gate with both his hands and when it opened inward he fell down at once. He scrambled up and rubbed his head and went straight into the hall. There the priests were all sitting at meditation, and when they saw Lu Chi Shen open the curtains and come plunging into the hall they leaped in fright and they bent their heads. Chi Shen went to the long couch, and suddenly gagging in his throat he leaned over and vomited. The priests could not bear the vile odor of his vomit and they exclaimed and covered their noses and mouths with their hands. But Lu Chi Shen, after he had vomited, climbed on the long couch and unloosed his girdle and tore open his robe.

Just then the dog's leg fell out of his bosom. Lu Chi Shen cried, "Good—good! My belly is empty!"

And he picked up the dog's leg and began to gnaw it. The priests, seeing this, covered their faces with their sleeves, and the two priests sitting on either side of him ran to a distance and hid. Chi Shen, seeing them thus, tore off a piece of the dog's meat and looking at the priest above him, he cried, "Put some in your mouth, too!"

But the priest only pressed his sleeve against his face. Then Chi Shen said, "You will not eat, then?" And he turned and stuffed the meat into the mouth of the priest below him.

It was now too late for this priest to escape to hide, for even as he was getting down from the couch Lu Chi Shen caught him by the ear and forced the meat into his mouth. Three or four priests opposite him on the couch exhorted him not to behave thus, and Lu Chi Shen threw down the dog's meat and lifted up his fist and hit them again and again with rattling blows upon their shaven crowns. By now all the priests in the hall began to shout and they all went to their cupboards and fetched their clothing and their brass bowls to go away from the temple. Such a thing is called the Great Dispersion in a temple, and how could the master of the temple hall prevent them?

Lu Chi Shen did but give a leap. Most of the priests hid in the temple veranda. The master of the temple and the dean did not tell the abbot but they gathered together working priests, laborers, chair bearers and stove tenders, some two or three hundred persons in all, and they took sticks and forks and poles and tied up their heads in kerchiefs and together they went rushing into the hall. Lu Chi Shen, when he saw them, gave a great roar, for he was weaponless. He rushed into the Hall of Meditation and pushing over the sacrificial altar before the god, he pulled out two of its legs and leaped out again. The priests, seeing him come at them so fiercely, all retreated to the veranda, dragging their staves. When Lu Chi Shen came swinging his two altar legs the priests surrounded him suddenly. But Lu Chi Shen laid about him east and west and north and south, only when he pretended to beat east he turned westward, and when he pretended to beat south he really turned northward and thus he turned about.

Thus Lu Chi Shen fought clean into the Hall of Laws and Ceremonials and there the abbot sat. He shouted out, "Chi Shen, you are not to behave so without manners! Let no priest move his hand!"

The crowds on either side, of whom some tens were wounded, now when they saw the abbot, retreated, and seeing them scatter thus, Lu Chi Shen threw down the altar legs and he roared out, "Abbot, you must help me!"

He was by now less drunk than he had been, his wine having subsided seven- or eight-tenths. But the abbot replied, "Chi Shen, you have wearied me too much. The first time you were drunk you upset all of us and I told your elder brother Chao of it. He wrote a letter to us asking the pardon of each priest. Now you have sinned greatly in being drunk beyond all manners, and you have soiled our pure customs, you have pulled down the pavilion and you have broken the guardian gods. Letting this pass, even, you have so disturbed the priests that they all wish to run away. This sin is no small one. On our mountain this temple has been for many hundreds and thousands of years a place of clear peace and incense burning; how can I allow a thing so defiled as you are to be here? Now come and live with me for a few days in the Hall of Guests. I will prepare a certain place for you."

Chi Shen went with the abbot into the hall, and the abbot called a working priest to go and tell the other priests not to go away but to return to their meditations. The wounded priests were to go and refresh themselves. The abbot then led Chi Shen into that hall and they spent the night there.

On the second day the abbot and the master of the temple took counsel together and they gathered some silver and prepared to send Lu Chi Shen to other parts. But first they must tell Chao. The abbot at once wrote a letter, therefore, and he sent temple attendants to go straight to Chao's village and tell him how all was come about. There they were to wait for a letter in answer.

The lord Chao, when he had seen the letter, was very unhappy in heart and he sent back an answering letter, and he said to the abbot, "The broken guardian gods and the pavilion I will at once bring silver to repair. Let the abbot send Chi Shen whither he will."

When the abbot had received this letter he told his attendants to bring a priest's black robe and a pair of priest's shoes, and ten ounces of silver. Then he called Chi Shen out from the hall and he said to him, "Chi Shen, the first time you were so drunken that you upset everything in the priests' hall; that we called a sin of carelessness. This time you have again been greatly drunken and you have broken the guardian gods and you have ruined the pavilion and you have so troubled everyone that the priests want to run away. In this place of renunciation of the world we have only peace and purity, and your behaving in such ways is very wicked. But I have considered the honor of your guarantor Chao and I give you this letter to a place where you can be at rest. Here surely we cannot tolerate you. During the night I had a vision. Now here are four scrolls of prophecy. Preserve them safely all your life and follow their teachings."

Chi Shen replied, "Teacher, I am your disciple and do you tell me whither I am to go. There I will live in peace and I will obey the four commands of my teacher."

Wu Cheng-en

NO BOOK of Chinese humor would be complete without Monkey Sun, the inspired creation that has for over three hundred years nourished the imagination and enriched the laughter of Chinese readers old and young. In English this simian saint has appeared first in the missionary Dr. Timothy Richard's translation of the original novel called A Mission to Heaven *and, more recently, in Arthur Waley's superb literary rendition published under the title* Monkey. *For my selection I have borrowed from my friend Chi-Chen Wang's translation and adaptation of the Monkey King's story (the first seven chapters of the book) because it is shorter and its humor more accessible. For the best commentary on this story I borrow the very illuminating dictum handed down by Mr. Lew Lehr by way of the newsreels: "Monkeys are the craziest people!"*

THE MONKEY KING

I

The Stone Monkey, Its Birth and Ascendancy

Far out in the ocean, due east of the country of Aolai, there was an island unfrequented by men. It was a haven for all kinds of wild animals, which roamed its forested hills and streamed valleys in primeval freedom, unmolested by hunters bent on wanton destruction. Among the immortals it was known as the Flower and Fruit Mountain because it abounded in fruit-bearing trees. This suited the monkeys—the chief inhabitants of the island—for they thrived on fruits.

Now on the summit of the highest mountain on the island there was a massive rock 365 inches high and 24 feet around, so fashioned by Nature that its height corresponded to the days of the year and its girth to the hours of the day. It had perched on top of the mountain for untold centuries and had been, during this indeterminable period of time, imbibing the wonderful essences of the heavens and the sun and the moon. One day it burst open with a thunderous crash and out of it rolled a ball-like object about the size of a watermelon. Presently

Translated by Chi-Chen Wang.

it stopped rolling and assumed the form of a monkey. The monkey sat up, rubbed its eyes and opened them, whereupon two rays of brilliant light issued forth and penetrated into Heaven itself and dazzled the eyes of the Jade Emperor on high sitting on his throne in the Ethereal Hall.

Telescopic Eyes and Telephonic Ears, two deities who constituted the eyes and ears of the Jade Emperor, were sent to the South Gate of Heaven to make an observation, and they soon returned and reported what had happened on the earth below. Some of the heavenly ministers were alarmed by the portent and suggested that the stone monkey should be destroyed before it became dangerous, but the Jade Emperor in his lovingkindness spared the monkey and allowed it to live.

The stone monkey was immediately accepted by the monkey tribe. They did not snub him because he had no mother, for they were not ruled by prejudices such as are found among men. All that they expected of a monkey was that it should look like a monkey, behave like a monkey, and be able to jump and swing from tree to tree as monkeys do. They cared not whether it had a mother, nor did they ask who its father might be. The stone monkey was able to do all these things and more besides, for he was larger than the other monkeys and excelled them in feats of strength and agility. He always led them in exploring strange corners of the island and was always the first to wade into unfamiliar streams. In a short time he came to be looked upon as their leader.

The life of the monkeys was carefree and full of fun. They scampered about the island during the day, climbing trees, gathering fruits, and bathing in clear streams, and at night they slept in·caves or under overhanging cliffs. Life went on like this for untold ages, for the monkeys did not know how to reckon time and regarded the seasons as alternating periods of cold and warmth, of scarcity and plenty, rather than four three-month periods into which the year is divided.

One hot summer day as the monkeys were bathing in the pool beneath the waterfall as they had done innumerable times before, one of them suggested that whoever dared to plunge through the waterfall and find out what lay beyond should be made their king. The stone monkey immediately accepted the challenge. He closed his eyes, held his breath, and dived into the waterfall. He did not have to hold his breath long, for the waterfall was in reality a screen of water hanging in space. He opened his eyes and found himself in a semicircular pool concealed from the outside by the waterfall and the overhanging cliff. A gentle slope led up to an opening in the cliff, which was otherwise sheer and perpendicular and could not be scaled. At the opening there was a stele with the inscription "Water Screen Paradise." Without a moment's hesitation the stone monkey ran up the slope and went past the stele, beyond which he found a passageway that led into a huge grotto with tables and chairs and beds and bowls and dishes, all cut out of stone and set out in orderly fashion as if begging for someone to relieve them of their idleness.

The stone monkey was too excited to stay long in the grotto. He rushed back to the anxious and chattering monkeys waiting outside and told them what he had found. Then, following his example, they dived through the screen of water and scampered into the grotto. There was plenty of light in the large hall hewn out of stone, for the sun shone through the jagged rocks that formed a sort of eaves for the grotto. The monkeys chattered with wonder and excitement and busied themselves with the stone furniture and utensils, moving them about endlessly until they had to stop from sheer exhaustion.

Then the stone monkey mounted a bench and demanded silence. "A monkey without faith," he said, "is like a cart without wheels or an ax without its handle. You have agreed to make him king who dared to dive through the waterfall. Now I have dared and have found for you this cave palace; I remind you of your promise!"

Thereupon the monkeys fell on their knees and shouted, "Yes, you are our king. Long live the king!"

And so it came about that a monkey born without a mother became the king of the monkeys in the Flower and Fruit Mountain. He ruled them wisely and well and taught them peace and good will toward their fellows such as we humans do not know even till this day.

2

The Monkey King Goes in Search of Immortality

Though in outward appearance and behavior the Monkey King was like his subjects, he differed from them in that he was often inwardly troubled by things which do not often trouble human beings, much less monkeys. One of these things was death, the awful significance of which was forced upon him by the death of an old monkey a few years after he became king. He was deeply depressed and became moody and would not play with the other monkeys as he was in the habit of doing though he was their king. He got into the habit of wandering off by himself and of sitting for hours crouched on the branch of an old pine tree pondering upon imponderable things.

"Something ails our king," the monkeys said, "and we must do something to cheer him up."

So they decided to hold a great feast for him. They spent days in gathering fruits and nuts and succeeded in getting together a much larger variety than was ever assembled before. At the banquet in the great hall they tried their best to amuse him. But their efforts were unsuccessful. He tried to be lighthearted at first, but then he suddenly realized that one of their number was not with them. His heart was again filled with sadness and his eyes filled with tears.

The monkeys were puzzled. "Why do you weep, O King," they asked anxiously, "when we have so much cause for rejoicing? Have we not all the fruit we can eat and this grotto to shelter us from the wind and rain? And do we not all love and honor you, O King?"

"It is true that we are free and have everything we need," answered the Monkey King. "But how long will this last? Didn't you see what happened to old Toothless? Where is he now? You must realize that we all have to reckon with the King of Death and have to go as old Toothless did when he calls. We are not free, therefore, so long as we are mortal."

These thoughtful words sobered the monkeys, and they too began to realize how short their happiness must be, and how much shorter yet if something should happen to them, as when they miscalculated the distance between two branches and fell in their leap. They too began to weep, and the feast became a scene of lamentation instead of rejoicing.

Finally the Monkey King spoke: "There must be some way to escape death. I must find the way. In the land beyond the ocean there must be wise men who have learned the secret of immortality. I shall set out in search of them and bring back the secret."

The very next day the Monkey King set out on a raft built of mountain pines and crossed over to the mainland. There he encountered human beings for the first time. For a few days he hid from them and watched them with curious and apprehensive eyes, but he gradually became bolder and managed to appropriate some clothes and dressed himself in them. In time he learned human speech and went everywhere asking people how one might become immortal. No one could tell him and all thought that he was foolish to have such a notion. He visited the monasteries in the mountains and talked with the Buddhist monks and Taoist priests, but he found that they too were more concerned with the things of this world than with the hope of immortality.

Just as the Monkey King was about to give up his quest and return to his native island, he encountered a woodcutter who directed him to the Wizard Supooti of the Monastery of the Three Stars, reputed to be an immortal of great magic powers. Following the directions of the woodcutter, he hastened toward the Fangtsun Mountains and located the monastery, which he readily identified by a large stele in front. He did not dare to knock on the gate but climbed on a pine tree and picked pine seeds to satisfy his hunger while he waited for someone that might chance to come out.

Presently the gate opened and a novice came out and asked who was loitering about.

"It is I, a searcher after immortality," the Monkey King said, jumping down from the tree.

"Then come with me," the novice said, "for the Master is expecting you."

The Wizard was in the middle of a discourse when the monkey was led to him, but he stopped to speak to the monkey and asked where he had come from.

"From the Flower and Fruit Mountain in the Eastern Ocean," the monkey answered.

"Put the untruthful monkey out!" the Wizard shouted angrily. "How can such a puny little thing like you come from so far away?"

But the monkey soon convinced him and was accepted by the Wizard as a disciple. He gave the monkey the surname of Sun, as monkeys are sometimes called *husun,* and named him Wu-kung, or Realizing-All-Is-Vanity. The monkey was better known, however, as Sun Houtze, or Monkey Sun, as he still looked very obviously like a monkey in spite of his human garb.

As a novice in search of immortality Monkey Sun was given the chores of the monastery to do. He carried water to the kitchen from the streams, cut firewood, and swept the courtyards. The discourses given by the Wizard sounded very dull and the monkey could make little of them, but as they were supposed to be of great benefit to the hearers, Monkey Sun listened attentively and tried to make of them what he could.

Thus years went by. One day the Wizard asked Monkey Sun if he would like to take up fortunetelling.

"What good would fortunetelling do?" the latter asked.

"It will enable you to do things that will bring happiness and to avoid things that will bring misfortune," the Wizard said, "and it will enable you to make a living by telling the fortunes of others."

"Would it give me immortality?"

"It would be like climbing trees for fish," the Master answered with a grin.

"I beg your pardon?" Monkey Sun said, not being used to metaphors.

"It means that you won't catch any fish."

"Then no fortunetelling for me."

"Would you like to take up meditation?"

"Would that give me immortality?"

"You'll be like a brick still in the kiln."

"What does that mean?"

"A brick in the kiln is only half-baked and will melt away in the rain."

"It means, then, that they will not last forever," the monkey said. "I do not want to study meditation."

"Perhaps you would like to study alchemy," the Master suggested. "This will teach you how to turn base metal into gold and how to make brews out of herbs that will prolong life."

"But would it make me immortal?" the monkey persisted.

"It is like fishing for the moon in the water."

"That means that you'll only get the reflection of the moon. I do not want to study alchemy."

Suddenly the Wizard became very angry. He struck Monkey Sun three times on the head, saying, "Perhaps this is what you want, choosy monkey that you are!" Then he turned his back on him and walked into his own courtyard, shutting the gate behind him.

The other disciples reproached the monkey for his lack of modesty and said that they had never seen the Master lose his temper before. Monkey Sun received these reproaches good-naturedly, for to him the punishment he received meant quite something else.

"The three strokes on the head," he reasoned, "meant that the Master wants to see me at the third watch of the night and the closed gate meant that I should enter by the back door."

So at the third watch that night Monkey Sun went to the back gate. He found it ajar as he had expected. He went into the Wizard's room and knelt down in front of the couch and waited for the Master to speak.

After a while he heard the Wizard whisper to himself, "I do not want to hide the secrets of my magic powers but no one seems really to want them."

"I want to learn those secrets," the monkey said.

"What are you doing here?" the Wizard asked, turning around.

"I have come in as you commanded," the monkey replied.

"It must be the will of heaven that you should learn the secret of immortality," the Wizard said. "Bend forward and I will give you the magic formula."

Monkey Sun obeyed and slowly repeated the mystic phrases after the Wizard. When he had learned the words by heart, the Wizard dismissed him, saying, "You can go now. Say the formula to yourself over and over again and meditate upon it. In time it will reveal the secrets to you."

Three years went by before Monkey Sun grasped the significance of the magic formula. Then the Wizard taught him the seventy-two transformations and the somersault whereby he could in an instant travel the distance of 108,000 *li*. He would have probably learned other magic powers from the Wizard if he had not allowed his vanity to get the better of him and caused him to display his abilities before the other disciples in disobedience to the Wizard's injunctions.

One afternoon as he and his fellow disciples were playing in the clearing outside of the monastery, he was asked what he had learned and whether he could transform himself into other shapes.

"Of course I can," the monkey said. "Tell me what you want me to change myself into and I'll do it for you."

A tall pine tree was suggested. Thereupon the monkey uttered the magic formula and said, "Transform!" No sooner was this word uttered than he had completely disappeared, leaving in his place a pine tree exactly like the one indicated. The applause that followed disturbed the Wizard and he came out to see the cause. The monkey quickly resumed his own shape and edged himself into the crowd, but this did not help him. The Wizard insisted on the truth and when it finally came out he said sternly to the monkey:

"Have I not told you repeatedly that you must not be vain and display what you can do before others? This vanity will bring destruction upon yourself and disgrace to me. I cannot let you stay here any longer; go away at once!"

All his entreaties failed to move the Wizard, who looked upon vanity as the greatest of all evils. Reluctantly and with tears in his eyes, Monkey Sun took leave of his master and the other disciples. In parting, the Wizard warned him never under any circumstances to reveal the source of his magic powers. "For I know you will get into trouble because of your vanity," he said, "and I do not want to be held responsible for it. I shall myself destroy you, if you ever whisper my name to anyone."

3

The Monkey King Avenges the Wrongs to His Subjects

With a slight wiggle of his waist, Monkey Sun crossed the ocean which had taken him several months on his previous passage. He found the monkeys in a sad plight, for during his absence a monster who called himself the King of Destruction had come out of the clouds from the north and terrorized in the island, killing and kidnaping hundreds of monkeys. So aroused was the Monkey King that he did not even take time to see his beloved Water Screen Cave. He jumped into the air, to the amazement of the monkeys, and headed toward the north until certain black emanations from below told him that he was near the abode of some evil spirit.

He alighted from the clouds in front of a cave and found some little monsters playing there. He seized one of them and said, "I would gladly dash your carcass to pieces except that I want to get a message to your king. Now go and tell him that the heaven-born Sage of the Flower and Fruit Mountain has come for revenge."

"Yes," the King of Destruction said when he heard the frightened little monster, "I have heard about this king of the monkeys, for they used to boast about him and to threaten dire consequences when he returned from his quest of immortality. Now let us see what manner of warrior he is." So saying he donned his black armor, seized his long-handled sword, and went out of the cave.

Now the King of Destruction was a giant thirty feet high and ten spans around the waist, and so looking straight ahead of him he was not able to see the monkey, who was hardly more than four feet tall. He looked around and around and wondered where his challenger was.

"Why don't you look down here, you eyeless devil, if you want to see your old ancestor?" said the Monkey King.

The King of Destruction then looked down and saw the monkey shaking his fist at him.

"I cannot fight you, little monkey," the King of Destruction said, bursting into laughter. "What would people say if I fought you? They would say that I am coward and a bully to fight one of only about a tenth of my size. So go back to your hills and I won't hurt you."

This infuriated the Monkey King, and he advanced toward the King of Destruction without another word. The latter regarded his adversary with amusement and threw away his sword and waited condescendingly for the monkey to strike first.

The monkey was very quick and threw the Devil King down several times by ramming against his legs, and before the latter could get up he hit him on the face. In his desperation the Devil King no longer cared for what the world might say; he picked up his sword to gain advantage over the monkey. The latter then decided to try his magic powers. He pulled out a handful of hair from his body, chewed them in his mouth, and spat them into the air, saying, "Transform!" and behold! they changed into hundreds of little monkeys, all rubbing their fists and eager for the fight. They swarmed around the Devil King, pulling at his legs, striking at his loins and back. They completely confounded the Devil King, and Monkey Sun, taking advantage of the confusion, snapped the sword from him and cut him in two with a single blow. With the aid of the monkeys, Sun made short work of the little devils, after which he set the cave on fire. Then with a wave of his hand he changed the magic monkeys back into hairs and stuck them back on his body. The real monkeys that the Devil King had captured remained, of course, and these were taken back to the Flower and Fruit Mountain by their king.

After the celebrations of his return and his victory, Monkey Sun divided the monkeys into companies and regiments and appointed officers over them. He showed the monkeys how to fashion weapons out of wood and drilled them in the arts of war. Then he flew to the capital of the Country of Aolai, drove the inhabitants to cover with a storm, and with the aid of his magic monkeys robbed the king's armory. Thus he outfitted his army of monkeys with real weapons, an impressive army forty thousand strong.

Impressed by the parades of the organized and militarized monkeys, the other animal tribes held council among themselves and all decided to join the monkeys. There were wolves, tigers, leopards, deer, foxes, hyenas, weasels, lions, gorillas, bears, wild boars, mountain bulls, goats, and so on—seventy-two tribes in all. Led by their own kings, they all went to pay homage to the king of the monkeys. Thus the army of the Monkey King was quadrupled. Under his direction Flower and Fruit Mountain was fortified and made impregnable as if it were built of iron and steel.

4

Monkey Sun Terrorizes the Oceans and Hell

Monkey Sun had been using the long-handled sword that he took from the King of Destruction, but he had always found it a clumsy weapon to wield. For one thing he had to assume a larger shape in order to use it, and one is never so comfortable in an assumed shape as when one is one's natural self. So one day, at the suggestion of four old monkeys, he went to the palace of Aukuang, the senior dragon king, who was famed for his marvelous treasure house in the deeps of the eastern ocean.

Aukuang first offered him a long-handled sword much like the one he had been using, but this the monkey refused, saying that he did not like swords. Next a nine-pronged battle fork was brought in by Captain Carp and Major Bass, who staggered under its weight, but after trying it Monkey Sun refused it because it was too light, though it weighed 3,600 pounds. Colonel Halibut and General Shark then brought in a huge halbert weighing 7,200 pounds, and again the monkey tried it and again he said that it was too light!

"But this is the heaviest weapon we have, great immortal," said the Dragon King, growing more and more uneasy at the manifest strength of his uninvited guest. Just then the Dragon Queen came out and whispered something to the Dragon King, who brightened up and said to the monkey, "We have a piece of iron that was used by the great Yü as a weight to measure the depth of the ocean. Perhaps it would suit the great immortal?"

Monkey Sun asked to see it and was led to the treasure house, as the iron was too heavy to be moved. In one corner the iron rod lay sparkling with a myriad bright rays. It was about a foot in diameter and twenty feet long, with two hoops around either end and close to one end a line of engraved characters reading: "As-you-like-it staff. Weight: 13,500 pounds." Monkey Sun raised it, tried its weight, and said, "Its weight is just right, but it is too big and too long. It would suit me better if it were smaller and shorter." Just as he finished these words, the rod became a few feet shorter and noticeably smaller around. The monkey tried it again and said, "It would be better yet if it were smaller still." And the treasure again grew smaller.

Returning to the reception hall of the crystal palace Monkey Sun said to the Dragon King, "This piece of iron suits me perfectly, but it reminds me of something else; it reminds me that I am sadly in need of some suitable armor worthy of the staff."

"I am very sorry that we do not have anything of that sort," the Dragon King said.

"I won't leave your palace until you have kindly obliged me," the monkey insisted.

"O great immortal," the Dragon King said, "why don't you go to some of the other oceans and see if you can find something there?"

" 'It is better to stay at one house than to call at three,' " the monkey quoted.

"I really have nothing in armor," the Dragon King pleaded. "If I had, I should be only too happy to present it to the great immortal."

"I am afraid that this staff wouldn't believe you even though I did," the monkey said, and brandished his new weapon, at which the Dragon King trembled with fear, the dragon princes were scared out of their wits, the turtles drew back their heads into their shells, and the fishes, shrimps, and crabs hid their heads in the mud.

"Please be careful with that piece of death-dealing iron," the Dragon King beseeched. "I shall find out whether some of my younger brothers can help you." He then summoned the iguana general and the ancient tortoise marshal and bade them strike the iron drum and the golden gong, whose magic notes resounded throughout the four oceans and which were struck only in great emergencies. Before the notes had died away, the three junior dragon kings had arrived—Auching from the southern ocean, Auchun from the northern, and Auyun from the western.

When they heard the cause of the emergency signals, the three younger brothers proposed that they should summon their forces and eject the monkey; but Aukuang begged them to be patient. "Let us meet his demands now," he said, "for he is a powerful being and I fear that nothing can withstand his iron staff. After he has left us, we can submit a memorial to the Heavenly Emperor, and have the monkey punished." His counsel prevailed and, the quicker to rid themselves of the unwelcome visitor, Aushun took off his boots made of sealskin, Auching his chain armor of pure gold, Auyun his helmet of purple gold with phoenix plumes, and gave them to the monkey, who immediately donned the outfit, mockingly thanked his hosts, and went away brandishing his staff.

Back in the Water Screen Cave, Monkey Sun stood the staff in the center of the great hall and then sat down on his throne. The monkeys all came forward and tried to lift the staff, but they were like dragonflies trying to shake a pillar of stone.

"Everything awaits its owner," Monkey Sun said, coming down and taking up the staff. "This precious thing has been lying under the ocean for thousands and thousands of years, but no one knew its worth until I came upon it, and I found that it is a magic staff that expands and contracts as the owner wishes." Thereupon he said, "Contract, contract!" until the staff shrank to the size of a small embroidering needle, which he easily concealed in his right ear.

Then he took the tiny needle out and said, "Expand, expand!" and it grew in an instant to its natural size. He played with it for a while, waving it over his head, parrying and attacking. Warming up, he went out of the cave and stretched himself saying, "Grow, grow!" until he was over a thousand times a thousand feet tall, his head towering in the clouds like a mountain peak, his eyes flashing like lightning, his mouth spouting hot steam like a volcano, his teeth like rows of huge swords. The magic staff grew with him and reached heaven above and hell below. The mountains quaked while he played with his staff. Then amid the awe and admiration of the worshiping monkeys and other animal tribes he resumed his natural size, changed the staff into a small embroidering needle, and put it in his right ear.

The Monkey King now delegated the four old monkeys who had been giving him good counsel on many occasions to supervise the training of his army. He made the two gibbons with red seats marshals and named them Ma and Liu; and made the two hylobates generals with the names of Bang and Boom. The King himself went everywhere in the universe, now that to travel ten thousand *li* was no more trouble for him than to nod his head. He made friends everywhere and became sworn brothers with six other kings of powerful tribes of wild animals, with whom he held many contests of strength and skill and jolly drunken feasts.

One evening after he had seen his guests off after one of these feasts he was overcome by sleepiness and fell asleep under a pine tree near the cave, guarded over by Marshals Ma and Liu and Generals Bang and Boom. In his sleep he saw two men approaching him with a summons.

They slipped a piece of cord around his wrists and dragged him away with them without a word. The King of the Monkeys was too sleepy to protest or care at the time, but when they came to a city with the legend "The Shadow World" inscribed over its gate, he started. "This Shadow World is the domain of the King of Death," he said aloud to himself. "How does it happen that I am here?"

"You are not mistaken," the two men said. "It is time for you to die and so we have taken you here."

"But I am not going any farther with you," Monkey Sun said. "Old Sun is outside of the three spheres and above the five elements. I am under the rule of no one and I shall answer no one's summons. How dared you bring me here?"

"Orders are orders," the two men said. "Come with us and save us the trouble of having to drag you by force."

The King lost his temper when the two men of doom tried to tug at the cords that bound his hands. He broke the cords with a wave of the hands, took the magic staff out of his right ear, expanded it to its natural size, and with two gentle blows crushed the two men into a mass of chopped meat.

"Since I am here," the King said to himself, "I might as well settle matters with the King of Death. I must let them know that Old Sun is not to be trifled with."

He stalked into the city and brandished his club as he went, sending the ox heads hiding east and west and the horsefaces scampering north and south. Some of them ran into the judgment hall of the King of Death and said, "Woe is Hell! A hairy-faced warrior with a beak like the Thunder God is fighting his way hither."

With the King of Death were his nine colleagues, each one the ruler of a different court. The ten kings hastened out to meet the invader.

"Who is it that is honoring us with his visit?" they asked.

"I am Sun Wu-kung, the heaven-born Sage of the Flower and Fruit Mountain," Monkey Sun said. "You ought to know that Old Sun is above your control. How dared you issue a summons on me?"

"Do not be angry, great immortal," the King of Death said. "There are people with the same names. Perhaps the servers have made a mistake."

"Nonsense," the monkey said. "It is said that the judge may be mistaken and the server may be mistaken, but the prisoner is no less a prisoner. So let me examine the book of life and death and see for myself."

The monkey was ushered into the hall of judgment. He seated himself on the throne of the King of Death and examined the books that Tsui Pan-kuan, chief clerk of Hell, brought him. He did not see his own name until he came to a book labeled "Simians," in which he found this entry:

Sun Wu-kung, a natural born stone monkey;
to die at the age of 324 of a natural death.

"I don't remember my age and I don't care," the monkey said. "I shall cross my name out."

The secretary passed him a brush after wetting it on the ink stone. With a heavy stroke he crossed out his name and the names of other monkeys that he could find. Thus it happened that some monkeys are immortal to this day.

"Now you can no longer claim me," he said, throwing down his brush. Then he walked out of the judgment hall and the city of the dead as unceremoniously as he had come, brandishing his staff. He stumbled and woke up.

"What a terrible dream," he said, yawning. "It is lucky that I came back at all."

He told the four generals about his dream, which they all knew to be more than a dream, and they rejoiced because they were now no longer under the rule of Death since their names had been crossed off the book of life and death.

In the meantime, the ten kings of the Shadow World gathered in the Green Cloud Palace for a conference with Ti Tsang, the supervising budhhisattva of the Shadow World. It was decided that a memorial should be submitted to Heaven with the request that the monkey be punished for its outrages.

5

Monkey Sun Spurns Curatorship of Horses

"Who is this troublemaker that has robbed the Dragon King and disturbed the natural course of life and death?" God said when he received the memorials of the senior dragon king and of the supervising buddhisattva of the Shadow World.

From the ranks of the heavenly ministers stepped out Telescopic Eyes and Telephonic Ears and said, "This is the same monkey born over three hundred years ago out of a piece of rock. No action was taken at the time, though a bright golden light issued from his eyes and pierced to Heaven through the clouds. He has since acquired great magic powers and become a most formidable being."

"We cannot let such outrages go unpunished," God wrathfully said. "Who volunteers to lead an expedition against the troublemaker?"

Before the martial deities could speak, the great White Star, noted for his stand for peace, hastened to plead for the monkey, urging that he should be forgiven since he was ignorant of his crimes and that he should be given a petty position in Heaven to keep him out of mischief.

The proposal pleased God. He commanded Kuei Hsing, the god of literature, to write the edict and sent White Star with the message to the Flower and Fruit Mountain.

As soon as Monkey Sun heard the edict of the Heavenly Emperor, he entrusted the affairs of the Flower and Fruit Mountain to the four generals and set out with the White Star. As he traveled much faster than the latter, he soon arrived alone at the South Gate of Heaven. There the guarding deities, ignorant of the edict, barred his way. As he was quarreling with the guards, the White Star arrived, panting a little because he had tried so hard to keep up with the monkey.

"Why did you fool me?" the monkey asked angrily. "Why are these people stopping me if God had sent for me as you said?"

"Please do not misunderstand," White Star said. "You have never been here before and you are not known. As soon as you have been given a position and your name has been added to the roster of heavenly officials, you can come and go as you wish."

This pacified Monkey Sun and he entered the South Gate with White Star. They passed through a series of palaces and halls, all made of precious stones and gold. Heavenly warriors in gold armor guarded the approaches. Arriving in the audience hall, White Star prostrated himself before God on his throne and reported the success of his mission, while Monkey Sun unceremoniously stood by. When God asked where the unknown immortal was, he only bowed and answered, "Old Sun is here."

This horrified the heavenly ministers. "Such rudeness is treason!" they said. "He does not prostrate himself and calls himself 'Old Sun.' He deserves death."

But God was more generous. "Sun Wu-kung has only recently acquired human knowledge," God said, "and does not know the rules of conduct. We forgive him." The heavenly ministers all cheered and praised God's magnanimity, prostrating themselves on the jade-paved floor, but the monkey could not bring himself to such abject humility.

Then God asked what posts were open to which the monkey might be appointed. The God of Appointments came forward and said, "All the posts are filled except one. The Equestrian Galleries have at present no one in charge."

"The monkey, then, shall be the curator of our Equestrian Galleries," God said.

"Long live His Magnanimous Majesty," the heavenly ministers cheered.

The monkey did not know what the curatorship of the Equestrian Galleries meant, but he decided that it must be a great honor since it required so much magnanimity to confer it upon him. When he was shown to his post he found that the Equestrian Galleries were nothing but a series of horse stables. But he was unfamiliar with heavenly ways and he did not want to betray his ignorance by any false move.

There were over a thousand horses, cared for by scores of grooms. Directly under him were the associate curator and the assistant curators, with whom he checked over the list of horses, assigned each groom his proper duty, and supervised everything himself with great diligence. The horses seemed to be especially tame in his presence. He was so quick and agile and managed the runaways so well that none dared to play any pranks on him. They fed well and grew sturdy and strong.

At the end of about two weeks, his assistants and grooms gave him a banquet.

"What kind of official is the curator of the Equestrian Galleries?" Monkey Sun asked toward the end of the banquet.

"It is as indicated by the title," they answered.

"Of what rank is it?" Monkey Sun continued.

"It has no rank," the assistants explained.

"Since it has no rank," the monkey said, "it must be a very great title indeed."

"No, no," they said. "It has no rank not because it is above ranking but because it is below ranking. It is a very menial position, and one gets no thanks for one's troubles. Take your case, for instance, O Chief. You have worked hard and the horses have grown sturdy and strong. The most you will get in return will be 'Good work.' On the other hand, you will be penalized and made to pay if anything happens to the horses."

"Is this, then, what the curatorship of the Equestrian Galleries amounts to?" the monkey asked, incredulously.

"That's all," they answered.

"Then why should anyone want such a job?"

"Well," the assistants said, "some people love horses and care nothing for thanks or honors, others love horse fanciers and get into their favor through their pets, still others manage to keep on believing that the Equestrian Gallery is as exalted an institution as its name pretends to be. For these reasons, there has never been any difficulty in filling the curatorships."

"I care neither for horses nor horse fanciers, and I shall not subject myself to such humiliations," Monkey Sun cried. "And I'd rather be a common thief than to deceive myself and think that I am something, when I know I am nothing." He became more and more furious as he went on.

"How dare they insult Old Sun like this?" he cried, thumping and upsetting the table. "Old Sun is king in his own right in the Flower and Fruit Mountain. How dare these blind fools make me a common groom?" He took his staff out of his right ear, shook it to its natural size, and broke up everything in his rage.

"Tell God that I think he is blind to have put me to such a lowly position," he said. "I am going back to my own world." With these words he flew out of Heaven and was soon over his native mountain and saw his subjects drilling under the four generals.

The monkeys all flocked to him. "Congratulations, O King," they said. "You must have attained great honors during all these years in Heaven."

"Years?" the King said in astonishment. "I have been in Heaven only about half a month."

"But you must remember that a day in Heaven is a year on earth," the four generals explained. "It is now fifteen years since you went away. And pray tell us what position you held there."

"It is a very embarrassing question," the Monkey King said. "I am ashamed to tell you, but the truth is that the Heavenly Emperor is blind and does not see my worth. He made me what he called very magnanimously the curator of the Equestrian Galleries. I thought it was an exalted position at first, but I just discovered it to be nothing but that of a common groom, so lowly that it is below ranking."

"We are happy that you are back with us, O King," the monkeys said. And a great banquet was held in honor of the Monkey King's return. In the midst of the banquet, the King of the Single-Horned Monsters came to pay homage to the Monkey King, bringing with them an imperial yellow robe as a present, and declared that nothing short of the title of "The Great Sage, Equal of Heaven" could be worthy of him.

Monkey Sun liked the title and assumed it immediately. Banners bearing the new title were made and flown from his flagpoles, and henceforward the monkeys addressed him not as King but as the Great Sage.

6

The Great Sage, Equal of Heaven

An expedition of the heavenly host, led by Lee Tien Wang, the pagoda bearer, and the mighty No Cha, his third son, was sent against the monkey for deserting his post, but the latter defeated the expedition with his prowess as much as with his magic. Lee Tien Wang sent for reinforcements, but again the White Star intervened.

"What is a title without office and its benefits?" he pointed out. "It would be much cheaper to give him the empty title than to fit out another expedition, which might fail as the first."

The Heavenly Emperor consented and the monkey appeared once more in the audience hall with the White Star, who prostrated himself before the throne and said, "Your unworthy servant has brought the ex-curator of the Equestrian Galleries."

"Sun Wu-kung, if you please," Monkey Sun said impatiently.

"Come forward, then, Sun Wu-kung," God said. "We confer upon you the title of Great Sage, Equal of Heaven, the highest honor we can give. We trust that you will be sensible to the honor we have conferred upon you and be worthy of it."

The heavenly architects were ordered to build him a palace. Two commissioners were appointed to wait upon him, the Commissioner of Quietude and the Commissioner of Serenity.

The Great Sage, though now the Equal of Heaven, was after all a monkey and knew nothing of the ways of Heaven. He was ignorant of the precedence of the various ranks, nor did he know the pensions that the various deities drew. But under the guidance of his two commissioners, he led a well-regulated life. He would get up early in the morning and have his breakfast. Later he would lunch. Still later he would have supper and presently he would go to bed. Between his round of meals and sleep he would make calls on the various deities in Heaven and the immortals in remote parts of the universe. Soon he came to know everyone of any consequence and with all these he was considered an equal. It was not a very exciting life, but since it was all part of being the Great Sage, Equal of Heaven, he felt that he should bear it with graciousness.

This went on for some time until one day it occurred to one of the deities that it would be wise to give the Great Sage something to do to keep him out of idleness and mischief. At his suggestion, God made the monkey the superintendent of the peach orchards of the Queen Mother, the Empress of Heaven.

Now the peaches of the Queen Mother were known as *pantao,* the fancy and delight of the immortals. There were 3,600 trees divided into three groups of 1,200 each; the first ripened every three thousand years, the second every six thousand, the third every nine thousand years, reckoned in the time as the mortals know it. Every year the Feast of Peaches was eagerly awaited by all in Heaven, for only then did the Queen Mother distribute the coveted fruit among her guests, which included only the greater deities and immortals. In fact, the heavenly ranks were distinguished as the Invited and the Uninvited.

There was no doubt that the Great Sage liked his position, for since his appointment he was no longer seen in the palaces of the deities and the abodes of the immortals, for he began to spend practically all his time in the peach orchards, and the news of his diligence reached God and God was pleased, and the Queen Mother anticipated a larger crop than formerly. But when the fairy maidens went to the orchards to gather the divine fruits, they were only able to fill three baskets from the first and second groups of trees. In the orchard of the nine-thousand-year trees they found nothing but green fruits. The superintendent, too, was nowhere to be found, though in the pavilion they found his clothes and hat.

Then as one of the fairies let a branch go, it sprang back and something fell from it.

"Look!" exclaimed a fairy in red. "It is a little monkey."

Before they had recovered from their surprise, the little monkey stretched itself and lo! it was the Great Sage! For the truth was that while the Queen Mother and others had taken his diligence as exercised in guarding and caring for the peaches, the Great Sage had been in the habit of sending away the attendants and of helping himself to the peaches, stripping himself of his clothes so that he could more freely climb from branch to branch. After he had eaten all he could hold, he would change himself into a tiny monkey so that he could nestle between some branches and take a nap.

"Who are you that you dare to come to steal my peaches?" the Great Sage asked, producing his staff from his right ear.

"Do not strike us," the fairies cried, falling on their knees, "for we are no thieves but the fairy maids that the Queen Mother has sent to gather peaches for the feast."

"Feast?" the monkey asked. "What feast is this?"

"The Feast of Peaches, of course," they answered, and told the Great Sage about this great social event of Heaven.

"It is strange that I have heard nothing about it," the Great Sage said. "Tell me, good fairies, who are those that have been invited."

"There has been no change in the guest list this year," they answered. "There will be the Buddha Sakyamuni of the Western Paradise and his principal buddhisattvas and lohans, and Kuanyin the goddess of mercy from the Southern Paradise, the three Ancient Ones, the four emperors, the greatest of the immortals, and so on."

"Do you know whether I am on the list or not?" the monkey asked.

"We do not know, but we have heard that there has been no change and gather therefore that the Great Sage has been left out."

"They are again deceiving me," the monkey thought to himself. "They give me the title of the Equal of Heaven and yet here I am, left out of the Feast of Peaches to which thousands of buddhas, immortals, and deities have been invited!" Then he pointed his fingers at the fairies, saying, "Stay, stay, stay!" and while the fairies became fixed like statues, he leaped into the air and went toward the Jasper Pond, where the feast was to be held.

Halfway there he overtook the Great Immortal with Bare Feet.

"Where are you going, Brother Taoist?" the monkey asked.

"I am going to the Feast of Peaches," Barefeet answered. "The Queen Mother has been gracious enough to include me on her list."

"So this fellow has been invited while I have not been," the monkey said to himself. "I shall show them that I am no fool." Then he said aloud as a bright thought occurred to him, "You do not know then that you are first to go to the Hall of Light?"

"No, but why the Hall of Light?" asked the unsuspecting Barefeet.

"God has decided to hold a rehearsal this year for the feast," the monkey said. "I have been asked to spread the news as I can somersault faster than anyone can travel."

"It is strange," said Barefeet, "that God should want to hold a re-hearsal first, as if this were the first feast ever held! But thank you for letting me know, Great Sage."

As soon as Barefeet was out of sight, the monkey shook himself and changed himself into Barefeet. In this disguise he went to the Jasper Pond. He was the first guest to arrive. No one stopped him, as the attendants at the gate knew Barefeet and knew that he was on the invited list. He entered the palace and wandered around until he came to the Tower of Gems, where the feast was to be held. In the side chambers he found the cooks, wine bearers, dishwashers, and others making ready for the feast. There were innumerable varieties of dishes such as dragons' livers and phoenix brains, to say nothing of sharks' fins, birds' nests, bears' paws, and other delicacies found in the world below. There were wines brewed from mashed jades and other precious stones, each of a different color according to the stone that it was made from.

The monkey's mouth watered at the feast before him, but there were the attendants to be got out of the way. Again his magic came to his aid. He pulled off some hair, chewed it, spit it out, saying, "Transform!" The hairs became sleep bugs and they flew upon the faces of the servants and almost immediately they began to yawn, their hands grew limp, their heads drooped, and they soon snored away as if they had never slept before in their lives.

The monkey then quickly helped himself to the viands and wines. He tasted all the jars, lifting them to his lips. He especially liked a colorless but most fragrant wine distilled from diamonds and he drank up the whole jar. Then fear seized him. "I must get away from here before the guests begin to arrive," he said to himself. He staggered to his feet and leaped into the air and somersaulted zigzag across the sky. He lost his way and found himself before the palace of Laotze, the first of the three Ancient Ones, who lived above the thirty-third heaven. He entered the palace but found no one in the halls that he entered, for Laotze was giving his discourse in the innermost hall. He went into the room where the magic oven was kept and was over-whelmed by the sight of five gourds of golden pills, more precious than the oldest peaches of the Queen Mother, that lay beside the oven. He took up one gourd and emptied a handful into his mouth. They tasted so good that he did not stop until he had finished all the gourds, which had taken Laotze aeons of years to prepare!

The pills had a sobering effect upon him and Monkey Sun began to

realize the weight of his offences. He fled out of the palace of Laotze
and made for the nearest gate of Heaven, and, casting a robe of invisibility over himself, he stole out of Heaven unobserved and returned
to the Flower and Fruit Mountain.

7

Monkey Sun Meets His Conqueror

One after another the robberies were discovered, but suspicion was
not fixed upon Monkey Sun until the Great Immortal with Bare Feet
grew tired of waiting in the Hall of Light and went to God with his
story. Telescopic Eyes and Telephonic Ears made their observations
and confirmed all suspicions by reporting that Monkey Sun was carousing with his sworn brothers in the Water Screen Cave.

Lee Tien Wang, the pagoda bearer, set out of Heaven with another
expedition, larger than any that had ever left Heaven. Nets were spread
over the entire earth so that the monkey could not make his escape.

Nine of the mightiest warriors from the heavenly host fought the
Monkey King, but for all their might and number they were no match
for their foe, and they soon had to flee from the battle. Then Lee Tien
Wang gave orders for a general advance of the heavenly warriors followed by a host of one hundred thousand. On his side, the Monkey
King ordered out his own army of monkeys under the four generals
and the armies of his allies of the seventy-two caves led by their own
chiefs. The battle raged from morning till sunset. While the Great Sage
fought singlehanded Lee Tien Wang, No Cha, and the twenty-eight
fierce stellar knights, the heavenly army closed in upon the monkeys
and the seventy-two tribes and captured all except the monkeys, who
escaped back into the Water Screen Cave. Then the Monkey King
resorted to his magic. He pulled off some hairs from his body, chewed
them, and changed them into a host of monkeys exactly like himself
both in form and might. Soon he scattered the forces of Heaven and
went back to his cave in triumph.

The four generals greeted him with three tearful cries and then three
laughs. He asked if they had become mad, but they answered, "No,
we cried because the King of the Singlehorns and the chiefs of seventy-
two tribes have been captured by the enemy together with their followers, and we laughed because you have come back in triumph."

"You need have only laughed," the Monkey King said. "War is a
series of victories and defeats. Tomorrow I shall win a greater victory."

In the meantime Kuanyin, the goddess of mercy, arrived in Heaven for the Feast of Peaches. She was puzzled by the tense atmosphere she found and inquired into the cause. As God was explaining things to her, a message came from Lee Tien Wang begging for reinforcements. Kuanyin sent Ma Cha, her disciple and the second son of Lee Tien Wang, to try the power of the Monkey King, but Ma Cha shortly returned in defeat.

"The monkey is truly an invincible warrior and mighty magician," Kuanyin observed. "Only one person can prevail against him and it will be necessary to summon this person."

"Who is this person you have in mind?" God asked.

"It is your own nephew, Erhlang, the god of Kuankou," Kuanying answered. "He is a mighty warrior and has one transformation more than the monkey. He distinguished himself in the campaigns which finally brought peace to Heaven."

Erhlang was accordingly ordered to go to the aid of the heavenly expedition and he immediately mobilized his archers and set forth for the Flower and Fruit Mountain.

"Our fight will undoubtedly end with a contest of transformations," Erhland told Lee Tien Wang. "So I beg you to train your magic mirror upon him so that we shall not lose sight of him."

With this precaution Erhlang went out and demanded battle, and was met by Monkey Sun. The two warriors were each surprised at the other's great prowess. They had never before met such a powerful adversary. They fought over three hundred rounds without deciding the issue. Erhlang then shook himself and changed himself to a ferocious monster of ten times ten thousand feet in height, with a dark blue face, red hair, and tusklike teeth. He raised his three-pointed and two-edged spear and thrust it at the monkey. This did not intimidate the monkey, since he was himself a frequent employer of such magic art; he changed himself to a corresponding monster and fought on as before.

But these transformations frightened Generals Ma and Liu and Marshals Bang and Boom and the army of monkeys. They deserted their banners and weapons and fled, closely followed by Erhlang's archers and his trained hounds and hawks. Hundreds of monkeys were captured that did not run fast enough to the cave.

The cries of the monkeys in their distress weakened the fighting spirit of their king. He resumed his natural size and ran for the shelter of his cave, but his way was blocked by the six sworn brothers of Erhlang. He put away his staff in his right ear and changed himself into a sparrow and flew away. The brothers of Erhlang were baffled, but when the latter came up he looked around and recognized the sparrow perched on a near-by tree to be the assumed shape of the monkey. He threw aside his spear and bow and arrows and changed himself into an eagle and swooped down on the sparrow.

The Great Sage then flew off the tree and changed himself into a big cormorant and flew up higher and higher in the sky. Erhlang lost no time in changing himself into an ocean crane and flew after the cormorant, which thereupon closed its wings and dived toward earth. He landed in a stream and changed himself into a carp. Erhlang followed closely after him and when he did not see the cormorant he concluded that the monkey must have changed himself into some sort of fish, and so changed himself into a fish hawk with a sharp, curved beak and skimmed along the stream looking for the monkey.

The assumed shape of the monkey was swimming downstream, and when he saw the fish hawk he stopped and thought to himself, "That is a strange-looking bird, something of a kite but without its distinguishing blue, something of an egret but without its distinguishing comb, something of a heron without its red legs. It must be Erhlang." So he turned with a splash and swam in the opposite direction.

This attracted the attention of the fish hawk and it flew after the carp and dove for it. The carp rolled and changed itself into a water snake and wriggled into the grass. Erhlang then changed himself into a long-legged stork with a powerful beak and made for the snake, which thereupon changed into a bustard and flew up again into the sky.

Now the bustard was the lowliest of the birds and the god from Kuankou did not want to degrade himself by coming in contact with it. So he resumed his natural form and shot at the bustard with his bow. The bustard seemed to have been struck, for it fell and rolled down a mountain slope. When Erhlang reached the spot, however, the bustard was no longer to be seen nor the monkey, for he had in the meantime changed himself into a temple. He kept his mouth open for the doorway and his teeth for the doors, while his tongue was changed into the idol on its pedestal in the center niche, and his eyes served as windows. But he did not know what to do with his tail, and after some cogitation he changed it into a flagpole at the back of the temple.

This last adventitious flagpole betrayed the monkey, for upon closer examination Erhlang laughed and said aloud, "This must be the monkey, for whoever heard of a temple with its flagpole in the back? If I enter the temple, he will close his mouth and bite me in two. I shall first break down the windows and doors."

Monkey Sun did not, of course, wait to have his teeth and eyes put out; he resumed his natural form and vanished under a cloak of invisibility. Erhlang looked for him in the mountains and valleys, but could not find him or anything suspicious. So he went to the camp of Lee Tien Wang and asked the latter to sweep the earth with his magic mirror. Lee Tien Wang did so and then laughed, saying, "You had better go right after him, for he is headed toward Kuankou, bent, no doubt, upon some mischief."

In the meantime the monkey had reached Kuankou. Changing himself into Erhlang, he went to the latter's temple, where the attendants knelt and kowtowed to him in greeting. He sat down in Erhlang's throne and said, "Let me see what the offerings are like since I went away." They brought him the three sacrificial animals—pig, ox, and lamb—promised by Li Hu. "I forget what we did for Li Hu, but let's hope that he did not give the three sacrificial animals for nothing. We shall have lamb for dinner tonight. And what else?" Then the attendants brought in a new robe offered by Chang Lung. "We have more need of a suit of armor," the false Erhlang said, mystifying the attendants. "Anything else?"

"That is all," they answered, "but there are many petitions that have come in."

Monkey Sun looked through the list: Some contained requests for sons, some for relief from illness, some for money, and others for general blessings. The gifts promised in return varied according to the nature of the requests. The monkey was reading through the list with great interest and thinking what a profitable business it was to be a templed deity when the real Erhlang appeared before the temple.

"Have you seen Sun, the Great Sage?" he asked one of the guards, but the latter stared at him in astonishment and finally pointed inside, and Erhlang recognized the monkey seated in his throne. The monkey rose, saying, "My child, this temple has changed its name to Sun, so run along now."

The two foes again closed in on each other and fought their way back to the Flower and Fruit Mountain. They fought many hundred rounds without either showing weakness, while the heavenly host looked on and God, Laotze, and Kuanyin watched from the South Gate of Heaven.

"Have I not recommended the right man?" Kuanyin asked God.

"They are indeed well matched," God answered.

"I shall give Erhlang some help," Laotze said, remembering that the monkey had stolen all his pills, and he took down an armlet of inde-structible steel and hurled it down at the monkey. It struck him squarely on the head and he fell down. Erhlang and his brothers seized him and bound him with a cord through his shoulder blades to prevent him from escaping.

God's patience had by now been exhausted and he ordered the im-mediate execution of the monkey. He was taken to the execution tower and bound to a post. The heavenly executioners tried to cut him with their swords, but they could not hurt him. They hacked at him with their huge axes, but that also made no impression on him. They galloped at him with lances, but the lances broke and the riders were thrown off their horses.

The God of Fire then ordered forth his men and poured out their flames on the monkey, but they could not burn a single hair on his body. The God of Thunder then struck at him with his annihilating hammer, but when the crashes ceased and the smoke cleared away, they found the monkey grinning as ever.

Then Laotze took him to his palace and put him in his magic oven and sealed it with a powerful spell and started the magic fire; for he realized that only by distilling out of the monkey the marvelous prop-erties of the *pantao* peaches of the Queen Mother and of his own pills to the amount of five brimming gourds could the monkey be rendered destructible. This magic process required forty-nine days, but the attendant of the magic oven, too eager to see the result, opened it before the final hour had expired, and the monkey jumped out as lively as ever. The staff was produced again from his right ear and Heaven was again thrown into confusion. The warriors of Heaven all gave way before him and he fought his way toward the Hall of Light to usurp God's throne.

Fortunately the thirty-six warriors of the Thunder Department were on duty at the Hall of Light and these put up a stubborn fight now that the person of God was threatened. An emissary was despatched to the Western Paradise to seek the help of the Buddha Sakyamuni.

When the Buddha arrived he commanded the heavenly warriors to withdraw and the warriors obeyed, knowing full well the wisdom and power of the Buddha. But Monkey Sun did not know the Buddha and he asked, "What manner of monk are you that you dare interfere with my fight?"

"I am the Buddha Sakyamuni from the Western Paradise," the Buddha answered. "Now tell me, little monkey, why you are warring against Heaven and disturbing its peace."

"I want God the Jade Emperor's throne," the monkey answered.

"You do not know what you are saying, ignorant monkey," the Buddha said. "Do you know that the Jade Emperor has lived in virtue and righteousness over a period of one thousand, seven hundred and fifty cataclysms, each consisting of one hundred twenty-nine thousand years, before he became God? You are a mere nothing in age."

"But age is not everything," the monkey said. "I want his throne and there will be no peace until he abdicates it to me."

"Now tell me," the Buddha said, "wherein you think you are worthy."

"In the first place, I am as immortal as he," the monkey answered. "Then I can wield a staff over ten thousand pounds in weight. I am capable of seventy-two transformations and I have eighty-four thousand hairs, each capable of the same transformations as I. And finally, I can turn a somersault and travel one hundred and eight thousand *li*. Now tell me if that does not entitle me to the heavenly throne."

"If you can somersault one hundred and eight thousand *li*," the Buddha said, "then you can surely jump out of my right hand. Now I wager that if you can somersault out of my hand, I shall invite the Jade Emperor to the Western Paradise to live with me and yield the heavenly throne to you. But you must promise to return to the Flower and Fruit Mountain and live in peace if you fail."

"Of course I can," the monkey said and jumped on the Buddha's palm and started to somersault with all his might, until he came to five pink pillars so high that their tops were lost in the clouds. Beyond the pillars seemed to be the blue void.

"This must be the end of the universe," he thought. "I must leave an inscription here to prove that I have been here." He took a hair off his body and changed it into a writing brush, and with it he wrote on the middle pillar these words: "The Great Sage, Equal of Heaven, visited this place." He also left some water on the pillar in the manner of dogs. Then he somersaulted back and jumped off the Buddha's palm, saying, "Now ask God to abdicate the throne to me!"

"But, my dear monkey," the Buddha said, "you have never left my hand."

"Of course I did!" the monkey said. "I not only left your hand but I was to the very edge of the universe. If you don't believe it come with me and I shall show you the proof, for I saw at the edge of the universe five pink pillars and I wrote something on the middle pillar as evidence."

"We need not go to the edge of the universe for the evidence," the Buddha said. "Look here and see for yourself." The Buddha opened his right hand and pointed to his second finger with his left, and there was Monkey Sun's own handwriting, not yet dry.

"And if that does not satisfy you, shameless monkey, smell this!" and he thrust his hand under the monkey's nose.

Baffled though he was, Monkey Sun's immediate reaction was incredulity and a desire to try again. So he again jumped on the Buddha's palm, but the Buddha turned down his palm and hurled the monkey out of Heaven. The monkey fell and fell until he struck the earth in a desert in the west and before he could get to his feet the Buddha's fingers closed over him, changed into five mountains, and imprisoned the monkey underneath.

His mission finished, the Buddha prepared to return to the Western Paradise, but the Jade Emperor begged him to stay for the celebration of pacification of Heaven that he had decided to hold. The Buddha consented and a feast was held, the splendor of which even surpassed the Feast of Peaches. During the feast the guarding spirits that had been detailed to watch over the imprisoned monkey reported that the latter had wriggled his head out of the five mountains. The Buddha then gave them a mighty charm, saying, "Paste this on the top of the mountains and the monkey will never be able to escape."

Then the Buddha bade God and the others farewell and set out for his own paradise. On his way he passed the mountains, which had settled tightly around the monkey, and he took compassion upon the monkey. He summoned the guarding spirits and said to them, "Feed him with iron balls when he is hungry and give him molten bronze when he is thirsty. When he has served his penance, someone will come to deliver him from his captivity."

Anonymous

A READER who is privileged to pore over an unexpurgated edition of Chin Ping Mei (Gold Vase Plum) *is probably too busy to look for humor. So the inclusion here of what may be termed the keynote passage from that coveted book, in both style and content, seems to be justified. Incidentally, the author, whom Arthur Waley surmises to be the Ming dynasty scholar Hsu Wei, derived his story of Hsi Men Ching and Pan Chin Lien from that other great Chinese novel,* Shui Hu Chuan, *from which we have taken our own Tattooed Monk.*

HSI MEN AND THE GOLD LOTUS

Life hastened onward, fleet as a spirited colt when it leaps over graves; swift as a weaver's shuttle the days and months flashed by. And with the end of the twelfth month, Yang, the Prince of Light, resumed his dominion, and now the season of plum blossoms had arrived.

One seductively radiant spring morning, Gold Lotus decked herself in her newest and most dazzling finery. She waited only until her husband had gone to take her accustomed place under the awning before the door. It is an old story that the encounters willed by Fate are mostly brought about by trivial chances. In short, the young woman was in the act of adjusting the prop that held up the bamboo awning above the door when a sudden gust of wind caused the pole in her hand to swing aside, so that it grazed the head of a passer-by.

Startled, and yet amused, Gold Lotus looked more closely at the stranger. He had the air of a man about town, and was perhaps thirty-five years of age. His handsome figure was clothed in a tunic of thin green silk; on his head he wore a fine tasseled hat, decorated with golden arrows whose pendants tinkled faintly as he moved. Around his waist he wore a golden girdle with a border of jade; on his feet were cotton socks of dazzling cleanliness, and light, thin-soled shoes. In his hand he carried a gold-spattered Sze-ch'uen fan. Altogether he was a very Chang Shong, a second Pan An; in short, such a smart

From *Chin Ping Mei:* "The Adventurous History of Hsi Men and His Six Wives."

cavalier as every woman's heart must desire. Such was the man who stood under the awning as Gold Lotus inquisitively measured him with her glance.

When he felt the pole graze his head, he stopped short, and was about to make an angry protest. But when he looked up he found to his surprise that he was confronting a seductive beauty. Her thick black tresses were piled upon her head: the kiss-curls, like raven's feathers, contrasted sharply with the snowy whiteness of her temples; her blue-black eyebrows were curved like the sickle of the new moon. The almond-shaped eyes met his with a cool, clear gaze; the cherry mouth exhaled a fragrant breath; her little nose was like rose-colored jasper; her full, rounded cheeks were delicately pink; her figure was slender and pliant as the stem of a flower, which could almost be spanned with the hands. Her fingers were like tender onion-shoots, carved out of jade; her small waist was supple as an osier. And then that tender body, white as rice powder, those full firm breasts, those tiny feet, peeping forth like twinkling stars, those smooth thighs! And there was something else—something tightly closed, something firm and youthful, something dark and cushioned . . . I know not what. Ah, who could ever tire of gazing at such charms!

Dark splendor of tresses rolled in a heavy knot;
Waves of fragrance well forth from its recesses.
It is transfixed with delicate arrows;
On one side is a flower stem with twofold bud.
A comb is rakishly set in the knot at the back.
Words cannot describe the sweep of the eyebrows:
Slender willow leaves curving above two peach blossoms.
The tinkle of earrings is faintly audible.
Under the small wide-armed jacket
Of clinging blue-green muslin
Shows the gentle swell of the jasper bosom.
Over the tunic, slashed in the mode of Hunan,
A short skirt of taffeta glistens.
From the open sleeve peeps a gayly-flowered lawn kerchief,
A sachet of perfume swings at her waist,
Above her breast is a button, and one at her throat.
Roving downwards, the eye beholds
Two tiny, nimble, gold-lily feet:

Blessed the dust over which they float
In their white satin slippers, artfully quilted,
And light as clouds!
She moves, and the red silken hose are revealed,
Caught at the knee with a border of flowers and birds.
Now and again, as she walks or sits,
A breeze entices from her under garments
A breath of a strangely piquant fragrance,
A breath of musk and the scent of orchids.
Only to look at her!—Where is the man
Who would not long to swoon in her embrace?
And to be derided by her
Would truly be mortal anguish.

This unexpected sight caused the stranger's anger to take flight to the far land of Java. The scowl on his face changed to a gracious smile. The young woman, however, very conscious of her awkwardness, raised her clasped hands in greeting, and said, with a deep bow:

"A gust of wind made me lose my hold, so that the pole accidentally hit his lordship! His lordship must forgive me!"

Straightening his hat, the person thus addressed bowed so deeply that his head almost touched the ground: "It was nothing at all. The lady may be quite easy."

Mother Wang, the proprietress of the tea room next door, who had observed the whole performance, now intervened, stepping forward, and amiably grinning.

"The noble lord got a real swipe as he was passing by!"

"Entirely my fault!" the stranger insisted with a courteous smile. "I hope the lady has forgiven me?"

"Please, please!" Gold Lotus exclaimed. "The gentleman has no reason to ask pardon!"

"Oh, please, I beg you!" He spoke with the greatest submissiveness, trying to give his voice a ringing and melodious tone. But his eyes, thievishly desirous, accustomed for years to lust after flowers and grasses that quiver in the wind of desire, clung to the beauty's body. At last, but not without looking back some seven or eight times, he turned to go, resuming his indolent, swaying gait, and waving his fan.

Mild is the air, and heaven smiles;
He comes forth for a stroll.

About to pass under the awning
He sees her there, so lovely and abashed.
Hardly come, he turns away from her,
Sending back to her many a burning glance.
Ah, springtide love, barely awakened,
Has robbed him of sense and strength.

The stranger's elegant and worldly appearance, and his cultivated manner of speech had made a deep impression on Gold Lotus. Had he not caught fire from her, would he have turned his head seven or eight times as he left her? If only she knew his name and address! She could not help looking after him until he disappeared from her sight. Then, and only then, she drew in the awning, closed the door, and went inside.

Worthy reader, who do you think this stranger was? He was none other than the chief of that band of dissolute fellows whose pastime it was to rage with the winds and sport with the moonbeams; their leader in plucking the blue flowers of the night, and rifling their magic fragrance; our wholesale apothecary, the most highly-esteemed Master Hsi Men.

Still saddened by the recent death of his ailing Third Wife, whom he had just conveyed to her last rest, he had left the house this day in search of distraction. He felt a longing to see his friend Ying Po Kui, whose company would surely cheer him a little. And now, on his way to call on his friend, he had this unexpected adventure under the awning of a strange house. He gave up the thought of visiting Ying, and turned homewards. Once indoors, he abandoned himself to his thoughts. What an adorable little bird! How could he ensnare her? Mother Wang, the teahouse woman next door—she could do the trick! A few ounces of silver were nothing to him. Without even allowing himself time for his midday meal, he hurried back to the tea house of Mother Wang, and seated himself comfortably on a stool beneath the penthouse.

"Aha, the noble gentleman had just the right buttery tone when he was here just now!" said the worthy dame, teasingly, with a cunning smile.

"Worthy adoptive mother, come here; there is something I simply must ask you. That little bird next door—whose wife is she?"

"Why, she's the younger sister of the Prince of Hell, the daughter of the Marshal of the Five Roads. Why do you ask me about her?"

"No nonsense! Please talk seriously."

"What, you don't know her? Her old man keeps the cookshop by the yamen."

"Ah, you must mean Yu San, who sells the date cakes?"

"No. If it were he, they would make quite a passable pair. Guess again, noble gentleman!"

"Do you mean the man who sells broth, Li San?"

"No, no. Even he wouldn't be a bad match for her. Guess again!"

"Well then, it might be little Liu Hsiao, with the crippled shoulder."

"Wrong again. Even he wouldn't be such a bad partner. Go on!"

"Worthy adoptive mother, I cannot guess."

"Aha! Then I'll tell you. Her husband is the pieman, Wu Ta."

"What! The Three-Inch Manikin, the Bark Dwarf?"

"No other!"

Hsi Men shook with laughter. But then he exclaimed, bitterly: "All the same, it is a pity this delicous mouthful of roast lamb should fall into the jaws of such a filthy dog!"

"Well, that's how it is always," sighed the old woman. "The dullest fellows ride the best horses and sleep with the loveliest women. The old man in the moon is partial to such unequal matches."

"Adoptive mother, how much do I owe you?"

"Nothing to speak of. Stay a little longer. We can settle the reckoning later."

"By the way, where is your son, Chao, employed at present?"

"If only I knew! The last I heard of him he had joined a traveling merchant from An Hui, and I haven't set eyes on him since then. I haven't the faintest idea as to whether he is alive or dead."

"A clever, wide-awake young fellow. You should have placed him in my care."

"Were my noble Lord to take an interest in him, his fortune would be made."

"We'll wait until he returns; then we'll talk of it again."

He rose and took his leave.

Less than four hours later he was back again at Mother Wang's tea shop. Taking a seat beneath the penthouse, he gazed fixedly at the door of the adjoining house.

"Would you like some plum broth?" the hostess inquired.

"Excellent idea. But plenty of vinegar in it, please."

A few minutes later, Mother Wang set before him a dish filled to the brim and a bowl. For a time he gave his attention to the broth.

"Adoptive mother, you know how to make this kind of plum broth to perfection. Have you much of it on hand?"

"What do you mean, on hand? This old woman has arranged marriages all her life."

"Who was talking about marriage? I was praising your plum broth."

"Excuse me, I distinctly heard you say how well I understood the art of matchmaking."

"Very well," he agreed, with a smile. "I have no doubt you could bring mountains together. Would you be inclined to play go-between for me sometime? If you do the job well, there will be a big reward for you."

"It pleases the gentleman to jest with me! What if your First Wife should come to hear of it? She would surely half pull my ears off!"

"Don't worry about that. My First Wife is a kind, sensible creature. The fact is that among the various women I have at home there is not one who really appeals to me. Perhaps you know of someone who might suit me? If so, you can make your proposal in perfect confidence. Even a divorced woman would do . . . ."

"Only a little while ago I had someone who would suit the gentleman on hand, but I'm not sure. . . ."

"Speak plainly! I am greatly interested."

"Well, then, as far as her outward charms are concerned, she is more than perfect. The only thing is, she is rather advanced in years."

"Well, sometimes a ripe beauty is not to be despised. How old is she? I am not so particular about a few years more or less."

"She was born in the sixtieth year of the sixtieth cycle under the Sign of the Boar, so she'll be ninety-three years at the New Year."

"What an old windbag you are!" Hsi Men exclaimed with a laugh. "You must always have your stupid joke!"

"Well, we must wet our agreement!" said the old woman, encouragingly.

"That suits me. And make the drink sweet and strong!"

It was late in the evening when Hsi Men left his observation post and returned home.

"Adoptive mother, I will settle the account tomorrow. Enter it in your books for the present. Is that agreed?"

"That's all right, that's all right. Honor me again soon!"

At home, Hsi Men found that he had no appetite, nor could he sleep, so full was his mind of the unknown beauty. Moon Lady attributed his moodiness to his grief for the loss of his Third Wife, and took no special notice of it.

Next morning, no sooner had Mother Wang opened her shop than she saw Master Hsi Men pacing up and down the street not far from the house.

"He's in a mighty hurry!" she thought. "How the fellow hankers for the syrup I've smeared on his nose! Well, he's fleeced the whole district, and now he's fallen into my hands! He shall pay a pretty price for his pleasure!"

It should be remarked that Old Wang was quite untroubled by moral scruples. For years she had been an active procuress and matchmaker, and an expert nurse and midwife; and lastly, she was a resourceful receiver of stolen goods.

She now disappeared inside the shop, and busied herself about the tea kettle. It was not long before Hsi Men stepped in under the penthouse and took up his usual post of observation. Mother Wang pretended that she had not seen him; she seemed to have no eyes for anything but the fire, which she was vigorously fanning.

"I say, adoptive mother, two bowls of tea!" her early customer called at last from the porch.

"Oh, it's you, noble gentleman!" she said, in pretended astonishment. "I haven't had the honor of your presence for the last few days. Please make yourself comfortable."

"Keep me company!" he invited her, as she set before him on the table two bowls of strong, dark-green tea.

"Ha, ha! I'm to keep you company!" she laughed in his face. "I hope you don't mean to seduce me?"

He could not help smiling; then he continued: "Tell me, has the fellow next door anything really good to sell?"

"Why, crisp biscuits, cabbage rolls, meat collops, puff pastries, mussel soup with dumplings, and warm spiced cheese."

"I suppose you are quite crazy! Come, let's talk sense for once! If your neighbor really makes decent pies I should like to buy forty or fifty of them."

"You had better wait until he comes out. It would seem less remarkable if you were to buy from him in the street rather than call at the house."

"There, of course, you are right." He emptied his bowl and went out into the street. He turned to the east, then faced about and walked toward the west; but again he turned, and again he passed the house.

Seven or eight times he marched up and down, at last he re-entered the tea room.

"Ah, my noble gentlemen! What happiness! It is days since I've had the honor of a visit!" the old worm greeted him ironically.

He drew a shining silver coin from his pocket and handed it to her. "Here, adoptive mother, in partial settlement of my score."

She pocketed the money, thinking: "All right, let the fellow go on believing he'll get her! This is enough to pay my rent tomorrow." Aloud, she said:

"It seems to me that there is something on your mind."

"Now how did you guess that?"

"It wasn't so difficult. Don't you know the old saying:

> Comes a stranger to this place,
> Question not unduly:
> You must learn to read his face
> Would you know him truly.

Ah, my dear gentleman, what strange and intricate histories such people as I have divined!"

"Listen: if you can really find out what is troubling me, at this moment, I will give you a prize of five ounces of silver."

"Oh, it won't take me long to guess that! I will whisper it in your ear right away: if you have been running your legs off today and yesterday, it's because of a certain person next door whom you can't get out of your mind. Well, am I right?"

"My congratulations! you've guessed it. I must admit that since I saw her yesterday standing before her door, I have no longer any control over my three souls and my six senses. Day and night I can find no peace or rest. I have lost all desire for food and drink, and if I try to do anything, I feel as though I were paralyzed. Can't you give me some good advice?"

"Well, I'll speak quite plainly. If I were to depend on my miserable tea room for a living, I might as well hire a ghost as night watchman. It is now three years since a few poor bubbles of steam have evaporated from my tea kettle. I remember it distinctly: it was on a cold and snowy day at the beginning of June. Since then my shop has been without a patron. Under these circumstances, I naturally had to turn to some other means of support. I have been a widow since my sixty-third year. How were my boy and I to live? Well, I earned my living by negotiating marriages and acting as midwife and nurse: I sold old clothes on commission, and I did a bit of procuring: also, I know a bit about cauterizing wounds and diagnosing sickness with the sounding-needle."

"Good heavens, but you're a versatile woman! Well, if you'll help me to an interview with my little bird, I'll pay you a fee of ten ounces of silver. That's as much as you'll need for your coffin."

"Ha!" said Mother Wang; "you were taken in at once! Why, I was only joking!"

"Then, worthy adoptive mother, ten good ounces of silver are yours if you can bring this about," Hsi Men repeated, urgently.

"Listen to me, my noble gentleman. In love affairs it's not so simple as that. What does 'love' mean today? Stolen love. And for that, six things are necessary: good appearance, money, blooming youth, ample time for loafing about, the gentle rigidity of a needle wrapped in cotton wool, and finally a something as strong as the thing of an ass."

"Frankly speaking, I can offer all six of these requirements. First, as regards my looks. I don't indeed wish to compare myself to a Pan An, but otherwise I can very well say—not so bad! Secondly, I have plenty of money to burn. As for youth, I may still count myself one of the younger generation. As for loafing, I've time to spare. If it were not so, would you find me so diligent a visitor? And as to gentleness, well, I'll let a woman strike me four hundred times before I so much as clench my fist. And finally, as for the sixth point, since my earliest youth I have been at home in all the houses of joy, and have reared up quite a nice little monster."

"Then so far everything is in order. But there is still one difficulty, on which such affairs are most commonly wrecked."

"And that is?"

"Don't be angry if I speak quite frankly, but a love affair like this often goes wrong because one begrudges the last one per cent of the expenses. I know you are a thrifty gentleman who doesn't thoughtlessly waste his money. That's where the difficulty lies."

"You need not worry about that. I shall do exactly as you wish."

"Good! If that's how it is, I know of a nice little plan for bringing you and the little bird together."

"Really! Then out with it!"

"First of all you must go quietly home. Three or six months from now we'll discuss the matter further."

"Stop! This is absolute torture! Think of the reward that awaits you!"

"Not so hasty, noble gentleman! It is true that the little bird is of humble descent—old Pan, her father, is nothing more than a little tailor outside the South Gate; but she is intelligent and cultured; she can sing and pluck the guitar, throw dice, and play chess; she knows by heart all the songs of the hundred poets; and she is thoroughly skilled in all the arts of the housewife. She learned to sing and play the guitar in the house of old Chang. You've heard of the wealthy Master Chang: it was he who gave her, free and gratis, to the Three-Inch Manikin as wife. As she is much alone in the house, and never goes out, I frequently keep her company. She often asks my advice, and she calls me, quite familiarly, her 'adoptive mother.'

"If you want to get your way, then take my advice; first buy two bolts of coarse silk, one blue and one white, also a bolt of fine white silk and ten ounces of the best cotton wool. Have it all sent here to me. Then I'll go over to her and ask to see the calendar, pretending that I want to find a suitable day to send for the tailor. If she does not offer to do the work herself, well then, we must give up our plan. On the other hand, if she tells me that I needn't send for the tailor, and that she will gladly do the work for me herself, then we have won one-tenth of the game. If, at my suggestion, she comes here to do the work, two-tenths of the game is won. I shall then put wine and food before her and urge her to help herself. If she declines and leaves without touching the food, then we must give up our plan. If, on the other hand, she accepts without a word, then the game is three-tenths won.

"You mustn't come here the first time. You mustn't show yourself until the third visit, some time in the afternoon. Dress yourself in your best, and before you enter announce your arrival by clearing your throat. Say that it's a long time since you've seen me, and you would like to drink a bowl of tea. Then I'll invite you to come in. If she gets up as you enter, and if I can't persuade her to stay, then we must give up our plan. If, however, she doesn't stir, then the game is four-tenths won.

"I shall then introduce you as the giver of the material, and emphasize your innumerable virtues. You, for your part, must praise her skill and dexterity. If she is overawed, and cannot answer you, then we must give up our plan. But if she should begin to talk with you, half the game is ours. I shall then immediately remark how extraordinarily fortunate this meeting is, since I am indebted to her for the labor. I could flatter myself a little on my ability to bring distant mountains together, and then I could suggest that you might make this an occasion for standing some wine in honor of the lady. You will naturally take my hint, and give me the money to fetch the wine. If now, in spite of all persuasion, she insists on leaving, then we must give up our plan. If, however, she remains seated, then the game is six-tenths won.

"I shall take the money, and as I go I shall ask her to stay and keep the noble gentleman company. If she objects, and gets up, and insists on going, then we must give up our plan. If, however, she does not get up, then things are going in your favor, and the game is seven-tenths won. When I return, I shall lay the table nicely, and say to her: 'Come now, put aside your work and drink a cup of wine with us. The noble gentleman won't want to have spent his money in vain.' If she refuses to drink at the same table with you, and gets up to go, then our plan has failed. If, however, she objects only in words, and keeps her seat, then our prospects are good, and the game is eight-tenths won. As soon as I see that the wine is making her merry, and that the talk is tending in the right direction, I shall pretend that the wine is all gone, and then I shall go out again to buy some more, and you must give me more money for the purpose. As I go out, I shall simply lock the two of you in. If she is frightened and makes a scene, then you must give up your plan. But if she calmly allows me to lock the door, then the game is nine-tenths won.

"There is yet one-tenth more to win, but before that is won, there are, of course, considerable difficulties to be overcome. When you find yourself alone with her, you must press her with sweet and winning words, and don't be afraid to use the speech of hands and feet. Everything will depend on you. Brush a couple of chopsticks from the table with your sleeve, as though by accident, and when you stoop as though to pick them up give her leg a familiar pat. If she is outraged, and makes a scene, then I shall come in and help you out of the scrape. Of course, if that happens, we shall have to consider the game as good as lost. But if she puts up with all this without a word, then all the ten-tenths of the game are won. But will you show yourself grateful afterwards?"

"You have thought it all out magnificently, adoptive mother!" exclaimed Hsi Men, with enthusiasm. "You almost deserve a seat of honor in the 'Hall of Those who Float on Clouds!'"

"There, there. I shall be content with the ten ounces of silver you promised me."

"Don't worry about that! Tell me, when is this plan to be carried out?"

"This very moment, while the Three-Inch Manikin is out, I shall go over to her and borrow the calendar and discuss the matter with her. Now, you have the silk and cotton sent here as soon as possible, and I shall have news for you this very night!"

"Rely on me! I shall keep my word," Hsi Men promised as he took his leave.

On his way home he bought three bolts of silk, and ten ounces of the best pure white cotton wool. He ordered his servant, little Tai, to wrap them up in a shawl and deliver them at once to Mother Wang. With unconcealed delight she received the gift, and immediately entered the neighboring house by way of the back door.

"The lady has not honored my wretched hovel for the last few days," she said, as she greeted Gold Lotus.

"I haven't been altogether well of late, so I haven't felt like going out."

"Have you perhaps a calendar in the house? This old woman would like to pick out an auspicious day for tailoring."

"What do you want to have made, adoptive mother?"

"Well, this old woman is plagued with ten woes and nine laments! The time has come to think of dying. And my son is not at home."

"Where is he, then?"

"He joined a traveling merchant and left for foreign parts. He has not written to me since, and from day to day I grow more anxious about him."

"How old is he?"

"Seventeen."

"Why don't you find him a wife? Then you would have someone in the house to give you a helping hand."

"That's true. Yet as long as I have to do without help I can't manage to go looking for a bride. But I shall talk to him about it directly he returns. Oh, I suffer so from breathlessness and coughing! I feel as if I'd been beaten all over. At night the pain is so bad that I can't close an eye. It is high time to think of my shroud. And now it happens that a kind and wealthy patron of mine, to whom I have been of some service from time to time, going to his house as sick-nurse, or finding him a maid or a concubine—this wealthy gentleman, in his thoughtfulness and sympathy, has presented me with the very stuff for a shroud. It has been lying on my shelves for over a year now. But I could never find the time to make it up. Still, in view of my condition I can't go on putting it off. Besides, it so happens that this is a leap year, with an extra long month, so that I can spare a few days for sewing. But first my tailor fleeces me outrageously, and then he leaves me altogether, with the excuse that he is swamped with work. These endless vexations! They are simply beyond words!"

"I don't know whether I could suit your taste; otherwise, adoptive mother, if you do not despise my help, I could find some time for you in the next few days."

"Oh, if only you would work for me with your precious fingers," the old woman said, "then I could die content! I have often heard people speak highly of your skill, but I did not venture to trouble you with my affairs."

"Why speak of trouble? You have my promise, and it is settled. Now take my calendar along with you and have someone select a lucky day."

"But, my dear little lady, please do not underrate yourself. Is it really necessary to get a stranger to read the calendar, when you yourself are so well versed in all the rhymed and unrhymed poetry of our hundred poets?"

"I have long forgotten all I ever knew," said Gold Lotus, jestingly.

"Excuses, excuses!" Mother Wang persisted, forcing the calendar upon her.

"Tomorrow and the day after are inauspicious," Gold Lotus declared, after she had studied the calendar for a while. "But the day after the day after tomorrow is a lucky day."

Mother Wang impatiently took the calendar from her hand and returned it to its place on the wall.

"Well, but why do we need an especially propitious day for it? The very fact that you are lending me a helping hand is enough so to speak, to kindle a lucky star for me!"

"As far as that goes, when a shroud is in question, an overcast day would really be more suitable for the work," Gold Lotus decided.

"As long as you are helping, any day will do for me, whether good or bad," Mother Wang eagerly agreed. "Then I may expect you tomorrow in my dreary abode?"

"Why, wouldn't you rather come here to me?"

"I should very much like to watch you working, but on the other hand, I have no one to look after the house in my absence."

"That is true. Then, tomorrow after breakfast."

That very evening Mother Wang told Hsi Men that he was to make his appearance on the third afternoon.

Gold Lotus kept her word. The following morning, as soon as her husband had gone out, she went to her neighbor's house. Mother Wang welcomed her with an especially strong bowl of tea, flavored with an infusion of walnuts and pine kernels. Gold Lotus measured and cut the material and began to sew. Old Mother Wang watched her intently, and loudly expressed her admiration. She was now past seventy, but she had never known such skill and dexterity. Towards noon the work was interrupted for a light meal, and then Gold Lotus was busy until the evening.

The Three-Inch Manikin crossed the threshold, with his pannier on his back, at the very moment when Gold Lotus re-entered the house. He noticed that her cheeks were slightly flushed.

"Where have you been?" he asked her.

"At Mother Wang's," she answered. "She asked me to help her to make her shroud. She kept me for dinner at noon."

"You should not have stayed for dinner. We are always accepting favors from her. It isn't that the mouthful of food is worth talking about, but still it's better that you should come home for your meals, so as not to be a burden to her. At all events, if you go there again tomorrow, give her a little money so that you can square the account.

> *The neighbors to whom we bid good day*
> *Are better than kinsfolk far away.*

That's an old maxim. We must keep on good terms with the woman. And if she refuses to accept anything in return, then you had better do the work at home."

Gold Lotus listened to him and was silent.

Next day she resumed her work in her neighbor's house. As noon approached she took from her sleeve three hundred copper cash and handed them to old Mother Wang.

"Here, adoptive mother, buy something to eat and drink with this."

"Why, what does this mean!" cried the old woman in surprise. "I have asked a favor of you—and now you want to put yourself to expense as well! Or perhaps my food isn't to your taste?"

"My imbecile of a husband wishes it. If you persist in spurning this little gift, I am to finish the work at home."

"Your honorable husband is a stickler for form, I must say. Well, if you wish, I will accept your gift," agreed the old woman quickly, for she saw that her scheme was in danger. She added a few coins from her own pocket, and bought some extra good wine and a few special delicacies for their dinner. Towards evening she bade farewell to her guest, with extravagant expressions of gratitude.

On the following afternoon the two women were seated at their sewing in Mother Wang's shop when they heard someone loudly clearing his throat outside, and immediately afterwards a voice called out:

"Hey, Mother Wang! It's a long time since I've seen you!"

The old woman screwed up her eyes.

"Who is that outside?"

"It's I," came the answer.

It was, of course, Hsi Men. He had hardly been able to wait for the third day, and now he punctually appeared before the tea shop in all his finery, with five ounces of silver in his purse, his gold-besprinkled Sze-ch'uen fan in his hand. Mother Wang bustled out to greet him.

"Ah, it is you. Do please come in; you are just in time to see."

And tugging at his sleeve, she ushered Hsi Men into the shop.

"Allow me, my dear little lady, to present to you the noble donor of the material, Master Hsi Men."

He, in the meantime, could not remove his eyes from this fresh, delicate face, over which was piled a cloud of luxuriant blue-black hair. She was wearing over her chemise of white lawn a slashed petticoat of peach-colored silk and blue satin trousers. As he entered she continued her sewing, and merely lowered her head a little. Hsi Men bent his back in a low bow and spoke his words of greeting in a musical tone. She laid her work aside and replied with a soft, "Ten-thousandfold happiness!"

"Just think, my noble Lord," old Mother Wang interposed, "until now I have not been able to get to work on the material with which you honored me more than a year ago. And I have to thank the helpful fingers of this lady for the fact that the work is being done at last. And how her fingers can sew; how accurately stitch follows stitch! One can scarcely believe it! Just come closer, noble gentleman, and see for yourself!"

"Marvelous! Simply divine!" he exclaimed.

"Now don't be so sarcastic!" said Gold Lotus with a smile, sinking her head still lower.

"Might I ask to what family the lady is related?" he inquired, pretending ignorance, turning towards Mother Wang.

"See if you can guess!"

"I have no idea."

"Then I'll tell you. But first, take a seat," and she gave him a chair facing Gold Lotus.

"Do you remember, the other day, as you were passing a certain house, you got a good crack on the head?"

"Oh, you mean when the awning prop struck me? Yes, and I wish I knew whose house that was!"

Gold Lotus bowed her head still lower, roguishly murmuring: "I hope that you are no longer offended at my carelessness."

"What? Please tell me, what do you mean?"

"Why, this is the lady, and she is the wife of my neighbor, Wu Ta," said Mother Wang, completing her introduction.

"Alas! That I have been so remiss in paying you my respects!" murmured Hsi Men.

Now Mother Wang turned to the young woman.

"Do you know this gentleman?"

"No."

"He is the honorable Hsi Men, one of the wealthiest gentlemen in this district. He enjoys the honor of personal acquaintance with His Excellency, the District Mandarin, and his fortune is numbered in ten thousand times ten thousand strings of a thousand cash. The Great Dipper in heaven would not be big enough to hold all his money. The large apothecary shop near the yamen belongs to him, and in his granaries there is such a surplus of rice that it is rotting there in heaps. Everything yellow in his house is gold; everything white, silver; everything round, pearls; everything that gleams, gems; and there, too, are rhinoceros horns and elephant tusks; and his First Wife is a born Wu, daughter of Wu, the Left Commandant of the city. She is a clever, capable woman, as I know, for it was I who arranged the marriage. But, tell me, Master Hsi Men, why is it so long since you last came to see me?"

"My daughter's betrothal has kept me busy for the last few days."

He spoke of his domestic affairs, and the conversation was restricted to himself and Mother Wang, the old woman doing her utmost to emphasize the wealth and brilliance of her patron. Meanwhile Gold Lotus continued to sew in silence, with bowed head, but she listened as she sewed.

How women do change, alack!
Now it is this, now t'other.
The husband turns his back,
And off they go to another!

With satisfaction the experienced Hsi Men realized that the beauty was one-tenth won, and it grieved him that he could not take possession of her at once. However, it seemed wiser to bide his time, and allow the old woman to carry out her plan, step by step. Now the important stage was reached where Mother Wang could suggest to her patron, after some circumstantial preparation, that he should send for a good bottle of wine in honor of the lady. Hsi Men pretended to be surprised.

"Well, you have taken me unawares, but fortunately I happen to have some money with me. Please take this." He dived into his pocket, and brought out an ounce of silver.

Gold Lotus signed to the old woman that she must not take it, but her objection was only a matter of form, since, after all, she did not rise from her seat. The old woman, therefore, paid no attention to her, but took the piece of silver and turned to go.

"Might I ask you, dear lady, to keep the gentleman company in the meantime? I shall be back directly."

"I really ought not to, adoptive mother," Gold Lotus shyly objected, but she did not move.

And so they were left alone together. Both were silent. His eyes were steadfastly fixed on her, and she, bent over her sewing, could not refrain from taking an occasional glance at him. It was not long before Mother Wang returned. At a cook shop she had bought a fat goose, a duck crisply browned, roast meat, and freshly baked fish, and also various choice fruits, and wine of the best quality. And soon the table was set with succulent dishes. The old woman beamed encouragingly at Gold Lotus.

"Come now, put aside your work, and drink a cup with us!"

"Oh, no, that would hardly be proper for me. Do you keep the gentleman company!"

"My dear little lady, what nonsense! It is expressly in your honor that he has just washed his hands!"

And without waiting for an answer, the old woman placed a few savory dishes before Gold Lotus. At the beginning of the meal there was still some affectation on the part of the beauty, and some courteous formality on the part of her gallant, but after the third course, when Mother Wang left the room for a moment to fetch more wine, his manner became less constrained.

"How many blooming springs has the lady seen?" he asked.

"I am twenty-five."

"Then you are of the same age as my 'Lowly Intimate.' Her birth took place in the year of the Dragon, on the twenty-fifth of the eighth month."

"Too great an honor! To name me in the same breath as your First Wife is to place heaven and earth on a footing of equality."

"Oh, Madame Gold Lotus has had the most refined education," interposed old Mother Wang. "Not only can she ply her needle and thread to perfection; more than that, she knows our hundred poets and all our philosophers by heart, to say nothing of the art of writing, chess playing, throwing the dice and laying the cards, interpreting signs, and similar arts, in which she's a past mistress."

"Where else could one find so many virtues united?" exclaimed Hsi Men in admiration.

"H'm, this old woman doesn't wish to venture an opinion, but tell me, among all the women of your household is there one to compare with Lady Gold Lotus?"

"You are absolutely right. You see, I cannot explain myself in a word, but I've had the most infernal luck. I never succeeded in bringing the right woman home."

"How about your deceased First, of the house of Chen?"

"Oh, we won't speak of her. It's true she was of humble birth, but how clever and circumspect! I could rely upon her in every way. What a calamity, that death should have taken her from me three years ago! If she were still alive, things would not be at sixes and sevens in my house. Five, seven mouths to be filled, but no one takes the trouble to see to the housekeeping. The proper mistress is lacking. My 'Lowly Intimate' is constantly ailing and leaves the household to look after itself. That is really why I go out so much, since at home I have nothing but vexation."

"Don't take it ill, noble gentleman, if I speak rather frankly; but neither your former nor your present First Wife could compare with Madame Gold Lotus in outward and inward merits."

"True, nor in charm and vitality."

"Still, you have a little friend in East Street, haven't you? Why not let me act as go-between for her?"

"Oh, the little Chang, who sings so drearily. Since I discovered that she has taken to going round the corner I am no longer interested in her."

"And little Li Kiao from the house of joy? You have known her for some time, haven't you?"

"She is now my Second Wife. Unfortunately, she knows nothing about housekeeping. Otherwise I would have made her my First."

"Well, you've always got on excellently with little Cho Tin?"

"Oh, don't speak of her! She was my Third. A little while ago she fell ill and died."

"Oh, dear! Now suppose I knew someone exactly to your taste, would there be any objection if I were to come to your house with my proposal?"

"Since my parents are no longer among the living, I am my own master. Who could interfere with me?"

"I was only jesting. How should I find the right person at a moment's notice?"

"Why shouldn't you? Alas, that I should be so unfortunate in marriage!"

"Why, the wine is all gone!" said the old woman, suddenly interrupting the conversation. "It always gives out just when one feels most inclined to drink! Don't scold me for being so careless. How if I were to fetch another jug of wine?"

Hsi Men thrust his hand into his purse, and drew out the other four silver coins.

"Here, adoptive mother, take them all, so that we can have enough in case we run short again."

The old woman thanked him and set off on her errand, but not before she had cast a searching glance at the beauty. The three large goblets of wine whose contents had passed between her lips had not failed to take their effect upon Gold Lotus. Desire was now kindled within her. She had by no means missed the significance of the conversation, although she had listened in silence, motionless, with her eyes on the ground.

With an ingratiating smirk, Mother Wang turned to the young woman. "I am just going to East Street, near the District Yamen; I know where I can get a first-rate wine. It will be some time before I return. Be so kind as to keep the gentleman company until then. There is still a little wine left in the jug there. Fill your cups from that when they are empty."

"Please don't go on my account. I don't need any more wine."

"Oh, you two are no longer strangers. Why shouldn't you drink another cup together? Don't be so faint-hearted!"

"Don't go!" Gold Lotus protested once more, but she did not stir from her seat.

Mother Wang opened the door, and fastened it again from the outside, tying the latch string to the door post. She then sat down outside it and began quickly to spin yarn.

The lovers were now shut up together. Gold Lotus had pushed her seat back from the table, and from time to time she glanced surreptitiously at her companion. Hsi Men was gazing at her fixedly with brimming eyes.

At last he spoke. "What did you say was your honorable family name?"

"Wu."

"Oh, yes, Wu," he repeated, absently. "Not a very common name in this district—Wu. Might the pastry dealer, Wu Ta, the so-called Three-Inch Manikin, be any relation of yours?"

She flushed red for shame. "My husband," she breathed, drooping her head.

For a moment he was stricken dumb, and looked wildly around as though he had lost his senses. Then, in a pathetic tone of voice, he cried: "What an outrage!"

"Why, what injury have you suffered?" she asked in amusement, eyeing him obliquely.

"An outrage to you, not to me!"

And now he began to pay court to her in long, flowery phrases, with many an "Honored Lady" and "Gracious One." Meanwhile, as she fingered her coat, and nibbled at the seam of her sleeve, she provided an accompaniment to his speech, without stopping her nibbling, in the shape of a spirited retort, or a mischievous sidelong glance. And now, on the pretext that the heat was oppressive, he suddenly drew off his thin, green silk surcoat.

"Would you oblige me by putting this on my adoptive mother's bed?" he begged her.

She turned away from him with a shrug.

"Why don't you do it yourself? Your hands are not paralyzed," she replied, merrily nibbling her sleeve.

"Well, if you won't, you won't."

With outstretched arm he reached over the table and threw the garment on to the stove on which the old woman slept. His sleeve caught on one of the chopsticks, and swept it to the floor, and—oh, how providentially!—the chopstick rolled under her dress! As he was about to fill her cup again, and to offer her more food, it was only natural that he should miss one of his chopsticks.

"Is this perhaps your chopstick?" she asked with a smile, pressing her little foot on it.

"Oh, there it is!" he said, in pretended surprise, and he stooped; but instead of picking up the chopstick he gently pressed his hand on her gayly embroidered slipper. She burst out laughing.

"What are you thinking of? I shall scream!"

He fell on his knees before her.

"Most gracious lady, take pity on a wretched man!" he sighed, while his hand crept upwards along her thigh.

Struggling and throwing up her hands, with outspread fingers, she cried: "Why, you naughty, dissolute fellow! I'll give you such a box on the ears!"

"Ah, gracious lady, it would be bliss even to die at your hands!"

And without giving her time to reply, he took her in his arms and laid her down on Mother Wang's bed. There he loosened her girdle, and disrobed her. And now, sharing a pillow together, they also shared their delight.

Consider, worthy reader, that he who first possessed Gold Lotus was a feeble graybeard, the old moneybag, Chang. Now, this feeble graybeard, always with a drop on his nose, and his diet of bean-flour gruel —what sort of pleasure could he afford her? Then came the Three-Inch Manikin. The extent of his powers may be left to the imagination. If now she encounters Hsi Men, one long familiar with the play of the moon and the winds, a strong and upstanding lover, must she not at last experience satisfaction?

> Breast to breast—two mandarin ducks in love,
> Tumbling merrily about in the water.
> Head to head—a tender phoenix pair,
> Busy and gay, building their nest of twigs.
> She—fastening her red lips upon his cheek,
> He—firmly clasping her upturned head.
> Now the two golden clasps have fallen from her tresses,
> And the black cloud of her hair lies outspread over the pillow.
> His vows, deep as the sea and exalted as mountains,

And the thousand variations of his caress,
Banish the last lingering trace of reserve,
As a cloud is driven headlong by the wind.
Overcome by his tender violence
She utters a cry of bliss, like the song of the goldfinch.
The sweet saliva gathers in her mouth
And she thrusts out her tongue in voluptuous pleasure.
Through all the veins and arteries of her willow-lithe body
Heavily pulses the brimming, resistless tide of delight.
But now the panting breath of her cherry lips is more languid,
The dusk of twilight settles upon her eyes,
Her skin is agleam with a hundred fragrant pearls,
Her smooth bosom rises and falls like hurrying waves.
Now—all the sweetness of stolen love consumed—
Two lovers have completed their mating.

The cloud had poured forth its contents. The two lovers were just making themselves presentable again when old Mother Wang suddenly flung open the door and entered. She clapped hands as though in amazement, crying: "Hi, hi, here's a pretty business!" And turning to Gold Lotus, where she stood in confusion:

"I asked you here to sew, not to go whoring! The best thing I can do is to go straight to your husband and tell him the truth, for he'll reproach me all the more if he discovers it behind my back!"

And she turned as if to go, but Gold Lotus, red with shame, held her fast by the coat.

"Adoptive mother, have pity!" she pleaded softly.

"On one condition only: from this day you must meet Master Hsi Men in secret whenever he wishes; whether I call you early in the morning or late at night, you must come. In that case I will be silent. Otherwise I shall tell your husband everything."

Gold Lotus could not speak for shame.

"Well, what about it? Answer quickly, please!" the old woman insisted.

"I promise," came the hardly audible reply.

Now the old woman turned to Hsi Men:

"Noble gentleman, you have had ten-tenths of your desire—now remember your promise! Otherwise . . ."

"Have no fear, adoptive mother, I keep my word!"

"There is still another point," the old woman continued. "I have your promises, it is true, but they are not worth much without visible proof. I propose that you exchange mutual pledges as evidence of your sincerity."

Hsi Men immediately removed a golden hair clasp and made it fast to the curls on the nape of Gold Lotus's neck. She, however, took it from her hair and hid it in her sleeve, for she feared that her husband might notice it and grow suspicious. For her own part, she did not want to provide any memento of the incident, but before she could prevent it Mother Wang had drawn a flowered handkerchief of fine Hangchow silk from her sleeve and thrust it into Hsi Men's hand. They drank a few more cups of wine, and then Gold Lotus rose and slipped home through the back door.

"Tell me, have I done well?" Mother Wang asked Hsi Men.

"Excellently! I am deeply indebted."

"And she is well versed in the art of love?"

"Oh, she is a very daughter of delight . . . There is no describing it!"

"Then don't forget the reward you promised!"

"I shall send it to you as soon as I get home."

The old woman laughingly quoted the lines:

> *"The eye already sees the conquering banners wave;*
> *Now from afar the ear hears the triumphant blast!*

Still, I hope I shan't have to climb out of my coffin to collect the mourners' fees from you!"

Tsao Hsueh-chin

AMONG both mice and men there is the tradition that the city slicker should make a joke of his country cousin. The wide-eyed wonder of the rustic when planted for the first time in Times Square or on Nanking Road, in front of the Sunrise Teahouse, in prewar Shanghai, is always a source of amusement to the sophisticates. To describe such a situation the Chinese have a time-honored phrase: "It is like Liu lao-lao in Takuanyuan [Garden of Spectacular Sights]." Anybody who knows anything about the Chinese novel knows that Hung Lou Meng (Red Chamber Dream) *belongs to the lovers Pao-yu and Tai-yu; but, so far as the present comedy of manners is concerned, Old Dame Liu has the stage and steals the show.*

LIU *LAO-LAO*'S FIRST VISIT TO THE GARDEN OF SPECTACULAR SIGHTS

I

Although the Yungkuofu was not unduly large, there were over three hundred mouths from master to servant, and mistress to maid. Although the household duties were not unduly burdensome, there occurred daily at least a score of tasks and cares to be attended to. For one who attempts to unravel the story, the problems are as perplexing as a mass of hemp with a thousand loose ends. While we were at a loss as to what to use for further development of our story, there came to the Yungkuofu an obscure family which was only remotely related to the Chias. This family, then, will serve our purpose.

The surname of this family was Wang. The grandfather was a petty official in the Capital and was acquainted with the grandfather of Phoenix (Wang Feng-chieh). Impressed by the wealth and prestige of the more fortunate Wangs, this petty official had "joined family" with them as the nephew of Phoenix's grandfather. After the death of the petty official, the family returned to the farm and was survived by the grandson named Little Dog, his wife Liu-shih, their son Pan-erh, and Ching-erh their daughter. They lived with Liu-shih's mother, Liu

From *Dream of the Red Chamber*, translated by Chi-Chen Wang.

lao-lao (Old Dame Liu), a widow of advanced age and wide experience.

They were now in poor circumstances. In a good year, they were able to manage with the products of their small farm, but this year found Little Dog unprepared for the winter. One day he drank some wine in order to forget his troubles, and having nothing better to do amused himself by baiting his wife and children. Liu-shih did not have the courage to remonstrate with him, but Liu *lao-lao* at last intervened. "Son-in-law," she said, "I beg your pardon for using my tongue. But we must know our place and eat according to the size of our bowl. You were used to luxuries when your father and grandfather were living and formed the habit of heeding the head and forgetting the tail when you have any money and of becoming quarrelsome when you are without it. That is not the way of a man. There is plenty of money to be made in the Capital for those who are capable. It doesn't help things any to pick quarrels at home."

"Of course you can talk sitting there on the *k'ang*," Little Dog retorted. "I may say that you talk mostly nonsense. How is money to be gotten so easily in the Capital? Do you suggest that I should go and rob?"

"I suggest nothing of the kind. But we ought to be able to think of something. It is certain that the silver nuggets will not hobble into our house themselves."

"I wouldn't be sitting around here doing nothing if there was anything to be done," Little Dog said. "I have no relatives that are tax collectors or friends that are officials. What could I do? If I had any they might not want to have anything to do with me."

"One never can tell," Liu *lao-lao* meditated. "It is said that 'Man must try though his success depends upon the will of Heaven.' We must do our part and perhaps Buddha will help us to succeed. Now your grandfather once joined the Wangs of Chinling. Twenty years ago they used to take good care of your family, but since then your family and theirs have drifted apart because your people have been so proud of their poverty. I visited them once with Daughter. They were not a bad sort, especially their second daughter who is now the wife of Cheng *lao-yeh** of the Yungkuofu. The Wangs are not in the Capital now, but you can go to see Madame Wang, who may still remember us. I understand that she has become even more kind and

* Term of respect, meaning "Old Sire."

charitable since she is older. If they would only do something for us, it would be worth while trying: a hair from their body is bigger than our waist."

"Mother is right," Liu-shih said, "but how can we present ourselves in front of their gate with such ungainly features and awkward tongues? The keepers of the gate will probably not announce us. It would be like deliberately slapping our own cheeks."

But Little Dog was tempted by the prospects of such a visit. So he said, "Since Mother was there once before, why don't you go now and see how the wind blows?"

"I?" Liu *lao-lao* protested. "It is said that the gate of the Marquis is as inaccessible as the Ocean. Who am I to attempt such a mission? Besides, the servants do not know me."

"That does not matter," Little Dog encouraged. "Supposing you go with your grandson and call on Chou Jui, the servant that Madame Wang brought over to the Yungkuofu when she was married. My father once did him a favor and he will help us if you see him."

"Well," the old woman said reluctantly, "I suppose I shall have to go. You being a man cannot humble yourself to such a visit, and Daughter is still too young to be going around. I shall go then and see what I can do. An old face is thick and will stand some slapping."

2

Liu *lao-lao* was up before dawn to prepare for the journey. She taught Pan-erh a few sentences and set out for the city. With some difficulty she located the home of Chou Jui and was met by Chou Jui's wife.

Greetings being over, Chou Jui's wife asked Liu *lao-lao* whether she was passing by or whether she had come with a purpose.

"I have come partly to see you and partly to offer my humble greetings to *ku-tai-tai*.* If you can arrange an interview for me it will be my great honor; but if you can't then you can mention it to her sometime."

Chou Jui's wife guessed the real purpose of the old woman's visit. She recalled that her husband once was involved in a lawsuit and was helped by Little Dog's father, and she felt obliged to do what she could to help Liu *lao-lao*. Besides, she wanted to show her prestige in the

* Term of respect referring to a female member of the family in the "aunt" stage. Here, of course, it is Madame Wang.

Chia household. So she said: "Rest assured, *lao-lao*. After you have come all the way from the country I cannot think of letting you go away without seeing the Buddha herself. Strictly speaking, this falls outside of our duties, but as you have come to us as if we were somebody and as you are a relative of *tai-tai* I shall make this an exception and do what I can for you. I must tell you, however, that it is not the same now as it was a few years ago. Now *tai-tai* does not attend to affairs herself, having given Lien *erh-nai-nai* the household duties. And who do you think this Lien *erh-nai-nai* is? She is *tai-tai's* niece, Phoenix!"

"Really? I saw her once when she was a mere child and thought that she was destined to be a woman of many blessings."

"She entertains all the guests. You can afford not to see *tai-tai*, but you must see her if you do not want to go home empty-handed."

"*A-mi-to-fo*," Liu *lao-lao* said. "I thank you for your enlightenment and leave everything to your kindness of heart."

The maid was sent to reconnoitre while Chou Jui's wife told Liu *lao-lao* more about the Yungkuofu. Liu *lao-lao* expressed surprise that a woman of about twenty like Phoenix should be entrusted with the affairs of Yungkuofu. "Ah, but she is a very capable young lady," Chou Jui's wife said. "She is as pretty as a picture and has at least ten thousand heads. And such wit and tongue. Ten eloquent men cannot match her. You will see for yourself."

While Chou Jui's wife went to talk to Patience, the confidential maid of Phoenix, Liu *lao-lao* rehearsed Pan-erh again in the lines that she had taught him. Finally she was ushered into Phoenix's room to wait. The perfume made her dizzy and she felt as though she were treading on clouds. Everything in the room was strange and dazzling. Liu *lao-lao* nodded her head in admiration and murmured in praise of Buddha. She was led to a room to the east and was greeted by Patience. Mistaking her for Phoenix, Liu *lao-lao* was about to address her as *ku-nai-nai*, but Chou Jui's wife saved the situation by saying that it was Patience *ku-niang*.*

Slowly a rhythmic ticking came into the consciousness of Liu *lao-lao*. K-dong, k-dong . . . It seemed to her like a sieve being pushed back and forth along its rails by indefatigable hands. She looked around and discovered a boxlike effect hanging from a pillar in the outer room. The sound she heard was caused by a swinging object,

---

* *Ku-niang* is usually applied to the daughters of the house, but it is used sometimes as a mark of respect in referring to the more favored of the maids.

like the weight of a scale, that dangled from the bottom of the box. "What could that be and what could it be for?" Liu *lao-lao* thought, then suddenly she was startled by the dong! dong! that issued from the box. Seven or eight strokes followed in regular succession. She was gathering courage to ask what it was, but was interrupted by the maids who warned them that Phoenix was returning to her apartment. Patience and Chou Jui's wife got up and said: *"Lao-lao* will please wait here and make herself at home. We shall inform you when *nai-nai* is ready to receive you." They went out to meet Phoenix. Liu *lao-lao* held her breath and waited. About twenty women approached the outer room which was soon filled with the rustling of their skirts. Presently dinner was spread and the maids and servants gradually withdrew as they received their instructions from Phoenix.

3

Phoenix had finished her dinner and was sitting on the *k'ang* stirring the charcoals in her hand stove with a pair of brass tongs. Patience stood by with a tea tray. As Liu *lao-lao* entered the room she said, without looking up, "Ask the guest please to come in." She seemed to be surprised when she looked up and saw Liu *lao-lao* standing in front of her. While she was making a motion to get up from the *k'ang,* Liu *lao-lao* had already kowtowed several times before her.

"Chou *chieh-chieh,** don't let the guest do me such an honor. Why didn't you tell me before that she has been waiting? I am young and do not know the proper form or address to use."

Pan-erh had hidden behind Liu *lao-lao's* back and would not come forward to make his bow and say his lines, in spite of the careful rehearsals he had had. Phoenix said, smiling: "The relatives have all drifted away from us. Those who know say that our relatives neglect us, but those who don't would say that we have forgotten them."

"A-mi-to-fo," Liu *lao-lao* murmured. "We have not come because we have seen such hard times and did not want to slap *ku-nai-nai* in the face with our disgraceful presence. What would the servants think if they saw such relatives of yours?"

"Don't say such disgusting nonsense," Phoenix remonstrated. "It is said that even the Emperor has three or four poor relatives. So how must it be with you and me! Besides, we are a mere empty show, try-

---

* "Elder sister," here term of respect to an older servant.

ing to keep up with the traditions of the ancestors' illustrious past."
Then turning to Chou Jui's wife she asked, "Have you told *tai-tai* that
there is a guest here?"

"Not yet," Chou Jui's wife answered, "as we were waiting for *nai-
nai's* orders."

"You may go and inform her if you will," Phoenix said.

Chou Jui's wife returned with the report that Madame Wang was
busy and that Phoenix was to entertain the guest and thank her for
her kind visit. If the guest had anything to say she could say it to
Phoenix. Liu *lao-lao* said, "I have no other purpose except to visit *ku-
tai-tai* and *ku-nai-nai.*" Chou Jui's wife, seeing that Liu *lao-lao* was
letting her modesty defeat her purpose, prompted her, saying that she
need not be awkward about it if she had anything to say, that *ku-nai-
nai* was just like *ku-tai-tai.* Liu *lao-lao* blushed embarrassedly before
she spoke.

"I should not mention such a thing on this my first visit," she stammered, "but since I have come such a long distance to seek your generosity, I might as well say it. Well, I have come with your nephew
because his father and mother are so poor that they scarcely have anything to eat. Winter is coming on so we have come to you." She then
pushed Pan-erh forward and said to him: "Tell *ku-nai-nai* what your
father said. What did we come for? Tell *ku-nai-nai.* Is that all you
can do, eat, eat, and eat?"

Phoenix did not wait for Pan-erh to recite his lines. She said: "There
is no need of your speaking. I understand." Then to Chou Jui's wife:
"Has *lao-lao* had her breakfast?"

"I started from the country before dawn so I did not have time to
have breakfast," Liu *lao-lao* answered. A guest dinner was ordered.
Phoenix excused herself, charging Chou Jui's wife to see that the guests
had enough to eat. After retiring to her inner room, she sent for Chou
Jui's wife and asked her what Madame Wang actually said.

"*Tai-tai* says that they were not related by blood but only by joining
family some years ago in the time of *tai-lao-yeh.** They have not come
for some years now, but when they used to come they were never sent
away without something. *Tai-tai* says that if there is anything they
want now, *erh-nai-nai* can use her own discretion and give them something."

"I wondered why it is that I knew nothing about them," Phoenix
said. "So they are not really relatives. . . ."

* "Grand Old Sire."

4

Liu *lao-lao* had finished her dinner and came in with Pan-erh to thank Phoenix; they were licking their lips and smacking their tongues in gratification. Phoenix said to them, smiling, "I understand perfectly what you said a little while ago. Among relatives, we should take care of those who are in need before they open their mouths. But it is impossible for *tai-tai* to remember everyone. Besides, I have been taking care of things lately. You must appreciate the fact that although we seem prosperous, actually it is not at all easy for us to manage. It is the truth, though few would believe it. But today you have come from a long distance and this is the first time that you ask us for help. It is impossible to let you go away barehanded. Fortunately *tai-tai* gave me today twenty taels of silver for making clothing for the maids. If you do not mind the insignificance of the amount, you can take it."

Liu *lao-lao's* countenance sank during the first part of Phoenix's speech, but she brightened up when she heard the unbelievable sum of twenty taels that she could have. "Ah," she exclaimed, "I know that times are hard and that it is difficult to manage, but it is said, 'A camel that dies of starvation is larger than a fat horse.' A hair from *ku-nai-nai's* body is larger than our waist. . . ."

Chou Jui's wife tried to stop her from these homely remarks, but Phoenix did not seem to mind them. Patience brought the parcel of silver and in addition a string of cash. "Take this silver and make some clothes for the children," Phoenix said. "Come often when you have nothing to do, as relatives should. I shall not try to detain you as it is growing late and you have a long way to go. Give my best wishes to everyone that I should be remembered to." She stood up as she finished the words. Liu *lao-lao* thanked her profusely and went away with Chou Jui's wife. She offered a small piece of silver to her guide but the latter declined it, as such small sums were nothing to her. . . .

LIU *LAO-LAO'S* RETURN TO THE GARDEN OF SPECTACULAR SIGHTS

I

Arriving at Phoenix's apartment, Patience found that Liu *lao-lao*, the distant relative of Madame Wang, who had come some two or three years ago, was again there. She was accompanied by Chou Jui's wife who had introduced her on the occasion of her first visit. On the floor there were sacks containing dates, pumpkins, and vegetables such as the farm produces. It happened that Phoenix was in the Matriarch's room. The Matriarch overheard Chou Jui's wife when she went to tell Phoenix and wanted to see Liu *lao-lao,* as she felt a desire to talk with someone of her own age.

"You are in luck," Chou Jui's wife told Liu *lao-lao.* "I was whispering to *nai-nai* that you are thinking of going home before it got dark. *Lao-tai-tai* heard me and asked who Liu *lao-lao* was. *Nai-nai* told her, and she said that she would like to see you. You are lucky indeed. Please come with me immediately."

"Look at me!" Liu *lao-lao* said. "How can I see anyone, the way I look? Please tell *lao-tai-tai* that I have gone already."

"Do not be afraid," Patience assured her. "Our *lao-tai-tai* is kind and generous to the poor. She will be good to you."

Pao-Yu and the young ladies of the Takuanyuan were all in the Matriarch's room when Patience entered with Liu *lao-lao.* The latter was dazed by the bejewelled ladies that she saw, but she perceived an aged lady lying on a couch with a beautiful maid massaging her legs, and concluded that it must be the Matriarch. She curtsied profusely and said, "Greetings to the ancient goddess of longevity." The Matriarch returned the greeting and asked her to sit down.

"How old are you?" the Matriarch asked, calling her an old relative.

"Seventy-five," Liu *lao-lao* stood up and answered.

"See," the Matriarch said to those present, "how strong she is, and yet she is older than I am. I don't know how useless and dependent I shall be when I am of her age."

"But we are born to labor while *lao-tai-tai* is born to enjoy the blessings of heaven," Liu *lao-lao* said. "What would become of all the farm work if we were like *lao-tai-tai?*"

"Are your eyes and teeth all in good condition?" the Matriarch asked.

"Yes, they are all in good condition," Liu *lao-lao* answered, "but this year the left molar is beginning to get loose."

"I am quite old and useless," the Matriarch said regretfully. "My eyes are faded, my ears deaf, and my memory unreliable. I do not see many visitors now for fear of betraying my infirmities. All I do is to eat whatever my teeth can chew, sleep when I can, and amuse myself with my children and grandchildren when I need diversion."

"That is *lao-tai-tai's* blessing from heaven," Liu *lao-lao* said. "I would like to do those things, but I can't."

The Matriarch was pleased with the rural visitor and with her simplicity. She asked her to stay for a few days. Phoenix, seeing that the Matriarch liked Liu *lao-lao,* also urged her to stay, saying that though the Yungkuofu was not as large and spacious as her farm, they did have a few vacant rooms in which she could stay.

2

The day following the Matriarch, accompanied by her daughters-in-law and grandchildren, visited the Takuanyuan and showed Liu *lao-lao* the sights. Liu *lao-lao* was greatly impressed by everything. "We used to get pictures for the walls at New Year time," she said; "pictures of palaces and great mansions. We always thought that such houses as those in the pictures did not exist, but now I see your garden is much prettier than the pictures. How wonderful it would be if you could get some painters to draw the garden and let the country folks improve their knowledge!"

Dinner was served in Quest Spring's apartment, the Autumnal Study. Loyal Goose, the Matriarch's beloved maid, suggested to those present: "*Lao-yeh* has companions to amuse him at dinner in the outer apartments. Why can't we have a female companion to-day?"

Li Huan, who was not given to jokes, did not understand, but Phoenix applauded the suggestion and plotted with the maid to entertain the Matriarch and others at the expense of Liu *lao-lao*. The maid took the old woman outside and gave her certain instructions, saying in conclusion: "These are the customs of this house. You must follow them carefully if you do not want people to laugh at you."

"Rest assured," Liu *lao-lao* answered, "I shall do as *ku-niang* has taught me."

The old woman was seated near the Matriarch on a little table. Ordinarily, Loyal Goose did not do the menial tasks, such as passing towels and wafting the fly brush, but on this occasion she stood behind the Matriarch so that she could direct the campaign. She winked at Liu *lao-lao* to remind her, and the latter said to her: "Do not worry, *ku-niang*. I shall do everything as you told me."

After seating herself, Liu *lao-lao* was confronted with a pair of old-fashioned ivory chopsticks covered with gold. They were heavy and square and quite impossible to manage. "These implements," she said ruefully, looking at the chopsticks, "are heavier than our iron prongs. How can I handle them?" Then several maids came with covered trays with dishes of various kinds. After serving the Matriarch, Phoenix picked out a bowl of pigeon eggs and placed it in front of Liu *lao-lao*. When the Matriarch picked up her chopsicks and said ceremoniously, "Please!" Liu *lao-lao* stood up and said with great solemnity:

> Liu the old dame, the old dame,
> Her appetite's given her a well-earned fame,
> She'll eat a whole cow as easily as you say her name.

She then sat down as if she had performed a sacred rite. At first everyone was astounded and did not know what to make of it, but as soon as they realized the humor of the situation, they all burst out into a fit of violent laughter. Hsiang-Yun spilled the tea that was in her mouth and Black Jade choked with laughter, leaning upon the table, crying and groaning. Pao-Yu fell convulsively into the arms of the Matriarch, who was herself calling Pao-Yu all sorts of pet names hysterically. Madame Wang, knowing now that it must have been the work of Phoenix, put up admonishing fingers at her, but could not say a word. Some had to leave the table; others tried heroically to recover themselves and help those whose clothes were soiled by the general upsetting of cups and bowls.

Phoenix and Loyal Goose were the only ones who kept their gravity. They stood by Liu *lao-lao* and urged her to eat.

She surveyed the pigeon eggs and said: "Well, well, even your chickens are more elegant and delicate than ours. See what pretty tiny eggs they lay." At this everyone burst out laughing again.

"The rascal Phoenix must be up to mischief again," the Matriarch said. "Don't take her advice, Liu *lao-lao*."

Phoenix continued to urge Liu *lao-lao* to help herself. "Go ahead and eat," she said. "These eggs cost a tael of silver each and won't be good cold."

But the pigeon eggs were hard to manage, especially with the unwieldy chopsticks that Phoenix had given Liu *lao-lao* on purpose. After chasing the eggs in the bowl with her chopsticks for some time, she finally succeeded in capturing one. As she brought her mouth toward the egg and the egg toward her mouth and the two were about to meet, the egg slipped and fell to the floor, causing a fresh outburst of laughter. The Matriarch then ordered the maids to have another pair of chopsticks brought to Liu *lao-lao*. The new pair was made of ebony, covered on both ends with silver. Liu *lao-lao* remarked that after all their plain wooden chopsticks were the best for practical purposes.

"But the silver serves a purpose," Phoenix said, "for if the food is poisoned, the silver will show."

"Poison!" Liu *lao-lao* exclaimed. "If this is poison, then our food is all arsenic. Even if this is poison, I wouldn't regret it if I should die. It will be a pleasant death."

The Matriarch, whose pampered appetite was none too good, was delighted to see how Liu *lao-lao* enjoyed her food.

The old woman, it turned out, was not as unconscious of herself as the maids imagined, for when Loyal Goose apologized to her later for making fun of her, she said: "There is no need of apologizing. I am glad that I succeeded in furnishing *lao-tai-tai* some amusement."

3

In the afternoon, after visiting the various courts in the Takuanyuan, the Matriarch took Liu *lao-lao* to the convent in one corner of the Takuanyuan, where Exquisite Jade was living. The nun asked the Matriarch and her train to go into the inner hall, but the latter declined, saying that she had just used meat and did not want to desecrate the holy ground. Pao-Yu, who was acquainted with the fastidious habits of the nun, watched her closely to see how she entertained her guests. The nun presented tea to the Matriarch with her own hands in a *haitang*-pattern tray of carved lacquer on which was an exquisite Ch'eng *yao* cup (Ch'eng Hua period, 1665-88 A. D.).

The Matriarch asked her what water it was, after taking the cup, and the nun answered that it was rain water saved from the year before. The Matriarch drank half the cup and gave the rest to Liu *lao-lao*, saying, "You taste this tea, too." Liu *lao-lao* did so. When asked how she liked it, she said that it was too light. The rest were served with Kuan *yao* cups. The nun then tugged Black Jade and Precious Virtue by their dresses and took them into another room. Pao-Yu followed, curious to see what the nun had to say or offer to them. He found that Exquisite Jade was making some special tea for them. He entered and said: "So here is partiality! I insist on having my share."

The nun poured the tea into two cups of different patterns, of the rare Sung period (960-1225 A.D.), and gave them to Black Jade and Precious Virtue. To Pao-Yu she served the tea in her own cup of white jade.

"Is this also last year's rain water?" Black Jade asked, sipping tea.

"I did not think that you were so ignorant," the nun said, as if insulted. "Can't you tell the difference? This water is from the snow that I collected from the plum trees five years ago in the Yuan Mu Pan Hsiang Temple. It filled that blue jar there, and I have saved it all this time. It was buried under the earth and was opened only this last summer. This is the second time that I used it. How could you expect rain water to possess such a lightness and clarity?"

Black Jade also knew the nun's fastidiousness and perversity, so she said nothing. One of the attendants came in with the cups that the visitors in the outer hall had used, but the nun stopped her and told her not to put away the Ch'eng *yao* cup. Pao-Yu concluded that it must be because Liu *lao-lao* had used it. "What a pity to discard the cup!" he said to the nun. "Why not give it to that old dame? She will be able to realize a good sum from it."

"Give it to her yourself if you want to," the nun said; "fortunately I have never used the cup. If I had, I would break it before I would give it to her."

"Of course," Pao-Yu agreed. "Tomorrow I shall send someone to bring over a few buckets of river water for you to wash the floor where she stood."

"That will be excellent," the nun said. "But tell your men to leave the buckets outside the gate. I shall have the maids bring them in."

4

At supper there were games of impromptu verses and Liu *lao-lao* again amused everyone by her crude compositions. It was a full day and a strenuous one for the Matriarch, who was not used to visiting more than one or two places in the Takuanyuan at a time. As a result she was ill the next day; Chiao-chieh, the daughter of Phoenix, was also ill. Liu *lao-lao* offered some homely advices about how to avoid the evil spirits and how to keep out of the way of others. It was because of the wanton disregard of these elementary taboos, she said, that people got illness.

Liu *lao-lao* left with many presents in clothing, family remedies, foods, and money from the various members of the Yungkuofu. She was asked to come back whenever she wanted to. Since then she visited the Chias frequently, bringing with her simple gifts of the farm and taking with her valuable things in return.

Li Ju-chen

CHINESE who have read Gulliver's Travels—and there are many of them—marvel at the fact that the same idea was employed in a popular Ch'ing dynasty novel called Chin Hua Yuan (Romance of the Mirrored Flowers). The date of the Chinese work, around 1825, places it many years later than Swift and makes it the only known case of invention in which we cannot claim that the Chinese thought of the idea first. Nevertheless, there not being any evidence of Li's ever having studied the English language, I am going to exonerate him from any possible charge of plagiarism. The strange lands and peoples encountered in the Mirrored Flowers actually out-Gulliver Gulliver's Travels and include, besides the famous Land of Gentlemen and Land of Women, such utopias as Black-Teeth Country, Two-Faced Country, Small-Men Country, Busy-People Country, etc. No less an authority than Dr. Hu Shih has given us the interpretation that Li Ju-chen, a man, was one of China's early feminists, and his book a social satire dedicated to the advancement of women's rights.

The story, significantly, was set during the short reign of the famous Empress Wu (A.D. 690–705) of the T'ang dynasty. In Heaven, where most Chinese novels begin, the Goddess of Flowers had refused a request by the Moon Maiden to have her flowers blossom out of season. This winter day, however, after a contest of drinking and versification with her talented lady-in-waiting, Wan-erh, the Empress issued a capricious decree to have all the flowers in bloom the following morning. The incredible happened through negligence on the part of the Goddess of Flowers. Thereupon, she, along with the fairies of the ninety-nine varieties of flowers, was banished from Heaven to the "red dust" (mortal world). Twelve of the flowers were scattered in lonely countries overseas, and it was in their quest that the voyage was undertaken which led to so many strange lands.

A VOYAGE TO STRANGE LANDS

I

In which a bachelor of arts passed his examinations but did not get his degree, and the God of Dreams pointed out the way but did not reveal the goal.

The Goddess of Flowers was born into a well-to-do and cultured family in the province of Ling-nan. Her father was a *hsiu-ts'ai,* or bachelor of arts, by the name of Tang Ao. Her uncle, Tang Min, was also a *hsiu-ts'ai,* but he had already renounced his aspirations for a political career and settled down to a quiet and leisurely life as a tutor. Tang Ao, on the contrary, was politically ambitious, but a certain restlessness of disposition had thus far prevented his success in the higher examinations. He was apt to spend more than half of every year in travel, which tended to distract him from his studies.

When his wife gave birth to a daughter, a strange fragrance filled the room. It was neither musk nor sandalwood, but changed its character continually till in the course of three days a hundred varieties of perfume were detected. The neighbors marveled and called their street the Lane of the Hundred Fragrances.

Just before her labors, the mother dreamed of climbing a colored cliff of unusual steepness; hence she named her baby Hsiao-shan, or Little Mountain. Hsiao-shan was precocious, and showed at the age of four a great fondness for reading. She had a wonderful memory and remembered everything that she read. She studied under the tutelage of her father and uncle, and became in a few years an accomplished scholar. Besides her literary talents she evinced unusual qualities of courage and daring, and was often found playing with the lance and staff, much to the alarm and disapproval of her parents.

When Hsiao-shan was thirteen her father went again to attend the examinations at the capital. One evening following his departure Hsiao-shan and her uncle happened to talk about learning and examinations.

"But tell me, Uncle," asked Hsiao-shan suddenly, "when do the examinations for women occur? I suppose since there is a division for

Translated by Chi-Chen Wang and Ethel Andrews.

men there must be one for women also. I should like very much to prepare for them."

"I have heard of a women's division in medical books, but never in the examinations," Tang Min answered with a smile. "And although our ruler is a woman there have never been any female ministers in court. Are you thinking of passing the examinations yourself and trying to become an official? Like father, like daughter, I suppose."

"But don't you think we ought to have women serve the proprieties at court since our sovereign is a woman?" objected Hsiao-shan. "If there is no opportunity for women even in the examinations, what is the use of my studying? I would do better to take up sewing and embroidery."

So Hsiao-shan put away her books and took up needle and thread. But she soon found this womanly occupation not so nearly to her liking as reading and composing verses, and so returned to her books. Endowed with more than ordinary talents, she soon made her mind such a veritable storehouse of knowledge that her uncle often found himself at a considerable disadvantage when they composed verses and sang songs together. Before long Hsiao-shan had acquired the reputation of a genius in the district.

Meantime Tang Ao had passed the imperial examinations and won second place, which put him in line for official preferment. But unexpectedly a censor submitted a memorial to the throne accusing him of having taken blood vows with the rebels who had previously conspired against the Empress. Unfortunately, this happened to be true; although Tang Ao had not himself taken part in the rebellion. As a result of this memorial Tang Ao was deprived of the honors that he had recently won and nothing remained to him but his original degree of bachelor of arts.

Disillusioned and weary of life, Tang Ao had no heart to return home, and began to entertain ideas of abjuring the red dust. Finally he decided to seek distraction and oblivion in travel and, armed with funds which his brother had sent him for his expenses at the capital, set out alone on an extensive journey throughout the empire, "making use of carriages over land and of ships over water."

Six months later, as winter was giving way to early spring, Tang Ao found himself back in his native province of Ling-nan, not far from the house of Lin Chih-yang, his wife's brother. He was still in no mood to see any of his relatives, but he was at a loss where to go. He told his boatmen to fasten the boat along the river bank and stepped ashore with no particular purpose in mind. After walking aimlessly about for a time he found himself in front of an ancient temple bearing the inscription "God of Dreams."

"Life is indeed nothing but a vain dream," Tang Ao mused as he stood looking at the inscription. "But what am I to do now in the middle years of my life? Should I abjure the red dust and go in search of the Tao and immortality, or does my destiny lie in some other direction? Perhaps the God of this temple will enlighten me."

With these thoughts in mind he entered the temple, and after doing homage to the god sat down beside the shrine and prayed silently in his heart. Presently a young boy with flowing hair came to him, saying that his master desired his presence. Tang Ao rose and followed the boy to a hall in the rear compound, where he was met by a venerable man. "What is your esteemed name and in what do you wish to command me?" asked Tang Ao.

"My name is Meng [homophone for character meaning dream] and I live in this temple," replied the old man. "You have just now expressed a desire to renounce earthly ambitions and go in search of the Tao and immortality. May I ask what you consider your merits, and how you propose to accomplish your desire?"

"I have no merit to speak of," said Tang Ao. "But I have always supposed there was nothing more to this quest of the Tao than to forswear the red dust, to suppress the seven affections and the six passions, and to devote one's whole life to silent meditation."

"It is not so simple as you think," said the old man, laughing. "The methods you propose would merely serve to prolong your life a few years and prevent ill health. The immortal Kuo was right when he said that those who wish to enter the ranks of the immortals must possess the fundamental virtues of loyalty, filial piety, and benevolence. Without these virtues you would not succeed even if you sat in silent meditation a thousand years. I wonder if you realize that to become an 'earthly immortal' one must have accomplished three hundred good deeds, and thirteen hundred if one wishes to enter Heaven. For you who have accomplished none of these things to go in search of immortality is like a man climbing a tree to catch fish."

"I realize that I am ignorant and stupid by nature," said Tang Ao humbly, "but I hope you will enlighten me. I have spent my life struggling for political position and influence that I might restore the rightful heir to the throne and deliver the people from their trials. Alas, I have failed miserably. What is there left for me to do?"

"It is very much to be regretted that you have not fulfilled your purpose," said the old man more kindly. "But remember the saying: 'Who knows but that it might be a blessing for the Tartar to have lost his horse?'" * Then he paused a moment and said, looking at Tang Ao gravely, "Not many years ago, Heaven punished all the flowers for disobedience, sending them down to earth to suffer the trials of the wheel of incarnation. Twelve of these flowers are now scattered in lonely countries beyond the seas. If you should take compassion upon them and go forth yourself into strange waters, you might be able to return them to their original homes. For such an act of piety you might conceivably enter the Penglai Mountains, and find your name upon the golden roster of the immortals. In fact I will even go so far as to tell you that all this is decreed for you by fate, and will take place despite your apathy and pessimism."

As he finished speaking the old man vanished. Tang Ao rubbed his eyes and looked around. Could he have been dreaming? Beside him stood the statue of the god, whose features he now saw to correspond with those of the old man in his dream. What was it he said about the exile of the flowers? Tang Ao was confused. It was a pity he could not have inquired further as to the names of the flowers and where they were to be found. One thing, however, he remembered—the old man had commanded him to go forth into strange waters, and certainly nothing could be more to his taste. But how accomplish such a trip? Then he remembered that his brother-in-law, Lin Chih-yang, was a trader in foreign countries, and often undertook long voyages. Tang Ao decided to visit him immediately. Rising to his feet, he once more bowed to the idol whose help he had so successfully invoked, and returning to his boat he ordered his boatmen to set off in the direction of his brother-in-law's house.

As he walked toward Lin's house, he noticed carriers busy as ants loading bales of merchandise, and at once sensed preparations for a voyage. Entering the house he was ushered into the inner apartments and warmly welcomed by Lin and his wife. Wan-ju, his niece, also came out to meet him.

"My niece was not studying when I saw her two years ago," said Tang Ao as he greeted her. "Now her face reflects a scholarly air. Has she been neglecting her sewing and taken up books like my daughter?"

"Yes, she seems bent on studying," replied Lin. "I have bought her a number of books, but have been too busy to teach her myself."

* See page 32 for Liehtze's story of "The Old Man Who Lost a Horse."

"Do you know, Brother-in-law, that nowadays if a girl studies, she stands a better chance than a man?" said Tang Ao bitterly.

"What chance could she have?" asked Chih-yang incredulously.

"Haven't you heard about the lady Wan-erh and the honors that have been showered upon her by the Empress?" said Tang Ao, and then recounted the extraordinary events that the reader is already acquainted with. "As a result of these events," he concluded, "the Empress has instructed her ministers to seek out all the talented girls throughout the empire and report them to the throne. Families with daughters are therefore giving them every opportunity to study. The audiences have not been held as yet, but when they are no girl need fear obscurity if she has talent. I think it would be a pity not to encourage your daughter since she seems to have talent."

"I don't know how talented she is," said the girl's mother, "but I wish you would instruct her a little. Lately she has been copying the calligraphy of ancient masters; will you look over her work?"

Tang Ao asked to see the exercises, and after some apologies the girl produced a set of copies of the rubbings from Han stones. Not only were they perfect copies of the ancient calligraphy, but in some cases actually better than the originals. Each stroke showed strength and grace. Tang Ao was overcome with admiration.

"If given the opportunity she will make a great name for us all," he sighed.

"It was my fond hope," said the father, "that when you had passed the higher examinations and become established at the capital in some official position I might send her to you and have her study with your daughter. How unfortunate that the story of your fraternal vows came up just as you had achieved success!"

Tang Ao nodded assent. Having no wish to discuss his misfortunes, he hastily brought the conversation round to the subject nearest his heart. "You seem very busy, Brother-in-law. Are you by any chance going on another voyage?"

"Yes," said Lin. "Because of illness I have not been able to make a voyage for several years; but now that I am well I feel that I cannot stay at home any longer doing nothing. Seafaring is a hard life, but it is my profession. Besides, you know the saying: 'Even the resources of an entire mountain cannot support one who only sits and eats.'"

"Since my misfortunes came upon me," said Tang Ao, "I have been trying to distract my mind by traveling, but, having now visited all the famous mountains and waters of the empire, I long for some new sights to divert me and help me rid myself of the depression from which I have been suffering. It is providential for me that you are going on another voyage. Will you not take me with you? I have sufficient money, and will not be a burden to you."

"What is this talk of money when you and I are relatives!" exclaimed Lin, and turning to his wife: "Listen to what our brother is saying!"

"Our ship is large," said his wife. "There is plenty of room on board, and one person more or less makes no difference. As to food and drink, that is hardly worth mentioning. But we must warn you that seafaring is not the same as traveling by river. To anyone not used to the life it might be a miserable experience. You are a scholar accustomed to daily baths and tea served all day long. On board ship baths can only be taken sparingly, and even tea cannot be drunk to one's heart's content. We are inured to the life and do not mind it, but I fear you would miss your comforts and could never stand the hardships."

"Moreover," added Lin, "on the high seas all our movements are dictated by the wind. It is impossible to foretell whether the trip will take one year, or two or three. You had better think it over carefully, Brother-in-law."

"I fully appreciate all the difficulties," said Tang Ao. "I have heard you say before that fresh water has to be used sparingly on board; and as it happens I do not care greatly for tea, while a bath is something I take or not according to circumstances. Why should I be afraid of storms and high waves when I have sailed on the Yangtze and the great lakes? Furthermore, now that I have renounced all worldly ambitions, I shall attend no more examinations; and how long the voyage may take is a matter of indifference to me."

"Since you seem to have made up your mind, far be it from me to try to dissuade you," said Lin. "Have you told your wife?"

"She knows my general intentions," replied Tang Ao. "But if you are afraid of her blaming you, I will write to her again."

There was nothing for Lin but to consent. Tang Ao had his baggage brought up to the house, dismissed his boat, and sent a letter home telling of his plans. He tried to press a package of silver upon his brother-in-law, but on Lin's refusing to accept it, he gave it to Wan-ju for paper and brush money.

At Lin's suggestion he went out to purchase some merchandise which he might be able to sell in such countries as they intended to visit. Presently he returned with a great number of flowerpots and several loads of iron.

"Flowerpots are 'cold goods' that won't sell," objected Lin, "and what do you intend to do with the iron?"

"I thought there might be flower lovers in the lands we are going to visit," replied Tang Ao. "But if not, we can use them to pot any unusual flowers we come across. If we cannot sell the iron, it will at least make excellent ballast."

Lin shook his head doubtfully. "You may be right," he said. He knew the merchandise could not be returned.

Everything in readiness, the travelers set out for the ship, which lay anchored at the mouth of the river, transferring their effects down the stream by sampans. As soon as everyone was on board they set sail with a favorable breeze. It was the middle of the first moon and the weather was delightful. Within a few days the ship reached open ocean. Tang Ao paced the decks gazing in wonder upon the boundless expanse.

"I now appreciate Confucius' saying," he observed to his brother-in-law, "that it is indeed folly to talk about water to one who has seen the sea."

Actually, Tang Ao's life on board was very pleasant. He spent much of his time teaching his little niece, who proved a very apt pupil, while her mother saw to his comforts. No one considered the question of time, for seafaring persons are accustomed to being governed by the whims of the wind. Lin was at first unable to believe that Tang Ao had really renounced his career, and worried for a time about the examinations. Gradually, however, he came to realize that his brother-in-law meant what he said, and ceased to prod him. With a favorable wind behind them the travelers sailed on, hardly aware, as one day succeeded the next, of how fast they were going, nor of the miles they traveled.

II

In which it is shown how one can fly by eating the right kind of grass, or acquire literary taste by taking the proper kind of herb.

The only thing that preoccupied Tang Ao was the mission to search out the exiled flowers which the God of Dreams had revealed to him. It was with this in mind that he had bought the flowerpots, though he did not tell his brother-in-law about it. Now he asked Lin to let him go ashore whenever they came in sight of land. Lin, who had a great respect for his brother-in-law, was inclined to humor him and often accompanied him in his tramps.

One day the course of the ship was blocked by an imposing range of mountains rising out of the sea.

"How magnificent!" cried Tang Ao. "I have rarely seen anything finer!"

"This is the greatest mountain range to the east of the empire and is known as the East Notch," Lin informed him. "I am told too that the scenery is very beautiful. If you are so disposed we will cast anchor here."

The name excited Tang Ao's fancy, for he was well read in the ancient geographical works and readily recognized it. "The East Notch!" he exclaimed. "In that case we cannot be far from the Country of Gentlemen and the Land of the Cloud Riders."

"How does it happen that you know all this?" said Lin, greatly impressed by his brother-in-law's knowledge.

"I have read about them," admitted Tang Ao modestly. "It happens that for a long time I have been eager to visit some of these countries. I understand, for example, that the Country of Gentlemen is a true utopia, where consideration for the next man is more important than profit for oneself; and that in the Land of the Cloud Riders the inhabitants cannot walk as human beings do but ride upon clouds. All these variations in the warp of human nature have a great fascination for me."

"You will see many strange sights as we go along," said Lin. "There are the Indefatigables and the Winged People, not to mention the famous Country of Women, where the women run the government while the men attend to the household affairs. But I will not spoil your pleasure by anticipating." And he gave orders to the sailors to cast anchor as close to the shore of the island as possible.

The ship was moored at the foot of the high mountain. Steep cliffs rose abruptly on either hand. Lin and Tang Ao, taking the precaution of arming themselves with rifle and sword, left the ship and slowly ascended the tortuous path up the mountainside. At the top a magnificent panorama spread out at their feet. For a moment Tang Ao gazed in admiration at the view; then he remembered his mission and began to search for flowers.

"Next time we had better bring our pilot along," remarked Lin. "He can tell us all about these places."

"What is his name?" inquired Tang Ao, still hunting for flowers.

"His real name is Tou Chiu-kung, but the sailors have named him Know-not-much because he knows everything under the sun. He used to be a student, but he turned to trading after he failed in the examinations. He did not do very well, and has turned pilot for a living. He is more than eighty years old, but he is still very energetic and can walk like the wind. He and I are not only good friends, but distant relatives as well."

Just at this moment Tou Chiu-kung appeared on the side of the mountain. Lin called to him and introduced him to Tang Ao.

"I have seen you before on the ship, but we never had an opportunity for conversation," said Tang Ao politely. "Allow me to welcome a fellow student."

As the three men walked on down the path, suddenly a pebble fell from the sky and struck Tang Ao on the head. He looked up but failed to discover its origin. Lin pointed to the far mountainside where a flock of birds were busy picking up pebbles and flying away with them.

"What are those birds doing?" asked Lin of Chiu-kung.

"In ancient times," said Chiu-kung, "the youngest daughter of the Emperor Divine Farmer was drowned in the eastern sea. Her soul did not disintegrate but transformed itself into this bird, which has multiplied; and remembering the sea as its mortal enemy, it has been engaged ever since in picking up pebbles and dropping them into the ocean in a futile endeavor to fill it up."

"I always supposed the expression dropping pebbles to fill the ocean' was merely the result of an idle fancy," remarked Tang Ao. "I must say I admire the spirit of this little bird. They put to shame people who are afraid to undertake any difficult task and who come to the end of their lives without a single accomplishment."

"What in the world is that tree?" Lin suddenly exclaimed. They looked up and saw a colossal tree with bearded sheaths like rice, each over ten feet long.

"This is the famous wood rice," said Chiu-kung, examining it. "How I would like to take a grain home with me for a souvenir! What excitement it would create!" And he began searching about on the ground beneath the tree. The others joined him, and presently Lin came upon a huge grain of rice three inches wide and five long.

"When it is cooked this grain must measure not less than a foot!" he exclaimed.

"That's nothing!" said Chiu-kung. "I once ate a grain of rice which satisfied my hunger for a year!"

"How could you find a pot large enough to cook it in?" asked Lin incredulously. "As a matter of fact, I don't believe you!"

"I don't wonder, for I could hardly believe it myself," said Chiu-kung. "Later I heard that emissaries from the Land of Shadow used to bring this rice as tribute to the court of the Yellow Emperor."

"Now I understand," said Lin, "why archers say with great show of regret when they miss the target by more than a foot that they missed it by a grain of rice. It must have been a grain of this rice swelled by cooking!"

"You are too cruel," said Tang Ao, smiling. "It is bad enough to suggest that they missed the mark by a grain of such dimensions without suggesting that it was swelled by cooking as well. If the archers heard you, I am afraid you would get your face slapped."

Of a sudden they espied in the distance a little dwarf riding on a diminutive horse about seven inches long. To Lin, who was still hunting for rice, this spectacle afforded no interest, but Chiu-kung immediately dashed off in pursuit. Tang Ao had also seen it at the same moment and lost no time sprinting after him. The little dwarf rode off faster than ever. Chiu-kung, no longer as young or as strong as he used to be, stumbled just as he was about to catch up with his quarry. This delay gave the dwarf time to get away. Tang Ao continued his chase, and caught up with the little fellow half a *li* beyond. He seized it and ate it up without further ado, just as Lin and Chiu-kung came up.

"What is all this about a little dwarf on horseback?" said Lin. "Where is he now? I certainly saw you put something into your mouth. You could not possibly have swallowed both man and horse. What have you done with it?"

"It is known as the 'flesh fungus,'" explained Tang Ao. "I have recently read about it. It is said to confer long life to those who eat it! This dwarf seems to answer the description and I thought it could do no harm to try. And forgive me for not offering it to you, my elder brothers."

"Truly each drink and each mouthful is decreed by fate," said Chiu-kung with a sigh, for he had also read about the supernatural properties of this curiously shaped fungus. "Of us three, Brother Tang must have the favored destiny!"

"If this fungus confers immortality, then Brother-in-law must by now be an immortal and will never require food again," said Lin. "Which reminds me that I am extremely hungry after all this exertion. Haven't you got a leg or even an arm of the creature left?"

But the fungus was gone, and Lin was obliged to go hungry. The three wandered on. Suddenly Tang Ao leaned over and plucked a blade of grass by the roadside. Taking a seed from the leaf he put the blade into his mouth and swallowed it. Then placing the seed in his palm he blew upon it, and lo! it grew into a second blade of grass about a foot long. He blew three breaths and instantly it became a blade of grass three feet in length, whereupon he promptly swallowed it.

"There will be no grass left in the mountains if you go on like this!" exclaimed Lin. "May I inquire what this is you are eating now?"

"It is known as aerial grass," said Chiu-kung. "Whoever eats it will have the power of standing on air."

Lin was incredulous though he began hunting around for another blade of the remarkable grass.

"By all means then let me eat some," he said, "so that when I return home I can catch the thieves hiding on the roof of the house!"

"This plant is very rare," said Chiu-kung. "During all the years I have been roaming beyond the seas this is my first encounter with it."

"I refuse to believe that anyone can stand on air no matter what he eats!" protested Lin, abandoning his search. "Just let me see Brother-in-law try it!"

"I doubt if it has had time to work yet," said Tang Ao. "Still I don't mind trying."

He gave a little jump into the air, and to the astonishment of himself and everybody else shot up to the height of about fifty feet. There he stood still with perfect ease and seemed in no danger of falling.

Lin, greatly exhilarated by the spectacle, cried out, clapping his hands, "There is no doubt about it! Brother-in-law is actually treading on blue clouds!" Then looking up at Tang Ao, he continued, "Try walking a few steps! If you can walk on air it will certainly save shoes and stockings!"

Tang Ao signaled that he would do so. He raised his foot to take a step, but before he knew it he had fallen back to the ground.

Lin was excited beyond measure. "There is a jujube tree over yonder," he said looking around, "with great big jujubes on top! Why not jump up and get a few for us?"

They walked over to the tree and found that it was at least a hundred feet high. "I am afraid that it is beyond my reach," said Tang Ao. "I was only able to jump up about fifty feet, as you saw a while ago. I can't possibly reach to the top of that tree. It would be as absurd as the toad aspiring to the flesh of swans."

Lin considered the problem for a moment, then with sudden inspiration cried, "You might rest a moment after your first jump, and then jump again, as if climbing a ladder."

Tang Ao shook his head doubtfully. He did not care much for this suggestion, but finally he yielded to Lin's importunities and agreed to try. He jumped into the air, rested for a moment, and jumped again. Immediately he felt himself falling lightly like a kite whose line has been cut, and once more landed on the ground.

"Why didn't you jump up instead of falling down?" asked Lin somewhat peevishly.

"I did jump up," retorted Tang Ao, "but I fell in spite of myself."

Chiu-kung could not repress a smile. "You must have some support to take off from," he said. "If Brother Lin's idea were practicable you would eventually reach Heaven."

"I smell a clear fragrance," said Tang Ao suddenly.

"It seems to come from the direction of the wind," said Chiu-kung. "Let's follow it."

And the three went off, each his own way in search of this new mystery. Tang Ao passed through the forest, climbed the steep cliff, and looked about him. Presently he noticed growing out of the crevices of the rocks by the roadside a red plant about two feet high and in color an exquisite shade of vermillion. For some moments he studied it, then suddenly recalled to mind an item from the book known as *Guide to Foods for the Gods:* "The red plant resembles a small mulberry tree, with a stem like coral, with juice like blood. Gold and jade when mixed with it melt into a soft paste. Whoever eats of this paste will rise above the red dust and enter the ranks of the immortals."

Tang Ao had no gold with him but he took a jade ornament from his hat, and plucking the plant from the mountainside he rubbed them together. Instantly the jade melted into a red paste. He put it into his mouth, and in a moment became aware of a unique fragrance penetrating his brain and marrows. Also his vitality began to increase wonderfully. Very much pleased, he wondered if his bodily strength could have increased likewise. Espying by the roadside a broken stone monument which might weigh some five hundred pounds, he lifted it without effort. He tried jumping into the air with it, and to his aston- ishment was able to attain the same height as before.

Just then Chiu-kung and Lin came up and asked him how his mouth got so red. Tang Ao described what had happened. Chiu-kung imme- diately recognized the red plant of immortal qualities, and again con- gratulated Tang Ao on his good fortune. Lin looked skeptical, but as he was about to speak he saw that Tang Ao was in some distress. "What is the matter?" he inquired. "Are you melancholy at the pros- pect of becoming an immortal?"

"The red plant is giving me a pain in the stomach!" exclaimed Tang Ao; and as he finished speaking a convulsion seized him, forcing from him a succession of certain unpleasant sounds.

"How do you feel now?" asked Lin. "Evidently the red plant has driven out all your impurities. Do you feel somewhat empty inside?"

"It's perfectly extraordinary," said Tang Ao after a moment's reflec- tion, "but since eating that plant, not only has my vitality increased a thousandfold, but my ears are more acute and my eyes more pene- trating than ever before. At first, all the books I ever read came back to me, as well as everything I ever wrote, both poetry and prose; but since my stomach-ache I can only remember about a tenth of what I have written."

"There is nothing strange about that," said Lin bluntly. "The red plant must dislike the other nine-tenths so much that it has driven them out of you. The remaining tenth is evidently inoffensive and is still with you. I am curious to know whether your favorite brain child, the composition with which you won your last examination, has been spared by the red plant?" Then without waiting for Tang Ao to reply he continued, "Perhaps when you decided to publish your literary exercises, you will not have to consider what to include and what to leave out yourself; you can just omit the nine-tenths objected to by the red plant. The remaining one-tenth will probably make a very success- ful *Selected Works*! If you made the selection yourself you would un- doubtedly include too much, and publish as poetry much that the red plant would otherwise mercifully relieve you of. Really it is a great pity," said Lin, warming to his subject, "that this plant is not more abundant. For people trusting to their own judgment usually consider everything they write literature, while the red plant evidently feels quite differently. If we could only take it home and feed it to certain literary people I know, we could save endless labor involved in carving printing blocks! Why don't you eat some of it, Chiu-kung? Haven't you any manuscript you want to publish?"

"It is true that I have some manuscript," replied Chiu-kung, "but I am afraid that after the red plant had driven out the bad parts there would be nothing left. How about taking a little yourself?"

"I? Why should I bother with it?" said Lin. "I certainly don't intend to publish any cookbooks or wine classics!"

"What do you mean?"

"Merely that I am not a scholar like you and Brother-in-law. My soul is nothing more than a wine bottle and a rice bag; and if I published anything, it would have to be something in the culinary line. But I must say I have enjoyed myself very much today seeing all these unusual things. No wonder Brother-in-law is so addicted to wandering! It is an excellent form of diversion."

III

In which it is proven that a beast may be almost human, and that a man may be no different from a beast.

As the travelers were thus chatting and walking, they suddenly came upon an apelike animal on the mountainside. It was about four feet in height, but its tail was almost half again as long. It had long, fine hair and a long, black beard. It was crying piteously by the side of a dead animal.

"What a fine beard that creature has," remarked Lin. "I wonder what makes it cry so?"

"It must be mourning for the dead animal," said the well-informed Chiu-kung. "It is known as the *kuo-jan* and is remarkable for its loyalty to its kind. Its skin is much prized and hunters often use a dead *kuo-jan* as bait, for it would watch over the dead animal and mourn for it and would not run away even at the approach of danger. Some hunter must have left that dead body there, and will soon appear and bag his game without any difficulty."

Suddenly a strong gust of wind arose from the mountain and roared through the trees. It was an ominous and hair-raising wind and the three travelers withdrew in alarm into the deep recesses of the forest. As they did so, a huge striped tiger came down the mountain in the wake of the wind, and rushed up to the *kuo-jan*. The living ape trembled with fear but refused to abandon the dead one. The tiger roared like thunder, opened its mouth that looked like a basin of blood, and snatched up the dead ape. Just then an arrow shot out of nowhere and hit the tiger squarely in its face. The huge beast dropped its prey and leaped into the air with a tremendous roar of rage, and then fell dead on the ground.

Chiu-kung could not restrain himself from applauding vigorously.

"What miraculous archery!" Chiu-kung applauded. "And how instantaneously the blood has curdled!"

Asked what he meant by the latter remark, Chiu-kung explained that the arrow had been treated with poison derived from certain plants which caused the blood to coagulate instantly when it was introduced into the blood stream. "But it's the fine archery that turned the trick, for the skin of the tiger is thick and hard to pierce. The archer has apparently hit the tiger right in one of the eyes, which explains the remarkable speed with which the poison took effect. From the way the tiger fell, it must have died in mid-air, before it reached the ground. I should like to see who the archer is, and give him my congratulations."

Then a little tiger came from the direction whence the arrow had come. It stopped in front of the dead tiger and then, to the surprise of the travelers, it stood upon its hind legs and cast off its skin, whereupon it turned out to be a beautiful girl in a white archer's coat and fisherwoman's kerchief, carrying in her hand a carved bow. She drew out a sharp knife from her waist, cut open the tiger, and tore out its heart. Then she came down the mountainside in the direction of the travelers, with the tiger's heart in one hand and the tiger skin under her arm.

"So it is only a huntress after all!" cried Lin. "How brave she is for her age! Let me give her a scare!"

So saying, he raised his rifle, touched off the fuse, and fired an empty shot into the air. The startled girl looked up and saw the three men. "Do not shoot!" she cried, "for you'll see that I intend no harm as soon as you hear my story!"

She came up to the travelers and curtsied. "What are your names, honored elders?" she asked. "And where do you come from?"

Tang Ao introduced his friends, adding that his own family name was Tang, and that they all came from the Middle Kingdom.

"I know of a man by the name of Tang Ao in Ling-nan province," said the girl. "Could he by any chance be a relative of yours?"

"That is my own name," said Tang Ao in astonishment. "How do you happen to know the name?"

But the girl had fallen on her knees. "Forgive me, Uncle Tang!" she cried. "Your niece did not recognize you!"

"What is your name," asked Tang Ao, puzzled, "and why do you address me as uncle? Who else is there in your family? And what are you going to do with the heart of that tiger?"

It turned out that the girl was the daughter of Lo Pin-wang,* one of the leaders in the rebellion against the Empress, and a sworn brother of Tang Ao. After the failure of the rebellion he had disappeared, while his aged father had escaped the country, taking his granddaughter and her mother. Eventually they had come to these mountains and established themselves in a deserted ancient temple where they were able to live in seclusion and safety. But the year before their house had been wrecked by a stampede of wild animals caused by a tiger, and her mother was mortally wounded in the wreckage. "That is why I vowed to exterminate the tigers in these mountains," the girl concluded. "I am taking the tiger's heart as an offering to my mother's spirit."

Tang Ao was deeply moved by this story and asked the girl to take him to her grandfather. They soon arrived at the temple, where they found the old grandfather, Lo Hung, whom Tang Ao had not seen for years. He sat down with the old man and talked about the past, while the girl retired to offer the heart of the tiger upon the altar of her mother.

The old man said that since he was now over eighty years of age he knew that he would never live to see his own country again, for he was still a fugitive from the wrath of the Empress and dared not venture to return. His great sorrow was to see his granddaughter expatriated so young, and burdened with an old man. Finally he asked Tang Ao if he would consider adopting the girl as his own daughter and taking her back to China with him. Tang Ao consented readily, and promised to do everything he could for the girl. Red Lotus herself, however, refused to leave her grandfather. "My grandfather is advanced in years," she said, "and needs my constant attendance. Besides, I have taken a vow to kill all the tigers in this region to avenge my mother's death. There are still two tigers left and I cannot go away and break my vow."

In vain did her grandfather remonstrate with her. Finally Chiu-kung

* Early T'ang poet and best remembered for his manifesto against the Empress, considered a flawless masterpiece of prose.

suggested that they might leave her with her grandfather for the present and stop for her on their return voyage.

"What if I should not return?" said Tang Ao significantly.

"What are you saying, Brother-in-law?" cried Lin in alarm. "We all set out together and we shall return together. What do you mean by saying, 'What if I should not return?'"

"Do not be alarmed, Brother-in-law," Tang Ao assured him. "There is no particular significance in what I said. I was merely considering all the possibilities." Then turning to Red Lotus he said, "I appreciate your determination to fulfill your filial duties and I am sure that Heaven will reward you for it. We shall most certainly come for you on our return voyage. Perhaps by that time a general amnesty will make it possible for you to return to our homeland with your grandfather."

"Would you be passing through the country of Hsien Wu?" asked Red Lotus. "Cousin Enduring Fragrance, Uncle Hsueh's daughter, is living there now according to a letter she sent me recently by a silk merchant. We are sworn sisters and have taken a vow that we would never go back to our homeland unless we could go back together. Would you take a letter to her?"

"Hsien Wu is one of the countries that we shall have to visit," said Chiu-kung. "It would be no trouble at all since Brother Lin has business to attend to there."

Presently Red Lotus finished her letter and the travelers took their leave.

"Is it true, Chiu-kung," asked Lin, apropos of Red Lotus and tigers, which formed the chief topics of their conversation as they walked back to the ship, "is it true that tigers and leopards only eat those who have done evil deeds in their former lives?"

"That is only true in a manner of speaking," answered Chiu-kung. "The fact is, tigers and leopards never attack any human beings at all. They only eat other beasts, and if they occasionally attack men it is only because those men are in reality beasts in human forms. To the animals the difference between human beings and other creatures lies in the halo that envelops the heads of human beings. The tiger is as afraid of this light as it is of fire, and it gives people with this light a wide berth. But men of evil lose their light and as a consequence they appear no different from other beasts to the tigers and leopards. The size of the halos varies, too, according to the degree of one's virtues. A man who has done only good deeds has a halo tens of feet in height.

From the presence of such a man not only do tigers and leopards flee in haste, but even ghosts and demons keep as far away as they can. And did you not notice that the tiger did not attack the *kuo-jan* that was mourning for its comrade? That was because in its loyalty to its kin it was almost human."

"If that is true," Lin said, "how do you explain the fact that good men are known to have been killed by tigers? I know of a man who was noted for his devoutness. He fasted regularly and chanted the name of Buddha. But one day he was devoured by a tiger while on a pilgrimage to one of the sacred mountains!"

"Then the man must have committed sins which outweighed his conventional virtues. There are degrees of good and evil and the sum total of one is carefully weighed by Heaven against the other. The man you mention may have committed sins so great that in the face of them his petty observances of the Buddhist rules may be no more than a cup of water against a wagon of fuel on fire."

"The man was not very obedient to his parents," Lin admitted, "and he is known to have committed adulteries."

"That's exactly it," said Chiu-kung. " 'Of all evils, adultery heads the list; of all virtues, filial piety comes first.' How could a man like that expect to atone for his great sins with petty fasting and lip service to the Buddha?"

As they thus chatted, they soon reached their ship. Lin showed the large grain of rice to his wife and Wan-ju and they both marveled at it. Then they set sail and in due time reached the shores of the Country of Gentlemen.

IV

In which customers try to buy as dearly as they can and shopkeepers attempt to sell as cheaply as possible.

Tang Ao had heard a great deal about this land where the inhabitants universally practiced proper conduct and spurned gain and was eager to observe its customs and manners. And so while Lin went about attending to his business interests, he and Chiu-kung set out for the capital of the country. As they approached the city the first thing that caught their eye was the inscription over the gate: "Virtue Man's Only Treasure." In the city itself they were impressed by the air of prosperity and peace that reigned. The dress of the inhabitants was the same as in their homeland and the visitors soon found that they also spoke the same tongue.

After Tang Ao found this out, he stopped an old man and asked him how it was that they were able to overcome the passion for personal gain so universal elsewhere. The old man, however, was unable to enlighten him; it appeared that he did not know what the word "gain" meant. Nor was he aware that his country was known to neighboring countries as the Country of Gentlemen.

"They do not appear to be conscious of their own virtues and reputation," said Chiu-kung, "but there is no question that the reputation is well earned. Did you not notice how the plowman kept well within his own land and how everyone stepped off the road to yield the right of way to the other fellow? And notice how courteous they are in manner and speech, whether rich or poor, noble in rank or humble in station."

Presently they came to a thoroughfare where they noticed a porter buying goods at a stall. He was holding his purchase in one hand while he waved the other in indignant protest.

"Elder Brother," he was objecting to the storekeeper, "you ask too little for this high-grade merchandise. It makes me very uncomfortable, for I cannot take advantage of you like this. Pray raise your price, otherwise it will look as if you had no intention of doing business with me!"

"Extraordinary!" whispered Tang Ao, nudging his companion. "Did you hear him asking the storekeeper to raise the price?"

"The fact is," they heard the storekeeper say, "I have already asked you such a big price that I am frankly ashamed; and I did not expect you to treat me this way. Besides, my unworthy goods are not sold on the one price basis. I have already allowed for a large profit, yet here you are trying to raise the price on me! If Elder Brother feels he must injure himself thus, I must request him to take his patronage elsewhere."

"These arguments certainly sound refreshing coming from the seller," whispered Tang Ao.

"Not only do you try to pass off high-grade goods on me for an insignificant price," the porter protested, "but now you accuse me of trying to injure myself! Do you call that being fair? You cannot expect this younger brother to be so easily deceived; for, after all, each of us possesses a mental abacus with which to figure things out for himself."

Thus they argued for several minutes. The porter finally lost patience. He paid the low price insisted upon by the storekeeper, but attempted to leave with only half the goods. The storekeeper became indignant at this and would not let him go. No one knows what the end might have been, had not two old men passing by been called in as arbiters. Having heard both sides of the story, they decided that the porter should pay the low price and take 80 per cent of the goods.

Tang Ao and Chiu-kung nodded their heads in approbation; and as they moved on down the street, they could see that everywhere it was the same—customers trying to increase their prices, storekeepers beating them down. Suddenly they saw a farmer emerge from a store with a package under his arm. The storekeeper inside weighed the silver with which he had been paid, and after examining its quality ran after the farmer.

"Please wait a minute!" he called out. "There has been some mistake! We are accustomed here to second-grade silver, and since Your Honor has just paid in first-grade silver, you are entitled to receive an allowance. Such small matters may be of no importance to a wealthy person like yourself, but mean a good deal to this younger brother who does not care to accept charity."

"Why wrangle over such a trivial matter?" said the farmer. "If there is anything over, credit it to my account."

"That is impossible!" cried the storekeeper in alarm. "Only last year a customer left some surplus here and has never been back for it! Thus, you see, I have contracted a debt for the next life. If he does not return, I shall have to spend all my time in the next life trying to repay him, perhaps by being transformed into a donkey or a horse to slave for him! And now you propose that I take the chance of contracting another debt for still another reincarnation. No! No! Much better settle the matter now!"

And the insistent storekeeper finally induced the farmer to take some more merchandise. As he returned to his stall, still grumbling over his surplus and the unfair deal, suddenly a beggar appeared.

"Aha!" exclaimed the storekeeper. "This beggar is undoubtedly the reincarnation of some person who took advantage of someone else in a former life." And he promptly weighed out all the surplus silver and gave it to the beggar.

Tang was deeply impressed with all these proceedings, and declared to his companion that the country most certainly deserved its name.

"We are certainly lucky to have a chance to visit this wonderful country," he said to his companion. "Let us walk on and discover for ourselves what else there is to see." And even as he was talking he saw coming toward them two venerable gentlemen with complexions like those of children, and hair white as the plumage of the crane. Their faces reflected a nature as gentle as the spring breeze, and their carriage and demeanor showed culture and refinement. Tang Ao and Chiu-kung, realizing that these gentlemen were not of the common herd, stepped reverently aside; whereupon all four raised their hands in salutation and asked one another's names. The two old gentlemen were found to be brothers with the family name of Wu and the given names of Chih-ho and Chih-hsiang.

"So the two elders are descendants of the sage Tai Po," said Tang Ao. "Pray forgive my lack of reverence."

"May we be enlightened as to the land whence you have come and the mission that has brought you here?" inquired the first brother. Tang Ao explained their origin and family connections.

"So you come from the Celestial Empire!" exclaimed the second brother with a bow. "It is indeed rare good fortune to meet you, for as scholars you two worthies represent the aristocracy of the Celestial Empire, the land of the sages. Unfortunately, this younger brother was not notified of your coming, and has neglected to welcome you properly; but he begs you to forgive him in your ocean-like generosity."

"Since you two gentlemen have come from the faraway Celestial Empire," said the first brother, "we make bold to claim the privilege of acting as hosts and of offering a cup of tea. Our poverty-stricken house is only a few feet away, and if the worthies will deign to honor us, we will beg them to bend their steps thither."

Tang Ao and Chiu-kung were delighted by the courtesy of the brothers and followed them to their house. The grounds were surrounded by a thick hedge, overgrown with green vines, instead of the usual wall; the entrance was through a gate of thatched wood. Just inside there was a pond in which lotus and water chestnuts grew in abundance, while beyond stood an open, airy hall shaded by a bamboo grove. In the center of the hall was a tablet with this inscription signed by the King himself: "The Country Retreat at the Wei River," in allusion to a legendary minister who lived in obscurity on the shores of the Wei until he was discovered by King Wen.

"They must be people of some consequence," said Chiu-kung to himself. "Else they would not have a laudatory tablet presented to them by the King."

"This younger brother and his friend," Tang Ao said, addressing his hosts, "have just had the good fortune to observe the scenery and customs of your honored land, and are convinced that its fame as the Country of Gentlemen has not been exaggerated."

"Whatever knowledge and civilization belongs to this remote corner of the ocean is due to the influence of the Celestial Empire," replied the first brother with a bow. "Your culture, your music, your ethics have long been the wonder of us barbarians. How dare we call ourselves gentlemen? We can only hope that our reflection of your great country has not been too much of a travesty. At the same time," he added, "there are certain usages in your country which through our stupidity we fail to appreciate. Since we are fortunate enough to have you two gentlemen here today, we hope you will deign to enlighten us."

"Does your interest lie in affairs of state or in the social usages of our country?" asked Tang Ao.

"A sage now occupies the throne of the Celestial Empire," said Chih-ho, "and the acts and policies of the government are perfect and beyond criticism in every way. We who live in the ignorance of these remote shores not only dare not presume to offer any criticism, but also can find nothing to criticize. It is about your customs and manners that we want to seek enlightenment."

"Pray proceed," Tang Ao said, "and we shall tell you what we know."

Thereupon the brothers launched upon a series of observations about the Middle Kingdom which filled the travelers with a sense of shame and humiliation.

V

In which it is shown that forms of barbarism may prevail in a civilized state and that superstitions can plague an enlightened people.

"I have been told," said Chih-ho, "that in the matter of burial, people in your honored country do not follow the axiom that peace for the dead lies in an early interment. Instead, actual burial is often delayed for years and sometimes even for generations because the descendants cannot find an auspicious plot of ground according to the ideas of the geomancers. As a result, the temples are filled with coffins waiting for burial and the fields dotted with ghastly brick structures that serve as temporary tombs. Moreover, permanent burial sometimes never takes place because family fortunes decline to a point where it becomes impossible to have a proper burial. Is this the way to bring peace to the dead?

"Furthermore, the geomancers, too, have their parents. If they know of a good plot of ground, why should they not bury their own parents there? If indeed there is anything to geomancy, why is it that so few geomancers have prospered? It seems to this uninformed person that it is not only vain to seek good luck for oneself through the remains of one's parents but also very unfilial. I am inclined to believe that blessings and calamities depend not upon where the remains of one's parents are buried but upon one's own deeds. The *Book of Changes* says, 'Those who have accumulated good deeds will have a surplus of blessings.' In the matter of burial, therefore, the only considerations are that it should take place as soon as possible and that the site should be high and safe from possible floods. This is my uninformed opinion and I should like to be enlightened."

Before Tang and Chiu-kung could answer, the other brother said: "I have been told that in your country you celebrate the Three Dawns, the Full Month, the Hundred Days, and the Complete Year of your children. On these occasions you slaughter many pigs and sheep and chickens and ducks for the feasts. Now it is said that the virtue of Heaven is the love of life; if by causing one child to be born scores of other lives are sacrificed, why should Heaven bless people with children? Parents burn incense at one temple and make promises at another to insure the health and long life of their children; yet at the same time they kill many lives in their name. It is a well-known fact that the children of poor families have a better chance of reaching maturity than children of rich families. Though the fact that the poor cannot afford the feasts may not be the only reason, one may well learn a lesson from it.

"Another custom of your country that I have heard about is that of relinquishing one's children to the Buddhist temples in the belief that that will bring them health and long life. This practice may be harmless for those who are immediately concerned, but it is detrimental to the regular course of the interplay between the male and female principles and indirectly helps to bring about adultery and illicit relations between the sexes. It is my opinion that one Buddhist monk or one Taoist priest less will make one chaste woman more. Of course, not all monks and priests are guilty of adultery, but it cannot be denied that those who have such tendencies are in a particularly advantageous position to tempt innocent and ignorant women."

"I have been told about a peculiar institution in your land known as lawsuits," Wu Chih-ho broke in before the travelers could say a word. "I have come across the word in books, but as the thing is unknown in our country I have never been able fully to comprehend its meaning. Upon careful inquiry I found that lawsuits in your noble country arise from many diverse causes. Sometimes they arise from petty quarrels, sometimes from disputes in money matters, but at the bottom of all is the lack of patience and tolerance. Once the matter is brought to the courts, it becomes a procession of charges and counter-charges, of deliberate lies and unmitigated falsehoods; the litigants become like people possessed, each trying to do the other the greatest possible injury. More often than not both sides come out with less money than they started with, to say nothing of the humiliation and the bodily punishment that they suffer in court.

"But even more inexplicable are those persons who instigate the foolish and ignorant to sue in order to profit thereby, people who specialize in making something out of nothing, people who clutch at the thin air and pounce upon gray shadows. If they are discovered, they always have time to flee justice while their unfortunate clients are left to suffer for their ignorance. Such people are, of course, monstrous, but it seems to me that these creatures could not flourish if it were not for the vindictiveness and avarice of the victims themselves.

"Another custom in your country that has puzzled me is the killing of plowing oxen. I had thought at first that it was exclusively for the purpose of sacrifice, but I found upon careful investigation that it is done solely for profit and that the meat is eagerly bought by gluttons with perverted tastes. These people seem to forget that man cannot live without the five grains and the grains cannot be cultivated without the plowing oxen. Instead of trying to repay these faithful beasts, they feast upon them! What could be more unkind? One may argue that one did not kill the oxen oneself, but if no one ate the meat no one would kill the unfortunate animals. At first glance, the butchers appear to be chief sinners, but after all they are but ignorant wretches and cannot be expected to know better. Moreover, who knows but that the unfortunate beasts may be reincarnations of butchers in their former lives? So it is the opinion of this ignorant person that the purchasers of oxen meat should be regarded as the chief culprits.

"I understand also that it is the custom of your land to hold extravagant banquets at which innumerable dishes are served. The guests sit down first to more than ten dishes of fruits and cold tidbits. After wine has gone around two or three times, small dishes known in the south as 'little eats' and in the north as 'hot fries' are served, with a minimum of four to eight varieties and a maximum of over twenty. The main dishes do not begin until after these things, when rare and rich dishes are served in huge plates and oversize bowls, from eight or nine courses to well over ten. The truth is that the guests are satiated before they come to the end of the 'little eats' and the rest is nothing but an empty gesture very much like offerings to the spirits.

"But what astounds one most about these extravagant feasts is that a dish is not esteemed for its flavor and taste but for its cost. Because of this, bird's nest is most highly prized because it is the most expensive dish there is, costing as it does ten times more than any other dish. They seem to overlook completely the fact that it looks very much like the homely transparent vermicelli and has no more taste than chewing wax. Actually the guests might as well have been served with a bowl of vermicelli in chicken broth, but to the host he could not have been any more extravagant if he had served chips of the finest silver. A host should, of course, do the best to give pleasure to his guests and provide one or two dishes out of the ordinary. But then taste should be the only consideration. For the host to spend money so that the guests may chew wax—that is something beyond our comprehension.

"Bird's nest is bountiful in our land and is extremely cheap. It is used by the poor for food and costs only one-tenth the price of grains. But because it is tasteless, even the poor resort to it only in extreme necessity such as during periods of famine. Mencius has said: 'Fish is something I like, bear's paw is another.' The former is esteemed because of its fresh taste, the latter because of its rich texture. What could be the reasons that prompt your people to esteem the bird's nest? Because it is tasteless? Then why not chew wax? Because it acts as a tonic? But a banquet is no place to serve such things. Because it is rare and helps the hosts to exhibit his wealth? Then why not put an ingot of silver in each dish? If the custom is carried to its extreme the time may come when rich people will serve fried pearls or stewed jade in order to distinguish themselves."

"Another thing that I have heard about your country," Wu Chih-hsiang said, "is the prevalence of priestesses and nuns, women fortune-tellers and spiritual mediums. These creatures are allowed to enter the inner chambers to take advantage of the ignorance of women. Sometimes they do no worse than make away with money or clothing, but more often they set themselves to stir the passion of innocent women by lewd stories of wine. As soon as they perceive that they have a receptive victim they begin to describe in glowing terms the wealth of So-and-so or the handsome features of Such-and-such. Finally they would suggest secret meetings in the temples and monasteries under the guise of pilgrimages. Once a woman falls into their traps she cannot escape though she be pure as jade or cold as ice.

"In extreme cases men come into the household disguised as women to deceive the innocent girls and destroy their chastity. Such things are bad enough in themselves; imagine the shame and degradation should the misdeeds be known! It is precisely because of this fear of exposure that the victims dare not turn against their temptresses. The ignorance of women is chiefly to blame for this state of things, but the heads of families are also responsible for their lack of vigilance in preventing such evil associations. Men have only themselves to blame if they find themselves wearing the green cap of the cuckold. The ancients were ever careful in guarding the virtue of their women; they would never have allowed such vile creatures to enter their gates."

"I have heard that your country has a practice known as foot-binding," Wu Chih-ho said. "I understand that it is most painful at the beginning and causes a girl to cry day and night. Sometimes the skin is broken and the flesh exposed. During the worst period the victim can neither sleep nor eat because of the excruciating pain. I used to think that it was a form of cruel punishment inflicted on disobedient daughters, but later I found that it was all done in the name of beauty. Now does one shave off pieces of the nose to make it smaller or level off a high forehead? Why should crippled feet be regarded as beautiful? Did Hsi Shih and Wang Ch'iang, two of the most beautiful women of their time, cut off half their feet to make themselves beautiful? To my mind to cater to this perverted taste is no different from trafficking in obscene articles.

"Also I should like to mention the custom of your country in arranging marriages according to the pronouncements of the fortunetellers. I admit that in certain adverse circumstances it does no harm for a man to consult a fortuneteller. But marriage concerns the whole lifetime of a man and a woman and should not be trusted to luck. If such considerations as good character, parity of age and features, suitable family background, if such considerations have been met satisfactorily, what is the use of looking further? Is it not said in the *Chronicles of Tso* that one consults the oracle only in case of doubt? The most absurd thing is the belief in the south that it is unlucky to take a wife born under the sign of the sheep and the similar belief in the north that it is unlucky to have a woman born under the sign of the tiger. If a woman is useless if born under the sign of the sheep or is bound to be a shrew if born under the sign of the tiger, then what must women be like if they happen to be born under the signs of the rat and the viper? Can anyone claim that the wives of henpecked men are all born under the sign of the tiger or that all who are born under the sign of the ox are doomed to toil and hardship?"

There was no telling how much longer the inquisition would have gone on had not a servant come in at this point and announced that the King was coming to make a call in person to discuss certain matters of state with the two brothers. Chiu-kung thought to himself: "So they too resort to this harmless deception in order to get rid of guests who have stayed out their welcome. But they seem to go even further than we do by announcing that they have to receive the King!"

They rose to take their leave and the Wu brothers expressed their regret and begged to be allowed to pay a return call at their ship as soon as the King had gone. On the street Tang Ao and Chiu-kung noticed street cleaners busily engaged in sweeping off the dust and sprinkling water over the streets as if in preparation for the approach of some royal personage. Chiu-kung realized then that he had misjudged their hosts in thinking that they had secretly motioned to the servant to announce the King.

They returned to the ship and were presently joined by Lin, who had not had a very profitable day in the city because many ships had called during recent years. As they were about to weigh anchor, messengers arrived from the Wu brothers bearing gifts, including ten baskets of squash and ten baskets of bird's nest for the sailors. The brothers themselves arrived shortly afterward and brought greetings from the King himself. After they had exchanged courtesies, the brothers took their leave.

The sailors were overjoyed for this chance to taste the delicacy that they had heard so much about in their native land. They cooked it with the squash and sat down eagerly to the feast. Their faces fell on tasting the food. They insisted that it was nothing but common transparent vermicelli and refused to eat it and picked out only the squash.

Being a better informed man than the sailors, Lin bought the remaining baskets from the sailors at a low price. "What a piece of good luck," he said to his friends. "No wonder the magpies have been chattering around the ship all day!"

Wu Ching-tze

BECAUSE *for many centuries the only way a man could become a high official in China was through a series of competitive examinations, people fell into the habit of studying not for the sake of knowledge but solely to pass the examinations and secure a government appointment. This made for poor scholars and even worse men; it also resulted in innumerable heartbreaks and an occasional joke. The practice was particularly abused during the last two imperial dynasties, Ming and Ch'ing. The requirements for the literary degrees of* hsiutsai *(the Chinese B. A.),* chu-jen *(M. A.),* chin-shih *and* han-lin *(Ph. D.) became as rigid as their modern Western counterparts and held their aspirants under an influence ten times more pernicious. Wu Ching-tze, who scorned the examinations himself, satirized the products of this system in his famous novel from which the following excerpts are taken. His characterization can be a great deal less sympathetic than the ones chosen here. There is the story of Scholar Yen, a miser, who unconscionably prolonged his deathbed scene by holding up two fingers to indicate a wish and refusing to die until he was satisfied. The gathered members of the family tried to guess his wish but all failed. Finally, his concubine, who had been recently made wife upon his first wife's death, said, "I know, Master, your wish. You disapprove of the two wicks in the lamp where one would do." The dying man nodded and, upon the extra wick being removed, gave up his spirit.*

TWO SCHOLARS WHO PASSED THE EXAMINATIONS

How the Schoolmaster Chou Chin Obtained and Lost His Situation

I

In the province of Shantung, prefecture of Yenchou, district of Wenshang, there was a village called Hsueh-chia-chi, with a hundred some families, all engaged in agricultural pursuits. At the entrance to the village stood a temple to Kuanyin, which was attended by only one monk, and which constituted the meeting place of the villagers when they had community affairs to discuss.

From *Ju Lin Wai Shih:* "An Unofficial History of the Literati," translated by Chi-Chen Wang.

Toward the end of the reign of Ch'eng Hua, when peace and prosperity reigned in the land, such a meeting took place on the eighth day of the first month of the new year, the occasion being the lantern festival. About breakfast time Shen Hsiang-fu, in charge of the meeting, arrived at the temple with seven or eight men. The monk greeted them, but Shen immediately began berating the monk. "Now, *hoshang*, during the New Year season, at least, you might be a little more generous with incense and candle at the altar of the Buddha and show something for the offerings that pour in from the ten directions! Look at the glass lamp, my friends! It is only half full!" Then pointing to an old man more neatly dressed than the rest, he continued, "I need not mention anyone else. Master Hsun here sent you fifty pounds of oil New Year's Eve. Instead of offering it to the Buddha you have put it away to grease your frying pan!"

The monk listened to this tirade good-humoredly. Then he took out a pewter pot and filled it with tea leaves and water and put it on the fire to boil. Master Hsun was the first to broach the subject of the lantern subscriptions, but Shen said that they should wait for his brother-in-law. Just then a man entered, bleary-eyed, face dark as an iron pan, a few yellow hairs on his chin, a bailiff's cap tilted on his head, wearing a black cotton garment as greasy as an oil keg, and holding a riding whip in his hand. He greeted the people briefly and placed his buttocks on the seat of honor. This man's name was Hsia, the high bailiff appointed from Hsueh-chia-chi the year before.

"*Hoshang*," he commanded. "Take my donkey to the manger in the back yard, unsaddle it, and feed it well. After this I have to go to a New Year's banquet at Master Huang's opposite the Magistrate's yamen." After giving these directions he raised one of his legs and began pounding his side with his fist, saying, "I am no longer happy and carefree as you people who work the land. On the occasion of this great festival, who of the various officers of the Magistrate does not send me greetings? And pray how am I to avoid paying them New Year's calls? Day after day I have to mount that donkey and go in and out of the city until my head spins. And then that son of a turtle had to stumble and bruise me in the side."

"I suppose that was why you were not able to come to my meager fare on the third?" Shen asked.

"Quite so," answered Hsia. "I have not had a moment's leisure since New Year's Day. I could not have eaten of all the dinners though I had two mouths. Take Master Huang, for instance, who has invited me today. He stands high with His Honor the Magistrate. He has shown me a great honor by asking me and it is absolutely necessary that I should go if I did not want to incur his displeasure."

"I thought Master Huang has been away on a mission for His Honor since before the New Year," Shen said. "Who is going to act as host since he has neither brother nor son?"

"Ah, of course you wouldn't know," Hsia explained, unabashed. "Today's banquet is given by Master Li of the constabulary. Since his house is not large enough, he has arranged for the use of Master Huang's house."

Finally the conversation turned upon the subject of the lantern festival. "I feel disinclined to bother with such things any more," Hsia said. "Formerly I used to take charge year after year and I don't know how much money I lost making up for the defaults of those who put down their names on the donors' list but who later found excuses for not paying. Moreover, I shall be unable to see all the lantern processions that everyone in His Honor's service is giving, let alone your little affair. However, I shall contribute something since you have asked me to come, whoever may take charge. Master Hsun here may give a little more than the rest as he has more land and a larger store of grain. The others may contribute according to their means. You will have no difficulty."

No one presumed to disagree with the high bailiff. The Hsuns were assessed half the expenses while the other families made up the remainder, in all about three taels of silver. The monk brought out some cakes, jujubes, melon seeds, dried bean curd, chestnuts, and candies and served them on two tables, pouring the tea first to Hsia. Then Shen said, "My son is growing up and there are others who have children of age for school. We must get a tutor and start a school here in the temple." This proposal was seconded and it was agreed that they should try to get a good tutor from the city.

"I have someone for you," Hsia said. "He was formerly tutor at the house of Ku, the magistrate's secretary general. His name is Chou Chin, and he is about sixty years old. He headed one of the examinations of the previous magistrate but never obtained his degree. He taught three years at Squire Ku's and last year the young squire obtained his degree, at the same time as Licentiate Mei of our village. At the celebration the squire himself offered the tutor three cups of wine and escorted him to the seat of honor. When he was asked to choose the play, he named the one in which Liang Hao became Optimus at the age of eighty. The squire was displeased, but as the play progressed it turned out that Liang Hao's pupil became Optimus at the age of eighteen, at which the squire's displeasure vanished. I can get this Mr. Chou for you if you like."

This was agreed upon and on his return to the city Hsia engaged Chou Chin at twelve taels a year, with a daily allowance of two tael cents for boarding with the monk. The tutor was to go down to the country after the lantern festival, school to begin on the twentieth.

2

On the sixteenth the villagers sent their shares of the provisions to Shen's house, where a welcome dinner was prepared for the new tutor, with the Licentiate Mei as the assisting guest. At the barking of the dog outside, Shen went out and ushered the tutor in. He wore an old felt cap, a homespun silk robe much worn at the elbows and seat, and a pair of old shoes. He was dark of complexion and had a gray beard. The Licentiate Mei slowly rose to his feet upon Chou Chin's entrance and was introduced to him. When the latter heard that Mei was a licentiate, he would not consent to take the place of honor. "In age Scholar Chou is the senior," the villagers urged. "He need not stand on ceremonies."

"But you do not know," Mei said to them, "that according to our rules an old friend never compares age with a young friend. But it is a different matter today, so let Elder Brother Chou take the seat of honor."

For during the Ming dynasty it was the custom to call the students who had obtained their degrees "friends" and to call those who had not "young friends." Thus a licentiate was called an "old friend" though he might be only in his teens, while a student remained a "young friend" so long as he did not pass his examination, though he might be eighty. It is like a girl marrying: when she is just married, she is known as the "new mistress," but later simply as the "mistress"; but if she is married off as a concubine, she remains the "new mistress" all her life.

But to return to our story. At Mei's insistence, Chou Chin took the seat of honor. The villagers had plain tea, but two jujubes * were put

---

* Jujube, *tsao*, is a homophone for *tsao* meaning "soon" or "early"; hence the placing of the jujubes was a symbol of the wish that the two scholars would soon achieve higher honors.

in the cups of the two scholars. Then wine was poured and Chou Chin drained the cup that was offered him. But when the food was brought on, consisting of pork, fish, chicken, and so on, and when at the word "please" the company set upon the dishes with gusto, Chou Chin did not raise his chopsticks. He explained that he had once vowed to touch no meat for the recovery of his sick mother and that he had adhered to the diet for over ten years.

"Such vows are worthy indeed," the Licentiate Mei said. "My maternal uncle used to adhere to a vegetarian diet, but later, after he had passed his examination, when the director of studies sent him some sacrificial meat from the Confucian Temple, my grandmother said he must break his vow, for if he refused to eat the meat the Sage might feel offended and send him bad luck. The Elder Brother here will surely have to break his vow too when sacrificial meat is sent to him this fall."

The villagers applauded this speech and all drank to Chou Chin's success at the autumn examination, but sensitive to his repeated failures, Chou flushed red at the allusion.

"Where is your relative today?" someone asked Shen. "Why has he not come to dinner?"

"He had to go to a banquet given by Master Li, chief of the constabulary," Shen answered.

"Master Li stands well indeed with the new magistrate," someone else said. "He must take in a thousand taels a year. Only he is fond of gambling, unlike Master Huang, chief of the lictors, who has saved his takings and built houses like palaces."

"Your relative has been sailing in a favorable wind, too, since he received his appointment," Master Hsun said. "In two or three years he will have got where Master Huang is now."

"He is doing fairly," Shen said. "But to get to Master Huang's position will take a few years of dreaming."

"Dreaming?" said the licentiate suddenly, only catching the last word. "There is something to be said for dreams." Then turning to Chou Chin he asked, "Have you, Elder Brother, had any significant dreams before examinations?"

"I have never had any," Chou said.

"I had a dream the year when luck enabled me to pass," Mei said. "It was New Year's Day. I dreamed I was in the mountains. The sun fell out of the skies and hit me right on the head. I woke up in a sweat, my head still tingling. I did not understand it at the time, but coming to think of it now, dreams do have a meaning sometimes."

3

The students were as stupid as so many heads of oxen and would sneak out to play brick or ball the minute Chou Chin took his eyes off them. But Chou Chin was used to their ways and managed them as well as might be expected. Soon two months went by and the weather grew warmer. One day after the noon meal he went out of the back gate and strolled along the river. Though the countryside was monotonous with fields, there were a few peach and willow trees on the river bank and the pink and green was pleasant to the eye. A fine rain began to fall; Chou Chin sought shelter under the gate, from which he watched the mist-enveloped landscape. The rain fell thicker and thicker. A boat appeared from the distance and as the boat drew nearer Chou Chin could make out a man sitting under the straw canopy and two servants squatted at the stern. The man stopped the boat at the landing and came ashore with his servants. He wore a scholar's cap, a blue satin robe, and black shoes with white painted soles. He was about thirty years old. He greeted Chou Chin briefly as he entered, saying to himself, "So this is a school." Chou Chin followed him and bowed to him, to which he returned half a bow, saying, "I suppose you are the teacher? Where is the monk?"

The monk appeared at this juncture, saying, "So it is Your Honor Wang. Please sit down, while I go and make some tea." Then he said to Chou Chin, "His Honor Wang passed at the last provincial examination. Please entertain him while I go to get tea." The graduate did not stand on ceremony; he sat down on the bench that his servant had placed at the position of honor while Chou Chin sat at the lower place. He asked Chou Chin's name, and the latter, now apprised of the visitor's status, referred to himself as "your junior student" when he answered.

During tea Chou Chin remarked that he had read the graduate's examination essay with great diligence. "The last two paragraphs are especially exquisite," he said.

"I did not write those two paragraphs," the graduate said.

"The senior is being modest," Chou Chin said. "Who else could have written it?"

"I really did not write it, but no human hand wrote it either," the graduate said. "It was like this: During the first session, it was getting late and I had not yet finished the first essay. I wondered what was wrong, for I usually wrote easily. I fell into a doze and saw five blue-faced beings come jumping into my cell. The middle one touched me on the forehead with a big writing brush and they went jumping out. Then a man with a gauze hat and red robe and golden belt came in, and, touching me on the back, said, 'Rise, Sir Wang!' I was frightened and woke in a cold sweat. I took up my brush and began to write quite rapidly and automatically. From this we can see that spirits and deities do present themselves at the examination halls. I respectfully submitted this to the literary chancellor in charge of the examination and he said that your younger brother here must have the destiny of achieving high honors at the metropolitan examinations."

At this point a student came up with his calligraphic exercise for criticism. Chou Chin told the student to lay it on his desk, but the graduate told him to go ahead with his work as he himself had business to attend to. So Chou Chin went back to his desk while the graduate gave directions to his servants to bring in the food basket from the boat and to ask the monk to cook some rice for them. Then he returned to Chou Chin and signified his intention of staying for the night. Catching the name of Hsun Mei on the schoolboy's calligraphy exercise, he started, murmured unintelligibly to himself, and made faces. Chou Chin did not see fit to ask him about it, but when he rejoined his visitor, the latter asked him, "How old is that student?"

"Just seven," Chou Chin answered.

"Did he begin school this year? And did you give him the name Mei?" the graduate asked.

"Your junior student did not give him the name. When he began school his father asked the new licentiate of the village, Friend Mei, to give him a name. Friend Mei suggested naming the boy Mei, after himself, for good luck in the examinations."

"It is a good story," the graduate said, laughing. "I dreamed on New Year's Day of seeing the metropolitan list. My name was on it, it goes without saying, but the third name was Hsun Mei, a native of Wenshang. I wondered how this could be since there is no provincial graduate in this district by that name; who would ever thought to find the name borne by a child student? Could it be possible that I should pass the metropolitan examination at the same time as he?" He laughed again, saying, "Dreams cannot be depended upon after all. In the examinations literary ability counts for everything, to be sure."

"Sometimes dream portents come true," Chou Chin said. "Friend Mei said that on New Year's Day of the year when he passed his prefecture examination he dreamed that the sun fell on his head."

"That is an even more unlikely story," the Graduate Wang said. "If the sun fell on his head to portend his licentiate degree, then should not the sky have fallen upon me to portend my greater success?"

The servants brought the graduate's supper: chicken and fish, duck and pork, and rice and wine all over the table. The visitor did not invite the schoolmaster to share the feast with him but ate by himself. Later the monk brought in Chou Chin's supper, a dish of salted vegetable, some rice, and a pot of hot water. After a while they bade each other good night and retired. The following morning brought fair weather, and the graduate left with as little ceremony as he had come. The floor was littered with chicken and fish bones and other refuse which Chou Chin had to spend all morning sweeping away.

The story went around that the Hsun boy was to be a *t'ung nien* * of the Graduate Wang, and the other boys began to taunt him and call him Hsun the Metropolitan Graduate. The parents of the other students felt offended too and taunted the boy's father, Old Master Hsun, by addressing him as "Your Honor," which annoyed the poor simple soul all the more because he could do nothing about it. Then Shen Hsiang-fu privately explained to the people that His Honor Wang never really said anything of the sort, but that the schoolmaster, impressed by the affluence of the Hsuns, had made up the story in order to curry favor with Old Master Hsun. "I was told," he said, "that the Hsuns sent to the temple some meat and bean curd the other day and had on several occasions sent bread and rolls. That's why!"

The villagers could not hide their displeasure and Chou felt increasingly uncomfortable. But because he had been recommended by the high bailiff Hsia they did not dare dismiss him. However, they soon found that Hsia was not pleased with him either, as he had not called often enough to show his gratitude, and they let him go at the end of the year. Chou Chin was thus left without a position upon which he could depend for a living, and he found it increasingly difficult to make ends meet.

* "Same year," a term designating the relationship between persons who pass the triennial metropolitan examination together. Though such persons might never meet one another, they were supposed to be as close to one another as, or closer than, classmates in the modern school system.

The Rise of Chou Chin and His Career

I

One day his brother-in-law Kin came to visit him. Seeing the plight he was in, Kin said to him, "Be not offended with what I am going to say, Brother-in-law. You know well by now how difficult it is to achieve honors at the examinations. One should not spurn a ready rice bowl, the most important thing in the world after all. Are you going to be neither wheat nor chaff all your life? I am now going to the provincial capital with some merchants to buy goods and we need someone to keep the books for us. Why don't you go with us? You have no one home to take care of and you will not lack anything while you are with us."

Chou Chin was glad of this opportunity and readily consented, and on an auspicious day he set off for the provincial capital with the merchants. After settling in the guest quarters of a wholesale house he went out for a stroll. On the street he encountered large gangs of masons and carpenters and learned that they were on their way to the provincial examination hall that was being prepared for the triennial examination. Chou Chin tried to edge into the grounds to get a view of the cells, but was driven away by the gatekeeper's whip. Later he returned with his brother-in-law and the other merchants, the wholesale merchant acting as guide, and they were allowed in after bribing the gatekeeper. Reaching the Dragon Gate, their guide said, "Master Chou, this is where the honorable students come." At the entrance to a row of cells he said, "This is the Cell Series One. You can go in and take a look if you like." Chou Chin went through the entrance and stopped at Cell Number One. At the sight of the neat cell with the bare table and bench, the cell that he had never sat in though he had taken the district examinations all his life, Chou Chin was deeply moved. Tears welled up in his eyes, and he gave a deep groan and slumped unconscious over the table.

After his companions recovered from the panic that this had thrown them into, they revived him with some water that they secured from the workmen and assisted him to his feet. But the sight of the writing table again upset him; he beat his head against it and burst into lamentations. "Are you mad?" his brother-in-law asked. "Why are you crying as if you had a death in your house?" Chou Chin heeded not the disturbance he was creating. He cried and rent his clothes and would not be consoled. Finally they had to carry him forcibly out of the examination halls while he cried and struggled until he foamed blood from his mouth. They stopped in a tea hut and persuaded him to take some tea, which quieted him a little, though he continued to sigh and sob enough to break one's heart.

"What could be on Master Chou's mind that he cries like this?" one of the merchants asked.

"Friend, you know not the circumstances," Kin replied. "This relative of mine is not a man engaged in trade by choice. He has been a scholar and has studied diligently and attended the examinations for more than a score of years without attaining the degree of licentiate. The examination halls must have brought back his past dreams and frustrations and made him lose control of himself." This touched the true chord in Chou Chin's heart and he burst anew into crying, unmindful of the crowd in the tea hut.

"Master Kin is in a way to blame," one of the merchants said. "If Chou is of the scholarly rank, he should not have been brought into our midst."

"But he is destitute," Kin explained, "and he has no teaching situation just at present. Else I would not have advised him to trod the common road of tradesmen."

"Your relative appears to be a man of talent and scholarship," another merchant said. "That must be why he feels so keenly his failing."

"He has talent and scholarship," Kin said, "but what can one do if fate is against him?"

"He can enter the provincial examination as a collegian," the merchant said. "Why should he not purchase the degree and take the examination this year? If he should pass, he would have fulfilled a lifelong ambition."

"I have been thinking of that too," Kin said, "but where is such a large sum of money to be obtained?"

Chou Chin had stopped crying by this time. The merchant said, "We ought to be able to manage with all of us here. If Mr. Chou passes the examination and becomes a mandarin, the few taels of silver would be nothing to him. And what if he cannot repay it? Are not we who roam about the lakes and rivers always losing money here and there? This would be a worthy cause. What do you think, my friends?"

"'The princely man is ever eager to assist in a meritorious undertaking,'" the generous merchants all said. "'To pass by a worthy cause without lending a hand is cowardice.' Of course, we shall be glad to help. But would Scholar Chou deign to accept our help?"

"You are my parents in a rebirth," Chou Chin said. "Chou Chin shall repay you though he may have to do so in future reincarnations as your donkeys or horses." He prostrated himself and kowtowed to the good merchants, who returned the obeisance. Presently they returned to their quarters, Chou Chin no longer crying but chatting and jesting with the rest.

2

The requisite fee of two hundred taels was paid into the provincial treasury, and in due time Chou Chin received his certificate. And he was able to sit in one of the cells the sight of which had moved him beyond himself. His luck turned at last; he wrote easily and well and on the day the list was posted he found his name on it. He returned to Wenshang and paid the customary calls on the magistrate and the director of studies, while the submagistrate came to call on him as his "junior student." Many residents of Wenshang came to him to claim relationship, including many who were not related to him at all, and many others came to renew old acquaintances where no previous acquaintanceship had existed. Shen Hsiang-fu, hearing the news, came to congratulate the former village tutor with presents of four chickens, fifty eggs, and sweetmeats that he had bought with the money that the villagers of Hsueh-chia-chi had contributed. For a month Chou Chin was busy receiving visitors and presents and attending banquets given in his honor.

Then he went to the capital for the metropolitan and the palace examinations, both of which he passed without difficulty. He was appointed to a post in one of the boards and three years later promoted into the censorate and appointed literary chancellor for the province of Kwangtung.

He had with him the usual retinue of advisors, but because of his early struggles he was determined that he would read the papers himself as far as possible so that no meritorious talents should be buried. At Canton he was inaugurated with appropriate ceremonies and he began his duties by examining the students of Nanhai and Panyü, districts embracing the provincial capital. Sitting in the entrance hall he watched the students file in, some old, some young; some well-featured, some with "eyes of the musk deer and eyes of the rat"; some respectably dressed, others in ragged clothes. Straggling at the end was a pathetic-looking candidate, thin and sallow, his hair and beard streaked with white; he wore an old felt cap and a nondescript linen gown which was insufficient even for the warm climate of Canton, for the year was then in the twelfth month. The Grand Examiner could not help noticing his pathetic face and the way he shivered as he received his papers.

Cannons were fired, the gates locked and sealed. On the last day of the sessions Chancellor Chou again sat in the entrance hall and had no difficulty in recognizing the shabby candidate when he turned up with his papers; his linen gown, its threads weak from age, had a few more torn places than when he went into his cell, a great contrast to the purple robe and embroidered sash that the examiner wore.

"Is your name Fan Chin?" the examiner asked, looking through the roll book. The student answered that it was. "How old are you?"

"In the book the age of this student is put down as thirty, but actually it is fifty-four."

"How many times have you attended the examinations?"

"This student began when he was twenty, so it has been over twenty times."

"Why is it that you have never passed?"

"It must be because his compositions were bad that Their Excellencies did not deem it just to pass him."

"That is not always so," the examiner said kindly. "You may leave; I shall read your papers with care."

The examiner was not pleased with Fan's paper on the first reading. But as no other papers came in then and as he had taken pity upon the pathetic candidate and wished to reward his perseverence if he could find the least merit in his work, he read it again and liked it better. He was about to read it for a third time, when another student came up with his paper and begged for an oral examination.

"What do you want an oral examination for since your paper is here?" the examiner asked with a smile on his face.

"This student has exercised in all forms of verse," the student said, "and he begs Your Excellency to give him an extemporaneous test."

Thereupon Chancellor Chou's countenance became stern. "His majesty the Son of Heaven has prescribed the regulation essay for the examinations," he said. "Why should you, my friend, presume to talk about the poetry of the Han and the T'ang? As a student you should devote your energies to the form of essay prescribed instead of dissipating them on unorthodox pursuits. Furthermore, this examiner has come here by imperial command to weigh the merits of the prescribed essays; did you think that he is here to engage in idle talk with you on miscellaneous studies? From the fact that you have sought vain fame through idle pursuits it is not difficult to conclude that you have neglected your true duties and that your essays are filled with superficialities not worth looking into. Come, attendants, show this man out!"

Nevertheless, Chancellor Chou looked through the paper of Wei Hao-ku, the student who had incurred his displeasure. It was clear and fluent and he decided to pass him. Then he read Fan Chin's essay for a third time. Only then did he realize how perfect and flawless it was. Nodding admiringly, he said to himself, "What exquisite work; even I could not understand it until the third reading! Truly it is a masterpiece, each word a pearl! How many great talents must have been suppressed by stupid and careless examiners!" He put three circles on the outside of the paper and gave it first place. Wei he gave the twentieth place.

On the day of the interview the examiner warmly praised Fan Chin's work; he urged Wei Hao-ku to concentrate upon the regular studies and to desist from miscellaneous subjects. On the following day when he set off on his circuit, Fan Chin went thirty *li* outside of the city to bid him farewell. " 'The Dragon head belongs to the mature talents,' " Chou quoted to Fan Chin. "Your time has come, I have no doubt of your passing the provincial examination; I shall await your arrival at the capital after I have reported to His Majesty." Fan Chin knelt down and kowtowed in gratitude. He stood and gazed at the receding sedan until it disappeared around a spur of the hills.

How Fan Chin Was Deranged by His Sudden Success and How He Was Cured

I

Fan Chin then hurried home, to a village about forty *li* from the city. He lived with his aged mother and his wife, the daughter of the village butcher Hu, in a small decrepit house with but one courtyard. They welcomed him warmly and were about to light the fire to cook supper when his father-in-law came in with a large section of tripe and a bottle of wine.

"Since the unlucky day I gave my daughter to you in marriage I don't know how much I have had to put up with from you, the devil of poverty himself. Now I don't know what good deed of mine has brought you good luck and enabled you to become a licentiate, but I have brought some wine to congratulate you."

Being very much in fear of his father-in-law, Fan Chin took all his thrusts in good humor and said aye to everything he proposed. While his mother and his wife were preparing the meal, Butcher Hu continued as he heated the wine, "Although you are now a licentiate and a member of the gentry, you mustn't dare put on airs before me, seeing that I am in a respectable trade and your father-in-law, but you must remember that most people you see around, such as the farm laborers and the scavenger men, are common people, and that if you should bow to them and sit with them and in other ways treat them like your equals, you would be degrading your position and bringing disgrace on me besides. You are a very simple and softhearted man, so I have to tell you all these things and warn you against blunders that would make you a laughingstock." Then he called to the womenfolk to join them, saying, "Sister, you must have a hard time of it eating nothing but pickled vegetables and plain rice. You too, daughter, come and eat with us. I wonder if my daughter during the ten-odd years since her marriage ever saw pork fat as much as two or three times!"

It happened to be also the year of the provincial examination and Fan Chin, urged by his friends, had planned to go. He approached his father-in-law for help, but the butcher spat in his face and said, "Don't you let things go to your head. Just because you have become a licentiate, you want to eat swan's dung like the proverbial toad. I was told that you passed not because of your work but because the examiner saw how old you were and took pity on you. Now you want to be a graduate! You must know that a graduate is the incarnation of some literary star from heaven. Have you not seen His Honor Chang in the city? His family is rich and he is well featured with square face and big ears. You ought to take a look at your monkey face in your own water before you dream of feasting on droppings from the swan. You had better give up such notions and let me get you a teaching post so that you can earn a few taels to feed your ne'er-would-die mother and your poor wife. I make only a few tael dimes on good days; if I give everything to you and let you throw it in the water, do you expect me and my family to feed on the northwest wind?"

Fan Chin slunk away. But he remembered the words of the examiner that his time had come and he decided to go at all cost. He went without his father-in-law's knowledge and returned home without waiting for the publication of the list. On the day when the list was to be posted there was no food in the house and at the command of his mother Fan Chin went to the market with the family's solitary hen, one of their principal assets as it was a good layer, with the hope of selling it and with the proceeds buying some rice. Before he had gone long the sound of gongs was heard and three horsemen came galloping into the village. They asked for His Honor Fan, saying that he had passed the examination.

Fan's mother was frightened at first but emerged when she realized that they were the proclaimers. The first group of proclaimers was followed by a second and a third, and they all clamored for reward money. Fan's mother—Her Ladyship, as the messengers called her—begged one of the neighbors, who had gathered in the courtyard, to fetch her son. He was found at the far end of the town with the hen in his arms, shuffling slowly along the market street, timidly expectant.

"Congratulations, Mr. Fan!" the neighbor said to him. "You have passed! Please hasten home, for your house is filled with people."

Fan Chin thought that the neighbor was jesting and so walked on unheeding. The neighbor caught up with him and tried to relieve him of his struggling burden. "Why are you annoying me?" Fan Chin protested. "You do not want to buy the hen."

"But you have passed and you must go home and take care of the proclaimers."

"Do not jest with me, neighbor," Fan Chin said. "We are without rice and I must sell this hen before we can eat."

The neighbor lost his patience; he took the hen away from Fan and dragged him home. In the central room Fan Chin caught sight of the printed poster with his name filled in:

Report of Victory

His honor Fan Chin *of your honored house has passed the Provincial Examination of Kwangtung, winning the* seventh *place. . . .*

He glanced over the poster; then as if not trusting his senses, he read it aloud to himself.

"Ah!" he exclaimed at last, clapping his hand. "So I have passed!" He had hardly finished uttering these words when he slumped unconscious to the ground. His mother hurriedly poured some water down his throat and revived him.

"Ah! I have passed, passed!" again he shouted, laughing and clapping his hands. He bolted through the gate, scattering the proclaimers and the neighbors right and left. Not far outside the gate he strode right into a muddy pond. By the time he had struggled and freed himself his hands were covered with yellow mud and he was dripping wet all over. There was no stopping him. Still laughing and shouting, he ran away in the direction of the market place.

The neighbors looked at one another and said, "The new nobleman has gone mad!" They tried to comfort Fan's mother and wife and sent two men to follow and look after the madman. Some went home and brought chickens, eggs, spirits, and other provisions that the villagers prized, for the entertainment of the proclaimers. Fan's wife went into the kitchen and cooked the things, crying all the while. When the things were ready, they were served on tables that one of the neighbors had brought. The chief topic of conversation was, naturally, what was to be done about the new graduate.

2

"I know of a way, but I do not know whether it can be carried out," one of the proclaimers said at last. "His Honor has been overwhelmed by the happy news. His heart has been stopped up by the rising phlegm. Is there anyone that he is mortally afraid of? All we have to do is to have the man he is most afraid of slap him in the face and tell him that it was only a joke and that he has not passed after all. This new shock will loosen the phlegm and enable him to spit it out. The pressure on his heart will be relieved and his reason restored."

The idea appealed to the villagers immediately and someone was sent to find the butcher, who, as all the village knew, inspired the greatest fear in Fan Chin. The emissary met him coming toward Fan Chin's house with a huge cut of meat and a load of coppers. But when told of the situation and asked to wield his mighty palm he hesitated.

"Though he is my son-in-law," he said, "he is now a graduate and therefore a star incarnate. And a star from Heaven must not be touched. I have been told that if one strikes a star from Heaven the King of Hell will punish him with a hundred strokes of the iron rod, and send him to the torture chambers of the eighteenth hell, and there to suffer forever."

"Enough," commented a sharp-tongued neighbor. "You, Master Hu, who have butchered hogs all your life, must have thousands of strokes of the iron rod credited to your account in the other world. What is another hundred strokes or so? They will probably not get to this hundred before the club is worn down to nothing. On the other hand, the King of Hell might commute your sentence from the eighteenth to the seventeenth hell if you cured your son-in-law."

"Let us not jest at a time like this," the proclaimer said. "Master Hu, you must put away your scruples and try to cure His Honor."

Unable to withstand the importunities from all sides, the butcher reluctantly gave his consent. He drank two cups of spirits to fortify his courage, banished his newly found scruples in regard to his son-in-law, and tried to resume his former swagger as best as he could; he rolled up his greasy sleeves and went in the direction of the market place, followed by some of the neighbors.

"Dear relative," said Fan Chin's mother, somewhat alarmed, "give him a good fright, but please do not hurt him."

They found the new graduate holding forth before the temple, dishevelled and smeared with mud, clapping and shouting, "Passed! Passed!"

Forbidding as one of the escorting generals in a funeral procession, the butcher went up to him and thundered, "You ne'er-would-die beast! Passed! Passed what?" and gave him a resounding blow in the face. All the neighbors laughed. But the butcher was frightened by what he had done, his hand trembled and he dared not strike again. Nor was a second blow necessary, for the first had felled Fan Chin to the ground. The neighbors hurried up to him, rubbed his chest and pounded his back until they brought him to. The butcher felt a dull pain in his palm and could not bend his hand. He repented his rashness and said, "Indeed a star from Heaven should not be touched. I am being punished for my sin." He bought a plaster from a drugmonger and put it on his hand.

"How did it happen that I am here?" Fan Chin asked.

"Congratulations, Your Honor," the neighbors said. "You have passed, but you were upset a bit by the news. You are well now, so please return home and send off the proclaimers."

"Yes, indeed," Fan Chin said. "I remember now. I won the seventh place." He did up his hair and washed his face in a basin borrowed from the drugmonger. Catching sight of his father-in-law he prepared himself for another scolding but the butcher said to him humbly, "Your Honor my worthy son-in-law, it was not that I was impudent, but your honored mother wished that I should try to persuade you."

"It was a good earnest blow, Master Hu," said the sharp-tongued neighbor. "The pork fat that His Honor Fan will wash off will doubt-less fill half a basin."

"Master Hu," said another, pointing to his plastered hand, "you won't be able to use that hand to kill pigs tomorrow."

"What should I do with pigs?" the butcher retorted. "As long as I have His Honor for my worthy son-in-law, I don't have to worry about means of support the rest of my life. As I have always said, no one has such talents and features like my worthy son-in-law. I have good eyes, my friends; I pride myself for being able to recognize a noble face. That was why my daughter remained unmarried until she was over thirty though many rich families sought the match. I knew that my daughter had the destiny of a mandarin's lady. You see, it has come true."

After refreshing himself with some tea that the drugmonger pre-pared, Fan Chin went home, with the crowd following respectfully behind him. The butcher kept tucking at his coat, straightening out the wrinkles. "His Honor is here!" he shouted as they reached Fan Chin's house.

3

The proclaimers were sent off and the neighbors gradually dispersed. But just as the household, including the butcher, was about to sit down, a well-dressed servant came in holding ceremonial calling card above his head. "His Honor Chang to pay his respects to His Honor Fan who has just passed!" he said pompously, as his master's sedan stopped in front of the gate. The butcher hastily hid himself from the august visitor in his daughter's room while Fan Chin went out to meet his fellow graduate with a confident air with which circumstances had endowed him. The latter's name was Chang Ching-chai. He had served a term as magistrate and was one of the most important members of the gentry of the district.

"Though we live in the same district," the caller said, "fate has not thrown us together. Your junior student has heard your great name, but he has not presumed to call. From the official register," Chang con-tinued, "I find that your honored hall master, the underexaminer T'ang, magistrate of Kao-yao, was a student of my late grandfather. So it is that we are close family friends." *

* It must be remembered that these relationships were fictitious and of an ex-officio character. The Magistrate T'ang was probably no more an actual student of Chang's late grandfather than Fan was a student of the Magistrate T'ang, who was in all probability only an honorary examiner.

Looking about him Gentryman Chang noticed how disencumbered Fan Chin was with material things, whereupon he took from his servant a packet of silver and gave it to Fan Chin, saying, "I have nothing to show my esteem of you, but pray accept this fifty taels. And your residence is really not suitable for you and will prove inconvenient for receiving. I have a vacant house inside the East Gate, passably clean though not very commodious, which I presume to present to you and beg you to move into it as soon as possible so that I shall be able to wait upon you and improve myself in your company." Fan Chin made several attempts at refusing, but gave in when the retired official said that he could not interpret the refusal in any other light than that Fan Chin did not care to recognize their intimate relationship.

Only after the distinguished caller had gone did the butcher venture out of his daughter's room. Fan Chin took two pieces of silver and gave them to him, saying, "I am grateful to you for the five thousand coppers you brought. Here, take this silver, which must be over six taels."

The butcher took the silver but did not withdraw his hand, saying, "You had better keep it yourself. The money I brought was a present."

"But you see I have a great deal more at present," Fan Chin insisted. "When I have spent all, I shall ask you for help."

"I shall keep it then," the butcher said, putting the silver in his pocket. "Now that you have made friends with His Honor Chang you need never worry about lack of money. He has more silver than the Emperor himself! He is one of my customers; his household buys four or five thousand pounds of meat a year even when there are no celebrations, weddings, or funerals. What is money to him!" Then he said to his daughter, "That plagued brother of yours complained this morning when I brought the money. 'His Honor your brother-in-law is not the same as formerly,' I said to him. 'This is nothing to him, for people will send silver to his house,' said I. And now it is indeed so. I'll take this silver home and throw it in the face of that short-lived slave!" He went away happy and murmuring a thousand thanks.

And indeed many came to wait upon Fan Chin and to vie with one another for his favor. Some gave him land, some estates, some offering themselves as servants in the hope that they would someday reap benefits from the graduate's future official career. In two or three months Fan Chin had maids and servants and money and ample provisions. He moved, at the gentryman's insistence, into his new house in the city, on which occasion a celebration was held lasting three days, with banquets and theatricals.

On the fourth day, after breakfast, the venerable lady of the house walked around the house and watched the maids at work. "Be careful with the things, sisters," she said, "for they belong to other people."

"Why other people?" they said. "They all belong to you, Venerable Lady."

"How could we have so many fine things?" Fan's mother said.

"Indeed they are yours," the maids assured her. "Not only these things, but even we and the house belong to you!"

The old lady surveyed the fine porcelains, the chopsticks inlaid with silver, and caressed them with greedy eyes. Then she laughed and exclaimed, "And they are all mine, mine!" She fainted and fell to the ground. Efforts to revive her failed and when the physician was summoned he pronounced her condition beyond the power of man, an opinion concurred in by other physicians called in for consultation. At eventide the venerable lady breathed her last and "returned to Heaven."

Anonymous

THE CHUANGTZE in this story is supposed to be the same man whose philosophical and essentially humorous outlook on life is indicated in the first section of this anthology. It is interesting to note the way in which stories about Chuangtze are used here as a springboard for a bizarre flight of fancy, obviously on the part of some woman-hater.

THE INCONSTANCY OF MADAME CHUANG

I

In the latter days of the Chou Dynasty there lived a famous worthy surnamed Chuang. His personal name was Chou and his courtesy name was Tzu-hsiu. He was born at Meng I in the country of Sung and he held the office of constable under the Chou Dynasty at Chi Yuan.

He was a disciple of the founder of the Taoist faith, a great and holy personage whose surname was Li, his personal name being Ehr and his courtesy name, Poyang. The hair of this man was white at his birth and he was in consequence always known as Laotze, "The Old Child."

Now Chaungtze used frequently to sleep in the daytime, and when he did so he used to dream that he was a butterfly, flitting lightly over garden and copse and meadow. Such dreams were most agreeable to him, and on waking he used to flap his arms up and down as though they were butterfly's wings. He had indeed a most unusual mind, and this dream was very often repeated.

One day he was discussing the Canon of Changes with his master, Laotze, and he told him about his dream. Now Laotze was a true Holy One and had knowledge of the three phases of existence, The Past, The Present, and The Future; and he expounded to Chuangtze concerning The Past.

He explained that after Chaos was first divided at the creation, Chuangtze had existed as a white butterfly at the time when Heaven first produced water and the water caused the life of plants and made

Translated by E. Butts Howell.

the flowers blossom forth. The white butterfly, he said, had subsisted on the essence of countless flowers and had received the benefit of the rays of the sun and of the moon. It had thus achieved Release and had become immortal; its wings were as big as the wheels of a cart, and it flitted off to the Jasper Lake. And there it picked and stole the buds of the P'an Peach and in punishment was pecked to death by the wondrous bird that keeps watch over the flowers which bloom below the throne of the Royal Mother of the West.

The soul of the butterfly, however, he explained, did not suffer annihilation, but was subsequently reborn into the world in the body of Chuangtze. And because the latter thus came of no ordinary origin, and since his heart was steadfast in the Way, Laotze was his teacher and instructed him of the pureness of the Doctrine of Inaction.

And on this day Laotze was expounding the former life, and Chuangtze felt as though he had suddenly been awakened out of a dream. He felt the wind again under his arms just as if he were again about to flit off on the wings that he had possessed in his former existence. The successes and the failures, the losses and the gains, of this life he regarded as but the passing of clouds or as the flowing of water, in value not worth a hair. And Laotze knew that Chuangtze had a clear understanding; so he expounded to him the secret of immortality as conveyed in the Five Thousand Character Classic of the Canon of Virtue.

This teaching did Chuangtze absorb, and in seclusion he purified his soul by meditation and prayer. In due course he became able to metamorphose his frame and to cause simultaneous apparitions of himself to be visible in different places. He then resigned his office as constable which he had held at Chi Yuan, and, taking leave of Laotze, became a pilgrim in search of the Way.

But although he had cleansed his heart and had become a Taoist devotee, he never eliminated from his practice of life the relationship between husband and wife, and was actually married three times. His first wife died of disease at an early age. His second wife he divorced on account of wrongdoing.

The present story is told of his third wife, a woman of the Tien family, the clan-name of the State of Ch'i. For Chuangtze had in his wanderings visited that country, and the damsel's father, Tien Tsung, appreciating his sterling worth, had given him his daughter in marriage.

Tien Shih much exceeded in beauty either of the two former wives of Chuangtze, for her complexion was like ice or snow for purity, and her deportment resembled that of a heavenly fairy. Now Chuangtze was no mere seeker after pleasure, and his behavior to his wife was characterized by the utmost respect, but yet he derived as much enjoyment from her society as a fish obtains satisfaction from being restored to the water.

Prince Wei of Ch'u heard of the superiority of Chuangtze and sent messengers to him bearing gifts—two thousand taels of pure gold, one thousand rolls of brocade, a decorated chariot drawn by magnificent horses—and asked him to become his Prime Minister.

But Chuangtze refused with emphasis.

"The sacrificial ox," he said, "is decked with costly silks and his mouth is continually full of grain and hay. He sees the ox which is harnessed to the plough existing but by labor and bitterness, and he prides himself upon his superior lot. But the day comes when he is led to the great temple preceded by the sacrificial axe. Then he wishes, but in vain, that he could change places with the ox at the plough."

Thus Chuangtze refused the prince's presents and returned with his wife to his homeland and dwelt in seclusion among the mountains of Nan Hua near Ts'ao Chou.

II

One day he was wandering among the foothills and he noted the deserted graves situated all round him. He reflected that there was no distinction between young and old, but that all met there in the end, that the common lot of all alike was the tomb, and that no one could come back again to life.

He pondered thus, sighing deeply, and as he walked farther he came upon a young woman dressed in the white robes of mourning and bending over a newly-made grave, the soil of which was still moist. She sat by the side of the grave and fanned it vigorously with a silken fan, pausing not at all in her efforts.

Chuangtze, in surprise, approached her and asked her who she might be, thus engaged among the graves fanning the earth, and what might be the reason of her action.

And the young woman did not rise to reply, but continued her fanning as she answered him. Her voice was as beautiful as the fluty notes of the oriole, or as the early song of the swallows in the spring time. But the words that she uttered were far from being in accordance with the canons of propriety. Nevertheless—

Though shame should crush the utterer of sentiments so vile,
Her words to many a hearer's face would surely bring a smile!

"This grave is that of my husband," she said. "He, having unhappily died, his body is buried in this place. And while he was alive we loved each other deeply, and when death took him we could not bear to part. Nevertheless he told me with his dying words that if I wished to marry again I was at least to wait until, the funeral having been duly performed, the earth on his grave should be dry.

"Now I am anxious that the earth on his grave, which is, as you see, a recent one, shall dry as quickly as possible. It is for that reason that I am fanning it."

"The lady is surely overanxious!" thought Chuangtze to himself with a bitter smile. "She says that her husband was very fond of her; what, I wonder, would she have done had this not been the case?"

But he merely said to her: "If you wish, madame, that this new earth shall quickly become dry, the matter presents no difficulty. Your arm is evidently lacking in strength to fan sufficiently vigorously, and I, although without talent, am willing to exert my efforts on your behalf."

Then the woman rose and made a deep obeisance to the sage, thanking him warmly; and with both hands she gave over to him the little white fan. Thereupon Chuangtze, muttering some Taoist incantation, made several passes up and down the grave with the fan, and the moisture in the soil forthwith disappeared altogether and the earth became dry.

At this, the woman laughed aloud from her exceedingly great pleasure.

"I am indeed under a deep obligation to you, sir," she said, "for your help." And with her slender fingers she detached a silver pin from her hair and offered it to the sage as a present, together with the fan itself. Chuangtze refused the silver pin but accepted the fan, and the overjoyed woman departed.

The sage was greatly perturbed by the incident, however, and returned to his house, where he sat alone under his thatched eaves and gazed, musing, at the little silken fan as it lay before him. Anon he sighed and murmured the following verse:

"Only who in past existence met as bitter foes
In this life can meet together; thus strife ever grows!
Had he known her love to be as feeble as his life,
How could he have taken to him such a fickle wife?"

Now Tien Shih, Madame Chuang, happened to be standing just behind him at this moment and heard these despondent words. So, coming in front of her husband as he sat, she asked him what might be their meaning. Chuangtze was a true sage and had attained the Way, and he and his wife were always wont to address one another in terms of respect.

"Wherefore are you so sad, sir," she asked; "and where did you obtain this fan?"

Then her husband related to her the details of his encounter with the woman. "So you see, madame," he ended, "this fan is a thing to dry earth with. And she gave it to me because I had put forth my strength on her behalf!"

On hearing the story, Tien Shih reddened with anger, and, addressing heaven, she exclaimed how unspeakably shameless was the conduct of the woman in question, and remarked that no other creature so vile as she could possibly be found.

But Chuangtze answered her in verse, as follows:

"A man and wife together live; how well does she behave!
But when he dies how often grows a wish to fan the grave!
A tiger's picture shows his skin, but not the inward part;
And men are known from face alone. Who knows the secret heart?"

At these words Tien Shih became exceedingly enraged. The old saying has it that "hatred takes no heed of relationship and rage obliterates propriety!" And in her anger she lost sight of decorum and spat into the face of the sage, her husband.

"Although in a sense it is true that all are alike," she said vehemently, "yet at the same time there are the wise and the foolish, the good and the bad! How can you venture thus lightly to class together all the women under heaven? It is not fitting to confuse good people and bad people in this manner! Do you not fear to cause offense in speaking thus?"

"Your words, madame," returned her husband, "are both boastful and without consideration. Supposing that I should be so unfortunate as to die. You, a mere girl, as pretty as a flower, as elegant as jade, would not wait five years, no, nor yet three, before you married a second husband!"

"A good official does not serve under two dynasties," replied his wife, "nor does a virtuous woman marry two husbands! Where have you seen any decent woman who drank the tea and slept in the bed, first of one family and then of another? If, unhappily, so great a misfortune as to lose my husband were to befall me, so shameless a deed as that which you have indicated could not possibly be perpetrated by your widow, not only in three or five years, but in all my life! For even when I dream at night I retain some decency of feeling."

"One can never tell!" said Chuangtze slowly.

Tien Shih then in her indignation swore a great oath.

"A woman is more virtuous than a man!" she cried. "Reflect upon your own conduct! That indeed was without either love or propriety. One wife dies and you get another; she is divorced and you take a third! And with you men, all are alike! We women say 'One saddle, one horse'; and I am one upon whom the greatest reliance can be placed. How could I then be willing to give others cause to talk about me in such a way that posterity would laugh me to scorn? You are killing me with wrongs!" And, so saying, she snatched the silken fan from her husband's grasp and tore it into fragments.

"There is no need for this display of anger," he said quietly. "I am indeed overjoyed to hear that you have formed so meritorious a resolution." And he spoke no more of the matter.

III

A few days later, however, Chuangtze suddenly sickened and took to his couch. Each day his condition became more serious and Tien Shih wept continually at the head of his bed.

"I am sick unto death," said the sage, "and we must soon part for evermore. What a pity it is that you tore to pieces that fan! Had it been retained I might have presented it to you so that you might fan my grave with it!"

"Oh, master," sobbed his wife; "do not, I pray you, doubt me. I am myself a scholar and well acquainted with the principles of correct behavior. I shall be faithful to you until the end of my life! I swear to you that I have no other intention, and if you still do not trust me I am willing even to kill myself now, before your eyes, and thus give proof of my sincerity!"

"It is enough!" murmured the dying man. "Now that I hear the words in which you express your virtuous determination, I, Chuangtze, shall be able to close my eyes when I die!"

And so saying, he breathed his last, for his end had come.

Bitter indeed were his wife's lamentations as she stroked his dead body! Then going right and left among the neighbors she obtained burial clothes and a coffin, and clothing herself in full mourning she wept all day and all night for a long while, behaving, when she thought upon Chuangtze's love and kindness for her, like one mad or drunken, and going without food and sleep.

All those who dwelt near by among the mountains had recognized Chuangtze as a modest and retiring sage, but those who came to pay their duty to him as he lay there were fewer than they who went to market upon market days.

IV

Now it fell out that on the seventh day after Chuangtze's death there arrived unexpectedly at the house a young scholar. His face was beautifully pale with study as though it had been powdered, and his lips were as red as vermilion. He was in fact unsurpassed in personal beauty and no one could have excelled him in grace. He was dressed in purple garments and wore a black official hat, a jewelled belt, and red shoes; and with him came an aged retainer.

He said that he was the grandson of the Prince of Ch'u and that in the previous year he had made arrangements with Chuangtze to be his pupil; and he added that he had come to pay his respects to his master.

And when he heard that Chuangtze had died a few days before, his grief was extreme. He quickly removed his colored garments and clad himself in robes of mourning which his servant brought for him out of his baggage. Then, suitably clad, he approached the coffin and kowtowed four times before it.

"Oh, my master," he cried, "your pupil is indeed unfortunate that he cannot profit by your instructions imparted verbally. I will wear for you mourning for one hundred days and thus display my feelings of dutiful respect." And so saying, he kowtowed again four times and then rose to his feet, his tears flowing freely.

He then requested to be allowed to see Tien Shih, who at first refused to receive him. The Prince, however, sent a message to her.

"According to the custom of ancient times," he said, "it was not necessary among families who were closely allied by friendly ties for the female members to live in seclusion. And in this case your humble servant has already established with the Master Chuang the relation between pupil and instructor."

So Tien Shih came out a few steps from the mourning chamber and received the Prince, exchanging greetings with him. And when she saw what a talented and elegant person he was, she was moved with admiration, experiencing a strong inclination towards him, and she much regretted that there was so little excuse for her to see him again.

"Although my master is no more," said the Prince to her, "I, his pupil, cannot forget my feelings of friendly respect towards him, and I greatly desire to beg the hospitality of his roof for one hundred days, firstly to observe fitly the stipulated period of mourning, and secondly that I may see what writings he has left behind him on record, so that I may even yet benefit by his instructions."

"As our respective families are mutually intimate already by reason of the relation between pupil and teacher," said Tien Shih, "I see no reason why you should not remain." And she forthwith invited him to share her evening repast, which was then ready.

When the meal was ended, she produced the writings of her husband called "The True Canon of Nan Hua" and "The Five Thousand Virtuous Sayings of Laotze," compiled by Chuangtze during his lifetime, and gave them to the Prince, who expressed his gratitude.

Now the room in which the coffin was placed was next door to that set apart for the Prince as his bed-chamber, and Tien Shih every day used her visits of lamentation over the coffin as an excuse to exchange greetings with the visitor. She soon fell deeply in love with him and they began to exchange amorous glances. But though he was only half in love with her, she was wholly in love with him, and she felt that it was fortunate that they were among the mountains and in so remote a spot, for if it should happen that she were to stray somewhat from the beaten track of propriety and virtue, there were but few who might gossip. She regretted very much that the period of mourning was not yet over, and she sighed as she reflected that when it is the woman who courts, it is difficult for her to take the initiative. So she determined to possess her soul in patience.

Thus about half a month passed and she became as amorous as an ape and as restive as a horse, so that she found no repose at all. She therefore called the old servant into her room secretly one evening and plied him long with the best wine and flattered him. At length she asked him if his master had as yet found a wife. The old man replied that his master was not yet married or even affianced, whereupon she asked him again what sort of a woman his master intended to choose as his mate.

"My master has already spoken to me about this matter," replied the old man, who by this time was half-intoxicated, "and has said that if he could only find some lady as beautiful as you yourself, madame, he would be perfectly contented!"

"Can this indeed be true?" exclaimed Tien Shih. "I fear that you may be lying to me!"

"I am already full of years," replied the old man; "how could I speak that which is not true?"

"May I then request that you will be the go-between in this matter?" asked Tien Shih, "and will arrange the match, if indeed it is true that your master is not unwilling to regard with favor one so unworthy as myself? For I would most gladly become his wife and his servant."

"My master has already mentioned it to me," replied the man, "and has remarked what a capital match it would make. But he said that such a thing could not be considered, for it would be an offense against propriety for a pupil to marry his instructor's widow. He fears lest scandal would result!"

"But the arrangement which existed between your master and my late husband came to nothing," replied Tien Shih. "No actual instruction from the mouth was ever transmitted. They cannot be considered therefore as having really been teacher and pupil at all. Moreover, we live here in a very remote spot among the mountains and the few neighbors that there are are very ignorant people and no scandal would be caused. Can you, sir, not devise some way out of the difficulty? If you could, I should be most glad to invite you to the wedding feast!"

The old man said that he would do his best in the matter and turned to go; and, as he was leaving, Tien Shih called him back and besought him that, if his master were to consent, he should come straight into her room at once and tell her, no matter what hour it might be, for, she added, she would be waiting up for him.

And after the man had departed she became exceedingly restless and anxious from expectation, and kept on peeping round the room where the coffin lay. She only wished that she had a rope tied to the ankle of that handsome young man so that she could pull him in and throw her arms around him.

It was then getting dusk and she felt that she could not bear the suspense, so as soon as it was quite dark she crept into the mourning chamber and listened to see if she could hear what was passing in the adjoining room.

All at once she heard a sound coming apparently from near the coffin, and she started with fright for she thought first that it might be her husband coming back to life again. So she went quickly back to her room and returned with a lighted lamp to find that it was only the old servant, who was lying fast asleep on the altar in front of the coffin, where he had lain down after his potations. She did not dare to upbraid him or even to rouse him from his torpor, so she went back to her own room and lay there awake listening to the night-watchman going his rounds and beating out the watches on his bamboo clapper.

Thus the night wore away, and when daylight came she saw the old man walking up and down in the courtyard, but he did not come to report to her the result of his interview with his master. Tien Shih could not bear to wait until he should come to her of his own accord, so she called him at once into her room and questioned him. He only shook his head, however, saying: "No use, no use!"

"What do you mean?" she asked in dismay. "You could not have conveyed my meaning properly to him!"

"Oh, yes, I did indeed," was the reply. "But the objections which my master raised were unanswerable. He said that there was no need to talk about your beauty, madame, which was sufficiently obvious, nor the fact that no relations as between master and pupil had been actually established. He brought forward other objections under three headings which prevented my coming back with a favorable reply."

"And what were these three objections?" asked Tien Shih.

"I will tell you, madame," he answered. "My master said that in the first place there was that ill-omened object still in the room there. He felt that he could not consent to a marriage ceremony being celebrated under such circumstances, and that moreover such a course would be an outrage on the canons of propriety.

"In the next place," the old man went on, "my master pointed out that Chuangtze and yourself, madame, were a very devoted couple and that your late husband was a celebrated worthy of well-known virtue. He feels that his own attainments cannot possibly compare with those of such a man, and he thinks that you would not be able to feel sufficient respect for him in consequence.

"In the third place, my master has brought hardly anything with him, for nearly all his clothes and other possessions have been left behind. To enter into a marriage with empty hands, bringing no wedding gift and no money for the wedding feast, was a thing, he said, not to be thought of. And therefore he is of opinion that the matter cannot be arranged for these three reasons."

"Not one of these three reasons is valid at all!" the widow returned. "That coffin has not taken root, as far as I know; there is an old out-house behind there which is now empty, and it will be easy enough to summon a few of the villagers to carry it out there. Thus is his first objection disposed of!

"As regards his second objection, I would tell you that the story about Chuangtze being of such celebrated and well-known virtue is a gross exaggeration. His domestic affairs were always most ill-regulated and everyone complained of his lack of virtue in the matter of the divorce of his second wife. It is true that Wei the Prince of Ch'u entertained a very high opinion of him and asked him to become his Minister, but Chuangtze knew very well that he was most ill-fitted for so high a position, so he fled away into this place. And only last month he went down into the valley by himself and there met a widow who was fanning her husband's grave so that she might marry again as soon as the earth was dry. My wretched husband sported with her, and, taking her silken fan, he fanned the earth dry for her!

"And he actually brought the fan back here; but I took it from him and destroyed it. A few days before he died, in fact, we had a serious quarrel about the matter! I would like to know if such an incident as that is a proof of our mutual devotion!

"Now your master," Tien Shih continued, "is a young man still, and is of great learning. He will most assuredly rise to a high official position. Furthermore, he has the rank of a prince. I, his handmaid, how-ever, am likewise of a royal house, for my father was Tien Tsung. We are equals in status and this match is clearly preordained by Heaven!

"His third objection is raised on the score of his having brought no money either for the marriage banquet or for a wedding gift. But this is a matter for the woman to decide. Who would wish to receive a gift under such circumstances? The omission of the customary marriage banquet is likewise a small matter.

"But, on the other hand, I, his handmaid, have saved some twenty taels of silver from my household expenditure. This money I freely give to your master so that he may provide himself with a new suit of silken robes. Please go and answer him in such terms as I have indi-cated. If he should agree, today is an auspicious day and we can im-mediately become united!"

So the old man took the twenty taels and returned to his master, who expressed his readiness to accede to Tien Shih's proposition.

And Tien Shih's joy thereat was as wide as the earth and as high as the heavens; she doffed her mourning robes and put on a new and brightly colored dress; she powdered her face and painted her lips with vermilion. Then, having sent out the old servant to hire a few of the rustics from the neighboring hamlet to remove the coffin of her late husband and put it down in the shed outside, she swept out the mourning chamber and laid out the table which had lately been used as an altar to serve as a table for the wedding feast. The following verse bears testimony to the situation:

The lovely widow added charm gains from her mourning weeds,
But that the prince a trifler is, alas! seems all too plain.
She that declared that no good steed more than one saddle needs
Today intends to break her vow and basely wed again!

V

And that evening, Tien Shih lighted incense-sticks in the center chamber where the coffin had been, and lit up the room with brilliant lamps. And the Prince appeared with a new tassel upon his hat and clad in new flowing robes, to meet his bride in her red jacket and her brocade skirt. And there they stood together in the light of the gilded candles, unspeakably fine in their jewels and beautiful garments.

They had already made their obeisance to each other and lovingly, hand-in-hand, had entered the wedding chamber to drink the cup of wine which was to make them one, when suddenly the Prince knit his brows as if with a spasm of pain, and stood as though rooted to the spot. A moment afterwards he fell forward to the ground, his two hands clutching at his throat, and gasped out that a frightful pain had suddenly attacked him! Tien Shih, being desperately in love with him, felt none of the customary bashfulness of a bride but hugged him to her bosom and tried to soothe him, asking him what ailed him. But the Prince was in such agony that he could not speak, and gasped as though at the point of death.

The old servitor, having heard his master fall, rushed in to lend his aid, and Tien Shih asked him whether the Prince had ever had a similar attack.

"Yes, indeed," was the reply; "my master has suffered in this way many times in the past. Once every year or so he has had such attacks and no ordinary drug can cure him. There is but one remedy that can do him any good!"

"And what is that?" Tien Shih asked eagerly.

"The court physician wrote out for him a very singular prescription," was the reply, "ordering for him no less than the brain of a living man, to be swallowed in hot wine! This strange medicine effects an immediate cure, and formerly when these attacks came upon him his father requisitioned and obtained the person of a condemned criminal, whose brain was removed upon his execution. But now, in this remote spot among the mountains, what can be done for him? He is, I fear me, lost indeed!"

"A living man's brain is truly unobtainable," answered Tien Shih; "but could not the brain of a man who has been dead for some time also be used?"

"The physician did say," replied the old man, "that the brain of a dead man could also be used, provided that he had been dead not more than one hundred days!"

"Ah!" gasped Tien Shih. "Would my husband, then, not serve? He has been dead only a matter of twenty days! Why not break open the coffin and obtain his brain?"

"But you, madame, can hardly be expected to agree to such a proposition as that!" the old man said quickly.

"I regard myself already as the wife of the Prince," replied Tien Shih. "I would give my own life to serve him if necessary with the utmost readiness. Why, then, should I hesitate about a few old bones which in any case would soon become a mass of corruption!"

So, telling the old man to support his master's head, she ran off to fetch the chopper which was used for the firewood, and with this implement firmly grasped in her right hand, and with a lamp in her left, she made her way rapidly to the shed where her husband's coffin had been placed. Then, placing the lamp on a bench and tucking up her sleeves, she grasped the chopper firmly in both hands, and, taking a sure aim, she delivered a mighty blow with all her strength!

A woman's force is but slight, and, as you would have supposed, hardly sufficient to cleave open a coffin. But Chuangtze was an exceedingly sensible man, and had left special instructions that his coffin was to be of common soft wood, not more than three inches thick, and the first chop brought away a great piece of wood. Several more blows followed and the coffin lid was soon split open. Then Tien Shih paused in her efforts, out of breath with the unwonted exertion.

But to her consternation she heard her late husband within the coffin give a loud gasp of disgust. Then, pushing aside the lid, he raised his body and sat up!

Tien Shih, although by nature the most relentless of persons, was after all a woman, and, being desperately afraid, all strength went from her knees, which knocked together in the extremity of her terror, while her head swam, her heart leaped in confusion, and the chopper slipped from her grasp to the ground.

"Help me out of this coffin!" exclaimed her husband sternly, and though she could scarcely summon up enough strength to do so, she assisted her husband to reach the ground in safety.

Chuangtze then raised the lamp and went with it into the house, followed by his wife. The latter knew that the Prince and the old man were waiting there, and rivers of cold sweat coursed down her frame, so great was her apprehension. She knew not which way to turn or what to do. But when she reached the house, she found to her amazement that the two men had disappeared!

And although her fear was still upon her she began to regain her courage to some extent and to think as to how she could explain the situation. So she said to Chuangtze timidly: "I, your servant, after your death mourned over you day and night without ceasing. Just now, however, I heard a slight sound coming from your coffin, and I remembered that among the men of old time there were stories of how the spirit of one that had died sometimes came back to him. I hoped that possibly you also were returning to the world, so I ran to fetch the chopper and hacked the coffin open. Thanks be to heaven and to earth that you have indeed recovered and come to life again. What wonderfully good fortune for me, your servant!"

"I thank you, wife, for your kind words," replied Chuangtze. "But there is one thing which I would ask you to explain, and that is the fact that you do not appear to have worn mourning for me very long! How is it that you are clad in all this gay attire—gold embroidered coat, forsooth, and decorated skirt?"

"I could never have allowed my ugly clothes to spoil the joy of opening the coffin," replied the cunning woman. "As I was about to secure the unspeakable happiness of seeing you again I put on gay attire as an auspicious omen!"

"Indeed!" said Chuangtze. "But there is yet another question that I should like to ask. Why is it that my coffin was not placed in the proper mourning chamber, but, instead, was put away in that outhouse? That could hardly have been also an auspicious omen!"

To this his wife could think of no suitable reply, and when Chuangtze's gaze met the table spread for the wedding feast he made no comment. But he ordered wine to be brought and when it came he filled and drained a great goblet many times.

Tien Shih, not being a very clever person, thought that she had succeeded in deceiving her husband and began to hope that they might perhaps live again a happy life together as before. So she put her two arms on the table by the wine bottle to be ready to ply her husband with wine, and began to cajole him with fair words and affectionate gestures. But Chuangtze, who was beginning to show signs of intoxication, seized a pen and wrote these four lines of verse:

> "Upon my death I sundered all the ties that bound us twain,
> Now it is I who bear no love, while you would love again;
> Should we renew our former life of fond connubial bliss,
> Above my head once more I'd dread to hear the chopper hiss!"

And, seeing these four lines, Tien Shih was entirely abashed with shame and hung her head, not daring to utter a single word.

But Chuangtze went on writing:

> "Long have we lived together now with no affection true;
> The old man was no sooner cold than you would wed anew,
> The coffin lid was hacked to bits by your relentless hand,   ..
> You did not even wait until the grave-mound dry was fanned!"

And then at last he spoke.

"I now order you," he said, "to look upon the forms of two friends of yours!" and raising his hand he pointed out through the open door.

His wife turned her head and looked, and there she saw the forms of the Prince and his old servant as if about to enter! She leaped into the air with terror, and then turning round again she saw that her husband had disappeared! But when she looked again towards the door, the other two were no longer to be seen. Where indeed were they?

As will have been guessed, however, ere now, these happenings were all due to the miraculous power that Chuangtze possessed which enabled him to transform himself and to project his body.

Tien Shih was almost terrified to death and felt that she had indeed been irremediably shamed, so, taking off her embroidered silk girdle, she tied the end to one of the beams above her head and thus hanged herself and died.

Alas! Alas! How sad!

But this time death was genuine enough and there was no pretense. And when Chuangtze saw that the breath of life had departed from her, he cut down her body and laid it in the coffin with the splitten lid. Then he took one of the earthen rice-bowls from the table and, tapping upon it with his finger and making it ring again in rhythmical measure, he leaned against the coffin and sang the following song, accompanying himself upon the bowl:

> "She and I were born alike,
> Who knows how, who knows why?
> She was no true wife to me,
> No fit husband I!
> Rashly we two were wed,
> Under one roof lived we;
> The silver cord of my life was snapped,
> Another suitor came speedily.
> The evil man thinks not on life or on death,
> Death and life are alike to him,
> But I saw down to her inmost soul,
> Death was her due for her cruelty grim.
>
> While she lives her passion rules her,
> Now in death the north wind cools her.
>
> She wishes to use my brain,
> A chopper keen she brings;
> Now I use her as a theme for my song,
> For she's gone to the cold Nine Springs.
> The chopper's crash I heard,
> I returned to life so dear,
> And when her spirit hears my song
> Its meaning will be clear.
>
> I break this wretched bowl and sigh;
> What is she? Who am I?"

And, having sung this song, Chuangtze composed these four lines of verse:

I bury you when you are dead,
But when I die, you haste to wed.
And if I really had been dead,
I wonder what folks would have said!

Then, his versification finished, Chuangtze laughed loudly and long and shattered the rice-bowl on the ground. And, setting fire to his house and its contents, he burned it utterly to the ground, reducing everything, including the coffin, to ashes.

Only the two Canons, "The Virtue of the Way" and "The True Canon of Nan Hua," were not consumed, but were picked up afterwards from the ruined house among the mountains, and thus were preserved unto this day.

VI

As for Chuangtze, he wandered far and wide and never took another wife. He is said to have met Laotze again at Han Ku Kuan and to have accompanied him from there and thus to have gained The Way and become a disembodied spirit.

Wu Chi did kill his wife without a cause at all, they say;
And Hsün Ling nearly died of grief when his wife passed away.
But let us think of Chuangtze's song about his erring wife,
And I, for one, will take him as a pattern for my life!

III

HUMOR—
PRACTICAL AND OTHERWISE
(All Time)

III. Humor — Practical and Otherwise
(All Time)

IN CHINESE, fiction is called "small talk" and jokes are called "laugh talk." Next to gossip a good joke is probably the most often repeated thing when folks get together and sit around and talk. In this section I have collected one hundred and nine "laugh talks." They differ from the specimens in Section I of this book in that they have been handed down from generation to generation more often by word of mouth than in recorded history.

There is no pretension to philosophy here. Whatever wit and wisdom may be found in these jokes is purely incidental. Anything for a laugh, and sometimes a sad truth is the funniest thing in the world.

The teller of these tales can feel definitely superior to his fellow beings—and his listeners likewise. They have a healthy disregard for other people's feelings and can cite you case upon case of physical defects and mental deformities, so long as they are not their own. They expose literary and military men alike, if anything, favoring the former. The scholar in China is traditionally poor and therefore easy to poke fun at; besides, he can't hit back—except, perhaps, with a joke! They take pride in the incompetence and glory in the downfall of teacher and student, doctor and priest, as well as sundry men of other trades.

In this he-he and ha-ha world every doctor is a quack (they seem to like to pick on the medical profession); every cook, a thief. The greedy guest visits the miserly host, and the impatient maiden marries the backward "son-in-law." It is always "son-in-law," in deference to the Chinese family system, which is further exemplified in the relationships between father and son, brother and brother, husband and wife. The henpecked husband is in a class by himself.

In Western terminology, there are the moron jokes, the tall tales, a few practical jokes, many more not so practical ones, and some that may safely be classed as fantastic. They form a cross section of the basic pattern of folk humor among the Chinese, or any other like-minded people, for that matter. Start telling one of them and before you know it you will be making your own variations and embroideries on the theme.

A Collection of One Hundred and Nine Jokes

THE CUSTOMER IS ALWAYS RIGHT

In old Peiping restaurant waiters are well known for their polite and efficient service. A visitor from the South one day dined at a famous Peiping inn and, midway through his meal, took notice of the ingratiating young fellow who hovered about and administered to his every wish. In a mood to make friends, the man started a conversation with his waiter.

"What's your name, young man?" he asked.

"Anything you say, sir," the waiter answered, all smiles.

"Well, I have two guesses. Your name is either Chang or Li."

"Both are correct, sir!" the waiter exclaimed.

"How can both be correct?" the customer asked.

"Well, sir," the waiter explained, "I was born in the Chang family but adopted into the Li family. That's why both your guesses are correct."

Then the customer asked the waiter how old he was. And again the waiter answered, "Anything you say, sir!"

"I would say, you are either twenty-three or twenty-five."

"Both are correct, sir!"

"Well, now, how can both of my guesses be correct in this case," the man protested.

"It's like this, sir. I *am* twenty-three years of age. But a fortuneteller told me that it is an unlucky age for me, so he changed it to twenty-five. That's why both your guesses are correct."

Finally the customer asked the waiter what month of the year he was born in. And once again the waiter bowed and said, "Anything you say, sir!"

"Maybe you were born in June, or maybe you were born in January."

"Both are correct, sir!" the waiter exclaimed, polite as ever.

"Come, come, certainly *that* can't be true!"

"Oh, yes!" said the waiter. "I was born in the month of June, but when I saw that it was so hot I went right back and didn't appear again until January."

This and the following items retold by George Kao.

THE CHAMPION MISER

In a certain village there lived two misers, Old Chang and Old Wang, both famous for their stinginess. For a long time the villagers could not decide which one of the two was the greater miser, and a sort of rivalry developed between them in the art of penny-pinching.

When the Mid-Autumn Festival came around, on the fifteenth day of the eighth moon, and it was the custom to exchange seasonal gifts, Miser Chang thought he would take the occasion to assert his claim as the champion miser. He painted a fish on a piece of paper and instructed his son to present it to his friend, Mr. Wang, with his compliments.

The "fish" was accepted by Old Wang with a great show of appreciation. As Confucian etiquette calls for reciprocity, Old Wang prepared to send Chang a suitable gift in return. He called aside *his* son and gave instructions to do thus and so.

Toward the end of the day Little Wang returned from his mission. "Did you do as I told?" Old Wang asked. "Oh, yes!" replied his son. "When I saw Mr. Chang I bowed to him and said, 'In return for your very substantial gift my father asked me to present to you this moon cake,' and I used the fingers of my hands to form the shape of a round moon cake."

Instead of being pleased, Old Miser Wang was outraged by his son's conduct, and he gave the boy a slap on the face. "Who told you to be so extravagant?" he shouted, extending the fingers of one hand to show how it should have been done. "Half a cake would have been enough!"

FIXING THE BLAME

A carpenter was hired to fix a bolt on the door. Through a mistake he put the bolt on the outside.

"The blind fool!" the owner scolded him.

"You're a blind fool yourself!" the carpenter retorted.

The owner asked, "How come I'm a blind fool?"

"If you had eyes," he answered, "would you hire a carpenter like me?"

THE BROKEN BUDDHA

A particularly shrewd lawyer was admiring a porcelain Buddha in a crowded curio shop. He inquired about the price.

"A hundred dollars," said the salesman with his nose in the air.

"How about thirty dollars?" the lawyer bargained.

"For thirty dollars you can only have the Buddha's little finger," the salesman sneered.

The lawyer did not say a word. He picked up a stone and knocked off a little finger from the exquisite figurine.

Shocked and furious, the salesman wanted to have the lawyer arrested.

"Here's the money and these are my witnesses," the lawyer said coolly. "You said yourself that for thirty dollars I could have the Buddha's little finger."

OLD CHANG

Old Chang was notorious for his habit of taking advantage of others. It got so the villagers began warning one another against him, and nobody dared pass his door.

One day there came a man with a slab of sandstone. He passed Old Chang's door, thinking that he had nothing to lose.

From his window Old Chang hailed the passer-by. Then he dashed out with his kitchen cleaver and whetted it vigorously on the stone. When he was done Old Chang dismissed his victim with a wave of his hand and said: "Be off! I have no use for you any more!"

DOG MEAT *

A beggar declared that he had sworn off eating dog's flesh, which people told him was absurd.

"I haven't tasted any for a long time," he said.

"Well," replied a bystander, "if you have sworn off biting dogs, dogs haven't sworn off biting you."

COOK'S HOLIDAY

A cook was chopping meat in his own home. When nobody was looking he hid a piece in his lap. His wife observed this and scolded him.

"Why did you do it?" she asked. "This is your own meat."

"Oh, I forgot," he said.

---

* Dog meat has always a comic flavor to the Chinese. Cf. Lu Chi Sheng eating dog meat in "The Adventures of the Tattooed Monk," page 92, and Lin Yutang's "Dog-Meat General," page 293.

TAILOR'S DILEMMA

A tailor was cutting a suit for his customer. He turned the piece of material over and over for a long time without being able to bring himself to use the scissors. The apprentice boy finally asked him why he hesitated, and the answer was: "If I cut something out for him there would be nothing for me; if I cut something for me there would be nothing for him."

A BIGGER WORD

The father wrote out a word and taught it to his small son.

The next day the son was hanging around when the father was mopping the table. With a corner of his wet mop the father traced out the word on the table and asked the son to read it.

The son did not know how.

"Why, this is the same word I taught you yesterday," the father said.

"It's grown much bigger overnight," the son answered wide-eyed.

APPOINTMENT WITH LORD CHOU

A teacher dozed off before his class. When he woke up he told a fib to his pupils to cover it up.

"I had an appointment with Lord Chou in dreamland," he said.

The next day one of his pupils followed his example and also went to sleep in class. The teacher waked him up with a stick, and said, "How dare you sleep in the class!"

The pupil said, "I, too, had an appointment with Lord Chou."

"Well, and what did Lord Chou say to you?" the teacher demanded.

"Lord Chou said, 'I didn't see your honorable teacher yesterday.'"

THE EARLY RISER

A merchant had a son who loved to sleep late. In spite of the father's repeated lectures against indolence, the lazy son still would not get up until the sun was high in the sky. Finally the merchant thought of applying the profit motive as an incentive to his son for early rising. "Don't you want to make some money?" he said to his son. "You know the old saying, 'Get up early in the morning, pick up a pot of lost gold!'" "In that case," answered his son, "the one who lost the pot of gold must have got up even earlier."

GOD OF THE TARGET

A military commander was just on the point of losing a battle when a god joined his ranks and turned defeat into victory. The general forthwith knocked his head on the ground before the god, and asked what his godship's name might be.

"I," was the reply, "am the God of the Target."

"And what have I, a poor general, done," inquired the commander, "to deserve the help of the revered God of the Target?"

"I am grateful to you," replied the God, "because in the old days when you were practicing archery, you never once hit me."

INTELLIGENCE TEST

A militiaman was on night patrol duty when he came across a man who violated the curfew. The man owned to being a scholar, home late from the examinations. The militiaman said, "If it is a scholar I'll have to give you a test." The scholar asked for a question, but after a long while the militiaman could not think of a single question. "It's your luck," he cried, "I ran out of questions tonight."

HOW TO BECOME A DOCTOR

A quack killed one of his patients and, as a result, was bound hand and foot by the bereaved family. At night he struggled loose, dived into a river, and made his escape.

His son was deep in the study of a medical tome when he got home.

"Never mind studying medicine, my boy," he blurted out. "It's more important to learn swimming."

THE BEST DOCTOR IN THE WORLD

The King of Hell sent one of his messengers to the world in search of the best doctor, with these instructions:

"When you see a doctor at whose door there are no avenging ghosts, then you will have found the best doctor in the world."

The messenger looked far and near, but there was not a doctor who had not a host of avenging ghosts gathered at his door. Finally, he came upon one where there was a lone ghost wandering in front of the door. The messenger said to himself, "That's a good enough doctor for me."

When he inquired he found that the doctor had hung up his shingle only the day before.

RATHER BE KICKED

A woodcutter stumbled upon a doctor with his load. The doctor was very angry and raised his hand to hit him. The woodcutter knelt down and begged forgiveness. "I'd rather you kick me instead," he pleaded.

The bystanders wondered about this and asked him why.

"I don't mind if he uses his feet," the woodcutter explained, "but I'm sure I won't live under his hands."

SHOES FIXED

A cobbler in all his career used only one pair of leather soles. When he resoled a pair of shoes the soles were sure to come off the customer's feet as soon as he stepped out of the shop. The cobbler would follow his customer, pick up the soles, and use them all over again on the next customer.

One day he followed a customer out as usual but failed to find the soles. "There goes my business now!" he wailed. When he came back he found the soles—this time dropped inside of the door.

IT'S A DATE

A man was miserly to the extreme and he never gave a party. One day one of his neighbors gave a party in his house. Someone saw it and asked his servant, "Is your master giving a party today?" The servant said, "If you expect my master to give a party you will have to wait until the next incarnation!" Hearing this, the master scolded the servant, saying, "Who told you to promise any dates?"

HORSE FLESH

A guest from far away came to call on horseback and stayed long. The house was full of chickens and ducks, yet the master expressed his regrets, saying that he dared not ask his guest to stay for dinner as there was nothing at home to offer him. Hearing this, the guest borrowed a knife and offered to kill his own horse for dinner.

"Well, sir," the host asked, "if we eat up your horse how do you expect to go back?"

"Oh," said the guest, "I'll be all right. Just lend me one of your chickens or ducks to ride back on."

NO USE FOR MONEY

A street entertainer had a monkey show, and one day after making the collection from an audience the monkey held on to a coin and refused to give it to his master. The man first tried to bribe the monkey with some nuts and biscuits, then he dangled a little embroidered jacket before the animal's eyes, but no matter what he did the monkey backed away and would not relinquish the money. Finally, in a rage, the man started cursing his partner.

"You dumb beast!" he cried. "If you do not care for food or clothing, then what do you want the money for?"

AN IMPATIENT SON-IN-LAW

"I understand that your honorable daughter will come to me with a dowry of fifty thousand dollars?" asked the future son-in-law.

"Yes," answered the would-be father-in-law, "but for the time being this sum of money is in my safekeeping. As soon as I die it will be hers, plus interest."

"About when will that be?" the future son-in-law wanted to know.

DINING IN THE DARK

A greedy guest happened to be invited to dinner by a stingy host. When dinner was served, the dishes that appeared on the table were few in number and inferior in quality. Whatever they were, the guest gorged himself and in a moment swept everything clean. The host felt so disgusted at this that he balked at bringing on any more dishes.

"It's getting dark," observed the guest. "Please, may I have a candle?"

"Why, it's high noon," the host replied, "why do you wish to light a candle?"

"If it isn't getting dark," said the guest, "how is it that I can't see a thing on the table?"

VEGETARIAN

Ting Erh asked his friend to stay for dinner, which consisted of only one modest dish of bean curd. To cover up his niggardliness he claimed that bean curd was so nutritious that it was like very life to him—he had never tasted anything that could compare with it.

Another day Ting Erh paid a return visit to his friend. A sumptuous meal was prepared for him but, remembering his favorite food, his friend saw to it that bean curd was served with each dish of meat and fish. Surprisingly, Ting Erh picked out the fish and the meat to eat and completely ignored the bean curd.

"I thought you said the other day that bean curd was like very life to you," the friend asked. "How is it that you don't even touch it today?"

"Ah," said Ting Erh, "but what do you care about life when you can get meat and fish!"

HOSPITALITY

The host asked his guest to stay and have a cup of tea. He then sent to his neighbor's to borrow some tea leaves. Meanwhile, the water was boiling and every time it boiled over some more water was added. This was repeated until the big kettle was about full, and still no tea leaves were to be had. Finally, in despair, the host's wife said to her husband, "This guest is such a close friend of ours we might as well have him stay for a bath."

TEETOTALER

On New Year's Eve a jug of wine and a dish of cheese were offered for sacrifice before the spirit of the Tai Mountain. Turning around after the ceremony and seeing a dog at the side, the master of the house ordered the boy to put the food away quickly. The boy took the wine inside, but before he could turn around and put away the cheese it was already devoured by the dog. "You fool," the master scolded. "Why didn't you take the cheese first? You know the dog doesn't drink."

SHORT CUT

After a drinking party the guests were all discussing as to who had the farthest to go to get to his bed. A somewhat inebriated guest spoke up and claimed: "Of all present I have the shortest way to go to hit the bed."

"Who said so?" the others chorused. "Of course, the host himself has the nearest bed."

"The host still has a few steps to take to get to his bedroom," the drunken guest mumbled. "But I . . . I'm already there."

COLD WINE

A man who loved to drink found a jug of cold wine in his dream. He was about to warm it up and drink it when all of a sudden he awoke.

"I should have had it cold!" he said with profound regret.

EXCITEMENT

A very excitable man and a very deliberate man were sitting together before a stove, having a drink. The long coat of the former was touching the stove and was beginning to catch fire. The deliberate man, seeing this, said quietly,

"There is a point which I have noticed for some time, and which because of your quick temper I hesitate to mention, though it would be equally right to mention it or not to mention it."

"And what is it?" inquired the other.

"Well," replied the deliberate man, "your coat is on fire."

His friend hurriedly pulled his coat away from the stove and jumped up in a rage, shouting:

"Why didn't you say so before?"

"Well," answered the deliberate man, "people do assert that you have a very excitable temper, and now I see that they are right."

FIRECRACKER

A nearsighted fellow picked up a firecracker and proceeded to examine it at the lamp. The firecracker caught the flame and went off with a bang. A deaf man who was near by asked eagerly: "What did you pick up just now that came apart as soon as you touched it?"

IMPATIENT FAIRIES

Tung Ying was a filial son, so God in Heaven sent a fairy maiden down to earth to be his spouse. All the other fairy maidens were bidding the chosen one farewell and they asked of her, "In case you find any more filial sons down there be sure to send us a word."

THE ROBBED BRIDE

A family was marrying a daughter to a poor man. The latter's family, fearing lest the engagement might be broken off, got together all their kinsmen to carry the girl off. The younger sister, coming out first, was inadvertently seized and taken off pickaback by one of the conspirators.

"Stop! Stop!" cried the elder sister when she saw what had happened. "There's a mistake; you have got my younger sister on your back."

The girl on the back, however, shouted out, "No! No! There's no mistake. Hurry on, and don't believe a word she's saying."

THANKS TO LORD CHOU

A girl who was about to be married off tearfully demanded of her sister-in-law:

"Whoever invented this marriage institution?"

"Lord Chou," answered her sister-in-law. So the bride told what she thought of Lord Chou in no uncertain terms.

At the end of the honeymoon and on her first visit back in Mother's home, the girl demanded of her sister-in-law where Lord Chou could be found.

"What do you want of him now?" the sister-in-law asked.

"I wish to make him a pair of shoes in gratitude," she answered.

WHO'S CRYING?

A bride on the way to her wedding cried all the way in a most heart-breaking fashion. The sedan-chair carriers were so moved that they said, "Young lady, how about letting us carry you back home?"

"The crying's stopped now," replied the bride instantly.

CO-OPERATION

On the way to a wedding the bottom of the bridal sedan suddenly dropped out. The carriers held a hasty conference, agreeing that it would not do for the bride to walk the rest of the way, and yet it would not do either to go all the way back and fetch a new sedan chair. Overhearing their predicament, the bride volunteered a suggestion, saying, "I have a way." The carriers were all delighted and asked her what it was. The bride answered, "You just mind your carrying on the outside, and I'll mind my own walking on the inside."

THE SEDAN CHAIR IS READY

On her wedding day the daughter cried as if her heart would break. When she heard that the sedan-chair carriers were looking all over the place but could not find the poles she said sobbingly, "Oh, Ma . . . tell them the poles for carrying the sedan chair are behind that door."

WANG ERH TAKES A WIFE

A man of Ch'u had two wives. His neighbor, Wang Erh, made love to the elder one and she scolded him. Then he made love to the younger one and she encouraged him.

Not long afterward the man with the two wives died. Wang Erh was asked: "Would you take the elder one to be your wife, or the younger one?"

"The elder," he answered.

"The elder one scolded you and the younger one was good to you," he was reminded. "How is it that you wish to take the elder?"

Wang Erh answered: "When it is another man's wife you wish her to be good to you. Now for my own wife, I want one who would not be good to others."

RICE

A certain man had an affair with another man's wife. One day when they were making love to each other the husband returned, and the wife hurriedly hid her lover in a sack. The husband saw that the wife was a little bit nervous and he began to look around and saw something moving in the sack.

"What is in that sack?" demanded the husband.

The wife couldn't find any ready answer.

"What is in that sack, I say?" demanded the husband again.

In his desperation, the lover in the bag shouted on behalf of the wife, "Rice!"

THE BOLD HUSBAND

Ten henpecked husbands formed themselves into a sworn society for resisting the poisonous oppression of their wives. At the first meeting they were sitting talking over their pipes and wine when suddenly the ten wives, who had got wind of the movement, appeared on the scene. There was a general stampede, and nine of the husbands incontinently bolted like rats through a side door, only one remaining unmoved to face the music. The ladies merely smiled contemptuously at the success of their raid, and went away. The nine husbands then agreed that the bold tenth man, who had not run away, should be appointed their president; but on coming to offer him the post, they found that he had died of fright.

HE DIDN'T MEAN IT

The shrewish wife died. The henpecked husband, gazing at her portrait, thought of all the wrongs he had suffered at her hands and made as if to strike her. A sudden breeze went by and the picture stirred. The man, frightened to death, quickly withdrew his fist and said, "Oh, I was only kidding."

THE MANLY WAY

A man was beaten by his wife and had to go and hide under the bed. "You come out this minute!" the wife commanded.

"A man's a man," he answered. "When he says he won't come out, there's nothing you can do about it. He won't come out."

A YARD OF OIL

A man hailed an oil dealer and wanted to buy some for his lamp. "How much for a pound?" he asked.

The dealer laughed. "In buying oil, you measure," he explained.

"Of course, of course!" the man thundered. "I meant to ask you how much for a yard."

RED CANDLES

A village magistrate who did not know how to read and write kept his accounts by making a picture of everything he bought. One day during his absence his superior came on an inspection tour and looked into his books. Puzzled and annoyed at this new system of accounting, the official crossed it all out with red ink. When the magistrate returned and saw what happened, he resented it. "What's the idea of buying so many sticks of red candles for your own office and charging them to my account!" he said.

WINE FOR BREAKFAST

A man was so poor he could have only the cheapest food, fermented rice cakes, for breakfast. Every morning when he went out he would be slightly tipsy from the fermented rice.

One day a friend saw him and asked: "Have you been drinking this early?"

"No," he answered, "I just had some fermented rice cakes."

When he went home and told this to his wife, she said, "Why didn't you just say you had been drinking wine? It would sound much more elegant."

The next day when his friend asked the same question he told him he had been drinking wine.

"How did you drink it," his friend insisted on knowing, "hot or cold?"

"It's toasted," he answered.

The friend smiled and said, "It is only fermented rice again."

When his wife learned of this she blamed him once more and said, "How could you ever refer to wine as toasted? Next time you must say you drank it hot." The husband said, "Now I know."

The next time he saw the friend he volunteered the information without waiting to be asked.

"This time I drank hot wine," he said.

"How much did you have?" the friend asked.

"Two pieces," he said, extending two fingers.

CUT-RATE GOODS

A stranger in Soochow was about to go shopping when somebody stopped him and put him wise.

"The Soochow folks have a habit of asking double of the real price," he was told. "So when you buy anything just see what they ask and pay half of it; then you won't be cheated."

The stranger bore this piece of advice in mind, and presently he came upon a silk-and-satin store. For any piece of goods for which two dollars was asked he would offer one dollar in bargaining; for anything a dollar fifty he would offer seventy-five cents.

The shopkeeper grew very angry and finally told the man: "If this is the way you do business, then you don't have to buy anything. How about this small store making you a present of two bolts of choice silk?"

"Oh, my! No!" the would-be customer replied, bowing. "This humble servant will accept only one."

INSOMNIA

Two brothers bought a pair of shoes between them. The elder brother wore the shoes all day long and had a good time. To get even the younger brother put the shoes on every night and paced up and down his room. It was not long before the shoes were all worn out. Thereupon the elder brother proposed buying another pair in common.

"Not on your life!" the younger brother said, "I need to get some sleep."

SHARE AND SHARE ALIKE

I

Ah One and Ah Two were talking about going into partnership to make rice wine.

"You put up the rice, and I'll put up the water," Ah One proposed to Ah Two.

"How are we going to split later on if I put up all the rice?" Ah Two wanted to know.

Ah One told him: "Trust me always to be fair. When the wine is made all I want back is the liquid; the rest is all yours."

SHARE AND SHARE ALIKE

II

Two brothers, who became partners in tilling their corn fields, began by considering what share each should take in the harvest.

"I," said the elder brother, "will take the top half, and you will take the lower half."

"Oh, come!" cried the other; "that is not fair."

"It is quite simple," replied the elder; "next year you shall have the top half, and I will have the lower half."

When next year came, the younger brother urged the elder to sow the usual crop of corn; but the elder refused, saying, "This year let's have a potato crop."

ALL QUIET

A young man who loved peace and quiet happened to live in between a coppersmith's and a blacksmith's and suffered acutely from the noises from morning till night. He used to say: "If these two should move away I would be so thankful I would give them both a treat."

One day the two smithies presented themselves simultaneously and announced: "We are both going to move now. We know you have promised us a treat if we move and so we are here to collect." Asked when they expected to move, they said tomorrow. The long-harassed resident was overjoyed and entertained his neighbors sumptuously.

After the feast he asked, "And where are you two going to move to?"

The two smithies answered, "Well, I'm moving into his house and he is moving into mine."

OUT ALL DAY

A man's shoes and socks were both worn. The shoes laid the blame on the socks; the socks, on the other hand, laid the blame on the shoes. So they appealed to God for justice. God could not settle the case, so he had the heels arrested as material witnesses.

"And how should I know?" demanded the heels. "I'm out in the streets all day!"

FROM FEET TO MOUTH

Said the feet to the mouth: "You are the luckiest thing on earth. You are forever getting the best of me. Here I am, running around all day, wearing myself out. And all for the sake of your eating."

Retorted the mouth: "Don't accuse me. How would you like it if I stopped eating so that you could stop running around?"

BIG DRUM

Chang-three said, "We have a drum at home so big, when you beat it, it can be heard a hundred miles away."

Li-four said, "We have a cow in our home so big, when she takes a drink at the south bank of the river her head reaches out and touches the north bank."

Chang-three shook his head and exclaimed, "How could there be a cow of that size!"

Li-four said, "If there weren't cows of this size, where would you get the hide to make that drum?"

THE BIG MOUTH

There were two men who both loved to brag. The first man said: "In my humble village we have a giant whose head touches the sky while his feet are planted on the ground."

"We have a bigger man than that in our humble village," boasted the second man. "His upper lip reaches to the sky and his lower lip touches the ground."

This puzzled the first man, who asked: "Then where would his body be?"

The answer was: "He has nothing but a mouth."

SEEKING CO-OPERATION

Mr. Wang and Mr. Li saw each other in the street.

"How is Mr. Chang lately?" Mr. Wang asked Mr. Li. "I haven't seen him for a long time."

"Oh, Mr. Chang is dead," Mr. Li answered without thinking, whereupon Mr. Wang expressed his utmost regret.

When the two had parted Mr. Li started worrying about what he had just said. How could he have said a thing like that, he thought, when Mr. Chang was very well and alive? The more Mr. Li thought about this the more he thought that something should be done about it. So he rushed over to Mr. Chang's home.

"Mr. Chang," he said, "just now I saw Mr. Wang and we were talking about you when unthinkingly I remarked that you are dead. Now Mr. Wang will probably be over today to pay his last respects to you.

In case he should come would you do me a favor? Would you try, somehow, not to give me away?"

A HIGH-BORN MULE

Two noblemen, taking a walk in the fields one day, happened to see a farmer whipping his mule with great vehemence. Unable to stand the sight, they called to the farmer to stop and gave him a scolding.

"You shouldn't be so cruel to your mule," they admonished, "even though it is a beast."

The farmer was very frightened by this and thought to himself that these high-born gentlemen must have been some relations of the mule's to intervene in this way on its behalf. So, all upset, he bared his head, rushed up to his mule, and offered his apologies.

"I beg you, please, to pardon me," he blurted. "Just now I really didn't know what I was doing. I didn't know that even you are related to such high-and-mighties in the court."

SUMMER HAT

A man wore a heavy felt hat out in the heat of summer. Presently he felt so hot that he paused in the shade of a big tree, took off his hat, and started fanning himself with it. After a while he felt cooler and he told a passer-by, well pleased, "It's a good thing I wore this hat out today, otherwise the heat would have got me."

ORGANIZER

A certain man, who was manager of a labor association, was in the habit of swindling the workingmen out of their earnings. When he died and went to the next world, the God of Purgatory was furiously angry with him, and condemned him to be punished in the black-dark hell.

"Gentlemen," said he to his fellow sufferers as he passed through the entrance, "here it is impossible to get a ray of sunlight; why not form an association for cutting a hole in the roof?"

This and the following items translated by Herbert A. Giles.

PROPRIETY

A cook, who went to a rich man's house to run a dinner party, stole a large piece of meat and hid it in his hat. The host happened to see him do it, and planned to make the cook bow so that the meat would fall out of his hat. To accomplish this, he thanked the cook for all his trouble, and added, "I must really make you a bow of thanks."

The cook, who also knew that the host knew, and was in terror lest the meat should fall out and put him to shame, hurriedly fell on his knees and said, "Master, if you bow to my humble self, I must return the compliment on my knees."

A BLIND CRITIC

A man who was blind in both eyes was very clever in recognizing things by his sense of smell. One day a scholar brought some documents to him to test his skill. "This," said the blind man, "is the *Romance of the Western Pavilion.*"

"How can you tell that?" asked the scholar.

"By the aroma of powder and paint which hangs around it," replied the blind man.

"And this?" inquired the scholar, handing him a second book.

"*The History of the Three Kingdoms,*" answered the blind man at once.

"But how do you know?" asked the scholar again.

"By the atmosphere," replied the blind man, "which is one of weapons and warfare."

Then the scholar, lost in astonishment, produced some essays of his own composition, and submitted them to his critic.

"Ah," cried the blind man, "these beauties are from your own hand."

"How could you discover that?" asked the scholar again.

The blind man replied, "Just by the smell."

CONFUCIUS BORROWING FOOD

When Confucius, while in the state of Ch'en, was in want of food, he bade his favorite disciple, Yentze, repair to the country of the Muslims and borrow a supply, explaining who he was and to what nation he belonged, further stating that it was because of their friendly relations that the request was made. At this Yentze cried out in anger,

"What! Are you, the great philosopher, going to wheedle these barbarians, whom hitherto you have cursed, into giving us grain?"

As it turned out, he came back without any; and then Tzekung, another disciple, begged to be allowed to go, saying that he had long been skilled in the art of flattery.

"You may go, my dear boy," said Confucius, to the great delight of Tzekung, who managed to obtain a hundredweight of fine corn, with further supplies to be obtainable on the journey home. When he got back, Tzekung handed in a written report to the Sage, who highly praised what he had accomplished, saying,

"You have indeed brought back with you a hundredweight of corn, but your literary style is atrocious."

THE USE OF BOOKS

A student of the Imperial Academy hired rooms at a Buddhist monastery for purposes of study. Every day he would wander about amusing himself; and in the afternoon, when he got back, he would call the boy to bring his books. The boy brought the famous *Anthology,* but when he had glanced at it, he said:

"Fetch the *History of the Han Dynasty,* and put it underneath." He looked at it, and said, "I want the *Historical Records";* and again after inspection, he said, "Bring some Buddhist sutras."

The boy in astonishment replied, "The three works I have brought are enough to fill your belly *; why want more?"

"What I want," said the student, "is to go to sleep, and have the books as a pillow."

A CLEVER PUPIL

A tutor, who was anxious to be permanently engaged, was always praising the great cleverness of his pupil. The father did not believe in what the tutor alleged, and called for a test, which was to consist of providing correct antithetical words (of importance in writing verse, etc.).

"Come, now," said the tutor; "I give you 'crab.'" To this the boy replied, "Umbrella," and the tutor loudly applauded him. The father could not make anything of this, so the tutor said, "I see what he

* A colorful Chinese way of saying "enough for you to read."

means. A crab walks sideways, whereas your son holds himself and the umbrella in an upright position. I call it excellent."

THE TUTOR'S SON

A tutor, who was bragging about his son's cleverness as a book student, ended by suggesting that he might join in the lessons of his employer's son. This was readily agreed to; and the tutor, on his return home for the holidays, said to his son, "Next year I am going to take you with me for a course of study. I have praised you to my employer, whereas in reality you are a hopeless idiot and cannot read a single word." Then he wrote down three words—"coverlet," "rice," and "father"—and bade his son learn them carefully in order to bring them out when asked. Soon after their arrival, the employer examined the boy about a few words, of all of which he showed himself totally ignorant.

"He is nervous," said his father; "let me write a few words down, and you will see that he really knows something." The first word was "coverlet," which the boy failed to recognize. "Think of what is on the top of your bed," hinted his father. "Grass matting," replied his son. "What is this?" asked the father, writing down "rice." Again the boy failed, and again the father helped him with, "What is it you eat at home?" "Corn meal," replied his son. Finally the word "father" was written down, and once more the boy made no answer. This made the father angry, and he roared out, "Who is it sleeps with your mother?" To this the boy replied at once, "My uncle."

THE GREAT LEARNING

A teacher who had set up a school was asked by one of his pupils to explain the Confucian doctrine of *The Great Learning*. The teacher pretended to be tipsy, and said, "You have unfortunately chosen a moment to put this question when I happen to be tipsy." Then he went home and told his wife, who said, "*The Great Learning* is the name of a book, and its doctrine is concerned with principles of right and wrong." Her husband nodded assent, and next day he said to his pupils, "You stupid fellows chose yesterday, when I was tipsy, to ask questions, and now today, when I am sober, you don't ask me any. There is no difficulty in what you wanted to know yesterday." Then he gave his wife's explanation; after which a pupil begged him to explain the words "To brighten bright virtue" (to exhibit one's own virtue and to encourage others to do likewise). At this, the teacher put his hand to his head and said, "Stop a bit; I feel under the influence of wine just now."

THE PRIEST AND THE TIGER

A priest, who had been out performing religious duties, on his way home came face to face with a tiger. In terror, he flung one of his cymbals at the animal and hit it. As the beast still came on, he threw the other cymbal. But as this, too, had no effect, he took his prayer-book and flung that after the cymbals; whereupon the tiger at once turned and fled to its lair. The tigress asked what was the matter, and the tiger replied,

"I have just met a rude priest. It was all right for him to hurl both his cymbals at me, for I was not scared. But when he threw his subscription list at me, I had to flee."

EVIL SPIRITS

A Taoist priest, who was walking through the burial ground of a prince's palace, was bewitched by a host of evil spirits. He obtained the help of a passer-by, who saw him safely home. Said the priest to his rescuer:

"I am deeply indebted to you for rescuing me, but I have no means of rewarding you. Here is an amulet which will keep off evil spirits. I beg you to accept it with my best thanks."

THE PRACTICE OF MEDICINE

A doctor who had doctored a man to death was severely censured by the man's employer.

"Here, you fellows," he cried to his servants, "come and give this doctor a poisonous beating."

The doctor on his knees begged for mercy; but the employer said, "If now you are privately beaten to death, you will escape punishment at the hands of the officials." Then the doctor proposed that he should take away the corpse and have it decently buried. This was agreed to; but the doctor was a poor man without resources, and he was obliged to get his two sons and their wives to help carry the coffin.

"Oh, dear," groaned the doctor on the way, "I have never had any practice in keeping step."

"Bah!" said the wife, "it is your practice as a doctor which has brought all this trouble on us."

The younger son called out: "The head end is too heavy and the feet end too light; it's impossible to carry it."

"Father, father," cried the elder son, "in future doctoring, better pick out only very thin patients."

THE DOCTOR'S WIFE

A doctor, who had doctored a man's son to death and was threatened with legal proceedings, agreed to hand over his own son for adoption. Later on, he managed to cause the death of a client's servant, and was obliged to give up the only servant he had. One night there came a knock at his door from a neighbor, who said: "My wife is having a baby. Please come and attend to her at once!"

"Ah, the blackguard!" cried the doctor to his wife. "I know what he wants this time—he wants you."

TOO BUSY FOR WORDS

A doctor fell ill and could not go on his rounds. This roused the ire of a patient who had paid him large sums without getting any better; so he sent a servant to curse the doctor. When the servant came back, his master said, "Well, did you curse him?"

"No, I did not," was the reply.

"'And pray, why not?"

"Because," answered the servant, "all the time I kept trying to curse him, he was being badly beaten, and I really couldn't get a word in."

A DOCTOR'S GIFTS

A doctor who lived at a distance said to the neighbors at his temporary home, "You have been very kind to me for some time, and now I have no parting present to offer you. I will, however, give each of you a prescription."

This the neighbors declined on the ground that they were not ill.

"You soon will be," rejoined the doctor, "if you take my medicine."

CHOOSING A CAREER

A doctor, a girl, and a thief died and appeared before the Judge of Purgatory.

"And what did you do," said the Judge to the doctor, "to earn your living in the upper world?"

"Your servant," replied the doctor, "practiced as a physician, and was able to raise dying people to life again."

"You scoundrel!" roared the Judge. "You dared to interfere with my prerogative? Away with him, lictors, to the caldron of boiling oil."

Then, turning to the girl, the Judge bade her give an account of her doings.

"I make love to gentlemen," replied the girl, hastily adding, "But only to those who have no wives."

"You might do worse," said the Judge. "Take a further span of twelve years' life on earth."

The thief came next. He said, "I have been a bad man in robbing people and spending their money in extravagance, but I will now make some restitution."

"You have only done what other people do," remarked the Judge. "I give you ten more years of life."

"Oh, dear, oh, dear!" cried the doctor to the Judge. "If that is the way you administer justice, only let me go back to the upper world. I have a daughter and a son, and I shall know what professions to put them into."

THE ART CRITICS

An artist who had painted a portrait said to his subject, "I wish you would refer this picture to the man in the street, in order to judge if the likeness is good or not."

The subject agreed, and the first person who was asked declared that the scenery was perfect. The second went into raptures about the clothes; so that when a third was consulted, he was told what the other two criticisms were and was invited to deal more with bodily characteristics. After many hum's and ha's, he said, "The beard is extraordinarily like."

SELF-PORTRAIT

A painter of portraits failed altogether in the matter of likeness. One day a friend advised him to paint portraits of himself and his wife and to hang them out for people to judge. This he did, with the result that by and by an old gentleman came along who, after gazing at the pictures, inquired the name of the lady.

"Why, that is your own daughter," was the reply.

"Then why," asked the father, "is she sitting out here with a stranger?"

WHO WON?

An indifferent chess player, who thought a lot of his skill, on one occasion lost three games. Next day, a friend met him and asked him how he had come off.

"I didn't win the first game," he replied; "and my opponent didn't lose the second. As to the third game, I asked him to agree to a draw, but he wouldn't."

COMMON CLAY

A maker of clay dolls gained a considerable profit on his sales. One day he said to his wife, "In future, I shall make the dolls with their hands in their sleeves; this will save clay."

The plan succeeded; and again he said to his wife, "I will make the dolls sitting down, so that we shall save still more."

There was the same satisfactory result, and then he said to his wife, "I will make them with their heads bent over in sleep. How will that do?"

When finished, his wife picked one up and said, "The saving is right enough, but the dolls have now lost all resemblance to human beings."

A BARGAIN

A wealthy man said to a very miserly fellow, "I will give you a thousand ounces of silver if you will let me beat you to death."

The miser thought over the offer for some time, and then replied, "Make it five hundred ounces, and half beat me to death."

LOSE FACE

A man who wanted to have his portrait painted offered such a small sum that it was not enough to pay for the brushes, paper, and paint. So the artist used common ink and cheap paper, and painted a man with his back to the spectator. The sitter was very angry and said,

"The features are everything in a portrait; why have you only painted my back?"

"Well," replied the artist, "I thought you might be ashamed to look people in the face."

ALL THAT MONEY CAN'T BUY

The Judge of Purgatory decided that a certain disembodied spirit should return to earth as a rich man.

"But I don't want to be a rich man," cried the spirit. "I only ask for a regular supply of food, with no worries, that I may burn pure incense and drink bitter tea, and thus pass through life."

The Judge replied: "Money I can provide, to any amount; but this peaceful, happy life you require is more than I can give."

MONEY IS LIFE

A farmer who had been planting eggplants, but could not make them grow, asked the advice of an old gardener.

"There is no difficulty about that," was the reply. "Under every plant bury a copper cash."

"How so?" inquired the farmer.

"With money," said the gardener, "there is life; without it, death."

RICH MAN: POOR MAN

A rich man said haughtily to another man, "I am wealthy, you are poor; why don't you behave deferentially to me?"

"That you have money," was the reply, "is no reason why I should be deferential to you, as it has nothing to do with me."

"If I were to give you half of what I have," asked the rich man, "what would you do then?"

"If we each had the same amount," answered the poor man, "I should be on a level with you; where would the deference come in?"

"But supposing that I gave you all," said the rich man. "I can hardly believe that you wouldn't be deferential then."

"In that case," replied the poor man, "I having all the money and you none, it would be for you to be deferential to me."

HE DOESN'T BELONG

A vulgar fellow built himself a very nice house, and stocked it with valuable curios, books, and paintings of all kinds. To a visitor who came to see the treasures, he said, "If you notice anything at all inappropriate, kindly point it out to me, and I will have it removed."

"Your collection is certainly very beautiful," replied the visitor, "but there is one item which should be taken away."

"And what may that be?" asked the collector; to which came the answer:

"Your honorable self."

MONEY TALKS

A man who had lost his way met a dumb man and asked for guidance. The dumb man made it clear by signs with his hands that he would only direct the stranger if he were paid for doing so. The stranger grasped his meaning, and handed him some money; whereupon the dumb man at once directed him by word of mouth.

"But why," asked the stranger, "unless you get money do you sham dumbness?"

"Because," answered the impostor, "at the present day it is only money that talks."

INTERPRETATION OF DREAM

A debtor said to a creditor, "I am not long for this life; last night I dreamed that I was dead."

"Yes," rejoined the creditor, "but dreams go by contraries, and to dream of death means that you will live."

"Then," added the debtor, "I had another dream; I dreamed that I was paying my debt to you."

MEAT DUMPLINGS

A man whose wife was ill asked her if there was anything she fancied to eat.

"If I could have some good meat dumplings, I think I could manage one or two."

So the husband got ready a dish of dumplings, meaning to share the meal with her; but while he was gone to get chopsticks, his wife finished up all the dumplings except one.

"Why don't you eat the last one?" he asked on his return.

"Well," replied the wife, "I don't think it would hurt me."

A FOOLISH BIRD

A guest at a dinner sat tight and showed no signs of leaving. At length the host called his visitor's attention to a bird on a tree and said, "As our last course has been served, wait till I cut down the tree, catch the bird, have it cooked, and tell the butler to bring up some wine. What do you say to that?"

"Well," replied the guest, "I expect that by the time the tree is down, the bird will have flown."

"No, no," said the host, "that is a foolish bird, and doesn't know when to go."

HOUSE FOR SALE

A guest invited to stay to dinner, when he had finished his bowl of rice, not seeing any more forthcoming, brought the fact to the notice of his host as follows:

"A friend of mine has a house which he wants to sell. Its beams are as big and round as this"—pointing toward his host with the mouth of his rice bowl.

The host saw the point, and called his servant boy to bring more rice.

"And how much does he want for his house?" asked the host.

"Now that he has enough to eat," replied the guest, "he would not sell it."

THE FEAST OF LANTERNS

Two relatives, one of whom was very precipitate and the other very deliberate, met one day on the road. The latter made a bow down to the ground and said:

"I am deeply indebted to you; I have put you to trouble at the New Year; I have put you to trouble at the Feast of Lanterns; I have put you to trouble at the Dragon Festival. I have put you to trouble at the Midautumn Festival; I have put you to trouble at the Chrysanthemum Fete; for all of which I have made no return; besides which there are many other occasions which, I am ashamed to say, I cannot remember."

When he had finished this long speech he got up, to find that his relative had disappeared. Asked when his honorable relative had left, a by-stander replied, "Oh, he went after the Feast of Lanterns, about six months back."

SLEEPY DOG

A deaf man went to call at the house of a friend, whose watchdog, as soon as it caught sight of him, barked loud and long. He paid no attention to what he did not hear, but went in; and after the usual compliments had been exchanged, he said to his friend, "I imagine that the honorable dog which guards your palace did not get much sleep last night."

"How so?" asked the friend.

"Well," replied the deaf man, "from the moment it saw me, it did nothing but yawn."

THE RUDE MAN

A shortsighted man who had lost his way saw a stone by the roadside with a crow sitting on it, and he mistook the crow for another man. After he had called out several times, asking for direction, the crow flew away, and he shouted after it, "I have spoken to you several times and you have made no answer. Now your hat has been blown away, and of course it is no business of mine to help you."

FOUR GENERATIONS

The son of a duke having obtained a princedom, his father was overjoyed. The son was rather astonished at this, and he invited his father to explain.

"Well, you see," replied the latter, "your father has gone one better than my father, and your son has gone one better than my son."

LIKE FATHER, LIKE SON

A father and son were both very stubborn and would never yield to anybody. One day the father had invited a guest to dinner, and told the son to go into the town and buy some meat. When he had done so, the son was just going through the city gate on his way home when he met another man face to face. Neither would give way, and there they stood, until at length the father went in search of his son. On seeing the boy, he said, "You hurry home with the meat. I will take over this fellow."

THE FOOLISH SON

A man who was going away to a distance said to his son, "If anyone comes and inquires for your Venerable One, tell him that your father has gone away on business; invite him in and serve tea."

Then, knowing what a fool his son was and fearing that he would forget what to do, he wrote down his instructions and gave them to his son, who put them in his sleeve and from time to time took them out to look at. However, as three days passed and no one appeared, he began to think there was no use in keeping the paper, and put it to the lamp and burned it. On the fourth day a visitor did arrive and inquired after the Venerable One. The boy felt in his sleeve for the paper, but not finding it, said to the visitor, "Gone!"

The visitor, much alarmed, asked when this had happened. To which the boy replied, "Burned last night."

REVENGE

An unfilial son was always knocking about his father, who devoted himself to his grandson, keeping him always at hand and cherishing him more and more. A friend asked the grandfather why this devotion to the son of an unfilial son.

"The reason is this," was the reply: "I want to bring him up to manhood that he may do a little knocking about on my behalf."

FILIAL PIETY

A father and son were chopping firewood together, when the father, who had the hatchet, accidentally wounded the son's fingers.

"You old pimp!" cried the son. "Are you blind?"

A grandson, who was standing by, hearing his grandfather cursed like this, and feeling much hurt, turned to his father and said, "You son of a bitch! How dare you curse your own father?"

HIS WIFE'S LOVER

A lady had a lover who lived next door. Hearing her husband come home, the lover jumped out of the window; but when the husband got in, the first thing he saw was a man's shoe. Cursing his wife roundly, he put the shoe under his pillow and went to sleep, saying, "Wait till tomorrow, when I will find out whose shoe this is, and settle accounts with you."

The wife kept awake until he was sound asleep, and then gently drew out the shoe and placed one of her husband's own shoes in its place. In the early morning, the husband got up and began again to curse his wife; but he soon discovered that the shoe was his own. Repenting of his behavior, he said to his wife, "I was wrong in my suspicions of you. I must have been the man who jumped out of the window."

THE WISDOM OF AGE

A man who had just married a middle-aged wife, noticing some wrinkles on her face, asked her what her age was.

"About forty-four or -five," she replied.

"Upon your betrothal card," said the husband, "you put down thirty-eight; I am sure you are more than that."

"I will tell you the truth," confessed the wife. "I am fifty-four."

The husband pressed her again and again but she stuck to fifty-four; so he planned a trick. He said, "Oh, I must go and cover up the salt, or the rats will eat it up."

At this the wife cried out, "What a joke! Here I have lived sixty-eight years, and I have never heard of rats eating salt."

CHANGING OF THE GUARDS

The wife of a certain constable was of a rather amorous disposition, so that her husband had to keep a watchful eye on her. One day when the constable had to take his turn on duty, he painted on the left side of her door the figure of a constable on guard, noting carefully its position. When a lover of the lady came along, he rubbed out the figure on the left, and painted another on the right panel. At his return from duty, the husband examined the door and saw that the painting was not his work. In a towering rage, he said, "What I put was on the left of the door; how has it now got to the right side?"

"Well," replied his wife, "I am astonished that you, who have been all these years in a public office, have never heard of changing guard."

MATCHING DREAMS

A girl and her sweetheart, who met after a short separation, both swore that they had been thinking all the time each about the other.

"Not a night," claimed the girl, "but I dreamed of your being with me and going about with me as usual, the dreams being caused by my constant thoughts of you."

"Oh, my dear," said the youth, "and I too have been dreaming of you."

"What kind of dreams did you have?" asked the girl.

"Well, to tell you the truth," replied the youth, "what I dreamed was that you weren't dreaming of me."

A LOSING PROPOSITION

A man asked a girl, to whom he had taken a fancy, how old she was.

"I am eighteen," she replied.

Then he was obliged to go abroad on business and did not see her for two or three years, during which time his financial ventures were unsuccessful. Upon his return, he once again met her and inquired her age. This time, the girl, who had evidently forgotten the previous occasion, said, "I am seventeen years old."

Upon this the man burst into tears and blubbered away without stopping. The girl asked him whatever was the matter, and he answered, "Your age is just like my capital, getting less and less; surely that is enough to make one feel miserable."

CLASSIC EXAMPLES

A husband wished to take a concubine. His wife said, "One man, one woman. What right have you to take a concubine?"

"Mencius tells us," retorted the husband, "that a man of Ch'i had a wife and a concubine; and he also speaks of the 'right behavior for women.' Concubines have been known from of old."

"If you go by such authority," argued the wife, "then I must get a second husband."

"How so?" asked the husband.

"Do we not read in *The Great Learning* that Madame Chang of

Honan had two husbands; and in Mencius that there were chief and secondary husbands?"

GRAPEVINE

A government clerk lived in great fear of his wife. One day she scratched his face to ribbons; and next day, when he went to his office, the prefect asked him what had happened. The clerk cooked up an excuse and replied, "Last evening, as I was enjoying the cool air, the frame of our grapevine came down with a run and caused these cuts on my face."

The prefect did not believe him, and said, "No, no; of course it was your wife who did that mischief. Here, you lictors, bring the woman before me."

The prefect had not counted upon his own wife being behind the screen and hearing the whole story. Wild with anger, she dashed out of the hall, while the prefect hurriedly turned to the lictors and said, "Wait a bit, wait a bit! It seems that my own grapevine frame is likely to come down with a run."

A TEA CONNOISSEUR

A countryman went up to town to see a relative, who entertained him with some choice tea made with water from a famous spring.

"Delicious! Delicious!" cried out the countryman, several times. "You, my old relative, are evidently a connoisseur."

"Is it the tea or the spring water," asked the host, "which takes your fancy?"

"I like it," replied the countryman, "because it's hot."

THE HIDDEN HOE

A man was at work in the fields when his wife called to him to come in to dinner.

"Wait a minute," he shouted back, "until I have hidden my hoe."

When he got in, his wife reproved him, saying, "You should hide your hoe secretly; to shout out, as you did, is the way to get it stolen."

Urged by her, he went back to look after his hoe, and found it gone. He hurried back, and whispered very softly into his wife's ear: "Someone has stolen it."

A GRASS ROPE

A man stole an ox, and was put in the cangue (large square wooden collar). A friend came along and asked him what crime he had committed to get this punishment. The thief said, "I was just walking along the street when I saw on the ground a grass rope. Thinking it was of no use, I made the mistake of picking it up and taking it home; and so I got into this trouble."

"But what is there wrong," asked the friend, "in thus picking up a grass rope?"

"Well," replied the thief, "there was something else tied to the rope."

"And what was that?" asked the friend; to which the thief replied, "A very small ox."

GRATITUDE

A man who had been condemned to be bambooed hired another man to take his punishment, paying him three ounces of silver for the job. The latter was very pleased with the money; but the magistrate ordered him to receive thirty blows, a few of which caused him such pain that he pulled out the money and with it bribed the jailer to lay on with a light hand. On being released, he went to thank the man for whom he had suffered.

"The money, sire, you kindly gave me, saved my life. Without it, I should have been beaten to death."

THE PRICE OF WHEAT

A man told his servant boy to go to Maple Bridge and ask the price of wheat. The boy went along until he came to Maple Bridge, where he heard a man calling out, "Come and eat my cornmeal"; and thinking that no payment was wanted, promptly ate up three bowlfuls. He was just going off when the cornmeal man asked for his money. This not being forthcoming, he gave the boy nine good smacks on the face, with which he hurried home.

"Well," said his master, "and have you found out the price of wheat?"

"I have found out the price of cornmeal," replied the boy.

"And what may that be?" inquired his master.

"Three smacks a bowl."

SPECIAL DELIVERY

It being very important to carry an official dispatch quickly, the runner was told to take a horse. He did so, and ran behind, urging the animal on.

"If you are in such a hurry," said another man, "why don't you get up and ride?"

"Six feet," replied the runner, "get over the ground faster than four."

CHANGE PLACES

The nose and the eyebrows were quarreling over their positions. The nose said, "All manner of scents I am the first to detect, and this counts as a great merit to me; but you, you useless creature, what merit have you, that you should occupy a higher place than I do?"

"I admit," replied the eyebrows, "the strength of your reasoning; but if you were placed above me, do you think people would be pleased?"

THREE PRECIOUS THINGS

A man who was in the habit of telling tall tales said to his relatives that he had at his home three precious things: an ox which could walk a thousand li * a day, a cock which uttered a single crow at each watch of the night, and a dog which could read books.

"If you have all these wonderful objects," cried his relatives, "tomorrow we will pay you a visit and hope you will let us see them."

The man went home and told his wife that he had been lying, asking her how he was to make good.

"That will be all right," replied his wife; "I have a plan."

Next day, when the relatives arrived, she declared that her husband had gone off early in the morning to Peking.

"And when will he be back?" inquired the relatives.

"Oh, in seven or eight days," answered the wife. Then when they wanted to know how he could possibly do the journey in such a short time, she replied, "He is riding our ox."

* Three hundred miles.

"And have you got the wonderful cock which keeps the watches?" asked the relatives just at a moment when the cock crew, and it happened to be noon.

"There you are," said the wife; "but this is not all. Our cock crows also at the arrival of visitors."

The relatives next wished to see the dog that could read books. "Well," replied the wife, "I will not deceive you. We are very badly off, and the dog has taken a situation as tutor."

TRAVELERS' TALES

A Shantung man had heard so much about the huge bridges of the south, that regardless of distance he set out to see them. On the road he met a Soochow man who was eagerly traveling to see the Shantung carrots, of the size of which he had heard marvelous accounts. The Soochow man suggested that in place of these long journeys, each should describe his own wonders to the other.

"As to the bridges," he said, "last year on this date, a man fell over the parapet, and his body has not yet reached the water. How's that for high?"

"'Tis high indeed," replied the Shantung man; "and as to the carrots, I may say at once that it would be a waste of time for you to go to see them. They grow to such a length that by this time next year they will be with you in Soochow."

IV

THE HUMOR OF PROTEST
(Modern)

IV. The Humor of Protest
(Modern)

THE philosopher Chuangtze once said: "When all under heaven is muddled it is no time for serious talk." The modern times in China are muddled times. In the old emperor days, up to the time of the first foreign war and the first "unequal treaty," the Chinese scene was at least all of a piece. Within the world of the Middle Kingdom values were consistent, and by those values scholars perfected their "eight-legged essays" and either passed the civil examinations and became officials or flunked them and taught school. The body-building and the soul-searching exercises which a new and humiliated China sought to undergo at one and the same time, in order the better to face the outside world, were not conducive to a straight face or to conformist conduct. Depending on individual genius, a man who had an impeccable English style, like Ku Hung-ming, could use his pen to tilt at Western imperialism in China; another who was schooled in the best tradition of the Chinese classics, like Lusin, could strike at the basic evils in the character of the average Chinese and make him out to be a fool.

There were certain ancient virtues which China must preserve, and there were many ancient faults which China must discard, and no man-made government could set an example of doing both without, knowingly or not, committing some ludicrous sins. During the initial years of the National Government in Nanking there grew up, therefore, a group of writers headed by the pre-American Lin Yutang and rallying around a literary fortnightly named, somewhat tongue-in-cheek fashion, after the Confucian classic *The Analects*. They popularized a new Chinese word, *yumeh* (humor), to convey the exact flavor of their writing, and it was their self-appointed job to play the jester to the new Kuomintang rule. There should be a place for such a magazine and such a group under *any* government, because the targets of their good-natured attack are nothing so much as cocksureness and hypocrisy.

As most of the selections here are taken from bound volumes of *The*

Analects, I cannot do better than to reproduce the ten-point credo which appeared at the head of each issue of that publication to sum up this spirit of protest in modern Chinese humor:

THE ANALECTS' CREDO

1. Don't oppose the Revolution.
2. Don't criticize those whom we don t think much of; but do criticize those whom we love and esteem (for instance, our Mother Country, contemporary militarists, promising writers, and revolutionists who are not absolutely hopeless).
3. Don't curse people right off the mouth. (Try to have humor without harm. There is no reason to call a national thief father, nor is there any need to call him a turtle's egg.)
4. Don't take somebody else's money; don't talk somebody else's talk. (We will not accept paid propaganda from any quarter, but we might, if we like, do free propaganda, or even counter-propaganda.)
5. Don't follow any elegant fad; even more, don't follow any powers that be. (Refuse to be a fan to opera stars, movie stars, society stars, literary stars, political stars, or stars of any other kind.)
6. Don't shout slogans for each other; oppose "goose-pimpleism." (Avoid all such terms as "scholar," "poet," and "my friend Dr. Hu Shih.")
7. Don't compose stuffy verses or sweet songs.
8. Don't uphold public justice and righteousness, only spout your frank private views.
9. Don't get rid of your bad habits (such as smoking, tea drinking, looking at plum blossoms, or reading); and don't advise your friend to quit smoking.
10. Don't say your own writing is no good.

It should be noted that every article included here was published before war came to China in 1937.

Ku Hung-ming

BORN in Malaya, steeped in the classics of German and English philosophy, Ku Hung-ming returned to China in the latter part of the nineteenth century "an imitation Western man," unable to speak Mandarin, without a queue, and dressed in a foreign suit. He lived to become a colorful anachronism and, in his own estimation, the last of the Confucian scholars. A stubborn individualist, Ku's two pet hates were the Western colonial mind and the new Republican China, and in demonstrating traditional Chinese virtues he sometimes went to ridiculous extremes in order to prove his point. He was the philosopher who told the pilgrim Somerset Maugham that he wore a queue as a symbol of the old China. He was the unregenerate rogue who, in defense of concubinage, pointed out that, whereas you always see a teapot with four teacups, you never find a teacup with four teapots.

JOHN SMITH IN CHINA

The Philistine not only ignores all conditions of life which are not his own but he also demands that the rest of mankind should fashion its mode of existence after his own.—GOETHE.

Mr. W. Stead once asked: "What is the secret of Marie Corelli's popularity?" His answer was: "Like author, like reader; because the John Smiths who read her novels live in Marie Corelli's world and regard her as the most authoritative exponent of the universe in which they live, move, and have their being." What Marie Corelli is to the John Smiths in Great Britain, the Rev. Arthur Smith is to the John Smiths in China.

Now the difference between the really educated person and the half-educated one is this. The really educated person wants to read books which will tell him the real truth about a thing, whereas the half-educated person prefers to read books which will tell him what he wants the thing to be, what his vanity prompts him to wish that the thing should be. John Smith in China wants very much to be a su-

Written in English, from *The Spirit of the Chinese People*, published 1915.

perior person to the Chinaman and the Rev. Arthur Smith writes a book to prove conclusively that he, John Smith, is a very much superior person to the Chinaman. Therefore, the Rev. Arthur Smith is a person very dear to John Smith, and the *Chinese Characteristics* becomes a Bible to John Smith.

But Mr. W. Stead says, "It is John Smith and his neighbors who now rule the British Empire." Consequently, I have lately taken the trouble to read the books which furnish John Smith with his ideas on China and the Chinese.

The Autocrat of the Breakfast Table classified minds under the heads of arithmetical and algebraical intellects. "All economical and practical wisdom," he observes, "is an extension or variation of the arithmetical formula 2 plus 2 equal 4. Every philosophical proposition has the more general character of the expression *a* plus *b* equal *c*." Now the whole family of John Smith belongs decidedly to the category of minds which the Autocrat calls arithmetical intellects. John Smith's father, John Smith, Senior, alias John Bull, made his fortune with the simple formula 2 plus 2 equal 4. John Bull came to China to sell his Manchester goods and to make money and he got on very well with John Chinaman because both he and John Chinaman understood and agreed perfectly upon the formula 2 plus 2 equal 4. But John Smith Junior, who now rules the British Empire, comes out to China with his head filled with *a* plus *b* equal *c* which he does not understand— and not content to sell his Manchester goods, wants to civilize the Chinese or, as he expresses it, to "spread Anglo-Saxon ideals." The result is that John Smith gets along very badly with John Chinaman, and, what is still worse, under the civilizing influence of John Smith's *a* plus *b* equal *c* Anglo-Saxon ideals, John Chinaman, instead of being a good, honest, steady customer for Manchester goods, neglects his business, goes to Chang Su-ho's Gardens to celebrate the Constitution, in fact becomes a mad, raving reformer.

I have lately, by the help of Mr. Putnam Weale's *Reshaping of the Far East* and other books, tried to compile a Catechism of Anglo-Saxon Ideals for the use of Chinese students. The result, so far, is something like this:

1. What is the chief end of man?

The chief end of man is to glorify the British Empire.

2. Do you believe in God?

Yes, when I go to church.

3. What do you believe in when you are not in church?

I believe in interests—in what will pay.

4. What is justification by faith?

To believe in everyone for himself.

5. What is justification by works?

Put money in your pocket.

6. What is Heaven?

Heaven means to be able to live in Bubbling Well Road * and drive in victorias.

7. What is Hell?

Hell means to be unsuccessful.

8. What is a state of human perfectibility?

Sir Robert Hart's Custom Service in China.

9. What is blasphemy?

To say that Sir Robert Hart is not a great man of genius.

10. What is the most heinous sin?

To obstruct British trade.

11. For what purpose did God create the four hundred million Chinese?

For the British to trade upon.

12. What form of prayer do you use when you pray?

We thank thee, O Lord, that we are not as the wicked Russians and brutal Germans are, who want to partition China.

13. Who is the great apostle of the Anglo-Saxon Ideals in China?

Dr. Morrison, the *Times* correspondent in Peking.

It may be a libel to say that the above is a true statement of Anglo-Saxon ideals, but anyone who will take the trouble to read Mr. Putnam Weale's book will not deny that the above is a fair representation of the Anglo-Saxon ideals of Mr. Putnam Weale and John Smith who reads Mr. Putnam Weale's books.

The most curious thing about the matter is that the civilizing influence of John Smith's Anglo-Saxon ideals is really taking effect in China. Under this influence John Chinaman too is now wanting to glorify the Chinese Empire. The old Chinese literatus with his eight-legged essays was a harmless humbug. But foreigners will find to their cost that the new Chinese literati who under the influence of John Smith's Anglo-Saxon ideals are clamoring for a constitution, are likely to become an intolerable and dangerous nuisance. In the end I fear John Bull, Senior, will not only find his Manchester goods trade ruined,

* The most fashionable quarter in Shanghai.

but he will even be put to the expense of sending out a General Gordon or Lord Kitchener to shoot his poor old friend John China-man who has become *non compos mentis* under the civilizing influence of John Smith's Anglo-Saxon ideals. But that is neither here nor there.

What I want to say here in plain, sober English is this: It is a won-der to me that the Englishman who comes out to China with his head filled with all the arrant nonsense written in books about the Chinese, can get along at all with the Chinese with whom he has to deal. Take this specimen, for instance, from a big volume, entitled *The Far East: Its History and Its Questions,* by Alexis Krausse:

"The crux of the whole question affecting the Powers of the West-ern nations in the Far East lies in the appreciation of the true inward-ness of the Oriental mind. An Oriental not only sees things from a different standpoint to [!] the Occidental, but his whole train of thought and mode of reasoning are at variance. The very sense of perception implanted in the Asiatic varies from that with which we are endowed!"

After reading the last sentence an Englishman in China, when he wants a piece of *white* paper, if he follows the ungrammatical Mr. Krausse's advice, would have to say to his boy: "Boy, bring me a piece of *black* paper." It is, I think, to the credit of practical men among foreigners in China that they can put away all this nonsense about the true inwardness of the Oriental mind when they come to deal practi-cally with the Chinese. In fact I believe that these foreigners get on best with the Chinese and are the most successful men in China who stick to 2 plus 2 equal 4, and leave the *a* plus *b* equal *c* theories of Oriental inwardness and Anglo-Saxon ideals to John Smith and Mr. Krausse. Indeed when one remembers that in those old days, before the Rev. Arthur Smith wrote his *Chinese Characteristics,* the relations between the heads or taipans of great British firms such as Jardine, Matheson and their Chinese compradores * were always those of mutual affec-tion, passing on to one or more generations; when one remembers this, one is inclined to ask what good, after all, has clever John Smith with his *a* plus *b* equal *c* theories of Oriental inwardness and Anglo-Saxon ideals done, either to Chinese or foreigners?

Is there then no truth in Kipling's famous dictum that East is East and West is West? Of course there is. When you deal with 2 plus 2

* Chinese employed by foreign firms in China to be agents between them and Chi-nese merchants.

equal 4, there is little or no difference. It is only when you come to problems such as *a* plus *b* equal *c* that there is a great deal of difference between East and West. But to be able to solve the equation *a* plus *b* equal *c* between East and West, one must have real aptitude for higher mathematics. The misfortune of the world today is that the solution of the equation *a* plus *b* equal *c* in Far Eastern problems is in the hands of John Smith, who not only rules the British Empire, but is an ally of the Japanese nation—John Smith who does not understand the elements even of algebraical problems. The solution of the equation *a* plus *b* equal *c* between East and West is a very complex and difficult problem. For in it there are many unknown quantities, not only such as the East of Confucius and the East of Mr. Kang Yu-wei and the Viceroy Tuan Fang, but also the West of Shakespeare and Goethe and the West of John Smith. Indeed when you have solved your *a* plus *b* equal *c* equation properly, you will find that there is very little difference between the East of Confucius and the West of Shakespeare and Goethe, but you will find a great deal of difference between even the West of Dr. Legge the scholar and the West of the Rev. Arthur Smith. Let me give a concrete illustration of what I mean.

The Rev. Arthur Smith, speaking of Chinese history, says:

"Chinese histories are antediluvian, not only in their attempts to go back to the ragged edge of zero of time for a point of departure, but in the interminable length of the sluggish and turbid current which carries on its bosom not only the mighty vegetation of past ages, but wood, hay and stubble past all reckoning. None but a relatively timeless race could either compose or read such histories: none but the Chinese memory could store them away in its capacious abdomen!"

Now let us hear Dr. Legge on the same subject. Dr. Legge, speaking of the twenty-three standard dynastic histories of China, says:

"No nation has a history so thoroughly digested; and on the whole it is trustworthy."

Speaking of another great Chinese literary collection, Dr. Legge says:

"The work was not published, as I once supposed, by Imperial authority, but under the superintendence and at the expense (aided by other officers) of Yuen Yun, Governor-General of Kwangtung and Kwangse, in the 9th year of the last reign of Kien-Lung. The publication of so extensive a work shows a public spirit and zeal for literature among the high officials of China which should keep foreigners from thinking meanly of them."

The above then is what I mean when I say that there is a great deal of difference not only between the East and West but also between the West of Dr. Legge, the scholar who can appreciate and admire zeal for literature, and the West of the Rev. Arthur Smith, who is the beloved of the John Smiths in China.

Lusin

WHEN Lin Yutang was "promoting" humor, Lusin went on record to say that he was against it, as he was against importing the Anglo-Saxon idea of "fair play." But he was being difficult. No truly great storyteller can be devoid of humor. As a matter of fact, Lusin's justly immortalized Ah Q, besides being a composite of Chinese weaknesses, is a comical character of whom cartoon strips have been made. More than that of anyone else, Lusin's humor is born of protest, even of wrath; and, thinking over what he writes, one feels like using the Chinese expression: "I am so angry I can laugh!"

AH Q'S VICTORIES

Not only were Ah Q's name and origin unknown, but his "life and deeds" were likewise clothed in obscurity. The villagers of Wei were interested in Ah Q only when they needed an extra laborer, only as an object of jibes and practical jokes; no one paid any attention to his life and deeds. Ah Q himself did not throw any light on the subject. When engaged in quarrels he would sometimes allude to his past, saying, "We used to be much better off than you! Who do you think you are?"

Having no home, Ah Q lived in the village temple and worked for people by the day, harvesting wheat, husking rice, punting boats. When his work lasted for a period of time he stayed at his employer's house. So he was remembered only when extra hands were needed; but this was mere labor, not life and deeds. During the slack season, Ah Q himself was completely forgotten, to say nothing of his life and deeds. Once an old man praised him, saying, "What a hard worker Ah Q is!" At that moment Ah Q, stripped to the waist, was standing idle, doing nothing at all. Others were not sure whether the old man was sincere or sarcastic, but Ah Q, not being so precise, was greatly pleased.

Ah Q was very proud and held all the inhabitants of Wei in contempt, even to the extent of sneering at the two students. Now a

From *Our Story of Ah Q*, translated by Chi-Chen Wang.

275

student might one day pass his examination and become a licentiate. The reason Their Honors Chao and Chien were so esteemed by the villagers was that, besides their wealth, they were fathers of students. But in spirit Ah Q had no special regard for them. "My son would be much better than they," he would assure himself. The few trips that he had undertaken to the city naturally contributed to his pride, though he had no use for city folks either. For instance, to himself and the people of Wei a bench three feet long and three inches wide across the top was a *ch'ang-teng,* yet the city people called it *t'iao-teng* *. This was absurd and laughable, he thought. In frying fish, people of Wei used pieces of green onions half an inch in length, but in the city they cut the onion up in fine shreds. This too was absurd and laughable. But what ignorant country louts were the villagers of Wei! They had never seen how fish was fried in the city!

Once much better off, a man of wide experience, hard working— Ah Q would have been a perfect man but for some slight physical flaws. The most humiliating of these were some scars on his head from sores he had had he knew not when. Although these were his own scars Ah Q did not seem to be proud of them, for he avoided the use of the word "sores" and all its homophones. Later by extension he avoided the words "shiny" and "bright," and still later even "candle" and "lamp" were taboo. Whenever these taboos were violated, intentionally or otherwise, Ah Q would become red in the face and would either curse or fight according to whether the offender was slow of words or weak of limb. For some reason or other Ah Q always came out the loser. He gradually changed his tactics and contented himself with an angry glare.

But the idlers of Wei only became more relentless after he adopted this new policy. As soon as they saw him, they would exclaim as though surprised, "Hey! how bright it has become all of a sudden!"

Ah Q glared.

"No wonder! We have a safety lamp hereabouts," someone else would remark, unimpressed by his glare.

"You haven't got it, anyway." This retort, which he finally hit upon, gave him some comfort, as though his scars were no longer shiny evidences of a by-gone affliction but something quite extraordinary, something to be envied.

As the idlers still would not let him alone, a fight usually followed. Ah Q invariably lost and ended up by being held by the queue while

---

* "Long bench" and "a strip of a bench" respectively.

THE HUMOR OF PROTEST 277

his head was thumped noisily against the wall. This was of course only an outward defeat. After his adversary had gone with the laurels of victory, Ah Q would say to himself, "I have been beaten by my son. What a world we live in today!" and he too would go off satisfied and spiritually victorious.

At first he thought thus only to himself; later he got into the habit of saying it aloud. This method of securing spiritual victory became generally known, so that an idler, holding him by his queue, would say to him:

"Now Ah Q, this is not a case of a son beating his father, but a man beating a beast!"

Protecting his hair with his hands, Ah Q would plead:

"You are beating a worm. I am nothing but a worm. How is that? Now let me go!"

Even after this humiliating admission the idler would not let his victim go without first banging his head half a dozen times against something convenient. "Surely Ah Q cannot claim a victory this time," the victor would think as he went away in triumph. But in less than ten seconds Ah Q would also go away in triumph, for he felt that surely he was the most self-deprecatory of men, and is not a superlative—the first or the most of anything—a distinction to be achieved and envied? Is not a *chuang-yuan* only the first in the ranks of the successful candidates in the triennial examinations? "So what are you, after all?"

After conquering his enemies by such ingenious means as these, Ah Q would go to the tavern, drink a few cups of wine, jest and quarrel a bit, and return, after scoring more victories, to the temple and would soon fall asleep with a light heart. If he happened to have any money, he would join the crowd of gamblers squatted around in a circle, his face streaming with sweat and his voice heard above every one else.

"Four hundred *cash* on the Black Dragon!"

"Hey! Here goes!" the dealer would shout as he uncovered the board, his face also streaming with sweat. "Here goes Heaven's Gate and Ah Q's money . . . No one seems to like Human Harmony."

"A hundred on Human Harmony! No, a hundred and fifty!"

Gradually Ah Q's money would find its way into the pockets of other perspiring gamblers. Obliged to withdraw from the inner circle, he would watch from the fringe, shouting and perspiring for the active participants. He could never tear himself away until the party broke up, when he would return to the temple with reluctant steps. The next day he would go to work with swollen eyes.

But "who knows that it is not a blessing for the Tartar to have lost his horse?" The only occasion on which Ah Q did win, he came near to tasting defeat. It happened during the village festival. There was as usual an open air theater and there were several gambling concessions near the stage. The gongs and drums sounded very faint in Ah Q's ears, as though miles away; he could hear only the barking of the dealer. He won and won, his coppers turning into dimes, dimes into silver dollars, silver dollars growing into a big pile. He was happy and excited.

"Two dollars on Heaven's Gate!" he shouted.

Suddenly a fight broke out, no one knew who against whom or why. When the commotion subsided and Ah Q crawled to his feet, the gambling concessions and the gamblers had all disappeared. He felt aches here and there, indicating that he must have received a few blows and kicks. People stared at him wonderingly. He went back to the temple with an air of preoccupation and after recovering his wits realized that he no longer had his pile of silver dollars. As most of the gamblers were from other villages, there was nothing that he could do.

A pile of bright, white silver dollars—and his at that—had all disappeared. He could not find any lasting satisfaction in saying to himself that his sons had robbed him, or in calling himself a worm. For the first time he felt something akin to the humiliation of defeat.

But again he turned defeat into victory. He raised his right hand and gave himself two good slaps in the face. This restored his humor, as if one Ah Q had struck another Ah Q, and, after a while, as if Ah Q had struck someone else—although it was his own face that tingled with pain. And so he lay down to sleep as victor, as pleased with himself as ever.

And he soon fell asleep.

Although Ah Q's list of victories was long and impressive, it was not until he was slapped by His Honor Chao that he became famous.

This was at the time when the gong-beating messengers brought news that the son of His Honor Chao had passed his examination. Ah Q had just drunk two cups of wine and was feeling effusive. He announced excitedly that it was a great honor for him because he and His Honor Chao were kinsmen and that he, Ah Q, was, come to think of it, three generations higher than the new licentiate in the family tree. This made a great impression on some of the bystanders. But the next day the village constable summoned Ah Q to His Honor's house. At the sight of Ah Q, His Honor turned red with fury and thundered:

"Ah Q, you knave! Did you say that I am a kinsman of yours?"

Ah Q was silent.

This infuriated His Honor still more; he advanced a few steps, saying, "How dare you blab such nonsense. How could I have a kinsman like you? Is your surname Chao?"

Ah Q did not open his mouth; he considered a retreat. His Honor jumped up to him and slapped him in the face.

"How could your name be Chao? You!"

Ah Q did not try to argue that his name was really Chao; he simply backed out with the constable, nursing his left cheek. Outside, the constable gave him a lecture and accepted two hundred *cash* from him for wine money.

After paying the constable Ah Q went to his room in the temple and lay down with indignation in his heart. Then he thought, "What a world this is getting to be, a son striking his father." At the thought that His Honor Chao with all his power and prestige was now his son, Ah Q became quite pleased with himself. He got up and went to the tavern singing "The Little Widow at Her Husband's Grave" and feeling quite proud of His Honor Chao now that the latter had become his own son.

The strange thing was that people actually seemed to respect him more. Ah Q liked to think that it was because of the new status that he had conferred upon himself, but this was not the case. If Ah Seven should have a fight with Ah Eight or Li Four with Chang Three, the incident would pass unnoticed in Wei; in order to merit gossip the incident must be in some way connected with a personage such as His Honor Chao. Then by virtue of the fame of the chastiser the chastised would become famous, too. The victim's position was, in other words, analogous to that of the Great Offerings in the Confucian Temple, offerings which, though domestic beasts like pigs and sheep, become sacred after the Sage has put his chopsticks to them. There was never any question that the fault lay with Ah Q. Wherefore? Because His Honor Chao could not be wrong. Then why was it that people respected him more than formerly? This is a little difficult to explain. Perhaps they were afraid that, even though he was slapped for it, there might be after all something to Ah Q's claim of kinship, and they felt it was better to be on the safe side.

Thus Ah Q basked in this reflected glory for many years.

One spring day as he was walking drunkenly on the street he espied Wang the Beard sitting against a wall in the sun, hunting for fleas in the coat that he had taken off. Ah Q felt an infectious itch. Now Wang was not only bearded but also mangy. Every one called him Mangy Beard Wang, but Ah Q dropped off the word mangy as it reminded him of his by-gone affliction. He held the Beard in great contempt, feeling that the mange was nothing unusual, not like a swarthy, unsightly beard. Ah Q sat down beside him. If it had been some one else Ah Q might have hesitated, but he was not afraid of the Beard. In fact, he was conferring an honor upon the latter by sitting down beside him.

Ah Q also took off his ragged coat and searched it hopefully, but, either because it had been recently washed or because of his lack of thoroughness he caught only three or four fleas after a long search. In the meantime the Beard caught one after another, putting them in his mouth and crushing them with a crisp sound between his teeth.

Ah Q felt only disappointment at first, but this feeling soon gave way to indignation. How humiliating that such a worthless fellow as the Beard should have caught so many, while he so few! He wished to vindicate himself by finding a big one but after a great deal of trouble he succeeded in finding only a medium-sized one. He put it into his mouth and bit it with determination, but he did not make as much noise as the Beard.

His scars grew red. Throwing his coat on the ground he said, spitting with disgust, "The damned worm!"

"Whom are you cursing, scabby cur?" the Beard said raising his eyes contemptuously.

If the challenge had come from one of the idlers in whose hands he had suffered ignominious defeat, Ah Q, in spite of the distinction that he had recently won and the pride that he took in it, might have been more cautious about taking it up. But he did not feel any need for caution on this occasion; he felt very brave. How dare the hairy face talk to him like that?

"Whoever cares to take it," he said, standing up, his arms akimbo.

"Are your bones itching?" said the Beard, standing up and putting on his coat.

Ah Q thought that the Beard was going to run, so he rushed forward and struck with his fist. But the Beard caught hold of it and gave it a jerk. As Ah Q fell forward, the Beard had him by the queue and was about to bang his head against the wall.

"A gentleman argues with his tongue rather than his fists," Ah Q remonstrated.

The Beard did not seem to care whether he was a gentleman or not. Paying no heed to the remonstrance, he banged Ah Q's head against the wall five times, then gave him a push that sent him sprawling six feet away.

In Ah Q's memory this must have been the greatest humiliation in his life. Heretofore the Beard had been the butt of his scorn, never had he been the object of the Beard's jeers, much less his blows. Could it be true, as rumored on the street, that the Emperor had abolished the examinations, and no longer wanted any licentiates and graduates, so that the Chao's prestige has been impaired and their kinsmen might be treated with impudence?

As Ah Q stood and pondered on this inexplicable event, the eldest son of His Honor Chien, one of Ah Q's foes and abominations, approached from the distance. Young Chien had first gone to the city and entered one of those "foreign" schools and then he had for some reason gone to Japan. Half a year later he came back a different man: his legs had become straight and his queue was gone. His mother cried often and his wife tried to throw herself in the well no less than three times. Later his mother explained that Chien's queue had been cut off by some wicked people after they had made him drunk. "He was to have been appointed a big mandarin," she explained, "but now he must wait until his hair grows again."

Ah Q did not believe the explanations, insisted upon calling Chien a fake foreigner and a traitor, and would curse him under his breath whenever he saw him. What Ah Q hated most was the man's false queue, for surely one could not be said to be a man at all with a false queue, and his wife could not be a virtuous woman since she did not try the well a fourth time.

The fake foreigner drew near.

"Baldhead! Donkey!" Ah Q muttered aloud as his passion and his desire for revenge got the better of him.

The baldhead unexpectedly rushed at him with a yellow varnished stick—which Ah Q called the funeral stick—and instantly Ah Q realized that he was going to receive a thrashing. He tightened his muscles and hunched up his shoulders and waited. He heard a whack and realized that he must have gotten a blow on the head.

"I was speaking of *him*," Ah Q protested, indicating a boy nearby. Whack! Whack! Whack!

In Ah Q's memory this must have been the second greatest humiliation of his life. Fortunately the whack-whack seemed to give him a measure of relief, as though ending some suspense for him. Furthermore, forgetfulness, a treasured trait which he had inherited from his ancestors, came to his aid, and enabled him to regain his complacency by the time he reached the tavern.

Just then a little nun from the convent went by. Ah Q had never let her pass without hurling an insult at her, even when he was quite himself. Now all the resentment that he had felt for his recent defeats and indignities turned against the hapless nun.

"I have been wondering why I have been so unlucky all day; so it's because of you!" he thought.

He went up to her and spat in disgust. The nun walked on without paying the slightest attention to him. Ah Q approached her, thrust out his hand and stroked her clean-shaven head, saying with an idiotic grin, "Baldhead! Hurry home. The monk is waiting for you."

"What has possessed you that you dare to touch me!" the nun said hurrying on, her face flushed.

People in the tavern laughed. Encouraged by the general appreciation, Ah Q pinched her cheek, saying, "Since the monk can touch you, why not I?"

The tavern laughed again. Ah Q became more pleased with himself and gave the nun another pinch for the benefit of the onlookers.

This encounter drove out the memory of Wang the Beard and of the fake foreigner, and avenged all his adversities of the day. He felt more lighthearted than the whack-whack had made him, so lighthearted that he positively floated on air.

"May Ah Q never have any offspring," sounded the pitiful voice of the nun as she hurried off.

"Ha! ha! ha!" laughed Ah Q triumphantly.

"Ha! ha! ha!" echoed the tavern.

THE CAKE OF SOAP

Mrs. Ssu-ming, with her eight-year-old daughter Hsiu-erh, was making paper ingots in the slanting sunlight when she suddenly heard the

Translated by Chi-Chen Wang.

thump, thump of slow and heavy footsteps of someone wearing cloth-soled shoes. Although she recognized the step of Ssu-ming, she did not stop to look up but went on with her work. When the footsteps drew close and stopped right by her side, however, she could not help looking up, and when she did so she found Ssu-ming engaged in reaching down into the pocket of his long robe underneath a horse jacket.

With a great deal of difficulty he finally succeeded in extricating his hand from his pocket and handed a small, oblong package, palm green in color, to Mrs. Ssu. As soon as she took the package in her hand she smelled an exotic fragrance which was something, and yet not quite, like the fragrance of olives; on the palm-green paper wrapping there was a golden seal and some elaborate patterns. Hsiu-erh jumped up to her and asked to see it but Mrs. Ssu pushed her away.

"Been to town?" she asked, as she examined the package.

"Mm, mm," he answered, also looking at the package.

The palm-green package was then opened, revealing another layer of thin paper, also palm green; and it was not until this thin paper was removed that the object itself was exposed. It was firm and smooth, also palm green in color, with a pattern impressed upon it. The exotic fragrance which smelled something but not quite like the fragrance of olives became stronger.

"Oh, what fine soap," Mrs. Ssu said, as she held the palm-green object up to her nose, as delicately as if she were holding an infant, and sniffed at it.

"Mm, mm, you can use that from now on. . . ."

As he said this, she noticed, his eyes were fixed on her neck. Her face felt warm from the cheeks down. She had always felt a roughness whenever she happened to touch her neck, especially behind the ears, and she had realized that it was due to an accumulation of ancient dirt. She had not paid the slightest attention to it, but now under his gaze and before the cake of exotic-smelling soap, she could not prevent the warmth in the face. Moreover, the warm feeling spread and soon reached to her ears. She made up her mind then that she was going to give herself a good scrubbing with that soap after supper.

"There were spots where mere *tsao-chia* soap won't do any good," she said to herself.

"Ma, give that to me," Hsiu-erh said, reaching out for the palm-green paper. Chao-erh, the younger daughter who had been playing out in the yard, also came running in. Mrs. Ssu pushed them aside, wrapped the soap as before, first in the thin paper and then the palm-green paper, and, reaching up, put it on the topmost shelf on the wash-stand. She gave it a final caressing glance and then turned back to her work.

"Hsueh-cheng!" Ssu-ming suddenly called, as if he had just remembered something, and sat down in a high-backed chair opposite his wife.

"Hsueh-cheng!" she also called.

She put down her paper ingots and listened but there was no answer. She felt apologetic when she saw her husband waiting impatiently with his head turned upward, and she called again at the top of her shrill voice, resorting this time to the boy's more familiar milk name.

This produced immediate results. The clap, clap of leather soles neared, and soon Chuan-erh stood before them wearing a short coat, his fat round face glistening with perspiration.

"What were you doing? Can't you hear your *dieh* calling?" she scolded.

"I was practicing *pa-kua-ch'uan*," he said and turning to Ssu-ming he stood respectfully and waited inquiringly.

"Hsueh-cheng, I want to ask you this: what is the meaning of *o-du-foo*?"

"*O-du-foo*? . . . Does that not mean 'a ferocious woman'?"

"Nonsense! Stupid!" Ssu-ming suddenly burst out angrily. "Do you mean to suggest that I am a woman?"

Hsueh-cheng was scared by the outburst; he withdrew two steps and stood more respectfully erect than before. Though he had secretly felt that his father's gait resembled that of the actors of old men's parts, he had never thought him as having any effeminate traits. But he was certain that he had given the wrong answer.

"Do you think that I am so stupid as not to know that *o-du-foo* means a ferocious woman and have to ask you about it? This is not Chinese but foreign language, let me tell you. What does it mean? Do you understand it?"

"I . . . I do not understand it." Hsueh-cheng became more and more scared.

"Huh, I have spent a lot of money in sending you to school and you tell me that you don't understand even this? So this is what they call 'emphasis on both ear and mouth'? The speaker of those foreign words was only about fourteen or fifteen years old, younger than yourself, and yet he was able to chatter glibly away, while you do not even understand it. Shame on you! Now go and look it up for me!"

Hsueh-cheng answered with a throaty "Yes" and backed out respectfully.

"The students are getting more and more impossible every day," Ssu-ming said indignantly after a while. "Even as far back as the Kuang Hsu period, I was one of the most outspoken advocates of modern education. But I never, never thought that schools would come to this: it is emancipation this and freedom that, but they never learn anything. I have spent lots of money on Hsueh-cheng, and it has all been spent in vain. It was with considerable difficulty that I got him into one of these schools where both Chinese and Western learning are given equal attention. You would think that he ought to learn something there, wouldn't you? And yet after a year he cannot even understand *o-du-foo*. They must be still teaching them by rote. What sort of a school do you call this? What have they turned out? I say they should be closed up, every one of them!"

"You are right, you can't do better than to close all of them," Mrs. Ssu said sympathetically, still engaged in making paper ingots.

"We don't need to send Hsiu-erh and Chao-erh to school. 'What's the use of sending girls to school?' Great-uncle Nine used to say, and how I attacked him for his opposition to girls' schools! But now I am inclined to think the old people are right after all. Just think, isn't it bad enough to have women parading about the streets, without their bobbing their hair? There is nothing I hate more than girl students with bobbed hair. In my opinion soldiers and bandits are more forgivable than they, for it is they that have corrupted and subverted morality. They should be punished . . ."

"That's right. It is bad enough to have men cut their hair off like monks without the women trying to imitate the nuns."

"Hsueh-cheng!"

The boy had at that moment come in with a small, thick volume with gilt edges, which he held up to Ssu-ming and said pointing to some page: "This looks like it, this one here."

Ssu-ming took the book, which he knew to be a dictionary, but the print was very small and the lines ran sidewise. He took it over to the window and squinted at the line which Hsueh-cheng had pointed to and read: " 'The name of a co-operative society founded in the eighteenth century.' Mm, that's not it—How do you pronounce this?" he asked, pointing to the foreign words.

"O-do-fo-lo-ssu." *

"No, no, that's not it." Ssu-ming became angry again. "Let me tell you that it is a bad word, a curse word, something applied to one like myself. Do you understand now? Go and try to find it!"

Hsueh-cheng looked at him but did not move.

"What sort of riddle is this? You must explain it more clearly so that he can look it up," Mrs. Ssu interceded, taking pity upon Hsueh-cheng's helplessness and showing some dissatisfaction at her husband's behavior.

"It happened while I was buying the soap at Kuang Yun Hsiang's," Ssu-ming responded, turning to her. "There were three students besides myself at the shop. From their point of view I was, of course, somewhat troublesome. I looked at six or seven different kinds without taking any as they were all over forty cents. I finally decided to take some medium-priced variety and bought the green piece over there at twenty-four cents. The clerk was one of those snobs that toady to the rich, with his eyes growing upward on his forehead, and he assumed a doggish snout soon enough. In the meantime the students were winking at one another and jabbering in the foreign devil's language. Later I wanted to open up the package and take a look before I paid, but the snob not only would not let me do it but became unreasonable and said a lot of unnecessary and unpleasant things, at which the students chimed in with their jabber and laughter. That particular sentence came from the youngest of them. He was looking at me when he said it and all the others laughed. It is clear that it is bad language." Then turning to Hsueh-cheng he said, "You'll have to look for it under the category of 'bad language'!"

Hsueh-cheng answered with another throaty "Yes" and withdrew respectfully.

"They are always yelling and yelling about the 'new culture' but what has the 'new culture' brought them to?" Ssu-ming went on, his eyes fixed on the roof. "Now there is no longer any morality among the students, no morality among society in general. If nothing is done about it China will certainly vanish from the earth. Just think how terrible that would be. . . ."

"What's that?" his wife said, indifferently.

"I have in mind," he said seriously, "a filial maid. There were two beggars on the street, one of them a girl, about eighteen or nineteen —not a very suitable age to be begging on the street, I must say, but

* Odd Fellows.

that was what she was doing. She was with a woman about sixty or
seventy, white-haired and blind, and they sat under the eaves of a cloth
shop begging for alms. People all say that she was a filial maid, the old
woman being her grandmother. Whenever she got anything she gave
it to her grandmother and willingly went hungry herself. But did anyone give anything to such a filial maid?" he asked with his eyes turned
on her as if testing her.

She did not answer but kept her eyes on him as if waiting, in turn,
for him to explain what happened.

"*Heng,* none," he answered the question himself finally. "I watched
them for a long time and in all that time only one person gave her a
small copper, while the rest looked on them as objects for their amusement. Moreover, a ruffian went so far as to say to his companion thus:
'Ah-fa, do not overlook this piece of goods just because it happens to
be dirty. All you have to do is to buy two cakes of soap and *k-chee,
k-chee,* give her a thorough scrubbing and she will be as nice a piece
of goods as you'll ever find.' Now just consider what sort of world this
has become!"

"*Heng,*" she said looking down at her work and then asked casually
after a long while, "Did you give her anything?"

"I? No. I couldn't very well give her just a copper or two. She was
no ordinary beggar. At least . . ."

But she got up slowly without waiting for him to finish his sentence
and went to the kitchen. Dusk was falling thick and it was suppertime.

Ssu-ming also got up, and went out into the yard. It was lighter outside than in the room. Hsueh-cheng was practicing *pa-kua-ch'uan* at a
corner near the wall in accordance with the admonition that he should
utilize the space where day and night met for this particular purpose
since there was not light enough to read but enough to exercise by.
Ssu-ming nodded slightly in approval and began to pace back and
forth with his arms crossed behind him. Presently the only potted plant
—a ten-thousand-year green—became lost in the darkness, a few stars
twinkled through the fleecy clouds, and night began its reign. Ssu-ming
became more vigorous and acted as if he was about to do great things,
to declare war against the corrupt students and the evil influences of
society. The braver and more vigorous he felt, the longer grew his
strides and the louder sounded his footsteps, until the hens and chickens, which had been roosting peacefully in their cages, became frightened and started to cluck and twit.

The appearance of lamplight in the hall served as a beacon summoning the family to supper and all flocked to the table placed in the center of the room. At the head of the table was Ssu-ming, who was fat and round-faced like Hsueh-cheng but had a thin moustache. Sitting alone on one side of the table and seen through the cloud of vapor from the hot soup, he looked very much like the god of wealth across the altar in his temple. On the left sat Mrs. Ssu and Chao-erh; on the right Hsueh-cheng and Hsiu-erh. The chopsticks clattered on the dishes and bowls like raindrops, and made supper a very lively affair, though no one spoke.

Chao-erh upset her bowl, spilling its contents over half the table. Ssu-ming glared at her with a fixed stare and did not relent until she was about to cry. Thereupon he turned to pick up a piece of tender vegetable which he had previously spotted in the communal bowl. But it had disappeared. He looked around the table and caught Hsueh-cheng in the act of stuffing the prized morsel into his wide-open mouth. There was nothing for him to do but to content himself with a chopstickful of vegetable leaves.

"Hsueh-cheng," he said looking at him, "have you found out the word yet?"

"What word?—Oh, that? No, not yet."

"*Heng,* just look at him. He has learned nothing but eat and eat! It would be better if you learned something from the filial maid, who, though she is only a beggar, gives everything to her grandmother and willingly goes hungry herself. But, of course, you students know nothing of these things. You have no fears and beliefs; you'll turn out exactly like that ruffian. . . ."

"I did think of a word, but I don't know whether it is right or not. What he said was perhaps '*o-er-de-foo-erh.*' " *

"Yes, yes, that's it, that's exactly it. But the way he said it sounded more like *o-du-foo.* Now what does it mean? You are of the same tribe as they and you ought to know."

"It means—I am afraid that I don't know what it means."

"Nonsense! You are concealing it from me. You are all bad eggs!"

"Even 'Heaven would not strike one who is eating.' What has come over you today that you act like this, 'striking the chicks and cursing the dogs' even at the supper table? What can you expect from them when they are only children?" Mrs. Ssu suddenly remonstrated.

"What's that?" Ssu-ming was about to continue his tirade, but he took a look at his wife and thought better of it, for her cheeks were

* Old Fool.

puffed out, her color changed, her triangular eyes flashing an ugly light. He said instead, "Nothing has come over me. I am only trying to impress Hsueh-cheng that he must try to learn some good traits."

"How can he learn since he cannot read your mind?" She was angrier than ever. "If he could read what's in your mind, he would have long ago lit the lantern, sought out the filial maid and brought her to you. Fortunately you have already bought a cake of soap for her. All you have to do now is to buy another cake and . . ."

"Nonsense! That's what the ruffian said."

"I am not sure of that. All you have to do is buy another cake and *k-chee, k-chee,* give her a good scrubbing, and set her up on an altar and peace will reign in the world again."

"What are you talking about? What has that got to do with it? It was only because I happened to remember that you did not have any soap . . ."

"That has everything to do with it. You have specially bought that for the filial maid. You go and give her, *k-chee, k-chee,* a good scrubbing yourself. I am not worthy of it, I don't want it, I don't want anything that was intended for the filial maid."

"Now what are you talking about? You women . . ." Ssu-ming parried, his face covered with a greasy sweat, just like Hsueh-cheng's after he had finished his *pa-kua-ch'uan* exercises, although it might have been due to the heat of the rice.

"What's wrong with us women? We women are much better than you men. You men are either cursing eighteen- or nineteen-year-old girl students or praising eighteen- or nineteen-year-old beggar girls. You haven't a decent thought in your heads. *K-chee, k-chee!* Shameless wretches!"

"Did I not say that it was a ruffian who said that? Have I . . ."

"Brother Ssu!" a loud voice sounded in the darkness outside.

"Is that you, Brother Tao? I'll be with you directly." Ssu-ming recognized the voice of Ho Tao-tung, known for his loudness, and welcomed him as if he were a messenger bringing an unexpected reprieve. "Hsueh-cheng, light a lamp right away and show Uncle Ho to the study!"

Hsueh-cheng lit a candle and led Tao-tung into a side room to the west, followed by another guest by the name of Pu Wei-yuan.

"Pardon me for not going out to meet you, pardon me, pardon me," Ssu-ming came out and said, raising his clasped hands in greeting and still chewing his last mouthful of rice. "Would you deign have a bite with us?"

"We have already selfishly preceded you," Wei-yuan said, also shaking his own clasped hands before him. "We have come to disturb you at night because we want to discuss with you the themes for the literary contest of the Ethical Literary Society, for don't you realize that it is a 'seventh' day tomorrow?"

"Oh, is today the sixteenth already?" Ssu-ming exclaimed.

"See how stupid of us!" Tao-tung shouted.

"Then we must send the themes to the newspaper office tonight and make sure that they get into tomorrow's edition."

"I have already drafted a theme for the essay contest. Take a look at it and see if it is all right," Tao-tung said, as he fished out a strip of paper from the carry-all improvised with a handkerchief and handed it over to Ssu-ming. The latter took it over to the candle light, unfolded the strip of paper and read slowly the following:

> *A proposed petition to be sent by the citizens of the entire Nation to His Excellency the President requesting him to promulgate a mandate commanding the study of the Confucian Canon and the Canonization of the mother of Mencius as a means of saving the declining morals and preserving the National essence.*

"Excellent, excellent," Ssu-ming said. "But it is not too long?"

"It does not matter!" Tao-tung said loudly. "I have counted it over and found that we do not have to pay anything over our reserved space. But how about the theme for the verse contest?"

"The verse contest?" Ssu-ming was suddenly reverential in manner. "I have one that I would like to suggest. It is: 'Ballad of the Filial Maid.' It happens to be a true incident and we ought to give it a wider acknowledgement. Today as I was walking on the street . . ."

"That will not do," Wei-yuan interrupted, shaking his hand in disapproval. "I have seen her myself. She must be a stranger in these parts, for I could not understand her and she could not understand me. I don't know where she comes from. Everyone said that she is a filial maid, but when I asked her whether she could write poetry, she shook her head. It would be much better if she could write poetry."

"We'll use this theme," Ssu-ming said, brushing aside his objection. "We'll add an explanatory note and have it printed in the newspaper. In the first place this will give her some deserved acknowledgment; in the second place it will furnish an opportunity to give the public a few shots of a much-needed needle of criticism. What has the world come to? I watched the two women for a long time but I did not see anyone give any money. Does that not show that people have no heart any more?"

"But, Brother Ssu," Wei-yuan again objected, "you are now 'cursing a bald head in front of a monk.' I was one of those who did not give anything. It happened that I did not have any money with me."

"Don't be so sensitive, Brother Wei. Of course it is another question with you. Let me finish: a big crowd gathered before them, but no one showed any respect. Instead they made fun of them. There were two ruffians who behaved especially badly. One of them said, 'Ah-fa, go and buy two cakes of soap and *k-chee, k-chee,* give her a good scrubbing. She'll be very good then.' Just imagine . . ."

"Ha, ha, ha! Two cakes of soap!" Tao-tung suddenly burst out in his loud guffaw, which vibrated in every one's ear. "You buy—ha, ha, ha-a . . ."

"Brother Tao, Brother Tao, please do not shout like that," Ssu-ming was frightened and spoke hastily.

"*K-chee, k-chee,* ha, ha, ha-a . . ."

"Brother Tao," Ssu-ming said seriously, "why do you insist on joking when we have business to discuss? Listen, we'll use these two themes and send them to the paper right away and make sure that they get in tomorrow's edition. I'll have to impose this errand on you two gentlemen."

"We'll be glad to do it, of course," Wei-yuan said eagerly.

"Ah, ah, a good scrubbing, *k-chee* . . . he, he . . ."

"Brother Tao!" Ssu-ming said with annoyance.

This quieted Tao-tung at last. Then they drafted the conditions of the contest. After Wei-yuan had copied everything out on letter paper, he went off to the newspaper office with Tao-tung. Ssu-ming escorted them to the gate with the candle and as he approached the hall on his way back he began to feel uncomfortable again, though he ended up by stepping inside after a moment's hesitation. The first thing to come under his observation as he entered the hall was the package of soap in green wrappers in the center of the table. The golden seal glittered in the lamplight and the delicate patterns could be seen.

Hsiu-erh and Chao-erh were playing, squatted on the ground in front of the table, while Hsueh-cheng was looking up words in the dictionary on the right side of the table. Farthest away from the lamp

Mrs. Ssu sat on the highbacked chair in the dimness, her face immobile and expressionless and her eyes staring vacantly at nothingness.

"*K-chee, k-chee,* shameless wretches . . ."

This seemed to have come from Hsiu-erh, but when Ssu-ming looked back he only saw Chao-erh scratching her face with her two little hands.

Aware that the atmosphere was none too favorable, he extinguished his candle and strolled out again into the yard, where he began to pace back and forth. The minute he forgot himself, the hens and chicks would begin to cluck and twit, whereupon he would make his steps lighter and walk farther away from the chicken cage. After a long time the lamp in the central room was shifted to the bedroom. Moonlight covered the ground like a sheet of seamless white muslin, while overhead the jade disc of the full moon shone between white clouds and showed not the slightest imperfection.

He was a little sad and felt himself a lonely man, as forgotten and neglected as the filial maid. He did not go to bed until very late that night.

But the services of the soap were enlisted early the following morning. He got up later than usual that day and found his wife bent over the washstand scrubbing her neck. The soap lather rose in billows, behind her ears, as foamy as water bubbles that form over the mouth of huge crabs. The difference between this and ordinary *tsao-chia* was as great as the difference that exists between heaven and earth. From then on there was always an exotic fragrance about the person of Mrs. Ssu which was something and yet not quite like the fragrance of olives. It was not until almost half a year later that she began to have a different odor, which, according to those who noticed it, smelled of sandalwood.

Lin Yutang

SINCE Lin Yutang has written about many things, including the present book, there is no call for me here to write about Lin Yutang, except to point out that all three specimens reproduced are early Lins, written before he was discovered for the American public. His letter to Mr. American is a museum piece today because "extra-territoriality" (extrality) in China is no more. But it should still make amusing, and profitable, reading to "Old China Hands" across the sea.

IN MEMORIAM OF THE DOG-MEAT GENERAL

General Chang Tsungch'ang, the "dog-meat general," had died, according to the morning's news. I was sorry for him and I was sorry for his mother and I was sorry for the sixteen concubines he left behind him and the four times sixteen that he had left him before he died. As I intended to specialize in writing in memoriams for the bewildering generals of this bewildering generation, I began with the Dog-Meat General first:

So our Dog-Meat General has died! What an event! It is full of mystic significance for me and for China and us poor folks who do not wear boots and carry bayonets! Such a thing could not happen every day, and if it could, there would be an end to all China's sorrows. In such an eventuality, you could abolish all the five *Yuan,* tear up the will of Dr. Sun Yat-sen, dismiss the hundred odd members of the Central Executive Committee of the Kuomintang, close up all the schools and universities of China, and you wouldn't have to bother your head about communism, fascism and democracy and universal suffrage and emancipation of women, and we poor folks would still be able to live in peace and prosperity.

So one more of the colorful, legendary figures of medieval China has passed into eternity. And yet Dog-Meat General's death has a special significance for me, because he was the most colorful, the most legendary, the most medieval, and, I must say, the most honest and unashamed of all the colourful, legendary, medieval, and unashamed rulers of modern China.

He was a born ruler such as modern China wants. He was six feet tall, a towering giant, with a pair of squint eyes and a pair of abnormally massive hands. He was direct, forceful, terribly efficient at times, obstinate, and gifted with moderate intelligence. He was patriotic according to his lights and he was anti-communist, which made up for his being anti-Kuomintang.

All his critics must allow that he wasn't anti-Kuomintang from convictions, but by accident. He didn't want to fight the Kuomintang; it was the Kuomintang that wanted to fight him and grab his territory, and, being an honest man, he fought rather than turn tail. Given a chance and if the Kuomintang had returned him his Shantung, he would have joined the Kuomintang, because he said the Sanmin doctrine can't do any harm. He could not be anti-Kuomintang, because he couldn't be anti-something-that-he-didn't-understand. He could drink and he was awfully fond of "dog-meat" and he could swear all he wanted to and as much as he wanted to, irrespective of his official superiors and inferiors. He made no pretence to being a gentleman and didn't affect to send nice-sounding circular telegrams, like the rest of them. He was ruthlessly honest, and this honesty made him much loved by all his close associates. If he loved women, he said so, and he would see foreign consuls with a Russian girl sitting on his knee. If he held orgies, he didn't try to conceal them from his friends and foes. If he coveted his subordinate's wife, he told him openly and wrote no psalm of repentance about it like King David. And he always played square. If he took his subordinate's wife, he made her husband the chief of police of Tsinan. And he took great care of other people's morals. He forbade girl students to enter parks in Tsinan and protected them from the men-gorillas who stood at every corner and nook to devour them. And he was pious and he kept a harem. He believed in polyandry as well as polygamy, and he openly allowed his concubines to make love with other men, provided he didn't want them at the time. He respected Confucius. And he was patriotic. He was reported to be overjoyed to find a bedbug in a Japanese bed in Beppo, and he never tired of telling people of the consequent superiority of Chinese civilization. He was very fond of his executioner, and he was thoroughly devoted to his mother.

Many legends were told about Dog-Meat's ruthless honesty. He loved a Russian prostitute, and his Russian prostitute loved a poodle, and he made a whole regiment pass in review before the poodle to show that he loved the prostitute that loved the poodle. Once he appointed a man magistrate in a certain district in Shantung, and another day he appointed another man to the same magistracy. Both men therefore arrived at the same office and started a quarrel. Each claimed that he had been personally appointed by General Dog-Meat. It was agreed, therefore, that they should go and see the General to clear up the difficulty. When they arrived, it was evening and General Chang was in bed in the midst of his orgies. "Come in," he said, with his usual candor. The two magistrates then explained that they had both been appointed by him to the same district. "You fools!" he said. "Can't you settle such a little thing between yourselves but must come to bother me about it?"

Like the heroes of Shui-hu, and like all Chinese robbers, he was an honest man. He never forgot a kindness, and he was obstinately loyal to those who had helped him. His trouser pockets were always stuffed with money, and when people came to him for help, he would pull out a bank roll and give a handful to those that asked. He distributed hundred-dollar notes as Rockefeller distributed dimes.

Because of his honesty and his generosity, he was beyond the hatred of his fellow men. The morning I entered my office and informed my colleagues of the great news, everyone smiled, which showed that everyone was friendly toward him. No one hated him and no one could hate him. China was then still being ruled by men like him, who hadn't his honesty, generosity, and loyalty. He was a born ruler, such as modern China wants, and he was the best of them all.

IF I WERE A BANDIT

"If I were a bandit," is a speculation which is most fruitful of new and ever widening avenues of thought. I do not think it is an idea that occurs to many of my compatriots, but I confess it holds for me a certain fascination. And can anyone blame me for this, when the prospects of a bandit are so very extraordinarily tempting, and when the problem of making a decent living is so extraordinarily difficult in this grand old China of ours? Supposing a bandit of China today is gifted with an unusual intelligence, but an atrocious bad taste, it will be little short of a miracle if he does not end up his career in the Peiping palaces and find his name in China's *Who's Who,* with a list of honorable titles comparable to those of our dear old Ts'ao K'un.

Now, of course, I am not qualified to be a bandit. Not only have I never killed a man (so far as I am directly aware), but also I lack all the admirable qualities which it takes to be a good bandit. A good bandit must be "a nice fellow" and have that divine inimitable sense of gay fellowship and camaraderie which I deplorably lack. A bandit chief must have all the necessary qualities of successful leadership, tact, knowledge of men, utter contempt of moral scruples, and, above all, a turncoat conscience. These are the qualities that I have noted in all successful leaders, and that I know I don't have. But suppose that I have them, and I can show you how to carve out a career until my name is a household word for integrity, patriotism, and honor, and parents, when reading eulogies of myself in newspaper editorials, will point to me and command their children: "Live ye like this man that ye may be a glory unto the Lord!"

In the first place, I would begin my thieves' job with calligraphy. A little effort each day spent over the ink slab would serve me handsomely a lifetime. The two necessary things for my imagined meteoric rise from bandit chief to A-1 Patriot (with a capital letter) are calligraphy and ability to draft circular telegrams. But I can hire a college graduate to do the latter, whereas I cannot very well hire a man to write scrolls and book covers for me and sign on my behalf. At least I don't like that. Now, calligraphy is an art which takes years of practice, and hence I would begin practicing it even while I was yet in my village stage. By the time I occupied a few cities, people would surely come to me for writing scrolls and book covers, and a beautiful handwriting would put me at once in favor with the local gentry and the educated class, and go a long way toward establishing my name as a patron of the arts and literature.

Armed with calligraphy and a good secretary for circular telegrams (preferably in the "four-six" style), I would invade a little port like Amoy. That requires about five hundred soldiers. I would need only about one hundred finely trained soldiers; the other four hundred could be opium-smokers, so far as the fighting is concerned. I can say this, because I have watched such battles. Perhaps thirty courageous men would do the trick. Circular telegrams and military notices would go simultaneously with the completion of the battle, which should last about two hours. These notices would say: "I love the people, I love the people, and I love the people." But I would not say anything about the lightening of taxation just yet. I might add: "I hate the foreigner, I hate the foreigner, and I hate the foreigner." These must be in Chinese characters. Then I would hire a college sophomore of the "good-morning-good-afternoon-good-evening-thank-you-excuse-me" type, and call on the different consulates and assure them of the protection of foreign life and property. In my circular telegrams, this Protection of Foreign Lives and Property stuff would be solemnly reiterated. But I would not say anything about protection of Chinese lives and property just yet. The foreign consuls would at once think I were a second Yuan Shihkai. On the rock of foreign good will shall I build my political destiny.

The stage from city bandit to a bandit of provincial importance would take about three years. For three years, I would lie low and consolidate my position. The logic of my position would force me to get rich. I must have a better and larger army against my rivals, and for this I must have money. In the name of national reconstruction and modernization of China, I would reconstruct the whole city of Amoy, or whatever city that may be. This should give me about a million dollars in three years, or two, if I am a fast worker. The profit from each yard of road-building is about twenty dollars, so that it would be in my interest to build longer and longer new roads. People would call me the model bandit, and I would make Amoy a model city, besides having a million dollars in my pocket.

With the million dollars, I can do wonders. With the offering of three months' back pay, I can buy over any navy that there is in China, and here begins my stage of provincial importance. Next, it would be an easy enough thing to start a humble beginning in air force. Everybody would be speaking about the model bandit with the model air force. My art of calligraphy would be mature by this time and I would become a strong advocate for Confucianism. I would decorate the descendant of Confucius, if he were in my province. I would be the champion of morality and religion. I also would have a few phrases of the Sanmin Doctrine at my fingertips.

Civil wars are bound to break out about this time, and here's the chance for my rising to national political and financial importance. I figure I could safely make three to four betrayals, but I would not overdo it. With three or four betrayals, I should have reached, politically, a position of national importance, and, financially, become the proud owner of a $5,000,000 account in the Hong Kong and Shanghai Bank, figuring at about 1,200,000 to 1,500,000 for each change of sides (figures are based on the current rates). Only God knows where I should end at this rate.

I would then be humble and good. My hobby would be the collecting of Sung editions of Chinese works, and I would ask my secretary (the same one who drafted the circular telegrams for me) to write commentaries on *Tahsueh* and *Chungyung,* and have them published in my name. And I am blowed if I don't receive a decoration from the French Government for promotion of oriental culture and international peace before I die.

It is all no use. The picture I drew of the meteoric rise of a bandit chief to A-1 Patriot is glaringly inadequate. My model bandit who proposes to get a million dollars in the name of national reconstruction by rebuilding the city of Amoy remains only a model bandit on paper, the whim child of a writer's imagination. I had said that if I were a bandit, I would get this million dollars in three years. I added that possibly I could do it in two, if I were a fast worker. I figured out I could get twenty dollars profit from each yard of road-building; hence the profit from building each mile (or 1,760 yards) would be $35,200, approximately $100,000 for every three miles, or a million dollars for thirty miles. There are not thirty miles of roads to be built in Amoy, but I could build the roads bad enough so as to require immediate and throughgoing repairs the very next year, and every year afterward. Hence the necessity for waiting three years. Now comes General F——, who is going to get two millions in two weeks by the end of August (about the time this article appears in print), and another six million dollars from the poor ransacked and pillaged K—— by November 30, in the name of training an army and building forts (*sic!*) to fight the communists. I said to myself when I read this: This is flesh and blood. It is Reality itself. The child of my imagination is only such stuff as dreams are made of. It is unreal, inadequate, lacking in the red corpuscles of a living and patriotism-breathing F——, and unfit to see the day.

General F—— is going to be immortal. I have no doubt about it. He will remain so in my mind and memory at least, forever a reminder of the paucity of my imagination and immaturity of my literary craftsmanship. How I would love to have him pose there for me, while I, a second Rodin come to earth, would hew and chisel out of a poor piece of ragged barren rock, a very image of the God of Militarism himself, with anticommunist indignation burning in his eyes and the thought of eight million dollars burning in his soul! How the very sight of him would strengthen our faith in Reality and scatter our romanticists and idealists as the golden chariot of Apollo riding across the blue firmament in the early dawn would scatter the fogs and the dews! Idealism must wither, and Romanticism evaporate into thin air at the very touch of his breath, while Realism, joining hands with Reality, feels too tickled to laugh and too bitter to shed a tear.

Even my vigorous heart, long nursed in the lap of Realism, felt a slight twinge, a creeping sense of burning shame . . . some violence had been done to my human nature.

That night I had a dream. I dreamed I was riding by a pond on a poor farmer's donkey. It was a sick, underfed, and half-lame donkey. The roads were treacherous. Splash . . . splash . . . splash! The donkey slipped, and I fell on the mudbank with the donkey. My clothes were dirty, but the poor creature broke his leg. The poor farmer offered to wash my clothes in the pond, whose water was clear and transparent. But I would not allow him. "Think about the poor donkey first," I said generously. The farmer kept silent, looking at me. Sorrow was written upon his face. The donkey was his only means of sustenance, his all. "What shall we do about his broken leg?" I said. "We cannot let the poor thing die like that. You give me a hundred dollars, and I will send for an ambulance and have the donkey sent to the Shanghai Sanitarium, and have a silver leg put to it." The poor farmer looked dumfounded. I got furious. "D'ye hear me?" I asked, pulling him by the shoulder. "Give me a hundred dollars, and I'll have a silver leg put to your donkey." The farmer looked as glum and sullen as ever. As he was not willing to produce the hundred dollars, I took him to his house, took all the furniture, and sold his house and garden on the spot for him for a hundred dollars. Then I bade him good-by, saying I would surely pay the hospital fees with it and return him the donkey with the silver leg. The poor man was sitting on the ground and I noticed his eyes did not move. I bent close to him and found they were made of clay. In fact, the poor man was made of clay entirely, I discovered. But there was something about the expression of his mouth in the clay figure that I didn't like. It was too deep for words.

Then I woke up. A kind of hot feeling surged up and burned in my cheeks so that it seemed indeed the clay man was heaping coals of fire on my head. I had a sense of nausea. Then it was that I realized I could never successfully become a model bandit. I had still one kind of feeling. It was *shame*.

AN OPEN LETTER TO AN AMERICAN FRIEND

My dear Mr. American:

Believe me I am no propagandist, for that is the last thing my friends are willing to give me credit for. But I wish to have a plain talk with you as between two nonpolitical people, about a topic concerning which I think there has been lately altogether too much senseless commotion. It is, namely, the thrilling topic of the abolition of extraterritoriality, which has kept your president, your Washington State Department, and all your consuls, merchants, editors, and press staff correspondents pretty busy. I understand your nephew is at present engaged in an egg-products business at Shanghai, so you will probably think you will begin by agreeing with me that this is a topic which concerns both of us across the Pacific personally. My purpose in writing this letter is to correct that wrong impression, and I hope you will end up by agreeing with me that it is a topic which concerns neither of us. I am a peaceful citizen, and have been out of jail all my life, and I have great confidence your nephew will keep out of jail also during his sojourn in China, until he can go back with a beautiful bride and three kiddies and buy up a big estate in South Carolina.

For, be it noted at the beginning, in talking about the abolition of extra-territoriality, it is not the civil code, but the criminal code and landing in jail that your consuls, merchants, and editors are worried about. Now it is with the purpose of allaying that fear that your nephew may be beheaded by some slant-eyed executioner, and of telling you that your Washington State Department is giving this topic altogether too much attention—it is with this single purpose that I am writing you this letter.

Of course your Washington State Department has the duty of protecting the interests of its citizens abroad, including those who are prone to get into foreign jails. In other words, your Washington Department is taking an insurance policy for some of its nationals who are "bad risks" (technically speaking), by making all of you, 98 per cent of whom are "good risks" and decent people, pay the premium.

Now, there is much to be said both for and against insurance. Mark Twain once wrote a witty article, called "The Danger of Lying in Bed," in which he succeeded in proving mathematically that there was no use buying an insurance against accidents when traveling by rail, and that the real peril lay not in traveling, but in staying at home.

Mark Twain traveled twenty thousand miles almost entirely by rail one year, and over twenty-five thousand miles another year, half by rail and half by sea, and up to the time he wrote that article, he had traveled sixty thousand miles in three years, *and never an accident*. On the other hand, there were 3,120 deaths in San Francisco and 26,000 deaths in New York annually. Taking that ratio as the standard, Mark Twain figured, there should be a million deaths each year in the United States. Out of this million, ten or twelve thousand are stabbed, shot, hanged, poisoned, or meet a similarly violent death in some other popular way, such as perishing by kerosene lamp and hoop-skirt conflagrations, getting buried in coal mines, falling off housetops, breaking through church or lecture-room floors, taking patent medicines, or committing suicide in other forms. The Erie Railroad kills from twenty-three to forty-six; the other 845 railroads kill an average of one-third of a man each; and the rest of that million, amounting in the aggregate to the appalling figure of 987,631 corpses, *die naturally in beds*. Therefore, Mark Twain concluded, "you will excuse me from taking any more chances on those beds. The railroads are good enough for me."

All this, of course, does not prove that railroad insurance against accidents is not strictly scientific, but that there need not be such a frightful scare, every time one buys a railway ticket at the station. And that is principally what I mean, with regard to the entirely inordinate anxiety you manifest for the peace and safety of your good nephew, should the extra-territoriality be abolished. Don't talk to me about Christian courage, when you feel you cannot send your nephew out here to China without first inquiring about the conditions of our prisons. Anyway, I don't like the suggestion; nor probably does your nephew. Why, I have traveled in your esteemed country, the United States of America, and have even dared to reside in New York without finding out first what the American code says about the difference between pilfering, burglary, and robbery and what are the legal punishments for assaults on women. And if I had occasion to find out these points, I would do it by getting tips from some cops, instead of asking our consul at New York to send Extra-Territoriality Commissions to the State Department at Washington. I have met a lone Chinaman keeping a laundry at Dresden without the aid of extra-territoriality or of any Chinese consul, by quietly and dutifully plying his trade. And American tourists, especially some of the world hikers, have gone through Poland, Rumania, and even red Russia, yes, even the much-hated red Russia, without so much as the shadow of extra-territoriality protecting them. American ladies have resided peacefully in Turkey, where extra-territoriality has been abolished, and where, your geography books say, they keep harems. And today there are several thousand Germans living in Shanghai, without my hearing of any of them landing in a Chinese jail. I myself have grown up for thirty-five years in China, without knowing what the Chinese law courts look like. No, sir, your nephew is quite safe over here.

The fact is, in my opinion, extra-territoriality belongs to the class of luxuries, on which the Nanking Government ought to levy a 50 per cent surtax. Your attitude seems to be: "Well, if it isn't exactly as dangerous as that, it is at least highly inconvenient. We do not know the Chinese laws and customs, and we do not know the Chinese language."

There you are hitting the nail on the head. Extra-territoriality is one of the modern conveniences you don't like to do without. But it is a "modern convenience" you can well afford only while your gunboats can at any time silence C. T. Wang when they choose to. When Turkey licked Greece, you gave up that luxury among the Turks. When Japan gave Russia a punch in the jaw, you also gave up that luxury in Japan, without seeming much the worse for it. Japan has, by incorporating certain clauses in their civil and criminal codes, made it mightily unpleasant for Americans to appear in Japanese law courts, but American businessmen have always found their way out and prospered by avoiding the Japanese law courts. I cannot boast yet that in the near future China may punch anybody in the jaw to win your respect, but I like to think that you will give up that luxury in China without any proof of our pugilistic skill. Anybody traveling abroad will have to put up with a certain amount of inconvenience anyway, as American residents in Berlin well know. Your coming to China exempts you from the income tax at home, and you are not even willing to learn to keep out of law courts over here, or to learn a few Chinese phrases, like the equivalents of English "Pardon me," "See you again," and "Good morning," which will contribute a lot toward that object? Why, it isn't a fair bargain at all. It is downright demoralizing.

The Shanghai Evening Post and Mercury, the only American paper in Shanghai, quoted in its editorial of February 18, 1931, a cable despatch from Washington (which I have not seen) to the effect that "the United States Government is reported as asking that 'foreign judges be maintained permanently in Chinese Courts,' and that they be authorized to assume jurisdiction 'upon the failure of the Chinese judicial officials to ensure justice.'" So far from thinking with the *Shanghai Evening Post* editor that the report is incorrect, I rather regard it as an able and representative statement of the devout wish of many of your compatriots over at this end of the Pacific. But I also think that only rich, idle people can afford to talk like that. Such a provision would be as beautiful as the luxurious swimming pools and dancing halls on the transatlantic ocean liners. It confirms my opinion that your Washington State Department should be transformed into a world tourist bureau, and that you are sending people out here, not for the purpose of money-making business, but in search of "modern conveniences." You don't know what a luxurious feeling it gives a fellow to ride around in a rickshaw—*extra-territorially*, i.e., feeling yourself above all the police, police regulations, laws, customs, and tribunals of the land. It is distinctly aristocratic. So long as you can afford it, by keeping a better and bigger naval armament than our toy gunboats, I have nothing to say.

This brings me to the question of paying premiums, which I referred to in the first part of my letter. It will do nobody any good to sleep entirely on a bed of roses and feel annoyed by a crumpled leaf. Extra-territoriality is demoralizing. It breeds bad manners, and it exempts the persons enjoying the privilege from the social obligation of being pleasant to one's neighbors. There are two classes of people enjoying extra-territoriality in this country, your nationals and our officials. Both of them have degenerated, and both of them would have behaved more respectably if they had not enjoyed that privilege. You know what I mean. A normal person stepping on his neighbor's toes would say, "Pardon me." An extrality fellow doesn't have to—and he doesn't do it. I am sending here three phrases which will help to improve the extrality fellow's manners, and which I beg you to copy out and forward to your nephew, for I am sure he hasn't learned them yet:

1. *Tui pu chu* .... Pardon me.
2. *Tsai huei* .... See you again.
3. *Nin hao* .... Good morning.

They are as common and as useful as the German *Danke sehr* and *Bitte schön,* and if your nephew will undertake to learn them, I will wager he will keep out of Chinese jails, until he returns with a beautiful wife and three kiddies to buy you that Carolina estate.

So pick up courage, my dear Mr. American, and don't let the extra-territoriality business worry you. It is an atrocious word any way, and ought to be abolished linguistically and lexicographically. And while we are on the linguistic ground, let me propose that its place be taken by a liberal use of those three phrases I have just written for your nephew. There is a closer relation between language and politics than you would suspect. For my part, I am willing to believe that the function of such phrases as lubricators of unnecessary social friction and promoters of international understanding and good will is greater and more important than all the diplomatic protection your Washington State Department is able to give your nephew. By refusing to use those phrases, your nephew has steadily declined to reveal to his Chinese business associates the human and essential gentlemanly side of his character. And let me assure you that when you, Mr. American, will care to reveal the essential gentlemanly side of your character, there is always enough essential gentlemanliness in your Chinese business associates to meet it.

Yours sincerely,

THE LITTLE CRITIC

Lao Sheh

UNTIL Rickshaw Boy *became a "runaway" best-seller in America Lao Sheh (Lau Shaw) was completely unknown outside of his own country. Yet he has been one of China's best-loved novelists for about fifteen years. His humorous equipment includes a skill in transcribing the Peiping colloquy that at times is peculiarly droll. For the benefit of Westerners he is now called the Mark Twain of China. The targets of his barbed pen are frequently those elements in Chinese bourgeois society who have been "gold-plated," or superficially exposed to the advantage of foreign culture. It used to be a favorite indoor sport among the Chinese to lampoon the inflated "returned student," a sort of counterpart of the innocent abroad. A classic tale of this school relates the downfall of one who had returned and boasted of his experience just once too often. Looking up to the sky, the young man sighed: "Ah, even the moon shines brighter in America!" At this the long-suffering father could stand it no more, and he slapped his son soundly on the face twice. Smarting under the blow, our unhappy hero came back with his final say: "Surely American fathers are better than ours—they never beat their own sons!"*

Lao Sheh's "Dr. Mao" is caricatured in the same spirit. Here is, however, more than satire of a type; it is written definitely with malice toward one—perhaps some particularly sorry individual whom he had known. As a class, the returned students deserve better.

TALKING PICTURES

Erh Chieh, or my second sister, had never seen a talking picture. But she already had a theory about it, as we all do about the things we haven't seen. The less facts there are, the more theories there must be. Like great men discussing politics, she also indulged in making up a theory about something she did not quite understand. She thought that the "sound pictures" were called by that name because the projecting machine was particularly noisy. Or else, it must be because of the fact that when the "electric men" "electric women"—by which she meant the stars of the pictures—kissed, a good deal of noise was pro-

Translated by Lin Yutang.

duced by the public applause. As she really believed in this latter theory, she didn't care much about going to see them, because she used to hide her face behind her fingers, when she saw the "electric men" kissing each other on the screen.

But, she was told, there are real talking and singing and laughter in sound pictures. She did not believe it at first, but when all reports confirmed this fact, she began to be curious.

Erh Lao Lao, or the second great auntie, was also getting curious. Besides, Erh Chieh had just won a lot of money from cards, and she was going to celebrate. Those invited included the second great auntie, the third maternal auntie, the fourth maternal sister-auntie, Little Bald-Head, Little Obedience, and "Number Four Dog."

As the second great auntie always went to bed at dusk, it was impossible for them to go to a night performance. It was decided that they should see the two-thirty show and should set out at twelve. This was considered early enough, because, after all, seeing a movie was only an amusement or an outing, as it were. When she had to meet people at the station, Erh Chieh used to go seven or eight hours ahead of the schedule. When Erh Chieh's husband was leaving for Tientsin last time, she urged him to go to the station three days ahead, because she was afraid he might not get a proper seat.

The point is that, when you leave early, you don't necessarily arrive early; otherwise what is the use of leaving as early as possible? When one agrees to leave by twelve, one is generally just about ready at quarter to one. It took the great auntie fifteen minutes to find her spectacles; she had them in her inside pocket all the time. Then the third maternal auntie was looking for her buttons, and she had ransacked through four trunks in vain for them, and decided finally to wear a simple dress. Number Four Dog finished his toilet in fifteen minutes, which was pretty good, considering the fact that he used to take over half an hour, and even then the policeman of the street had to give him lessons about washing his face.

Finally they were all outside the door, and were all set to start on the journey, when it was found that Little Bald-Head was missing. Back they came into the house to look for him, but could not establish his whereabouts. They agreed to give up going, because looking for Little Bald-Head was more important. Everybody began to take off his or her things, and went off in different directions to look for Bald-Head. After a while, Bald-Head appeared by himself; he had gone ahead, and was returning to see why they hadn't started and what had kept them so long. So they began to dress up again. It was a little late, but it didn't really matter; they could go by rickshaws.

The great auntie, whose opinion was respected on account of her age, used to haggle with the rickshaw coolies on the basis of one hundred twenty coppers being equal to one dollar, which obtained in the last years of the Manchu days. She hadn't been out much, and she was consequently inclined to think people were taking advantage of her old age, when they told her that a wheat cake cost three coppers. When the rickshaw coolies demanded two or three dimes for the distance of about one mile, she also considered they were taking advantage of her old age. She was going to show it to them. She would walk. Only when she started, nobody could tell whether her legs were carrying her forwards or backwards, and she didn't know herself. Apparently, the fourth maternal sister-auntie came to help her, but she in reality had put on high-heeled shoes when she realized she was going to see the movie, and she felt it was safer to go with some one. Of course, it was plain to everyone that if either of them were going to fall, they would fall on top of one another.

Thus they arrived at the theater, punctually at quarter past three. The performance had already started. Some one was to blame, probably the management. Punctuality in starting programs meant no allowance for human nature and no consideration for old age. It was inhuman. Erh Chieh felt like scolding somebody, but she decided not to show her temper.

They bought tickets, as was the proper thing to do. The moment they were shown in, Little Obedience refused to go in; it was so dark, and in all dark places were hidden red-eyed monsters. The darkness also reminded the great auntie of night, and night reminded her of going to sleep. She was feeling sleepy and "would rather go home with Little Obedience." So they began to hold a family council, which was not quite open to the audience in general. Erh Chieh insisted that the occasion was in honor of the great auntie, and if she went home, there was no point in their seeing the picture at all. As for Little Obedience, she could buy him some candy and keep him quiet. Furthermore, great auntie had already one foot in her grave, and if she died without seeing a sound picture, what could she tell the King of Hades, when she was asked? Erh Chieh's persuasion carried effect, and all decided to stay. There was the question of proceeding down the hall. The fourth maternal auntie held great aunt by the hand, the third maternal sister-auntie took charge of Little Obedience, while Erh Chieh took care of

Number Four Dog, and they proceeded down the dark and treacherous hall with hues and cries very much like Alpine tourists. There were ushers of course, but they wanted to sit in their own preferred manner. This manner was still a moot question. Were they to sit all in one line? Were they to separate? Were they to sit in front or at the rear? Erh Chieh was quite upset about it, while Number Four Dog was very vociferous and great auntie was feeling out of breath. The whole audience was forgetting about the picture and their interest centered around this great family. "Sh . . . Sh . . . Sh!" But Erh Chieh could make her voice heard above them all, and was giving brief and clear-cut commands, just to show them she was perfectly at home in society.

When the usher's flashlight—or "electric stick," according to Erh Chieh—was about used up, they made up their mind to sit down anywhere anyhow. But not exactly "anyhow." The question of superiority arose. It seemed entirely proper that great auntie, being the oldest in age and great in virtue, should sit inside. But great auntie protested out of politeness towards the fourth maternal sister-auntie: she had been married out and she was the hostess; the third maternal auntie was after all in the position of a daughter-in-law vis-a-vis the great auntie; Little Obedience was only a kid. Who was going to disentangle these social and moral relationships for them? It looked as if they were quarrelling from the vehemence of their respective humility, until some one among the audience cried out to God. After due noise and courtesy were made, they thought they would all sit down. But . . . they hadn't yet bought candy for Little Obedience. "Candy man!" Erh Chieh shouted rather loud, in fact so loud that the manager rushed in, thinking that the candy man had committed a murder.

When candy had been bought, great auntie thought of an important thing—she had forgotten to cough. Her cough, however, stirred up the "filial piety" of Erh Chieh, and she fell to discussing the number of days great auntie had yet to live. Old people like great auntie don't mind their children discussing their number of days, and were even willing to participate. "The other things I don't care much about," she said, "but I do want a golden nine-lock-puzzle. And don't forget about a pair of paper children to accompany me to my grave."

Now, this was a vast and practically endless topic, and was besides of absorbing interest. One thing recalled another, and one event brought up another event. Strange as it may seem, one could talk about family affairs with so much more zest when in a public theater.

In the midst of this interesting talk, the lights were turned on and people began to leave. Erh Chieh called for the seller of melon-seeds. One needed to chew melon-seeds when discussing family affairs.

The usher came and informed them that the performance was over, and the next one would be at eight o'clock in the evening.

So they had to leave. It was not till great auntie had gone to bed that Erh Chieh asked the third maternal aunt, "Come to think of it, what really is a sound picture?" After a little pause, auntie replied, "Oh, let it alone. I didn't hear anything, anyway." It was the fourth maternal sister-aunt who proved herself to have been a keen observer. She remarked that foreign devils let out smoke through their nose when they smoke. "These electric pictures are really wonderfully made. When the smoke comes out through the nose, it looks as if it is real." And they all assented in admiration.

DR. MAO

Language is a funny thing. Each person speaks his own language; he uses certain words and phrases in a manner all his own so that unless you understand him as a whole you will never understand what he is talking about. Because in all your life there are not many people whom you get to understand you had better not be overoptimistic about languages. A scholar in linguistics does not necessarily speak the same language as his wife, else how would you explain the fact that occasionally the scholar in linguistics is ordered by his Mrs. to kneel before the bed by way of punishment?

It has been three years since I first made the acquaintance of Dr. Mao. I still remember distinctly the circumstances under which we first met. As I had trouble understanding what he said I paid particular attention to his own interpretation and, along with this, I retained in my mind a strong impression of the circumstances. The reason I failed to understand him was not that he did not speak good Mandarin; his Mandarin, as a matter of fact, had passed the test of the Committee for the Promotion of the National Language with an even grade of 80. I could make out what he said very well, but I could not understand him. Even if he should write a short story in his own language and have it printed beautifully for me to read I would still fail to understand him, unless he were to accompany every sentence with careful annotation.

Translated by George Kao.

It was a fine, crisp autumn day, the trees just beginning to yellow and the butterflies were in a playful mood with the falling blossoms. It was that special kind of a day that makes it difficult for you to stay indoors at your desk, at the same time gives you nothing in particular to do once you go out. Several times I rose, then resumed my seat in a sort of dilemma. Finally I decided to go out and look up a friend, as if visiting a friend was something to do, a pardonable way of spending the time.

When I came out on the street I was still undecided which one of my friends to visit. Again, the fine day that it was suggested open country, and I thought of calling on my friend Lao Mei at Kwang Hwei University, which was located on a spacious campus outside the city.

Even before entering the house I could see from the courtyard that Lao Mei was in his room; the windows of his room were wide open, from one of which two freshly laundered handkerchiefs were hanging out to dry. I called out his name, and he instantly poked his head out, wearing a halo from the light of the sun shining on his hair. He told me to come on up, which I did in a hop-skip-and-jump. Upstairs, not only his room, but all doors and windows were thrown open, stamping little squares of sunshine on the floor. Lao Mei received me at his door, looking free and easy in his lounging jacket and slippers, apparently having no classes to teach that day.

"Nice day!" we both sang out in a two-worded hymn of praise.

There seemed to be another person in the room, some one I did not know.

With a gesture of the hand Lao Mei established contact between us and we both bared our teeth in a formal smile, preparatory to asking, "Your honorable name?" when Lao Mei settled it for us. "Mr. So-and-So. Dr. Mao." Once more we showed our teeth before I sat down on Lao Mei's bed. Dr. Mao leaned against the window sill, taking a position diagonally across from the door. Lao Mei pulled up a chair and sat backwards astride it; either they were very good pals, or Lao Mei did not have much respect for this doctor fellow, I thought.

Plunging into the usual patter with Lao Mei, I started giving the doctor the once-over. There was something funny about this man. He was in the "full armor" of a foreign suit, with everything where it ought to be. For instance, a handkerchief was carefully stuck in the outside breast pocket, a tiepin in the tie, a length of watch chain dangling across the lower portion of his vest, the correct shine on the tip of his shoes. His suit, however, looked as if it had seen at least three years' wear and his shoes appeared unnaturally thick, apparently re-soled. He wasn't *wearing* foreign clothes; he looked more like he had committed himself, under oath, to foreign clothes—the handkerchief must be there, the tiepin goes there, they were all a kind of duty, one of those religious commandments followed on faith. He did not give people the feeling that he was wearing Western clothes; he reminded people more of the filial son in mourning, wearing the painful and enforced raiment of hemp that custom decreed.

He kept his eyes on something across the room, and I soon discovered that there was a good-sized mirror near the door and he was surveying himself in that mirror. His face, now I saw, was hollow in the middle and bent at both ends, in the shape of a gold ingot. His sunken nose represented the bottom of the pit. His eyes, situated on the upper slope of the ingot, also appeared deep-set, like two little wells, with spots of black water where the pupils were. His chin stuck out on the lower slope of the ingot, the lower row of his teeth protruding more than usual, in a perpetual clash with his upper teeth.

He was of medium height, neither fat nor thin, his frame being just the right size on which to hang the suit of foreign clothes which he was under oath to wear. To top off his ingot-shaped head, there was duly grown a mop of black hair, oiled and brushed, again in an over-exercised sense of duty.

There he was, eying himself in the mirror, throwing his glances back and forth, as if appreciating his own beauty. But he looked odd to me. He had his back to the sun, so that the middle and concave portion of his face appeared somewhat dark. Every time my eyes rested on this dark and low spot on his physiognomy I hastened to turn and look out of the window to see if it had started clouding up. This doctor fellow even made people suspicious of the beautiful day that it was. He *was* a funny fellow.

His heart didn't seem to be in our conversation; at the same time he couldn't bear leaving us; he was bored, and because he was bored he paid special attention to himself. He made me think that here was a fellow who regarded living, like wearing foreign clothes, a kind of obligation.

I don't remember what we were talking about at the moment when he suddenly turned around his face, his low-sunken eyes closed momentarily, giving the impression that he was making a search in his heart. By the time he reopened his eyes the smile that was lurking around his lips changed its mind about coming out, and in its place escaped a little sigh. Most likely this was to show that he had not found anything in his searching his heart. Could be his heart was a complete void.

"How about it, Doc?" Lao Mei's tone bore out the suspicion that there was something disrespectful in his attitude toward the doctor.

The doctor seemed to be unaware of this though. Along with the sigh he sent forth a little noise—"Pugh!" as if the weather was excessively warm. "Too much of a sacrifice!" he said, placing his body in the arms of a chair and stretching his legs way out.

"Ph.D. from Harvard. Suffering foreign rats, eh?" Lao Mei must be pulling the doctor's legs.

"To be sure!" the doctor's voice was almost quavering. "To be sure, no human being should be asked to endure this suffering! No girl friends, no movie to go to," he paused, apparently unable to recall any other of his needs, creating quite a bit of suspense for me, and then summed up in an all-inclusive phrase: "No nothing!" It's a good thing his eyes were located in those low hollows or tears would surely roll off his face. I could swear he felt very badly indeed.

"And if it were in America?" Lao Mei prompted.

"Sure! Even in Shanghai—good movies, any number of girl friends," he paused again.

Outside of women and movies I guess there wasn't much on his mind. I tried to draw him out: "Dr. Mao," I said, "in the North here they have fine operas. Worth going to look at."

His face darkened, and it was a long while before he managed to come out with an answer. "From what I hear from my foreign friends, the Chinese theater is barbarous!"

That put a stop to our conversation. I became a bit tired of sitting. After a while I proposed that we go for a bath; there was a newly opened bathhouse in town, said to be a very good one. It was my intention to ask Lao Mei to go with me, but I couldn't very well not include Dr. Mao in the invitation since he was there and feeling so lonely.

The doctor shook his head: "That's dangerous!"

That got me puzzled again; I had always bathed out and had not been drowned yet.

"Female masseuse! Bathtub. . . ." He seemed really scared.

Oh, I got it. In his mind, outside of America, there is only one place —Shanghai, where there is the institution of the female masseuse.

"This is different from Shanghai," I went so far as to suggest.

"But where else in China can you find a place so civilized as Shanghai?" He deigned to give me a smile with this statement, a rather uncomfortable smile—his upper lip reached up almost touching his forehead, his nose completely sunken in.

"And Shanghai again cannot be compared with America?" Lao Mei was really making fun of him now.

"Sure," the doctor assented in all seriousness, "in America there's a bathtub in every home; in American hotels there is a bath to every room. You want to take a bath, all you need to do is to turn on the water—*hwa!* Hot or cold, mix them any way you like; if you want to change the water, *hwa*—you just let out the dirty water and turn on some fresh water, *hwa*—just like that." He poured forth this information all in one breath, his every "*hwa*" was liquid and frothy as if he was using his mouth to demonstrate the American hot-and-cold water faucet. In the end he added as an afterthought: "Chinese people are all very dirty."

While the doctor went "*hwa*" and "*hwa*," Lao Mei had put on his shoes and coat.

The doctor stepped out of the room before us and gave out with a "Well, good-by." He said this in a tearful and grating tone. He hated to see us go, for he was really lonely; yet he couldn't quite bring himself to go to a "Chinese" bathhouse with us, no matter how clean it was.

When we had walked downstairs and reached the courtyard I noticed the doctor at one of the upper windows gazing after us. The sun slanted toward his head throwing a little dark spot on his face which was the shadow of his nose. As he swayed his body slightly this little dark spot on his face appeared to be growing, now long, now short. When we were about to reach the school gate I turned my head and saw that he was still standing there, seemingly defying the sun all by himself.

Several times on our way to and in the bathhouse Lao Mei wanted to bring up the subject of Dr. Mao, but I didn't join in. He entertained a somewhat disrespectful attitude toward the doctor, and I didn't care to allow my impression of the man to be colored by his opinion, even though Dr. Mao didn't leave me with any too good an impression. I still couldn't quite understand him, all I felt was that he represented something half-baked or not altogether ripe; he was neither a Shanghai playboy, nor an offspring of overseas Chinese in America; he resembled neither a Chinese nor a foreigner. He seemed to me a man without roots. My observation might not be accurate, nonetheless I didn't wish to have any assistance from Lao Mei; I wanted to size him up to my own satisfaction. On the one hand, I felt that he was disgusting; on the other hand, I thought he was rather funny—I don't mean he would be fun to know, but funny in the sense implied in the old adage: "There are nine kinds of dragons, all different from one another."

Not long afterwards I found an opportunity. Lao Mei asked me to substitute for him in his classes. Lao Mei was that kind of a man; nobody knew how he managed it, but every term he would take a leave of absence of at least two or three weeks. This time the reason was, according to him, that his eldest nephew had been bitten by a mad dog. He must go home for a few days.

Lao Mei handed his keys to me; I was not going to sleep in his place, but I could rest between classes and prepare my lessons there.

After a couple of days I began to realize that I couldn't rest or prepare my lessons there either, for as soon as I went to Lao Mei's room Dr. Mao would move in. This man surely was lonely. Sometimes he even came in looking tearful, apparently having been weeping in his own room and rushed over at the sound of my arrival without waiting to dry his eyes. To be considerate, I always greeted him with a smiling face even though he didn't give me a moment's peace and quiet.

It was chrysanthemum time, but up in the North the bright autumnal days did not affect normal persons with the usual melancholia of the season. Dr. Mao, however, remained his doleful self. Every time I looked at him I had to take another look to see if the weather had changed. He had a way of manufacturing his own dreary and rainy atmosphere with which he surrounded himself and banished sunshine from the room.

It took me a few days before I began to learn to interpret the language he used. One thing good about him: he was never bothered by the fact that others wondered what he was saying. People could wonder all they wanted, he would still talk as he pleased. He totally ignored the fact that language was invented as a means of communication; when I talked with him I had to make believe that I was a talking machine and he was a talking machine; we both had our say without bothering about who understood what. No wonder Lao Mei liked to poke fun at the doctor; whoever heard of cultivating an intimate and mutually understanding friendship with a talking machine?

Regardless of what manner of man he was, I wanted to try to cure him of his ennui. It wasn't right for young fellows to carry on like that.

Of course I didn't dare suggest going to the bathhouse or to the theater. But there was nothing wrong about going for a walk.

"How can you take a walk all by yourself? Really!" the doctor gave out another of his sighs.

"Why can't you take a walk by yourself?" I asked.

"After all, you got to enjoy life, haven't you?" he lashed back.

"Oh!" I swear I didn't mean to be so dumb.

"Taking a walk all alone!" There was fire in his eyes when he said this, although they were still sunken.

"Well, then, how about my going along with you?"

"But you are not a girl," he heaved a long sigh.

Now I understood.

After a long pause he added another thought. "Chinese people are too dirty, you can't take any walk on the streets here."

We were obviously leading up a blind alley, so I tried another tack. "Find someone to go with you to some café, play tennis, or maybe read a novel all by yourself; practice calligraphy. . . ." I mentioned a whole string of ideas commonly employed by the average man to kill time with; with his foreign clothes *de rigueur* in front of me, I wouldn't dare suggest any more sensible preoccupation.

At least he was consistent in his reply. To sum it up in one phrase: no women, nothing can be done.

"Well, in that case, go and find yourself a girl!" Having sized up my objective, I let go with my big guns. "That's not such a difficult thing, you know."

"But, still, it's too much of a sacrifice!" He countered with the same shot in the dark.

"Huh?" At least this gave me a chance to practice looking blank; I would admit he had me confused.

"You got to buy things for her, haven't you? You got to take her to dinner, to the movies, haven't you?" he cross-questioned me as if he was a judge.

I said to myself: "What do I care?"

"Of course you got to. That's the American custom, and it must be done. But Chinese people are poor; me, a Ph.D. from Harvard, I get only two hundred dollars a month—I must ask for a raise! Where could I find the money for such an outlay?" Apparently he had launched on his favorite theme, and I was all ears. "Suppose you spent all that money, and went on smoothly and got yourself engaged, and then married, that wouldn't be bad, although it costs a lot of money to get engaged—you got to get her a golden ring, haven't you?—with the price of gold so high! And it costs a lot of money to get married, too,—you got to take her to some place for honeymoon, that's the custom in America. Then there's the home to furnish; you got to have a bed with box springs, a foreign-style bathtub, a sofa is a 'must,' and so is a piano, a rug for the living-room floor. Oh, Chinese rugs are not bad, even Americans are fond of them. Now, how much money *that* would cost you, all told. That is to say if everything goes smoothly. Suppose you spent a lot of money buying her things, taking her to movies, and in the end she ditched you, then what? All that money for nothing! Such things often happen in America. But Americans are rich, they can afford it. Take Harvard for instance, when boys and girls go together the money they spend on ice cream alone would be more than the Chinese can afford! Think of it——"

I waited a long while but he failed to continue. Perhaps he had lost the thread of his story, perhaps he was fed up with the conditions in this "China" of his.

I gave up. I couldn't do anything with this fellow, I would have to leave him to his troubles.

Before Lao Mei came back, every day I heard some more about American customs and Chinese barbarities. The only place that appeared passable was Shanghai; unfortunately there still were so many Chinese in Shanghai, considerably lowering the prestige of that city! He was a little afraid of Shanghai too, with its "wild chicks," robbers, killings, kidnapings, and sundry other dangers. All on account of the presence of Chinese. In his eyes, all Chinese are like the Chinese portrayed in American movies. "You must do things with the American spirit, you must see things the American way!" He always admonished me in these words, and when he became enthused about a subject—as he was whenever he was on the subject of America—he would break out in one of his rare grins. Just what is the American spirit? He was unable to enlighten me in a few words. He had to divulge it in his own sweet time by means of illustrative facts. For instance, a bathtub in every home, driving your own car, movie houses everywhere you go, a girl friend to every male, room temperature always above seventy in the winter, women are all good-looking, living room thickly carpeted. . . . Though I succeeded in laying all these facts end to end I still couldn't quite grasp what he meant by the American spirit.

Lao Mei returned, and I felt a slight letdown. I had hoped to make out Dr. Mao in one gulp, but with Lao Mei back I wouldn't be seeing the doctor every day. That was not Lao Mei's fault though. It turned out that the dog which had bitten his nephew wasn't a mad dog, so Lao Mei had to terminate his leave of absence.

Having handed over Lao Mei's classes and shown him where I left off, I asked him to lunch, inviting Dr. Mao, too, while I was at it. I wanted to see, after all, whether he could stand any "Chinese-style" entertainment, or whether he was just stuffy.

He declined, but only with thanks and sincere appreciation. "Really we young people should learn to be careful with our money. Why eat out? We must learn to save toward building our future little homes —the way Americans do, a bed with box springs, bathtub, electric heater"—he seemed like a man with a vision before his eyes, a vision of the modern Adam and Eve in a cosily furnished little paradise— "and a sofa, where husband and wife can read together from *Married Love*. That's true happiness. Really! We must learn to save a little now . . ."

I didn't wait for him to finish but simply grabbed him by the arm and marched him off between us. He had his own reason for not wanting to waste money, if what he said could be trusted. What I wanted to know was whether he would be capable of enjoying a nice meal when it was spread before him.

At the restaurant I soon discovered he was not capable of this enjoyment. He didn't help with the ordering; he was ignorant of the Chinese dishes. "You know, there are many Chinese restaurants in America, too. But after all, Chinese food is not hygienic. In Shanghai it's better, one can always go to a Western restaurant. Imagine a date with the girl friend for some Western chow. Not bad, eh?"

I had a mind to tell him he might as well change his name too, to "Dr. Moore" or "Dr. Maurice." Not bad, eh? But I couldn't quite bring myself to insult him like that. So Lao Mei and I ordered the dishes.

When the food was served, to be sure Dr. Mao did not exactly eat it with relish. Half of the time he was staring at the table in a sort of daze, his concave face a study of sadness. Lao Mei, always the joker, teased:

"If only there were two or three girl friends around, eh, Doc?"

The doctor suddenly came to and protested: "No, no. One boy, one girl. Three is a crowd. Really, cooking your own meals at home, a chicken dinner for two. What a life!"

"No parties ever?" Lao Mei was pretty good at this sort of dead-pan comedy.

"Americans don't make friends as indiscriminately as the Chinese. Chinese people go around too much with friends, no conception at all of the time wasted. That won't do at all!" Dr. Mao was practically lecturing Lao Mei to his face.

Lao Mei and I were so angry we had to laugh. At least there was a certain genuine honesty about the doctor. He honestly had no use for anything Chinese—except Chinese rugs. He was born in China—his greatest personal sacrifice! He couldn't help that. But he could spend his life hating all things Chinese, endeavoring with all his might to build a little home, American-style, with which to add to the everlasting life and glory of China. Of course, I found it hard to believe that the American spirit was all that he described. Yet I knew that what he did see he worshiped with a touching and devout faith. The bathtubs and the sofa were his credo. I also realized that if he acted in America the way he did in China he could not have seen very much. But he did see the movie houses in America and that the Chinese are dirty. What can you do about that?

But because of this I started to pay special attention to him. I could never cure him of his ennui, and I had no wish to spend my energy in this pursuit. I did, however, want to get to the bottom of him and see what made him the way he was.

I was no longer substituting for Lao Mei, but I still called on him often, thus seeing Dr. Mao frequently. Sometimes when Lao Mei was out, I would sit around awhile in Dr. Mao's room.

The doctor's quarters were sparsely furnished. A small bed, beside which stood two iron trunks, one big, one small. A small table, covered with a snowy-white tablecloth, on which were placed some writing materials, all made in America. Two chairs, one for people to sit on, the other permanently occupied by a typewriter. There was also a rocking chair with an oval-shaped dragon embroidered cushion on it, the type that was made to sell to foreign tourists. When he was free he would sit and rock in this chair, with the apparent intention of urging Father Time on with his rocking so that he might the more quickly reach his life's goal. There were a few foreign-bound books sitting on the window ledge. The walls were decorated with a "Harvard" pennant and a few photographs taken in America. Of all the things in that room the one most tinged with Chinese flavor was Dr. Mao himself, although he might not admit this.

I had been in his room more than once, but never had I seen him provide it with a pot of flowers or a painting or picture of any landscape. Every now and then he did stealthily pick a flower from the school garden, but it was only to make a boutonniere for his foreign suit. This man's ideals were entirely centered around the creation of a man-made, American-style, neat and cosy little home. I could picture the day this ideal little home came true, how he would surely keep the blinds down all day long and not pay the slightest attention to the outside world even if the sky should turn purple and the sun rise from the west. It would seem that, outside of his own self and his bit of American spirit, the universe and all it holds did not exist for him.

What happened between us constantly bore out this observation on my part: the scope of our conversation was limited to money, foreign clothes, women, marriage, American movies. Occasionally when I brought up some topic of politics, the state of society, arts and letters, or other matters that I recalled or that were the talk of the town he would never join in the discussion. He would unbend enough to impart a few words, however, if any one of these items happened to have any connection with America. But his approach would be entirely his own. For instance, on American politics, he would relate to me the following facts: when the American Senator So-and-so was married, how the bride and groom arrived at the church in swanky limousines, and how many special details of police were called out to keep the crowds back. It was the same way with other topics that came up for discussion. In his eyes and mind, government, art, and anything you could mention, were all glamorized adjuncts to married life and the middle-class civilization. As to China, does China have any government, art, and social problems to speak of? He hated most the Chinese movies; Chinese movies are rotten, everything else is rotten too. The most unsatisfactory thing about Chinese movies, to him, was that the men and women there didn't go in for kissing.

Several years of Harvard have imbued him with that much of the American spirit, I quite understood. But was he not born in China? Before he went to America had he not spent at least twenty-odd years in China? Why then was he so ignorant, so unfeeling about China?

I experimented many times to find out what his family background was, what his experience in work and study had been. . . . Hmm, that man could keep his mouth shut tighter than a rock! That was another strange thing about him, he was forever after others to talk to him but never willing to tell anything about himself.

I had known him for nearly a year. I was beginning to see that this honorable Ph.D. was not as simple as I had thought. Even if he were simple his simpleness was of another kind. He must have lived by some religious creed, which made him simple and yet mystic.

Since he didn't let anything drop from his own mouth I had to attempt anew my estimation of him on the basis of his outward appearance. Whenever I asked him something personal I would pay special attention to observe his face. He wouldn't answer my question, but his face was not exactly idle. He couldn't be a bad man, for his face gave him away. His deep mysticism didn't succeed entirely in overcoming his simpleness, yet he must remain mystic; that's what made Dr. Mao what he was today; otherwise, what was there to live for? A man must have something that he could point his finger to and identify himself with. Some people forever talk about this something; others keep it forever buried and hidden away in their hearts. The idea nevertheless is universal. Dr. Mao wished only to hide himself in his own heart. He did talk about the American spirit and about his ideal little home without end, but behind all this—it must be *behind*—did we find the real "he"?

His face, when I tried to question him, appeared hollower than ever. From the bottom of this hollow there came a dark cloud, spreading slowly until it shrouded his whole face. His eyes, never too much in evidence, now began to recede as if to disappear entirely. His crowded mouthful of teeth ground together a few times, his ears moved ever so little, all conspiring, as it were, not to reveal what secret he had in his heart. Then some light stole out from his eyes, the shadow on his face rolled up slowly into his hair. "Really!" he started saying, but whatever it was he said it would have not the least bit to do with what I asked. He was victorious again; a long while afterward he would still brush me with the corner of his eye.

To imagine that he was born an American Ph.D. would be one easy solution, but it would be too illogical for words. And since asking him proved of no avail, the only thing for me to do was to wait. After all, he couldn't very well spend *all* of his time rocking to and fro in that rocking chair.

Time has a way of sifting things out. Sure enough, waiting brought me results.

Summer vacation was approaching when one day I went to see Lao Mei. Of course, whenever I saw Lao Mei I also expected to see that personification of ennui. But this time the doctor failed to show his face.

"Where's our friend there?" I indicated with my head.

"Hasn't shown his face for more than a week now," Lao Mei answered.

"What happened?"

"They say he wanted to resign. I am not too clear what it's all about," Lao Mei chuckled, "you know he isn't exactly voluble with others about his private life."

"What did the others say?" I really became nosy.

"They say he had a three-year contract with the school."

"How many years is yours supposed to be?"

"None of us signed any contract. The school wrote us a letter of appointment at the beginning of the year."

"How come he alone had a contract?"

"The American spirit, you know; he wouldn't teach unless there's a contract."

Just like Dr. Mao.

"They say," Lao Mei continued, "his contract was drawn up in Chinese and American versions. This is a school run by Chinese, but the doctor did not have implicit faith in the Chinese language. They say the terms of the contract stipulated that within three years both parties to the contract must not seek to withdraw, must not demand a raise in salary on the one hand, nor a cut in salary on the other. The contract was duly signed, in the best American spirit. Nevertheless, at the end of the year, with summer vacation here, he demanded a raise in salary or he wouldn't come back after the summer."

"Oh." It took me some time to get it straight in my mind; then I asked, "What about the contract?"

"When you make a contract it's the American spirit, but when you break a contract it's the Chinese spirit." Lao Mei's epigrams were a bit too sharp for my comfort.

And yet this casual remark of his was fraught with significant meaning, at least to me who had been making a serious study of the doctor.

"What about the school?" I asked.

"They say the school refused to grant his request. Naturally, there's the contract."

"What about him?"

"Who knows. He never talked to anyone about himself. Even when he wanted to deal with the school it would always be through correspondence. He has a typewriter."

"If the school refused him a raise, you think he would quit?"

"Didn't I tell you? Nobody knows." Lao Mei was a little contemptuous of my concern. "If he quit he would be breaking his own word; but of this much I am sure, the school wouldn't go to court with him over the breach of contract; they haven't got that much time to waste."

"I suppose you don't know what's behind his demand for a raise? Oh, of course, I forgot!" I withdrew this question on my own, at the same time advancing another, "Don't you think somebody ought to speak to him?"

"You go to speak to him, not me!" Lao Mei gave a few more chuckles. "You ask him to dinner, he won't go; you ask him to have a drink, he won't drink; you ask him a few civil questions, he won't talk; and what he does talk about bores you stiff. How can you speak to this kind of a man and offer any friendly advice?"

"That's not entirely so; our friend sometimes can be a lot of fun."

"That depends on the way you look at it. A mental case can be a lot of fun to the psychiatrist."

Lao Mei sounded serious. After pondering it awhile, I asked him, "Lao Mei, I guess the doctor offended you in some way. I know you never had much respect for him, but . . ."

He laughed. "Pretty sharp, I'll hand it to you! Yes, the doctor is getting on my nerves. Women, women—morning, noon, and night! I'm getting tired of listening to him."

"This is not the real reason." I gave him another thrust. I knew Lao Mei's ways very well, he was not one to go for anybody easily, and if somebody really offended him he would generally keep it to himself. At first he treated the doctor rather lightly but without malice; that's why he did not hesitate to discuss the man; now the doctor must have really offended him, and, as a result, he would rather not talk about it. But after this prodding from me he couldn't hold back any longer.

"Well, it's just this," he chuckled again, somewhat forcedly. "One day the doctor asked me point-blank: 'Mr. Mei, you are an instructor also?' I said that was the appointment I got from the school; there was nothing I could do about it. 'But you are not a Ph.D. from America?' he asked. 'No,' I said, 'but, as for Americans doctorates, how many coppers a dozen?' He didn't say anything, but his face turned green. I didn't think much about the incident, but ever since then he seemed to regard me as a deadly enemy. He even went so far as to write a letter to the president demanding to know why Mr. Mei, who hasn't got a doctorate, was paid the same salary as someone with a

doctor's degree—and an American degree, at that. I don't know how
he ever found out what I was earning."

"Well, the president shouldn't have let you see the letter."

"Don't blame the president. It's the doctor himself who sent me a
carbon copy of his letter, but without a signature. I guess he considers
me not good enough for his company." Lao Mei laughed even more
forcedly. I guess all young people are proud like that.

"Hmm, perhaps he used you as his reason for demanding the raise."
I speculated out loud.

"Don't know. Let's talk about something else."

After I left Lao Mei, I figured that before summer vacation began I
would surely have a chance to see the doctor, and perhaps I could find
out something from him. Sure enough, one day I ran into him on the
street. He was walking hurriedly, his brows knitted, his hollow face
the shape of a spoon. He looked more like chasing after his own
shadow than walking.

"Where are you going?" I called to him.

"To the post office," he said, drawing out a handkerchief—not the
one tucked in his breast pocket—to wipe off his perspiration.

"Summer is here. Where do you plan to go for a vacation?"

"Really! They say Tsingtao is a very nice place, just like a foreign
country. Maybe I'll go there for a vacation. But . . ."

I knew exactly what that "But . . ." would lead to, so without waiting for him to get there, I asked: "Plan to come back after summer?"

"Not definite." Maybe it was because of the suddenness of my question, he made this slip of the tongue; of course "not definite" implied
the possibility of not coming back. He also realized this at once, and
hastened to cover it up by adding, "It's not definite that I'll go to
Tsingtao." He pretended that he missed my last question. "Must go to
Shanghai though. All the movies there you want to see. It's too much
of a sacrifice working in the North. No good movies to go to. Well,
come over to see us at the school to avoid being lonely." He started
walking away before he was quite finished, and with the first step he
practically broke into a run.

I didn't understand just whom he had in mind when he said "to
avoid being lonely." As to whether or not he planned to come back to
his teaching job I would have to wait until after the summer vacation
and see.

As soon as the examinations were over, we found that the doctor
had gone off, but he didn't take his things with him. According to Lao

Mei's deduction, the doctor must have gone elsewhere to look for a job. If he should be successful he would display his Chinese spirit and not come back for all the world, regardless how many years were specified in his contract. If he should fail to find a better job he would return to prove his American spirit. Things seemed to be developing somewhat along the lines of Lao Mei's deduction. We didn't want to expect the worst of people, but his actions didn't quite encourage people to think of him in any other direction.

After the summer I happened to be substituting for Lao Mei again. Why he took leave of absence this time perhaps he himself didn't quite know. At any rate, he neglected to tell me. As long as he could count on me as a substitute it didn't matter very much whether or not he had a reason.

Dr. Mao had returned.

Anyone would feel that to return like this was something of an anticlimax and rather face-losing—any one, that is, except the doctor himself. He was in high spirits. If he hadn't proved a sympathetic character when he was sad his grinning now didn't seem to help either. I guess he figured that his grin would indicate how happy he was inside; unfortunately his face would not co-operate. Every time he opened his mouth it always made me think he was going to yawn, until I noticed that there wasn't any tear in his eyes. Then I knew he was really grinning. Well, he could grin all he wished, but it wouldn't make me any happier.

"Did you go to Tsingtao?" I greeted him. He was standing outside his door.

"No. There's no life in Tsingtao. Really!" He grinned.

"Oh?"

"Come in. Show you something precious."

I followed him in like a fool.

His room looked the same as it did before, except for the addition of a mosquito net over his bed. He stuck his arm inside the net and came out right away with an object which he hid behind his back. "Guess what?" he said.

I didn't feel like playing.

"Let's hear your opinion. Are southern women nicer, or northern women?" His hands were still behind his back.

I would never answer this type of question.

When he saw that I didn't care to answer his hands came up in front and handed me a picture; then he put his head over my shoulder and grinned so broadly that I was really afraid the lines on his face would spread over to mine. He didn't say anything, but some kind of smacking noise kept emitting from his mouth.

It was a photograph of a young woman. It is always unsafe to judge a person's appearance by a photograph, so I'm not here to say to what degree this woman impressed me as beautiful. From what I could tell, she wasn't old; her hair was done up in an elaborate and intricate wave, her face smallish, eyes big, chin round. Anyway, not bad-looking.

"Don't tell me you are engaged, Doc?" I asked him laughingly.

The doctor was grinning so, he didn't know where to place his eyes and eyebrows. Still he did not say anything.

I took another look at the picture, and felt a wave of sympathy for its subject. Of course, I could hardly decide anything for her; still, if I were the girl . . .

"Too much of a sacrifice!" When the doctor finally found his voice it was the same old tune that he sang. "But this time it is worth it, really! Nowadays girls are really smart. Just twenty-one, and she catches on to everything, as if she's been to America! After I dated her to a movie the first time she insisted on going home no matter what I said. Smart girl! The second time we were at the movies she still refused to let me hold her hands. Just think, how smart that is! And I bought the tickets, too. Finally, when I took her to the movies again, then she let me kiss her once. Really! Worth spending any amount of money for! When I was leaving she saw me off at the station and even got some fruits for me. Yes, sure, worth spending a little money to get; she will always be mine now. I never believed in going for 'wild chicks,' it won't do no matter how much money you spend. And dangerous, too! From this day on I must start saving. . . ."

"You haven't been extravagant, you know." I interpolated.

"My God!" Imagine his eyes popping out from the bottom of the pit. "Not extravagant? A bachelor; meals, laundry, everything costs money! After you're married—'two can live as cheaply as one.' Cook your own meals, wash your own clothes. That's what they call teamwork between husband and wife."

"If so, why bother to save any more?"

"Well, you have to have a box-spring bed, haven't you? Got to have a sofa, and a piano in the living room, haven't you? Got to spend money for the wedding, and spend more for the honeymoon, haven't you? A home is a home, after all!" He paused and pondered for a moment. "You even need to spend money on the minister if you want to get married."

"Why have a minister?"

"That's to take your wedding seriously. In America all high-class people are married by ministers. Really!" He reflected once more. "Then, there are traveling expenses! She's from Shanghai; train fare for two from Shanghai to here; second-class, third-class trains in China are intolerable! You figure out how much that would add up to, you just figure it out!" He was mumbling in his mouth and counting on his fingers, without being able to arrive at any clear-cut budget. He no sooner knitted his brows than he broke out in a broad grin. "No matter how much, it's worth spending! Suppose you bought a five-thousand-dollar diamond; it's just to wear it so that others can see it, isn't it? Here's a southern beauty coming up north, all mine; I must show her off in all her glory, no matter how much it would cost. She's the most beautiful girl in Shanghai. Isn't that worth sacrificing for? After all, a man's got to sacrifice sometime."

I still did not understand what he meant by "sacrifice."

During the month or so I substituted for Lao Mei I got an earful of Shanghai, marriage, sacrifice, glory, box-spring bed. . . . Sometimes I even found myself writing these magic words into my lecture notes and had to start over again. He certainly got me all upset, too. I hoped Lao Mei would be back soon so that I could go off for a few day's peace and quiet. It's interesting to observe human nature, but when the human in question is sticky like a piece of New Year's cake then you could get stuck and get fed up.

There were five or six more days to go before Lao Mei was due back. At this point the doctor came up with a new twist. His life was like a skillfully composed essay. Just when the reader was beginning to get tired he would come up with a brilliant passage.

He had got over his period of ecstasy. Now, outside of class hours, you would find him in his room tap-tap-tapping on his typewriter. After each wave of tapping you would see the door open and the doctor emerge and make a beeline downstairs to the mailbox. He would make straight for the mailbox and come straight back to his room where he would start pacing the floor. You would hear him pacing back and forth, and then you would hear a long sigh, such a loud and doleful sigh as would raise the roof and blow his room down like a house of cards, burying himself under it. Once after sighing he came over to look for me, with a ghostly pale smile on his face. "Pugh!" He sniffed in my room as if the air was full of dust before he said anything. "I really envy you people. Not a care or worry on earth."

He always talked in such neat little riddles, giving others no chance to join in the conversation. Luckily, this time he was self-explanatory: "I can't live on like this, really! What's the use of crying, old Time won't listen to you and move any faster! I wish I could fly to Shanghai!"

"How many letters do you write a day?" I asked.

"What's the use, even if I should write a hundred! I told her already, I want to commit suicide! This is not life. No!" The doctor shook his head repeatedly to make his point.

"Good thing winter vacation is only three months away," I sought to console him. "Aren't you planning to get married then?"

He didn't answer at once, but started pacing my room. After a long time he said, "Even if tomorrow were my wedding day I'd still feel bad!"

I was searching my mind for some comforting words when, like a flash, he darted out of the room as if suddenly remembering something very important. The moment he disappeared in his own room there went the tap-tap-tapping on the typewriter.

Lao Mei finally returned. I didn't have any occasion to call on him again before the winter vacation came around. After New Year's he forwarded to me a wedding invitation, engraved in English. I felt rather delighted for Dr. Mao. He had reached his goal, perhaps from now on he could devote himself to some other of life's pursuits. . . .

Lao Hsiang

IN HIS more serious moments Lao Hsiang, or Wang Hsiang-cheng, worked in "Jimmy" Yen's world-famous mass education project at Tinghsien. This probably explains his ability to give us such an accurately observed picture of a village family's reaction to the son's modern-styled school. His story of the Tinghsien barber who dedicates himself to National Salvation reminds me of Frank Sullivan's piece in The New Yorker, *in the early New Deal days, wherein a little man heeds the call of President Roosevelt to "put his shoulder behind the wheel."*

AH CHUAN GOES TO SCHOOL

When a country boy is eight or nine years old, he is expected to help in the pulling of haystubs in the spring and in the weeding of the fields in summer; he should be able to carry bricks during the building of farmhouses or dig ditches for the irrigation of the garden, thus making himself worth half the labor of a grownup man. Who would want to spare such a boy and send him to school? But an official notice has been posted in the city that whoever fails to send his children above six to school is liable to be sent to prison. So Ah Chuan has to go to school.

On the first day Ah Chuan goes to school, he brings home eight school books. His grandfather and grandmother and his parents all come around to see the pictures in them, which compel their unanimous admiration. The grandfather says, "In our times, we never had such colored pictures in the Four Books and Five Classics studied at school."

"But these people in the pictures are not Chinese," Ah Chuan's father suddenly remarks. "Look here, the men and the children are all dressed differently from our people here. These are foreign boots, and this is foreign dress . . . this is called a dog-beating stick. It really all looks like the foreign preacher at the Shih-tse-chieh."

"This cotton-spinner, he also is a foreigner," says the grandmother. "We turn the spinning wheel with the right hand, while this one turns it with his left hand."

Translated by Lin Yutang.

"Why, when it comes to that, even this cartdriver isn't a Chinese. Whoever saw a cartdriver holding his whip in that manner?" says the grandfather.

Seeing them all so much interested in his books, Ah Chuan feels very happy, and says, "The teacher says that these eight books cost one dollar twenty cents." This quiet remark strikes the family like a powder explosion, and holds them in a spell of consternation.

It is the grandmother who breaks the silence.

"We are forced to send him to school, and now we are to pay for his books as well. Why, on the very first day he already spends over a dollar. Who can ever afford that? Even if we stop burning oil-lamps and go without lights for half a year, we can't spare that amount. Why, it is the price of eight bushels of maize!"

"It seems to me that when a boy is just beginning this work at school, he only needs one book," remarks the grandfather. "When that book is finished, he can go on with another. Isn't that right?"

"And you see," says the grandmother, taking up the thread of her thought, "there are only three or four big characters on a page. How can it be worth so much money? An almanac, with so many big and small characters in it only costs five coppers. It can't be worth the money."

After a long family council which lasts deep into the night, the family agrees to pay the price, as a piece of bad luck which has to be put up with. The final arrangement is that Ah Chuan's mother should sell her two pairs of earrings to make up the total amount. And his father says to him, "We're sparing your help in the farm, and sending you to school. You know it is hard for us. You are nine years old. You owe it to us to work really hard at school."

Although Ah Chuan is a mere farm boy, yet he remembers every word of what his father says. Next morning he goes to school at dawn. The servant at the school tells him that classes don't begin until nine. "Why, it is only half past five now, you are too early. The teacher is still in bed and the school rooms are closed. You'd better not wait, better go on back." Ah Chuan looks around at the school and sees that none of the pupils have come. He peeps in at the window and hears the snore of the teacher. He walks around the school building and finds all the doors closed. So he comes home.

Ah Chuan's father is just sweeping the yard, when he sees him coming home. He is really angry, for he throws away his broomstick and shouts at him, "You little scoundrel, good really only for holding a hoe! So you are running away from school on the very second day!" Ah Chuan is just going to explain, when his mother comes along and gives him a hearty slap on the cheek, and tells him immediately to go away and carry fuel and help in cooking the breakfast. It is needless to add that they are not really angry with Ah Chuan, but angry at the price they have to pay for the school books.

After breakfast, Ah Chuan goes to school again. The teacher is giving a talk on his platform on "The Importance of Punctuality." He is telling a story about a fairy with a bag of gold, waiting to give it to the earliest comer to school. Ah Chuan thinks that the fairy and the bag of gold all sound very nice, but does not quite understand what "earliest comer" means.

At half past three in the afternoon, when Ah Chuan's father has just finished his afternoon nap and is getting ready to go to work, Ah Chuan is already returning home. Luckily for him, his father sees that the teacher himself is taking a walk with his dog-beating stick, and so he lets it alone.

Six days have passed, and according to the regular school routine, the teacher has already taught Ah Chuan his first lesson. The text of the lesson is four characters: "This is mamma." Ah Chuan is really a good boy, for from the time he comes home till supper time, he keeps on reading "This is mam-ma." He presses his book with his left hand, and points at the characters with his right hand while he reads, as if the characters would fly bodily off the pages of the book at the slightest relaxation of his finger.

But his mother is sitting by and every time he repeats, "This is mam-ma," his mother's heart feels a slight tug, until she really cannot stand it any longer, and she snatches the book from Ah Chuan's hands and says, "Let me see. Which one is your mamma?" Ah Chuan tells her in all honesty that the one with high-heeled shoes and curled hair and a long gown is the mamma. On hearing this, the mother breaks out into a cry, which is a howl. Ah Chuan's father and grandparents all come round, thinking that a devil has gone into her, and ask what's the matter, but she only cries and will not explain. At long last, she only says, "Whoever did see such a monster in our village for a mother?"

So they all begin to understand that she is crying because of a sentence in the school book. And the father tries to calm her and says, "but the book doesn't say whose mamma. We will ask Ah Chuan to ask the teacher tomorrow whose mamma it is. Perhaps it is the teacher's."

The next morning, early at dawn, the mother wakes Ah Chuan up and dispatches him to ask the teacher about the question which has kept her awake all night. Ah Chuan realizes only after arriving at school that it is Sunday, that a Sunday is a holiday, and that the teacher got drunk last night and is still deep in his dreams. Ah Chuan comes home and tells his mother about it, which does not help her any. "Sunday be hanged!" she says.

On Monday, at the weekly inspirational talk, the teacher tells the pupils that they should try to ask questions. "Good boys should ask questions of the teacher when at school and ask questions of their parents when at home." Before he has finished his sentence, Ah Chuan stands up and says, "The national language book says 'This is mam-ma.' Can you tell me really whose mamma it is?"

"It is the mamma of any boy who reads this book. Is that clear?" the teacher explains in very good humor.

"I don't understand," says Ah Chuan.

"What don't you understand?" says the teacher, still in a very good humor.

"For instance, Baldhead Number Two is also studying this book, but Baldhead Number Two's mamma does not look like the one in the book," Ah Chuan replies.

"Baldhead Number Two's mamma is a crooked-armed one-eyed dragon," says Hsiao Lin, one of the pupils.

"Your mamma is a dead one anyway," retorts Baldhead.

"Now, now, be quiet," the teacher says, banging his stick on the blackboard. "We'll go on with the second lesson. This is pa-pa. You see carefully. The one with spectacles and parted hair is the papa."

In the afternoon, when Ah Chuan comes home, his mother is still waiting for the results of his inquiry. However, she hears him repeating from the book, "This is pa-pa," and she is afraid that her husband might accuse her of finding a new papa for Ah Chuan, and so she lets the question rest unsettled. But she is thinking in her heart, "What kind of a book is this! Gives people a lot of papas and mammas. Oh, what kind of a school!"

After a few days, Ah Chuan has learnt a new lesson, which says, "The cow prepares the meals; the horse eats noodles." He is reading it for the six thousandth time in the afternoon, with increasing bewilderment. He reflects that he has a cow and horses at home, that he has led them to the pastures himself, but has never seen a horse eating noodles, or a cow preparing a meal. But surely, the book can tell no lies. He would obey his teacher and "ask questions of his parents when at home." To his question, his father replies, "I have once seen a foreign circus in the city, and the horses can ring a bell and shoot a gun. It must be the cow and horses in a circus."

But Ah Chuan's grandmother protests. "I am sure that the cow is the Ox Spirit and the horse is a Horse Spirit, for they are wearing human dress, and only their heads haven't been changed into human form yet. The change of the head into human form would require five hundred years of piety and good work." And she goes on to tell them of wonderful stories of the spirits of the heaven and the earth and the winds and the rain. The result is that Ah Chuan wakes up at midnight in tears and trepidation, having just narrowly escaped the fangs of a winged wolf in the air.

The next morning, Ah Chuan asks his teacher, "Is this cow wearing a foreign dress a foreign cow?"

"You foolish child," answers the teacher, smiling. "The book is saying these things only for fun. There are really no cows that can prepare meals, nor horses that can eat noodles."

Ah Chuan is greatly delighted at this explanation, for he has been somewhat suspecting all along the reality of people in the books who "eat bread and drink milk and go into a park and play tennis-balls," which he has never seen, and now he knows that these are merely said for fun in the books.

Now Ah Chuan's class has come to an action story, and it is about a "tea party," and it is agreed that they should all contribute ten or twenty cents to buy oranges and apples and chocolates and have a real tea party. Ah Chuan knows what he will have to face at home, for every time he asks for money to buy some paper, it puts his grandfather into a fury, saying that the family will go bankrupt on account of keeping him in school. But the tea party described in the book seems so delightful, and he must think of some way of getting the money for his share in it. Consequently, his mother has been persuaded to sell two pieces of her hair decorations and tamper with the money reserved for buying cabbage seeds and give it to him.

Ah Chuan's grandfather has been suffering from consumption, and the cough and panting have been giving him much trouble. It happens this day that he has heard some one say that orange-skins will relieve the cough, and he comes home repeating to himself, "What is an orange-skin like? Where can I find orange-skins?" Glad of this opportunity to please his grandfather, Ah Chuan tells him that they are already getting some oranges in school.

"You are getting oranges in school! What for?" comes the old man's query.

"We are going to have a tea party."

"And what is a 'tea party'?" asks his grandmother.

"We learn this from the book. We get together to eat and have tea."

"What kind of a book is this now? Always talking of eating or playing, when it is not talking a dog language. No wonder that when a boy goes to school, he begins to grow lazy and greedy," says the grandmother.

"And even what they eat is all foreign food. There are no *pang-tse-mien* and *wo-wo* in the book, and no beancurd served with onion either," the grandfather says.

"Remember," says the mother, "you should bring home some orange-skins for grandpa."

"Now, wherever did you get the money for buying oranges?" queries the father.

"The teacher . . ." But before he had completed that lie, they hear Baldhead's cry in the next house on the east, and Baldhead's father is scolding him out loud, "Here is a family of seven or eight mouths, and we can't afford even to buy salt, and you want to buy candies!"

Then on the west side, they hear Hsiao-lin's uncle also creating an uproar. "Look here! I'm sparing this money, which I earn with the sweat of my brow, for you to go to school to buy books, to get you educated. I am not going to give you money for you to squander on sweets. Whoever invites you to tea must pay for it as well."

Now the whole show has been given away. Ah Chuan's father aims a good kick at him, but luckily for him, there is a table in between, and the table turns, crashing five or six bowls to the ground. It is his grandfather's opinion that he should stop going to school and grandma is of the opinion that he might eventually land in jail if he keeps on like this. After a long parley, the family agrees to let him try yet for a few days.

After this disgrace, Ah Chuan makes up his mind to work hard and recover his favor with the family. Every afternoon after he comes back from school, he keeps on working over his lessons till dark, unaware that Fate is lying in ambush for him in the form of a new lesson, and that his days at school are numbered.

For the grandmother has been feeling that since her son's marriage, her position in the family has not been quite the same, that her words are not listened to the way they were before. It happens that Ah Chuan has come to a new lesson and the words are: "In the family there are a papa, a mamma, and brothers and sisters." There is no mention of the grandfather and the grandmother. The realization penetrates into her old soul with all the force of accumulated anger and resentment. "Now, I am not wanted any more. I know I have no place in the family." And in her bad temper, the old woman picks up a brick and dashes it against an old cooking utensil and breaks it into pieces.

"Oh, don't be angry, mamma!" says Ah Chuan's father. "I have decided that we shall not send Ah Chuan to school to study books of this kind. I prefer to go into the county jail."

And next morning, Ah Chuan's father dismissed a hired farm hand, and the teacher makes a cross against Ah Chuan's name in the pupils' register.

SALT, SWEAT, AND TEARS

I hear the old people in the villages used to say that "When a catty of salt costs over a hundred cash of *chingchien,* then it is true that the officials are forcing the people to rebel, and there will be no peace." I am both happy and sorry to hear this, sorry because I am afraid we shan't have peace any more, and happy because that after the period of wars and turmoil, the price of salt will come down again. A hundred cash *chingchien* is only about fifty cash, or about five coppers. Now the salt authorities are trying to "increase the salt tax on the pretense of changing the standard of measurements." Even with the new standard, which has 1.6 ounce less in the catty, the cost of a catty of salt is already fifty-four coppers, or the equivalent of over a thousand cash *chingchien.* A peasant laborer's wage is eight coppers a day, and even then many of them are hanging about unemployed. A peasant woman sells her chicken for only ten cents, and for that, she has to go to the cities and sell it to the wealthy families. The salt officials seem never to have thought of the purchasing power of the people. Alas! how are we ever going to escape wars and turmoil? But the people of China are not thinking of rebellion: they have already learned the art of going without salt, viz., the art of eating their food without flavor.

Translated by Lin Yutang.

We know that merchants have proverbs like "Kindliness is the first virtue," and "Kindliness will bring you a fortune." But the salt merchants apparently do not need this virtue, because they have the monopoly. But we will leave their haughtiness and their high prices alone; there are other things, like pouring dirty water over the market salt and mixing sand and mud with it, which are marks of their privilege and nobility. "It is but natural and proper that they should be so," I thought to myself with envy. The psychology of these salt merchants is the same as that of the salt authorities: the people have to have salt under any conditions. As a matter of fact, there are many families which have embarked on a policy of cutting down the consumption of salt, and fifty to sixty per cent of the families do not know the flavor of salt for months. If it goes on like this, the salt merchants may have to shut up shop. (Note.—The writer of this article is working at Tinghsien with the mass education movement, and should know what he is talking about.)

In the north of my village, along the river, there is what we call the "salt land." Crude salt appears on the surface of the earth when the wind blows and the sun shines upon it. This salt has to be removed before the land can be cultivated. But this crude salt is "contraband salt." There are patrols of salt officials all over the place. I have seen several cases of peasants accused of "smuggling salt" and being fined and flogged for selling half a bushel of *hungliang*. If they dare to scrape this crude salt from the surface of the earth, I cannot guarantee them a decent burial. Therefore, the peasants have preferred to eat their food unsalted for months rather than scrape this crude salt. Thus the crude salt lies there, preventing proper cultivation of the land, but the farm tax and labor tax remain the same. Do our people grumble? "Grumble not against heaven, and murmur not against thy fellowmen," says our proverb. We bemoan our fate merely.

It is said that sour, sweet, bitter, hot, and salty are the five flavors of the art of cuisine. But one must have something to cook with first. Now there are no rice in their jars, and no vegetables in their fields. How could they eat salt with their empty mouth? Besides, salt is the only one among the five flavors which is subject to taxation. Perhaps our people who have already been bled white and squeezed to their marrow may one day abandon salt and take to pepper. There was a town called "No salt" in ancient times, and there was a man, Lu Hsiang-mai, who never tasted salt in his life. These things are recorded in books. How can you say therefore that salt is the daily need of the people? What worries me is that, after the people have taken to pepper, the salt administration may be replaced by a pepper administration, with pepper tax, pepper patrols, and pepper tax bureaus, and then people who eat contraband pepper will be punished like opium smugglers. Well, then, two out of the five flavors will be struck off the list, and the people may resort to the bitter flavor. But there is a time when the bitter-water well in the village may run dry.

Huainantse, the Han philosopher, once said, "The salty sweat flows and the throat gasps for breath." The commentary to this passage says, "Sweat is salty in flavor; hence the expression 'salty sweat.'" It wouldn't be a bad idea if our people became coolie carriers for the army or servants of the officials and run about so that we might perspire and taste the salt of our perspiration. They should be careful therefore not to let their "sweat drop on the earth" when "tilling it under a hot sun," as an ancient poem says. If the salt officials could provide a large cauldron, and cook the people in it, they would surely get a lot of salt from them, and this is a good way to prevent the unwarranted consumption of contraband salt. Some one may say, tears are salty, too. So our people might eat their food with tears.

It is recorded that in former times, when there was an urgent military message to be delivered, the imperial mail service used to cut a hole in a camel's belly and put salt in it. The camel, smarting under that pain, would start to run and cover a thousand *li* in one day. But even if our people were lucky enough to be camels, we wouldn't get salt, because there is the radio. We can't get salt in our belly.

The old women in the village used to say that "when big rats eat salt, their hair will come off, and they will be turned into bats, but with human beings, the effect is just the reverse: when human beings do not eat salt, hair would grow all over their bodies, making them look like hairy buffaloes." If so, we may, by abstaining from salt, escape the salt tax and have a covering to protect us against cold. Let's become hairy people.

NATIONAL SALVATION THROUGH HAIRCUT

Nobody likes to be blamed for the plight of the nation, for that's always the responsibility of the next fellow; on the other hand, everyone likes to be told that he and he alone is the man to save his nation.

Translated by George Kao.

He may not deem it proper to answer, "Oh, yes!" to this proposition right away, but in his heart he would assent and he would be flattered. And yet, as the saying goes, the one to unbell the cat must be the one who belled it; only he who has the courage to own up to being the chief sinner against his country is qualified to talk about being its savior. Such, anyway, are the views of a contemporary, called Master An, Yu-lin by name.

Master An is no scholar, nor is he a bigwig; he is a barber in the town of Tinghsien who possesses a fair amount of common sense. He maintains his offices on the premises of the Chinese Mass Education Promotion Association and, perhaps because of his baptism in mass education, he has long since taken down his traditional barber's shingle—"No National Affairs Discussed"—and burned it to ashes. Now he loves to read newspapers, and is particularly fond of discussing national affairs.

Master An said: "The bigwigs used to shout of national salvation through aviation, but now they have switched to promoting a movement for flying kites. What care must then be exercised by these plane-flying gentlemen, else they would run into the kites belonging to the bigwigs, resulting either in a plane crash or the ripping of a few kites. In either case, it would be bad. But it's bad enough that a nation should have found herself in such a mess that she should need 'salvation,' not to mention the various fancy means advanced for national salvation!" Thus he would keep his thoughts and sighs to himself, thinking that his glorious task of national salvation is as much incumbent on an outstanding figure of the tonsorial brotherhood as on representatives of any other field. Encouraged by this thought, he forthwith embarked upon a period of painstaking soul-searching to the neglect of his daily meals and nightly sleep. Finally, after twenty-four hours' experimentation, he came up with the invention of a brand new hair tonic which, being thrice put to the test, caused him to sing and dance with joy and to let out the cry, "Our nation is saved!"

With the method of national salvation ensured, Master An proceeded to complete his theory of national salvation. "China is about to perish, and the responsibility for this should be lodged in its entirety on the shoulders of the haircutting brotherhood." That is the premise of his "Theory of National Salvation." Not that he has been touched with megalomania, for he has his reasons. And this is how his reasoning evolved: Since the establishment of the Republic equality has been achieved for the Hundred Names, and the barber's political status is not lower than the rest. As a matter of fact, traditionally the barber may be considered more highly placed than most people by virtue of his profession, which deals with people's heads. Whether you be prime minister or prince consort, you will have to submit silently to the ministrations of the barber while he pulls at your hair or scratches your scalp. Inside the Imperial Palace, who else save the barber could ever wave a knife in His Majesty's face or scrape at his neck with impunity? As to technique, it's an open secret that the modern masseurs, who have been the rage of Shanghai of late, have plagiarized from the Chinese barber in one or two of his side lines. Even in fiction, where you see the superman whose powers include rubbing out an opponent with his finger, you will find it is also a heritage from the early founders of the haircutting brotherhood. Unfortunately, in the course of being handed down from generation to generation, much of this transcendental skill has been lost due to some individual barbers who were reluctant to impart professional secrets to their disciples, or even to their sons. This story, for instance, has been told: Once a barber understudied his father to learn the trick of rubbing people out with a finger. The father taught him how to rub out a man with the finger, but balked at teaching him the corollary lesson of reviving his victim, and whatever the barber did or said by way of imploring left his father unmoved. Finally the barber thought of a way. He rubbed out his own wife with a finger and begged his father to revive her so he could watch and acquire the trick. He never expected that his father would simply shake his head and refuse to budge, leaving his daughter-in-law to die a very unnatural death. Having failed once, the son thought of another scheme. This time he proceeded to rub out his grandfather before asking his father to demonstrate the method of revival. His father nodded his head, as if to say, "I know what you are up to"; after which he shook his head again as much as saying, "But don't think you can get away with it." From this kind of pernicious practice you can see how the haircutting brotherhood has degenerated from generation to generation until it has been generally conceded to be the lowliest of professions, and until even the barbers themselves have ceased to trust one another's hearts. And, since, as Mencius said, "There is no greater sorrow than the death of the heart," the state of the nation can justly be traced to the barber's heart.

Since the barber is responsible for this plight the nation is in, it is up to him to get the nation out of it. That is why Master An says, "These plans for national salvation which the bigwigs advance do not get at the root trouble of the thing. Any one who considers himself a patriot should lose no time in the promotion of National Salvation through Haircut, which is really the basic approach." To elaborate his thesis, he has issued the following dictum: "The weakened state in which the Republic of China finds itself is due to the fact that her citizens are no longer possessed of strong bodies. No matter how much they eat and sleep, the air is still filled with yawns and with cries of pain in the neck. It is certainly just that we are nicknamed the Sick Man of East Asia. But in *ancient* China it was quite different; the men were all seven-footers and as strong as oxen. It is only since the importation of opium and such that everybody began acquiring bad habits and letting the nation come to this pass. And why did the people take to drugs and poison to quench their thirst for joy? It must have been that they were at a loss to discover ways of enjoyment that produced no harm. In other words, if a barber could infuse his customer with a sense of infinite happiness once he was seated in the high barber chair, then you could count on one less customer in the market of the black drug. In this fashion, not only millions of dollars is capable of being saved every year, but also the nation's physique would be restored to the strength of oxen, elephants, or tigers. Could there still be any doubt then of the nation's being saved?"

The question remains: is it possible, after all, for the barber to afford a man the same happiness and satisfaction as he derives from drugs? To this we can answer without a moment's hesitation: More than possible! Just see, besides the traditional joys of having one's head shaved under the lamp, or of having one's ears picked against the sun, or of having one's back pounded so that the blood circulation may be restored, there is this new hair tonic invented exclusively by Master An. Its application is guaranteed to clear up your head, smoothe out your limbs, and to achieve other "incalculable results"!

A further question: Would all the barbers under heaven realize this theory of National Salvation through Haircut, and would they all be willing to adopt Master An's hair tonic or invent a similarly effective tonic of their own? That is why we say it is still up to everybody to *promote* this theory of National Salvation through Haircut.

Yao Ying

YAO YING is the Cassandra of The Analects *coterie, contributing to that magazine a regular letter from Nanking entitled* Ching Hua *("Capital Talk"). In it she comments freely on the antics of the "Party and Government Elders"—notably Wang Ching-wei and Chu Ming-yi, who have since played out tragicomic roles of the puppet in the war. This selection represents her interpretation of the last article in* "The Analects *Credo," and could be read as a satire on the literary man in government, as the Lin Yutang pieces are on the military.*

DON'T SAY YOUR OWN WRITING IS NO GOOD

Lately I have run into bad luck. It is not enough that I failed to win first prize in the Aviation Sweepstakes, I have to run into a lot of odd questions.

For instance, I did not participate in the legislative work behind the drafting of "The American Credo" and, furthermore, not being the judiciary, I lack the power to interpret law; yet there are people who keep bothering me with the question: Why list as one of the taboos the article which says, "Don't say your own writing is no good"? At first I gave no answer, but simply dismissed my inquirer as one of the "odd fellows I have known." But he repeatedly put the question to me and I repeatedly declined to answer. Finally, to avoid being bothered further, I decided to break my silence and, after having had a good meal, to write a few lines by way of interpretation. True, this may be charged to my lack of mellowness and reserve; but it is just as well, as only by writing can I disprove a theory that my own writing is no good.

There are a few points to be noted in the discussion of this subject. First of all, we must pay attention to the way this proposition is worded, namely, "Don't say your own writing is no good." To pursue the subject further and following the principle that two negatives make one positive, we ought to know that "Don't say your own writing is no good" is equivalent to "Say your own writing is good."

Lastly, inasmuch as the subject is couched in a negative fashion,

Translated by George Kao.

we must also consider the other possibility, to wit, "Don't say your own writing is good." Now let us consider these three propositions separately.

1. Don't Say Your Own Writing Is No Good

Writing is not an easy job; it is even harder to do a *good* job of it. That is why we would have to be considerate to ourselves even if we did not do a good job with our own writing. On the other hand, to fail to do a good job of writing does not do your "face" any good either. So naturally, according to the dictum that family shame must not be spread to outsiders, there is no great need for broadcasting the fact unless you have the mistaken notion that people will thereby take pity on you. If you do, let me tell you that such nice people are hard to find these days. Therefore, don't say it—that would be the correct thing to do! Besides, if you don't say it nobody else will be able to measure your height or fathom your depths. As long as he can see that you look cultured, dress well, and conduct yourself in an elegant manner, he will surely take you for one of those who do a good writing job. But if you should feel overly oppressive and must say it, then you must at least take a look around and observe the circumstances. I remember it was Lusin who gave the advice that when you discuss knowledge with others the best way is to be half-knowing, because if you are all-knowing people will envy and hate you and if you don't know at all people will hold you in contempt. This is really the voice of experience, worthy of our careful consideration.

Someone would ask this of me: Have I not seen these bigwigs who are so self-deprecating of their own scholarly attainments that to their superiors they are full of humbleness and to their colleagues they are modesty itself? And how is it that they have succeeded in becoming the bigwigs that they are? My answer would be that there are two sides to this half-knowing trick, both of which we must know to understand; for only those who are capable of obsequiousness to those above them can lord it over those who are under them. When you are seeing only one side of this dual personality it is no wonder that you are puzzled. (Of course, your superior official himself gets nothing but your obsequiousness; but as long as he can see that you are capable of lording it over the rest he will have no difficulty in believing that you are really a pretty good hand at writing.)

Following this policy, therefore, you would have to prepare two sets of declarations—one in which you say your own writing is no good and the other in which you say your own writing is very good. For if you make the mistake of saying too often your own writing is no good—of course you would only be joking—you should be careful lest people take you a little too seriously and confront you with your own words. In which case, beware of your rice bowl! Furthermore, society being what it is in its demands for self-promotion, you would run the risk of forfeiting the sympathy of your friends and the respect and admiration due you from your inferiors. That is why I say, even if your own writing *is* no good, the only wise thing to do is to keep your honorable mouth shut.

2. Say Your Own Writing Is Good

Our ancients have handed down a very popular saying, "When it comes to writing you always pick your own; when it comes to wives you always pick somebody else's." The discussion of other people's wives has always been a favorite indoor sport, even as it has been a human habit to advertise one's own writing by word of mouth. Or rather, I should say, a custom—a custom that has exerted far-reaching influence over this country of ours.

It is said that the officialdom of our country is largely recruited from the ranks of the literati. Even during their student days these literary men had already fostered the habit of saying that their own writing is good. By the time they have secured political power in their palms they have unconsciously carried over their pattern of writing and apply it to national affairs. Some of them go so far as to regard the whole problem of government as a piece of writing. Their political critics are always fond of discussing them in literary terms—"We don't know just how good a piece of writing he can make out of this." "Say, he is really writing a big essay out of a small subject." "How could he expect to cope with the situation with the style that he has got!" As to themselves, they are actually applying to politics the rules of composition that they have learned, all the while silently applauding themselves and organizing comrades into mutual admiration societies.

For instance, before a man is in he writes pamphlets decrying the state of the nation, mouthing patriotism and national salvation, and making such faces as if to say that he would rise and fall, live and perish with his nation. There is nothing that he writes, actually, that will not serve as overtures to some one or other of the bigwigs in order to secure for himself an appointment. Once a man is in he will be writing all the more furiously, writing proposals and memorials day in and day out, writing one thing and doing another. There will come a day when he will be out again. Then he can always take up a position among the Old Hundred Names, going in for detailed accounts of the sufferings of the common people and arraigning the authorities for their misdeeds count by count. He can even start writing out blank checks, promising in effect that once he is reinstated in office he will be the savior of the common people. All these introductions and conclusions, foreshadowings and fulfillments, climaxes and anticlimaxes —how closely they follow the art of writing and the rules of composition! And the way they beat their own drums and toot their own horns, is it not like literary men saying that their own writing is good? Even with an official who did not rise from the literati, once he has reached the top he will lose no time in staffing his office with writers so that, with their advice, he can engage in "writing" out his political career. That's why I say Chinese politics is literary politics; it is a kind of political game in which everybody claims that his own writing is the best.

I remember reading one of the strange tales in *Liao Chai* about a student named Miao who was annoyed at his guests because each said his own writing was good. He was so incensed, in fact, that he transformed himself into a tiger and devoured the guests. Although I feel that the student Miao overdid it somewhat, I cannot help wondering what he would do if he were alive today and were to see with his own eyes that this pernicious habit of the literati has already had its effect on politics and society. I would not dare lay all the blame for the bad politics which we have had of late at the door of the writing men; I only hope that these writing men will all rise and shed some of this bad habit.

3. Don't Say Your Own Writing Is Good

People will tell me this is politics and not everyone is a Student Miao. So why not say your own writing is good? I still think it is better not to say it.

In the *Collected Letters of Cheng Pan-Chiao* there is no self-advertising except this casual remark: "There are some good things here worth taking a look at." And to this day you still find people taking a look into his letters. On the other hand, our artists in revolt, who come out and parade their wares under the slogan of a "cultural renaissance" and are naturally much talked about, seldom are attractive enough to win a second glance from the public. Confucius once said: "People don't know him and still he is not peeved; is he not then a gentleman?" All this talk about gentlemen, of course, is an old Confucian trick; nevertheless there is more than a grain of truth in this idea of people not knowing you and your not being peeved.

Besides, there is no absolute standard by which to judge a piece of writing, whether it is good or bad. Take the four great prose writers of the classical school—Han, Liu, Ou, and Su. There are people who like the essays of Su, there are others who like the essays of Han, and there are those who choose the other two. Without being overly self-deprecatory, it is a fact that we are not regarded as the Han, Liu, Ou, or Su of today. Seeing that even the four classicists are variously evaluated, we had better not be oversold on the merits of our own writing.

In this day and age writing is not an easy job. If you are a writer of the aristocracy, you will be known as a *pu-erh-chiao-ah*.* If you go in for writing of the life of the poor, you will be regarded as an exponent of *pu-lo* † literature. If you uphold *fa-hsi-ssu-ti,* the *teh-mo-keh-la-hsi* people won't like you; if you come out in favor of *teh-mo-keh-la-hsi,* the *fa-hsi-ssu-ti* will not tolerate you. Mr. Chiang Mong-lin once made the remark that the best thing a literary man can do is write announcements for the militarists. Given these circumstances, it is extremely difficult to give birth to any good writing. So, what is there to say?

Again, whether a piece of writing is good or bad is for other eyes to see. It is not necessary to say your own writing is good, nor is there any use to confess that your writing is no good. I have often seen people who think their own writing is good and insist on inviting "criticism" from their friends and inferiors. Simply for the sake of face, the others have to tell them that their writing is good, and then they feel so good that they go around and repeat it to everybody they meet. To have it said that way is as good as not saying it.

I have said too much myself, and if I don't stop I am afraid I will be suspected of saying that my own writing is good. To sum up the above discussion, I might say that to say your own writing is good tends toward the optimistic and is too much; not to say your own writing is good, on the other hand, tends toward the pessimistic and is not enough; this leaves us only with the injunction "Don't say your own writing is no good," which hits the golden mean and is just right.

* Chinese transliteration for *bourgeois,* see page xxii.
† Short for *pu-lo-le-ta-le-ya* (*proletariat*).

Index of Titles

345